BESTSELLING BOOK SERIES

A+ Certification For Dummies, 2nd Edition

Cheat Sheet

Default system resource assignments

IRQ	Typical Assignment	I/O Address
1	Keyboard	060h
3	COM2/COM4	2F8h/2E8h
4	COM1, COM3	3F8h/3E8h
5	LPT2, Sound card	278h, 220h
6	Floppy disk controller	3F0h
7	LPT1	378h
10	NIC	300h
12	PS/2 mouse	064h
14	Primary IDE controller	1F0h
15	Secondary IDE controller	376h

CPU sockets and slots

- **Socket 7:** A 321-pin mounting for Pentium, AMD, Cyrix, and IDT processors
- **Socket 8:** A 386-pin ZIF-socket for Pentium Pro processor
- **Socket 370:** a 370-pin Celeron processor mounting
- **Slot 1:** A proprietary Intel connector for Celeron, Pentium II, and Pentium III processors
- **Slot 2:** A mounting Pentium II and III Xeon chips
- **Slot A:** A slot style used by AMD Athlon processors

Bus architectures

Architecture	Bus Width
Industry Standard	16-bit Architecture (ISA)
Intelligent Drive	32-bit Electronics (IDE)
Peripheral Component	32- or 64- itInterconnect (PCI) bus

File attributes (used with ATTRIB command):

- **Archive (A):** A file marked for back-up
- **Hidden (H):** A file that does not appear in directory listings
- **Read-Only (R):** A file that can be read, but cannot be changed or deleted
- **System (S):** A file used by the OS; not displayed in directory listings

Preparing a hard disk

SCANDISK	Check for media problems
FDISK	Partition the disk
FORMAT	Prepare the disk and load system files

DOS/Windows file systems

Operating Systems	File System
DOS	File Allocation Table (FAT) or FAT16
Windows 3.x	FAT16
Windows 9x	FAT16, VFAT, and FAT32
Windows NT/2000	FAT32 and NT File System (NTFS)

Laser printing phases

Cleaning, conditioning, writing, developing, transferring, fusing

For Dummies®: Bestselling Book Series for Beginners

P9-CCF-454

A+ Certification For Dummies, 2nd Edition

Cheat Sheet

DOS/Windows 3.x/9x memory management

Conventional memory	The first 640K of system memory
Upper memory area	The upper 384K of the (expanded memory) first megabyte of memory, above conventional memory
High memory area	The first 64K (less 16 bytes) of the second megabyte of memory
Extended memory	Any memory above the high-memory area

Windows 9x startup files

1. BIOS POST
2. Plug and Play (PnP) devices
2. IO.SYS
3. MSDOS.SYS
4. The Registry (SYSTEM.DAT)
5. CONFIG.SYS and AUTOEXEC.BAT
6. WIN.COM
7. Device drivers in Registry and SYSTEM.INI and VMM32.VXD
8. Windows 9x core components: Kernel, GDI, and User
14. Startup files

Windows 2000 files

- **Boot loader:** NTLDR
- **Multiboot entries:** BOOT.INI
- **Hardware configuration:** NTDETECT.COM
- **Windows 2000 kernel:** NTOSKRNL.EXE

POST error codes

Code	Hardware Group
1xx	Motherboard
2xx	Main memory
3xx	Keyboard
6xx	Floppy disk controller
14xx	Printer
17xx	Hard disk controller

Windows 9x files

- **Executable files:** BAT, EXE, and COM
- **Initialization files:** INI
- **System files:** SYS
- **Multiboot entries:** MSDOS.SYS
- **CD extension:** MSCDEX.EXE
- **Command prompt processor:** COMMAND.COM
- **Virtual device drivers:** VXD and 386
- **Program extension files:** DLL
- **Device drivers:** DRV

Memory types

- **DRAM (Dynamic Random Access Memory)**
- **EDO RAM (Extended Data Output RAM)**
- **RIMM (Rambus Inline Memory Module)**
- **SRAM (Static RAM)**
- **VRAM (Video RAM)**
- **WRAM (Windows Accelerator Card RAM)**

Hungry Minds™

For Dummies®: Bestselling Book Series for Beginners

A+® Certification
FOR
DUMMIES®
2ND EDITION

by Ron Gilster

Hungry Minds™

HUNGRY MINDS, INC.

New York, NY ◆ Cleveland, OH ◆ Indianapolis, IN

A+® Certification For Dummies®, 2nd Edition

Published by
Hungry Minds, Inc.
909 Third Avenue
New York, NY 10022
www.hungryminds.com
www.dummies.com

Library of Congress Control Number: 2001086260

ISBN: 0-7645-0812-1

Printed in the United States of America

10 9 8 7 6 5 4 3 2 1

2O/RY/QU/QR/IN

Distributed in the United States by Hungry Minds, Inc.

Distributed by CDG Books Canada Inc. for Canada; by Transworld Publishers Limited in the United Kingdom; by IDG Norge Books for Norway; by IDG Sweden Books for Sweden; by IDG Books Australia Publishing Corporation Pty. Ltd. for Australia and New Zealand; by TransQuest Publishers Pte Ltd. for Singapore, Malaysia, Thailand, Indonesia, and Hong Kong; by Gotop Information Inc. for Taiwan; by ICG Muse, Inc. for Japan; by Intersoft for South Africa; by Eyrolles for France; by International Thomson Publishing for Germany, Austria and Switzerland; by Distribuidora Cuspide for Argentina; by LR International for Brazil; by Galileo Libros for Chile; by Ediciones ZETA S.C.R. Ltda. for Peru; by WS Computer Publishing Corporation, Inc., for the Philippines; by Contemporanea de Ediciones for Venezuela; by Express Computer Distributors for the Caribbean and West Indies; by Micronesia Media Distributor, Inc. for Micronesia; by Chips Computadoras S.A. de C.V. for Mexico; by Editorial Norma de Panama S.A. for Panama; by American Bookshops for Finland.

For general information on Hungry Minds' products and services please contact our Customer Care Department within the U.S. at 800-762-2974, outside the U.S. at 317-572-3993 or fax 317-572-4002.

For sales inquiries and reseller information, including discounts, premium and bulk quantity sales, and foreign-language translations, please contact our Customer Care Department at 800-434-3422, fax 317-572-4002, or write to Hungry Minds, Inc., Attn: Customer Care Department, 10475 Crosspoint Boulevard, Indianapolis, IN 46256.

For information on licensing foreign or domestic rights, please contact our Sub-Rights Customer Care Department at 650-653-7098.

For information on using Hungry Minds' products and services in the classroom or for ordering examination copies, please contact our Educational Sales Department at 800-434-2086 or fax 317-572-4005.

Please contact our Public Relations Department at 212-884-5163 for press review copies or 212-884-5000 for author interviews and other publicity information or fax 212-884-5400.

For authorization to photocopy items for corporate, personal, or educational use, please contact Copyright Clearance Center, 222 Rosewood Drive, Danvers, MA 01923, or fax 978-750-4470.

Hungry Minds- is a trademark of Hungry Minds, Inc.

About the Author

Ron Gilster (A+ [1998, 2001], Network+, i-Net+, Server+, CCSE, CCNA, MBA, and AAGG) has been operating, programming, and repairing computers for more than 30 years. Ron has extensive experience training, teaching, and consulting in computer-related areas, including working on mainframes, minicomputers, and virtually every type of personal computer and operating system that exists. In addition to a wide range of positions that have included college instructor, Customer Service Manager, Data Processing Manager, Management Information Systems Director, and Vice President of Operations in major corporations, Ron has been a management consultant with an international auditing firm and has operated his own computer systems consulting firm.

Ron has authored a number of certification books, including *Network+ Certification For Dummies*, *I-Net+ Certification For Dummies*, *Server+ Certification For Dummies*, *CCNA For Dummies*, and *Cisco Networking For Dummies*, as well as several books on computer and information literacy, applications programming, and computer hardware topics.

Dedication

To my loving, patient, and understanding wife, Diane, and Mimi and Kirstie, who just want Daddy to come play.

Author's Acknowledgments

I would like to thank the virtual "cast of thousands" at Hungry Minds who helped to get this book published, especially Judy Brief, Katie Feltman, Amy Pettinella, James Sample, Robert Shimonski, Laura Moss, Jeanne Criswell, Laura Carpenter, Candace Nicholson, and a special thanks to Mica Johnson, who was on my side all the way.

Publisher's Acknowledgments

We're proud of this book; please send us your comments through our Online Registration Form located at www.dummies.com.

Some of the people who helped bring this book to market include the following:

Acquisitions, Editorial, and Media Development

Project Editor: Mica Johnson

Acquisitions Editors: Judy Brief, Katie Feltman

Copy Editor: Amy Pettinella

Technical Editor: James Sample, Robert Shimonski

Permissions Editor: Laura Moss

Media Development Specialist: Travis Silvers

Media Development Coordinator: Marisa Pearman

Editorial Manager: Leah Cameron

Media Development Manager: Laura Carpenter

Media Development Supervisor: Richard Graves

Editorial Assistant: Candace Nicholson

Production

Project Coordinator: Nancee Reeves

Layout and Graphics: Kristin Pickett, Heather Pope, Jacque Schneider, Brian Torwelle, Jeremey Unger

Proofreaders: Laura Albert, John Bitter, Nancy Price, Charles Spencer, York Production Services, Inc.

Indexer: York Production Services, Inc.

Special Help Mary SeRine, Christine Berman, Rebekah Mancilla, Sheri Replin

General and Administrative

Hungry Minds, Inc.: John Kilcullen, CEO; Bill Barry, President and COO; John Ball, Executive VP, Operations & Administration; John Harris, CFO

Hungry Minds Technology Publishing Group: Richard Swadley, Senior Vice President and Publisher; Mary Bednarek, Vice President and Publisher, Networking and Certification; Walter R. Bruce III, Vice President and Publisher, General User and Design Professional; Joseph Wikert, Vice President and Publisher, Programming; Mary C. Corder, Editorial Director, Branded Technology Editorial; Andy Cummings, Publishing Director, General User and Design Professional; Barry Pruett, Publishing Director, Visual

Hungry Minds Manufacturing: Ivor Parker, Vice President, Manufacturing

Hungry Minds Marketing: John Helmus, Assistant Vice President, Director of Marketing

Hungry Minds Online Management: Brenda McLaughlin, Executive Vice President, Chief Internet Officer

Hungry Minds Production for Branded Press: Debbie Stailey, Production Director

Hungry Minds Sales: Roland Elgey, Senior Vice President, Sales and Marketing; Michael Violano, Vice President, International Sales and Sub Rights

◆

The publisher would like to give special thanks to Patrick J. McGovern, without whom this book would not have been possible.

◆

Contents at a Glance

Cartoons at a Glance

By Rich Tennant

"Our automated response policy to a large company-wide data crash is to notify management, back up existing data, and sell 90% of my shares in the company."

page 537

page 523

page 7

page 55

"It appears a server in Atlanta is about to go down, there's printer backup in Baltimore, and an accountant in Chicago is about to make level 3 of the game "Tomb Pirate.""

page 231

"You know, this was a situation question on my A+ Certification exam, but I always thought it was just hypothetical."

page 403

"Drive carefully, remember your lunch, and always make a backup of your directory tree before modifying your hard disk partition file."

page 333

Cartoon Information:
Fax: 978-546-7747
E-Mail: richtennant@the5thwave.com
World Wide Web: www.the5thwave.com

Table of Contents

Part III: Getting Data In, Out, and All About 231

Introduction

● ●

*I*f you have bought or are considering buying this book, you probably fit one of the following categories:

- ✔ You know how valuable A+ Certification is to a professional personal computer (PC) technician's career and advancement.
- ✔ You're wondering just what A+ Certification is all about.
- ✔ You think that reading this book may be a fun, entertaining way to learn about computer hardware maintenance and repair.
- ✔ You love all ...*For Dummies* books and wait impatiently for each new one to come out.
- ✔ You're a big fan of mine and can't wait to read all of my new books.

Well, if you fit any of the first four scenarios, this is the book for you! However, I'm not certified in the appropriate medical areas to help you if you are in the last category!

If you're already aware of the A+ Certified Computer Technician program and are just looking for an excellent study aid, you can skip the next few sections of this introduction because your search is over. However, if you don't have the foggiest idea of what A+ Certification is, how it can benefit you, or how to prepare for it, read on!

Why Use This Book?

With over 20 years and layer upon layer of microcomputer hardware and software technology to study, even the most knowledgeable technician needs help getting ready for the A+ exams. This book is intended to shorten your preparation time for the A+ exams.

This book is a no-nonsense reference and study guide for the A+ Core Hardware exam (test #220-201) and the OS (Operating Systems) Technologies exam (test #220-202). It focuses on the areas likely to be on the exam, plus it provides background information to help you understand some of the more complex concepts and technologies. The concepts, processes, and applications on the exams are presented in this book in step-by-step lists, tables, and figures without long explanations. The focus is on preparing you for the A+ exams, not on my obviously extensive and impressive knowledge of computer technology (nor on my modesty, I might add). This book will not provide you with an an in-depth background on PC hardware and software. It will, however, prepare you to take the A+ Core Hardware and OS Technologies exams. In developing this book, I made two assumptions:

✔ You have knowledge of electronics, computers, software, networking, troubleshooting procedures, and customer relations, and need a study guide for the exams.

✔ You have limited knowledge of electronics, computer hardware, and the processes used to repair, maintain, and upgrade PCs and could use a little refresher on the basics along with a review and study guide for the exams.

If my assumptions in either case suit your needs, then this book is for you.

How This Book Is Organized

This book is organized so that you can study a specific area without wading through stuff you may already know. I recommend that you skim the whole book at least once, noting the points raised at the icons. Each part and chapter of the book is independent, and can be studied in any order, which should be helpful for your last-minute-cram before the exam. The following sections tell you what I include between the covers of this book.

Part I: First, Some Fundamentals

Part I begins with an overview of what to study for the A+ exam and other general information about taking the exam. It also presents background information on the concepts of electricity, electronics, and numbering systems. And finally, Part I covers the tools used in computer maintenance with an emphasis on electrostatic discharge protection and prevention.

Part II: Keeping the Smoke in the Box

Part II takes you down into the wonderful, incredible world of the motherboard and other electronic field replaceable modules (FRMs) found inside the case. This section is chock-full of information about the motherboard, memory, bus structures, power supply, disk drives, and other components found inside the case. Also covered in this part are the processes used to install, remove, troubleshoot, optimize, and upgrade these components.

Part III: Getting Data In, Out, and All About

You need to know about interfacing input, output, printers, and serial, parallel, USB, and FireWire connections, plus networking and data communications for the A+ Core Hardware exam.

Part IV: Putting the Hard in Hardware

Part IV has everything you need to know about the tools and best practices to use for repairing, maintaining, and configuring PC hardware. Read about disassembling and reassembling the PC, performing preventive maintenance, and the processes used to troubleshoot problems on the PC.

Part V: The Softer Side of Systems

This part of the book is focused on the A+ OS Technologies exam. The coverage includes installation, configuration, troubleshooting, and the comparative features of the various Windows operating systems (MS-DOS, Windows 3.*x*, Windows 95, Windows 98, Windows Me, Windows 2000 Professional, and Windows 2000 Server).

Part VI: The Part of Tens

This section provides additional motivation and study guides to help get you ready for the test, with advice about making sure that you're ready to take the test. This part also includes a list of ten great Web sites that offer study aids and practice tests.

Part VII: Appendix

This section gives you information about what's on the CD-ROM in the back of this book and how to use it.

Studying Chapters

A+ Certification For Dummies, 2nd Edition offers a self-paced method of preparing for the exam. You don't have to guess what to study; every chapter that covers exam objectives guides you with preview questions, detailed coverage, and review questions. This step-by-step structure identifies what you need to study, gives you all the facts, and rechecks what you know. The structure is as follows:

- ✔ **First page:** Each chapter starts with a preview of what's to come, including exam objectives and study subjects. Not sure that you know all about the objectives and the subjects in a chapter? Keep going.

- ✔ **Quick Assessment questions:** At the beginning of each chapter is a brief self-assessment test that helps you gauge your knowledge of the topics that chapter covers. Take this test to determine which areas you already understand as well as to determine which areas you need to focus on.

- ✔ **Labs:** Labs are included throughout the book to step you through some of the processes you need to know for the exam, such as installation or configuration of a particular component.

- ✔ **Prep Tests:** The Prep Tests at the end of each chapter gauges your understanding of the chapter's content. These Prep Test questions are structured in the same manner as those you may see on your exam, so be sure to try your hand at these sample questions.

Icons Used in This Book

Time Shaver icons point out tips that can help you manage and save time while studying for or taking the exam.

Instant Answer icons highlight tips to help you recognize correct and incorrect exam answers and point out information that is likely to be on the test.

Shocking Information icons point out ESD and other electrical dangers that you should be aware of for the test and on the job.

Warning icons flag problems and limitations of the technologies included on the exam and things to avoid when working with certain technologies.

Remember icons point out important background information and advantages of the technology that may appear on the exam.

Tip icons flag information that can come in extra-handy during the testing process. You may want to take notes on these tidbits!

Feedback

I'd like to hear from you. If an area of the test isn't covered as well as it should be, or if I provide more coverage than you think is warranted about a particular topic, please let me know. Your feedback is solicited and welcome. E-mail me at rgilster@gohighspeed.com.

Part I
First, Some Fundamentals

The 5th Wave — By Rich Tennant

BEING A+ CERTIFIED GAVE PHIL A KNOWLEDGE OF NETWORKING TO THE PC, TROUBLESHOOTING, AND OPERATING SYSTEMS VOODOO

Okay, Jerry-the bones are in place. Let's try it again.

In this part . . .

Not everything about the world of PC service technicians is on the A+ exams. There are some things you are just expected to know; for example, basic electronics, electricity, number systems, and the use of hardware, software, and electronic tools. CompTIA, the A+ test company, has assumed that you know this stuff or you wouldn't be either working (or wishing to be working) as a PC service technician or getting ready to take the A+ exams.

Before you begin preparing for the test, use this part of the book to learn about the tests and review some of the basic and underlying knowledge you need for the exams.

Chapter 1

The New A+ Certification Exams

A+ certification assures employers and computer owners that a PC repair technician has the requisite knowledge to build, upgrade, troubleshoot, and repair personal computer (PC) systems. The A+ exams measure the ability and knowledge a PC technician has after six months of on-the-job, hands-on training. Certified PC technicians are always in great demand, so passing the A+ certification exams is well worth the time that you spend preparing for the exams. A+ certification is a lifetime certification, meaning that you never have to take the test again (at least of this writing). So, if you are already A+ certified from either the 1996 or 1998 exams, then you don't need to take the 2001 exam. That is, unless you want to.

Who Is CompTIA?

Computing Technology Industry Association (CompTIA) is a membership trade organization that was formed in 1982 to promote standards of excellence in computer technology. Its goals are to develop ethical, professional, and business standards and provide educational opportunities to the industry. Its members include more than 8,000 computer resellers, VARs (value-added resellers), distributors, manufacturers, and training companies throughout the world (but predominantly in the United States and Canada). These companies range from large, multinational corporations to small, local computer repair shops and individual entrepreneurs. Visit CompTIA's Web site at www.comptia.com/aboutus/ for more information.

Why Get A+ Certification?

That's a fair question — why would you want to cram for a pair of tests and sweat bullets over taking them, just to get a piece of paper that says, "I know computer repair stuff?" Well, I can think of a number of good reasons, the first of which is the more than 260,000 A+ Certified Technicians worldwide that may be competing for the same jobs you are hoping to get.

What Do the A+ Exams Cover?

The exams are based on an industry-wide analysis of what a PC repair service technician with 6 months of experience should know to be considered competent. The results of this analysis were validated in a worldwide survey of thousands of A+ certified professionals.

The two A+ certification exams are the Core Hardware exam (exam number 220-201) with 70 questions on microprocessors, displays, storage media and devices, printers, modems, buses, and other hardware components of a PC; and the OS Technologies exam (exam number 220-202) with 70 questions. Each test is geared to measure your knowledge over a variety of technical domains.

Each test domain focuses on a specific area of technical service procedures, tools, and skills. Some domains are emphasized more than others, so the number of questions from any particular domain varies. Tables 1-1 and 1-2 list the domains and the percentage of coverage that each domain has on the total test, as well as the approximate number of test questions for each domain.

Table 1-1	A+ Core Hardware Exam Domains	
Domain	*Percentage of Test*	*Number of Questions*
Installation, Configuration, and Upgrading	30%	20–21
Diagnosing and Troubleshooting	25%	18
Preventive Maintenance	5%	4–5
Motherboard/ Processors/Memory	15%	10–12
Printers	10%	6–8
Basic Networking	15%	10–12

Table 1-2	A+ OS Technologies Exam Domains	
Domain	*Percentage of Test*	*Number of Questions*
OS Fundamentals	30%	20–21
Installation, Configuration, and Upgrading	15%	10–11
Diagnosing and Troubleshooting	40%	26–28
Networks	15%	10–12

For more information about the Revised A+ exams visit CompTIA's FAQ (Frequently Asked Questions) Web site at `www.comptia.org/certification/aplus/faq_revisions.htm`.

Who Can Get Certified?

A+ certification is open to anyone who registers for the exams, pays the exam fees, and passes the exams. You don't have to be a PC repair technician, work for a particular company, or have any prerequisite training to qualify for certification; you simply need to pass the exams.

How to Get Certified

The A+ exams are scored on what is called a scale method. This means that some questions and even some answers are worth more than others. The total possible points on each exam is 900. To pass the Core Hardware exam, you must get a score of 683; and to pass the OS Technologies exam, you must get a score of 614. The good news is that they spot you 100 points on each test.

You have 90 minutes to complete the Core Hardware exam and 90 minutes to complete the OS Technologies exam. You can take the exams on the same day or schedule them on different days. At one time, the tests had to be taken within 90 days of each other, but this is no longer required.

Where to Go

You can find a testing center and register for the exams online on these Web sites:

✔ **Prometric:** www.2test.com

✔ **VUE:** www.vue.com

How Much Does It Cost?

The cost of each exam is $132 U.S., or $85 if you or your company is a member of CompTIA. You can find discounted vouchers available for slightly more than the member rate if you shop around.

Chapter 2

Basic Electronics and Number Systems

· ·

Exam Objectives

▶ Identifying the concepts, terminology, and properties of electronics and electricity in the PC

▶ Identifying ESD (electrostatic discharge) and ESD protection devices

▶ Reading and converting binary, decimal, and hexadecimal number systems

· ·

*E*mbedded in the fundamentals of computer troubleshooting, repair, and maintenance is a knowledge and understanding of electricity, electronics, and number systems. You need to have a basic knowledge of electricity and electronic principles to even begin preparing yourself for the A+ Certification exams. Although no specific electronics or electricity questions are on the test, many questions assume a basic understanding of electricity concepts and terminology and the function of a few electronic components. Even if you know enough about electricity to repair a PC without destroying either the equipment or yourself, you may need a refresher on the names, definitions, concepts, and applications of electricity and electronics. Therefore, in this chapter I provide you with some groundwork that includes a very brief review of electricity and basic electronics.

Binary and hexadecimal number systems are used in the PC for addressing and data display. You may be asked to convert a binary number or two on the exam, and you can count on seeing binary and hexadecimal references in several questions. That's why this chapter takes a quick look at the binary and hexadecimal number systems. I also include a couple of labs to help you review the process of converting hexadecimal and binary numbers to and from decimal values.

Quick Assessment

Identifying the concepts, terminology, and properties of electronics and electricity in PCs

1 _____ measures the electrical pressure in a circuit.

2 _____ measures an electrical current's strength.

3 A semiconductor that can store one of two toggled values is a(n) _____.

4 Households use _____ current electricity.

5 PCs use _____ current electricity.

6 A(n) _____ is a device that can measure more than one property of electricity.

Identifying ESD and ESD protection devices

7 ESD stands for _____.

Reading and converting binary, decimal, and hexadecimal number systems

8 The _____ number system uses only the numbers 1 and 0.

9 The _____ number system uses the numbers 0–9 and the letters A–F.

Answers

1 *Voltage.* Review "Counting electrons."

2 *Amps.* See "Counting electrons."

3 *transistor.* Check out "Resistors, capacitors, transistors, and diodes."

4 *alternating.* Review "Switching from AC to DC."

5 *direct.* Direct yourself to "Switching from AC to DC."

6 *multimeter.* Check out "Measuring the current."

7 *electrostatic discharge.* Read "Don't Give Me Any Static."

8 *binary.* Review "Reading binary numbers."

9 *hexadecimal.* See "Working with hexadecimal numbers."

Understanding Electricity

Everything inside or attached to the PC system unit runs on electricity. Electricity is both the lifeblood and the mysterious evil of the personal computer. It's a flowing entity, measured in amps, ohms, and volts that should be approached with respect, if not outright fear.

Nothing helps you understand a complex technical topic better than a real-life analogy that you can relate to. I tried hard to come up with a new and original analogy to help you understand electrical properties and measurements and to dazzle you with my cleverness, but, unfortunately, I have failed. One analogy that I thought had a lot of potential involved Twinkies and beer, but it fell flat. So I am forced to use the same old water-in-the-hose analogy that you have probably seen and heard at least a thousand times. If you have heard it before, skip the next few paragraphs, but if it's new to you, read on.

Electricity flowing through a circuit is very much like water running through a hose. When you open a water faucet, the pressure in the water line forces the water to flow at some gallons-per-minute rate into the hose. Friction reduces the force and rate of the water before it exits the hose. When electricity flows into a wire from a source such as a battery, some of its pressure is lost to resistance in the wire.

The "electricity is like water in a hose" analogy points out the forces of electricity that can be measured. These forces are measured in volts, amps, and ohms. At the risk of running the analogy into the ground, Table 2-1 lists the water hose analogous element against its electrical equivalent.

Table 2-1	May the Force Be with You
Water Forces	*Electrical Forces*
How much pressure?	What's the voltage?
How much water is flowing?	What's the volume of the electrical current in amps?
Is there any friction in the hose?	What's the wire's resistance in ohms?

Table 2-2 may put this analogy into a little better perspective. The electrical measures are listed with a description and an example of how they're applied on the PC.

Counting electrons

The forces of electricity inside the computer can be measured, and each type of measurement tells you something different about the computer. I include the electrical measurements in Table 2-2 to provide you with an introduction to these units of measurement. Chapter 8 provides more information on the power used in the PC and how it is measured.

Table 2-2	Common Electrical Measurements	
Measurement	*Description*	*Application*
Amps	Measures a current's strength or rate of flow	The amount of current needed to operate a device; for example, a hard disk drive needs 2.0 amps to start up, but only 0.35 amps for typical operation.
Ohms	Measures a conductor's resistance to electricity	Resistance of less than 20 ohms means that current can flow through a computer system.
Volts	Measures the electrical pressure in a circuit	A PC power supply generates 4 levels of voltage: +5 volts (V), −5V, +12V, and −12V.
Watts	Measures the electrical power in a circuit	A PC power supply is rated in a range of 200 to 600 watts.
Continuity	Indicates the existence of a complete circuit	A pin in a DIN connector registers 5V on a digital voltage meter (DVM or multimeter) when grounded to another pin.

Measuring the current

The primary measurements of electricity are volts and amps. Volts measure pressure, and amps measure current. Current isn't needed to have voltage. When a water faucet is off, water pressure still exists. There is just no current. Likewise, when an electrical circuit is open, voltage (pressure) is still in the line although no current is flowing. If you touch the wire and close the circuit, the current begins to flow, and you can feel all of its pressure as a *shock*.

You can use a variety of devices to read the power and fury of an electrical current. Ammeters, ohmmeters, and voltmeters measure specific properties, but using a multimeter or DVM is more efficient for you to use because it combines these instruments into one tool.

Switching from AC to DC

Current is the flow of electrons in a wire. Electricity has two current types: AC (alternating current) and DC (direct current). AC is what you get from the outlets in your house or office, and DC is the type used inside the computer.

In alternating current, the current changes directions about 60 times per second, moving first one way, and then the other. The voltage changing rapidly from a positive charge to a negative charge causes the current to also switch the direction of its flow in the wire. AC power exists because it has advantages for the power company and for your household electrical appliances, but these advantages have little value on a low-voltage system like a PC.

When the flow of the electricity is in one direction only, it is direct current. What happens in direct current is that negatively charged particles seek out and flow toward positively charged particles, creating a direct electrical current flow. DC power maintains a constant level and flows in only one direction — always, predictably, and measurably, from a negative charge to a positive charge.

For example, wire a light bulb to a battery, and the current flows from the negative terminal to the positive terminal through the light bulb. Because the current of electricity causes heat and light in the right materials, the lighter materials in the light bulb glow.

The PC uses DC power. The PC's power supply converts power from the AC wall outlet into DC power for the computer. Peripheral devices, such as printers, external modems, and storage drives, including CD-ROM and Zip drives, use an AC power converter to convert AC power into DC power.

Okay, so the computer runs on direct current electricity. What does this fact have to do with the A+ exam?

When answering a question about the power supply, you must know what 3.3V, –5V, +5V, –12V, and +12V represent (3.3 volts, minus 5 volts, plus 5 volts, minus 12 volts, and plus 12 volts, which are DC power levels produced by the power supply).

Focus on the following electrical terms or concepts:

- ✔ Voltage and volts
- ✔ Amperes or amps

> ✔ Electrical resistance
>
> ✔ Ohms
>
> ✔ Watts
>
> ✔ Alternating current
>
> ✔ Direct current
>
> ✔ 5 or 12 volts DC current

Reviewing Elementary Electronics

Now that you know a little about electricity, you should review basic electronics principles. What follows is a series of definitions and concepts that both prepares you for any direct questions on electronics (not very many) and provides you with background information for questions in other areas. This stuff is pretty basic, so if you're an electronics whiz, you may want to skip over it.

Digital circuits

A digital circuit is an electronic circuit that accepts and processes binary data using the rules of Boolean algebra — the logic of AND, OR, NOT, and so on. Digital circuits are made up of one or more electronic components placed in a series to work cooperatively to achieve the logical objective of the circuit.

Conductors, insulators, semiconductors

A *conductor,* such as copper, carries an electrical current. An *insulator,* such as rubber, doesn't carry an electrical current, which is why a copper wire conductor is usually wrapped with a rubber insulator.

In the conducting electricity scheme of things, halfway between a conductor and an insulator is a *semiconductor.* Although its name technically means "half-conductor," it's really neither a conductor nor an insulator. When a semiconductor is zapped with electricity or light, it toggles to either a conductor or an insulator, depending on what it was at the time it was zapped.

The reason I mention semiconductors at all is because they are the building block of the computer. Electricity can hold the properties of plus or minus polarity. The electronics in the PC are designed to take advantage of this by storing electricity in one polarity or the other and assigning a numerical value to each. In the PC, these numerical values are the ones and zeroes of binary data (see "Reading binary numbers" later in the chapter). By using a semiconductor, which can be toggled between two electrical values, the result is a perfect place to store all of the binary values that course around inside of the PC.

Confused? Don't be. It's actually very simple: A semiconductor is simply an extremely simple on/off switch. Zap it once, it's on; zap it again, it's off. Zap it, on; zap it, off — and so on.

Resistors, capacitors, transistors, and diodes

These four electronic components are the building blocks on which virtually every electronic circuit in the computer is built. Each plays a distinctly different and valuable role in a circuit, as I explain in the following:

- ✔ A *resistor* acts like a funnel to slow down the flow of current in a circuit.

- ✔ A *capacitor* is like a storage bin to hold a charge. The PC has a few large capacitors that can literally kill you if you make contact with them, such as the capacitors in the monitor and in the power supply.

- ✔ A *diode* is a one-way valve that allows the current to flow in only one direction.

- ✔ A *transistor* is a semiconductor that stores one binary value.

- ✔ Transistors, resistors, capacitors, and diodes produce logic gates. *Logic gates* create circuits, and circuits make up electronic systems.

Don't Give Me Any Static

The term *static* has a variety of meanings in computer technology. To the computer technician, static means *static electricity* (electrostatic charge) and its evil twin — *electrostatic discharge* (ESD), also called electrical static discharge, that have the most importance. If you were a superhero named PC Repairperson, you would battle the evil nemesis ElectroStat Dis, a negatively charged evildoer of the first order. ESD, as it is infamously called, is the evil demon that lies in wait for the unsuspecting service technician who fails to don the sacred wrist strap before kneeling at the PC altar.

Throughout this book, you see repeated warnings, cautions, and preventive actions for ESD; something that can't be emphasized too much. Focus on preventing ESD damage.

Always wear a grounded wrist strap that's connected to either a grounding mat or the PC chassis when you work on any part of the computer (except the monitor). If you're curious about why you don't wear your strap when working on a monitor, see Chapter 10.

Static electricity is what makes your hair stand on end when you rub a balloon against your head. Of course, this assumes that you have hair — and that you'd have occasion to rub a balloon against your head. Static electricity also occurs when you walk across a carpet. Static electricity is not by itself a problem; the danger is in the discharge of the static electricity. You know, when you reach for the doorknob and zap! A blue spark as big as a towrope jumps from your finger to the metal. Although this may seem harmless (other than the pain), the potential for a lot of damage to a PC exists in that seemingly harmless spark. Remember that lightning is ESD in its most dreaded form.

This is on the test. Just because you can't feel an electrostatic discharge doesn't mean that it can't do harm to an electronic component. A human feels ESD at around 3,000 volts, but a mere 30 volts will do damage to electronic components. ESD is a far greater threat to the PC than anything else the PC service technician might do accidentally.

Looking at the dark side of ESD

Most PCs are designed to have some ESD protection as long as their cases are intact and closed properly. Cases are chemically treated or have copper fittings designed to channel electrostatic discharge away from the sensitive components inside.

The danger from ESD damage begins when the case is opened and the fragile components on the motherboard are exposed. When a human with a static electrical charge touches anything inside the case, the charge can travel along the wires interconnecting the various electronic components. One of the wires may lead inside a component, and when the charge gets close enough to a metal part with an opposing charge, the internal wires and elements of components can explode or weld together.

So, ElectroStat Dis is real, and it's YOU!

Take a look at some ESD facts:

- ✔ Most of the computer's electronic components use from three to five volts of electricity.
- ✔ An ESD shock of 30 volts can destroy a computer circuit.
- ✔ An ESD shock you can *feel,* such as on a doorknob, has around 3,000 volts.
- ✔ An ESD shock you can *see* carries about 20,000 volts.

The real problem with ESD damage is that not all of it is obvious. If an entire component is destroyed, you know it, and you replace the piece. When a component has been damaged but continues to work, though, days, weeks, or even months may pass before the component fails completely. More frustrating is intermittent partial failures that can't be isolated.

Eliminating static electricity

You can avoid static electricity. Good environmental preventive measures that help to eliminate, or at least reduce, static electricity are as follows:

- ✔ Always wear a ESD grounding strap on your wrist or ankle that is connected to either the chassis of the PC or to a grounding mat when working inside the PC.

- ✔ Treat carpeting inexpensively with antistatic chemicals to reduce static buildup. Aerosol cans of these chemicals are available in most computer or carpet stores. If your employer doesn't provide antistatic carpet treatment, ask for it.

- ✔ Store all electrical components in antistatic bags when not in use.

- ✔ Install a grounded pad under the PC. Before you touch the computer, touch the pad, and discharge any built-up static electricity.

- ✔ If all else fails, install humidifiers to replace moisture in the air. Keep the humidity above 50 percent. Dry air can cause static electricity.

However, when working on the monitor, do not, I repeat, do not wear a grounding strap. The monitor has a very large capacitor in it and a grounding strap invites all of its stored charge to run through your body — not always a pleasant experience.

For all my ranting and raving on the threat of ESD, it does have some good uses. For example, it's used to apply toner to paper in copy machines and laser printers and is used to clean the air of unwanted pollen, dust, and other debris.

Polishing Up on Number Systems

On the A+ exams, you encounter questions that reference hexadecimal addresses for items such as IRQs and COM ports. The ability to read and understand binary and hexadecimal values helps you understand some questions.

For example, one test question may ask you for the address of where BIOS is commonly located in memory. The answer choices listed are hexadecimal values such as A0000 to AFFFF, B0000 to BFFFF, C0000 to CFFFF, and F0000 to

FFFFF. Your ability to discern which of the numbers represents the range closest to the 1MB boundary for the upper memory area is your key to the answer.

Your ability to work with binary and hexadecimal numbers can also help you with questions related to troubleshooting and debugging situations, as well as on the job.

Reading binary numbers

The binary number system is the foundation upon which all logic and data processing in the PC is built. In its simplest form, the *binary number system* consists of only two digital values: 1 and 0. Because a transistor is a semiconductor that can only store one of two toggled values, the binary number scheme and the electronics of the PC are made for each other.

Binary values are the result of the number 2 being raised to various powers. This is true for all number systems. The decimal number system is based on values of the number 10 raised to increasing powers. For example, 2^3 is 8, and 2^{10} is 1,024. An 8-bit byte can store the value 255, which is a number that should sound familiar to you, because it is virtually the limit on everything in the PC.

You may see a question on the test asking you to convert a binary number such as 00000101 to a *decimal value* — you know, ordinary numbers. The key is to remember that each position represents a power of 2, starting with 0 on the right end up through 7 at the left end. For example, the binary number 00001010 contains

> $0 \infty 20 = 0$ (any number to the zero power is worth 1)
>
> $1 \infty 21 = 2$ (any number to the one power is the number)
>
> $0 \infty 22 = 0$ (two times two)
>
> $1 \infty 23 = 8$ (two times two times two)
>
> Totaling 10 (the remaining positions are all zero)

So, 00001010 in binary is the same as 10 in decimal. Just count the positions, starting from the right with zero, and then calculate the powers of two for each position with a one.

Follow the steps in Lab 2-1 to convert the numbers in your street address to a binary number. (If your house number is greater than 65,536, use a lower number.)

Lab 2-1   Converting Decimal to Binary

1. **Figure out the largest power of two values that can be subtracted from the number.**

   For a house number of 63,529, the largest binary value that can be subtracted is 32,768, or 2^{15}. Probably, a very scientific way exists to determine this number, but I use trial and error to find the largest power of 2 that can be subtracted from the starting number. For example, 2^{16} is 65,536 and that was too big, so I had to use the next lower power of 2. Because this value is 2^{15}, a 1 can be placed in position 16 of the binary number (remember the first power of two is a zero — so values of 2^{15} go in the 16th position. Got it?). I have 1000000000000000 for the binary number so far. This represents the following:

215	214	213	...	22	21	20
1	0	0	...	0	0	0

2. **Subtract 32,768 from your original number.**

   The difference in this example is 30,761. Repeating the process used in Step 1, the highest value that can be subtracted from this number is 16,384, or 2^{14}. The binary number is now 1100000000000000.

   Continuing the process through each remaining value of the original decimal number and for each digit in the binary number, the final binary number for this example is 1111100000101001.

How did your house number come out?

Of course, if you have one handy, you could use a scientific calculator to convert these numbers, but you won't always have one with you, so being able to convert decimal numbers to binary is a good skill for a PC repair technician to have. Luckily, you don't have to demonstrate this skill on the A+ test. You're not allowed to use a calculator on the test, anyway.

Addressing in binary

Because all data is stored as a binary value in the computer, the size of the computer's bus (8, 16, 32, or 64 bits) controls both the highest address that can be stored (and accessed) and the largest value that can be stored at any address. A 16-bit address bus can store an address or value of 2^{15}, or 32,768 — my lucky number! A 32-bit word length handles 2^{31}, or 2,147,483,648, and 64 bits stores a really big number with lots of commas.

The largest number that can be stored in a certain number of bits is calculated by raising two to a power represented by the number of bits minus one.

Working with hexadecimal numbers

The word *hexadecimal* means *six and ten,* and that's just what this number system is about. Whereas binary includes only zero and one, hex, as it's known to its friends, includes the decimal numerals 0 to 9 (the ten) and replaces the decimal values of 10 to 15 with the symbols A, B, C, D, E, and F (the six).

Expect to be asked for the hexadecimal number addresses of one or more IRQs, LPT, or COM ports on the test. For example, 2F8 is the default address of IRQ3 and COM2. The decimal equivalent of this number is unimportant, but the ability to convert hexadecimal numbers is a good basic skill for PC repair technicians, because you often need to convert a range of addresses to decimal to determine the size of a memory, storage, or address range. For example, the DOS DEBUG program gives memory locations in hexadecimal with a hexadecimal offset to indicate its size. You need to be able to convert this number to know how big an area it is.

Concentrate on the hexadecimal addresses of the IRQs, COM, and LPT ports and not the decimal equivalents of these hexadecimal values.

Converting hexadecimal numbers

As I show in Lab 2-1 earlier in this chapter, converting any nondecimal number system to decimal is a matter of knowing two things: the *radix* (base value) of the number system and the numeric value of each position. In binary numbers, each position represents a different power of two; the same holds true in any number system, including hexadecimal. The difference with hexadecimal is that each position represents a different power of 16.

The radix of a number is the value that 10 represents in that number's number system. The radix of decimal is 10, the radix of binary is 2, and the radix of hexadecimal is 16.

What is the decimal equivalent of the hexadecimal number A012F? Use the process in Lab 2-2 to convert it.

Lab 2-2	Converting Hexadecimal to Decimal

1. Because each position represents a power of 16, the A in A012F represents the positional value of 16^4. The A has the decimal equivalent of 10. So, this position is worth $10 \infty 16^4$, or 655,360.

2. The next position of value is a 1 in the position of 16^2, which is worth 256.

3. The next position has a value of $2 \infty 16^1$, or 32.

4. **The last position has the value of F (15) ∞ 16^0, or 15. Any number to the zero power is worth 1, so this is the same as 15 ∞ 1.**

5. **Add up the values: 655360 + 256 + 32 + 15. The sum is 655,663 — the decimal equivalent of A012F hexadecimal.**

Hexadecimal numbers are usually written with a small *h* following them. For example, the number used in the preceding lab is written as A012Fh. The h in A012h is a commonly used convention to indicate that a number is in hexadecimal form.

Hexadecimal numbers are by far easier to convert with a calculator, but knowing how to convert them can come in handy, especially when working with debugging and troubleshooting tools or when taking an A+ exam.

Prep Test

1 The decimal equivalent of 00000110 is

A ○ 8
B ○ 5
C ○ 110
D ○ 6

2 The number A06F is most likely from which numbering system?

A ○ Decimal
B ○ Binary
C ○ Hexadecimal
D ○ Octal

3 Electrical current is measured in

A ○ Amps
B ○ Ohms
C ○ Volts
D ○ Watts

4 What is the most common threat to PC hardware when being serviced by a technician?

A ○ ESD
B ○ Accidental breakage of a component
C ○ Improper tools damaging a component
D ○ Placing components on the wrong type of surface to work

5 Electrical resistance is measured in

A ○ Amps
B ○ Ohms
C ○ Volts
D ○ Watts

6 You should ground yourself with an ESD wrist strap when working on which of the following? (Choose all that apply.)

A ❑ Memory board
B ❑ Motherboard
C ❑ Hard drive
D ❑ System board

7 **The microcomputer operates on _____ current electricity.**

A ○ Alternating

B ○ Direct

C ○ Switchable

D ○ Directional

8 **The decimal equivalent of A00h is**

A ○ 44

B ○ 32,768

C ○ 2,560

D ○ 65,536

9 **Computer components can be damaged by an ESD charge of**

A ○ 2,000V

B ○ 30V

C ○ 30,000V

D ○ 3 to 5V

10 **What does ESD refer to?**

A ○ Electronically safe device

B ○ Electrical static discharge

C ○ Electric surge protector

D ○ None of the above

Answers

1 **D.** The binary number 00000110 is the same as adding 22 (4) and 21 (2) to get 6. *Take a look at "Reading binary numbers."*

2 **C.** A binary number consists of only 1s and 0s. An octal number has no digits higher than a 7; and this is obviously not a decimal number. Any number that has the characters A through F and 0 through 9 is a hexadecimal number. *Check out "Working with hexadecimal numbers."*

3 **A.** The strength of an electrical current is measured with an ammeter in amps. *Review "Counting electrons."*

4 **A.** ESD damage is far more common than any other damage inflicted by the repairperson or user. *Look at "Don't Give Me Any Static."*

5 **B.** Electrical resistance, or the amount of resistance in a conductor to the flow of electricity, is measured with an ohmmeter in ohms. *See "Counting electrons."*

6 **A,B,C,D.** Wear an ESD grounding strap when working all of these FRMs (field replaceable modules). The only part of the computer you don't want to be grounded to is the Cathode Ray Tube (CRT) — see Chapter 10 for more information. *Check out "Resistors, capacitors, transistors, and diodes" and "Don't Give Me Any Static."*

7 **B.** Household appliances operate on alternating current, but the computer operates on direct current. The power supply converts AC to DC. *Take a look at "Switching from AC to DC."*

8 **C.** A00h is the same as 10 ∞ 256 (16 ~2), or 2,560. *Review "Converting hexadecimal numbers."*

9 **B.** It doesn't take very much of an ESD charge to zap the internal components of a computer. *Check out "Looking at the dark side of ESD."*

10 **B.** ESD is the abbreviation for either electrical static discharge or electrostatic discharge; both terms are used interchangeably. *Zap over to "Don't Give Me Any Static."*

Chapter 3

Using the Right Tools

Exam Objectives

▶ Using common hand tools appropriately

▶ Applying diagnostic tools to troubleshoot and isolate problems

▶ Using a multimeter to measure voltage, amps, and ohms

*M*uch of the A+ Core Hardware exam relates to troubleshooting and diagnosing PC problems, and installing, configuring, and upgrading field replacement modules (FRM). Therefore, the PC service technician must have and know how to use the appropriate tools. The application of specific tools is a minor consideration of the A+ Core Hardware exam, but I believe that you must have knowledge of the repair process and the tools used to be completely successful on the test, as well as on the job.

The PC repair technician uses tools in two different situations: troubleshooting and repairing. Luckily, a single tool kit can be used for both situations. For example, a digital voltmeter (DVM) can be used to determine if an AC line carries the proper voltage and if a new FRM is installed properly.

You can do most customer-site diagnostics and repairs with about a dozen or so tools and a few pieces of software, so you don't need to carry around a suitcase full of stuff. On the other hand, a well-equipped tool kit ensures that you'll have the right tools with you and that you'll be ready for just about any situation.

The service tool kit can be divided into three groups: hardware tools, software tools, and measurement tools.

The A+ Core Hardware exam has very few questions on the specific uses of tools. You won't be asked the purpose of a screwdriver, how to use a pair of wire cutters, what a tweaker is, or the like. However, you might see a question about when a tool is used or which tools are used in a diagnostics situation. For example, you may be asked which tool is used to measure the power available from the power supply. (Answer: DVM.) Preparing you for this type of questioning is the primary mission of this chapter.

Quick Assessment

Using common hand tools

1 The _____ is an absolute necessity in any tool kit.

2 _____ is a supply item that's used for cleaning fans, grill work, inside the case, keyboards, and other parts of the PC.

3 _____ are used to diagnose a parallel or serial port on a PC.

Applying diagnostic tools to troubleshoot and isolate problems

4 The _____ is one of the most effective diagnostics tools available and runs every time you boot the system.

5 _____ software performs troubleshooting, system tune-ups, hardware checks, and system status.

Using a multimeter to measure voltage, amps, and ohms

6 A(n) _____ is a voltmeter, ammeter, and sometimes ohmmeter rolled into one.

7 The range of values used when measuring VDC is _____ to _____.

8 Placing one probe on a pin at an end of a serial cable and the other probe on a pin at the other end of the cable checks for _____.

Answers

1 *ESD wrist strap.* Review "ESD wrist strap."

2 *Compressed air.* Check out "Supplies."

3 *Loop-back plugs.* Look at "Loop-back plugs."

4 *BIOS POST.* See "The domestic tools."

5 *Diagnostic.* Visit "The foreign tools."

6 *Multimeter.* Review "Working with a Multimeter."

7 *3V to 12V.* Look at "Working with a Multimeter."

8 *Continuity.* Check out "Working with a Multimeter."

Hardware Tools

For the Core Hardware exam, you'll need a thorough understanding of the tools used to diagnose, troubleshoot, remove, and install FRMs in the PC. Your ability to appropriately use tools in troubleshooting, diagnosing, and repairing a PC is assumed in the A+ exams. If you have a fair amount of experience using tools to diagnose and troubleshoot PC problems, then you should at least skim this chapter. However, if you don't have much hands-on experience with these tools and how they are used, study this chapter, especially the section on multimeters.

There are literally hundreds of different types of hardware tools. Some tools are specific to particular tasks and others are more generic. Luckily for PC repair technicians, most of the necessary tools are fairly generic, which saves money when buying tools. The more specific a tool is to a task, the more it costs.

You can buy an adequate tool kit that has most of the basic tools you need at your local computer or electronics store or online for less than $20. (They often come in nifty little zippered cases.) When buying a tool kit, be sure that it has an electrostatic discharge (ESD) grounding wrist strap.

The PC repair technician's tool kit consists of two groups of hardware tools: the never-go-to-the-customer-site-without-these-tools and the tools-that-are-kept-at-the-shop-for-major-surgery. Like a doctor's bag, only the instruments and generic medicines that are needed for general care are carried in the bag, and the really strange and specific tools are left back in the operating room.

The following sections discuss the general categories of hardware tools, separating each category into those tools that go into the doctor's bag and those that should be left in the operating room.

Tools you shouldn't leave home without

Many tools should be carried to all customer sites. They're the staples of your tool kit. Don't leave home without 'em.

Screwdrivers

Screwdrivers are used in assembly and disassembly tasks, which are common activities in repairing and diagnosing PC problems. (You don't need a huge assortment of screwdrivers.) The screws used in the PC come in four general flavors: Phillips (cross-head recess or star), slotted (standard), hex head, or Torx. If you have one or two good screwdrivers for each type of screw, you'll never need to return to the shop to get the screwdriver you didn't think you'd ever need.

Know the different screw heads by sight, especially the Phillips and Torx.

Magnetic screwdrivers, although convenient, can be dangerous to the sensitive electronic components inside the computer. Take it from somebody with fingers like small tree trunks: Using a magnetic screwdriver to fish out a screw that has fallen inside the system case is tempting, but there are fragile electronic circuits that the electromagnetic field can damage. More than likely, poking around with the screwdriver is a greater danger than the magnetic tip. Regardless, I suggest you adopt a better-safe-than-sorry attitude and use nonmagnetic tools.

Needle nose pliers

While not completely necessary, you can use needle nose pliers to hold screws and connectors when your fingers are just too big. They also are handy for working with wire, and most needle nose pliers have a wire cutter near the hinge. I suggest carrying a set with you, just in case.

The handles on some pliers are plastic or rubber, which improve your grip, but don't protect you from electrical shock. Pliers that are insulated against shock are marked as such, but are very rare.

Parts retriever

This tool has a small set of retractable claws that extend when a button on the spring-loaded handle is pressed. After they are extended, you can place the claws around an item to be retrieved, such as the screw that fell onto the motherboard, and release the spring to grasp the item. This tool is a necessity and a safer choice than a magnetic screwdriver.

Diagonal cutters (dikes)

Manufacturers usually bundle all the cables, including the one you need, with cable ties. A small pair of diagonal cutters, also known as dikes, are useful for cutting cable ties and any other thick wire or plastic that you need to cut. Of course, cutting a cable tie should remind you to put some extra cable tie in your tool kit.

ESD wrist strap

This tool is a necessity in every tool kit for travel and in the shop. An *ESD wrist strap* (shown in Figure 3-1) is akin to the mask worn by the surgeon over his or her mouth and face. An ESD wrist strap is an elastic or Velcro wristband with a coiled wire that has a snap or clip at the end. The clip or snap attaches to a computer chassis or a grounding mat, or both, that grounds you and eliminates the potential for ESD damage from you or your tools.

Wear an ESD wrist strap (or ankle strap or heel strap if your workplace is equipped for them) whenever you open the system unit or handle circuit cards, such as the motherboard or expansion cards. The wrist strap must make two good contacts — with your skin at the wrist strap end and with a grounded surface through the clip or snap end.

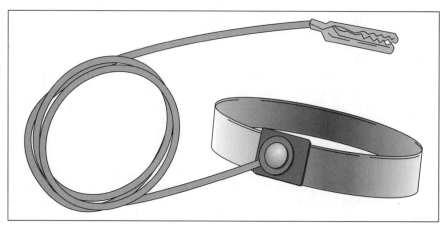

Figure 3-1:
An ESD wrist strap is an essential piece of equipment to have in your tool kit.

Follow these steps to ensure that both you and the PC are protected against ESD:

1. **Turn the PC's power switch to its OFF position. Verify that the power actually goes off.**

2. **Unplug the PC's power cord.**

3. **Ensure that you and the PC will not be in contact with any other grounded objects.**

4. **Place the PC on a flat surface that is free from metallic objects, electrical cords, power supplies, hydroelectric plants, and the like. Make sure that the PC is not touching another PC or any other electrical device that is plugged into an electrical outlet.**

An ESD wrist strap has a one-megaohm resistor located in its grounding cord. Never, for any reason, remove this resistor. If the resistor is damaged or is not working, replace the grounding cord or the entire wrist strap immediately. Dispose of the faulty cord or strap to avoid using it accidentally.

You can find just about anything you ever wanted to know about ESD and ESD protection on the ESDSystems.Com Web site provided by Desco Industries, Inc. at www.esdsystems.com.

Multimeter

One of the primary troubleshooting and diagnostic tools in your tool kit is a multimeter, also known as a digital multimeter or digital voltage multimeter (DVM). On the A+ Core Hardware exam, it is referred to as a multimeter. This tool, shown in Figure 3-2, is used to test or measure a range of electrical properties of the PC. The multimeter is covered in greater detail in "Working with a Multimeter" later in the chapter.

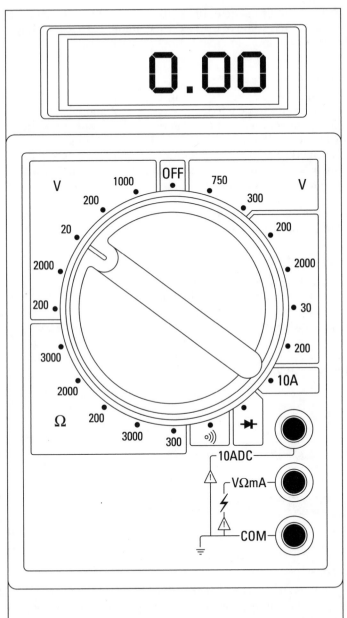

Figure 3-2:
A multimeter
is used to
test and
measure the
electrical
properties
of the PC
and its
components.

Flashlight

A flashlight is another must-have. Many gloomy shadows lurk inside the computer where screws and other small parts can fall. You may also need it to read some very small print on chips, labels, or circuit boards, such as the pin markings on a connector or version numbers on a ROM, that can be hard to read in the shadows inside of the system. A small high-beam flashlight comes in handy, although some of us need what amounts to a searchlight for finding small parts or components inside the PC's case.

Loop-back plugs

You rarely need to diagnose or repair a parallel or serial port on a PC. However, if it is necessary to isolate a port problem, *loop-back plugs,* which simulate a connection on a port, can be used to test the function of a port. Loop-back plugs, which are constructed by connecting the pins of a connector head together so that the data sent out is immediately sensed on the receiving pins of the port, are typically used in conjunction with a diagnostics software package, such as Pc-Check (`www.eurosoft-usa.com`), Norton Utilities (`www.symantec.com`), or CheckIt (`www.touchstonesoftware.com`). A loop-back plug performs a full operations test to determine if the cause of a communications error problem is in the port.

Operating tools

I carry a small set of dental and medical tools that includes angled mirrors (like those shown in Figure 3-3), hemostats, and probes. They have no specific repair purpose but come in handy when I need to see a connector or wire deep inside the computer or around a card or connector. You can find nonmedical versions (which are cheaper than medical versions) of these tools at most tool shops. Most good commercial tool kits available now include these items.

Figure 3-3:
Angled mirrors help see around corners inside the PC.

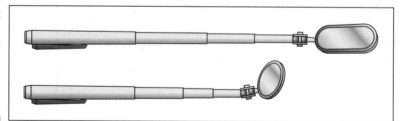

Sharp edge

When you need to cut through something that can't be cut with wire cutters or dikes, a utility knife or blade of some type can be just what you need. If you carry one with you, be sure that it has a retracting edge or snug-fitting cover. You may also want to include a small, good-quality pair of scissors in your tool kit. Just make sure that it has a cover or small case to keep you from stabbing yourself when you reach into the kit.

Vacuum

Anytime you open a PC, perform a little preventive maintenance. (See Chapter 17 — "Preventive Maintenance.") If nothing else, vacuum the system case to remove all of the dust bunnies that have accumulated inside since the last time it was cleaned (if ever). A variety of small vacuum cleaners designed specifically for PCs is available in both AC and battery powered models. Most have either a small brush head, like the one shown in Figure 3-4, or a relatively short hose on which brush attachments are mounted.

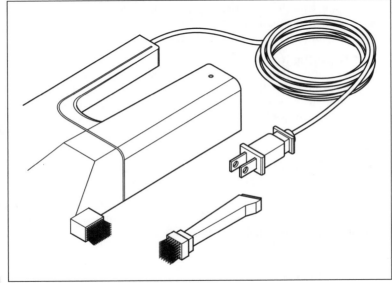

Figure 3-4:
A small hand-held vacuum cleaner helps clean out the system case.

Very few PC vacuums can be used to clean a laser printer. The toner in a laser printer can severely clog up any vacuum not specifically designed to handle it. Be sure that your vacuum can handle toner before you use it for that purpose.

Tools you can safely leave at the shop

The following tools and their uses may show up in test questions. These tools aren't used often enough to warrant lugging them around to every site, but that doesn't mean that they don't come in handy back in the shop. The following sections discuss tools that have specific purposes that aren't called to duty quite as often as other tools.

✔ **Wire cutters/strippers:** You rarely need to cut a wire in a computer or strip the insulator on a wire or cable. But when you do, you need a wire cutter or wire stripper. Most technicians use a tool that can be used to both cut and strip a wire. Should the repair require this level of activity, take it to the shop — where you have this tool waiting.

✔ **Chip tools:** You can use chip tools in two ways: inserting Dual Inline Packaging (DIP) chips and extracting DIP chips. Just about every commercial tool kit comes with a DIP chip inserter/extractor tool. DIP chips are rare (except on the snack table), so you may never be asked to insert or remove one. If you don't have an inserter/extractor tool, try using a slotted screwdriver or tweaker and then remove it with your fingers. Inserting a DIP chip with your hand often works better than the official tool and damages fewer chip pins in the process.

✔ **Soldering iron:** Many technicians say that a soldering iron is a useless tool and should be omitted from commercial tool kits. I agree that at a customer site, this tool should never see the light of day, but in the shop, it is handy for repairing cables and other tasks. As long as it's kept away from circuit boards, it can't do much damage.

Supplies

Not all hardware tools are actually tools in the common sense of the word. Some actually fall more into the category of supplies. Consider keeping the following supplies close at hand. They're cheap, easy to find, and may save your bacon sometime:

✔ **Electrical tape:** The black plastic kind, for wrapping wire ends and insulating other components is handy for covering the flashing time on a VCR.

✔ **Compressed air:** Handy for cleaning fans, grill work, inside the case, keyboards, and so on. Compressed air comes in handy-dandy aerosol cans. Place a thin, plastic tube in the spray head to pinpoint just where you want the air to go.

✔ **Soft, lint-free cloth:** Or should I say, the proverbial "soft, lint-free cloth." Just about every preventive maintenance or cleaning instruction for any part of a PC calls for this. Good for cleaning the glass and plastic components of the computer and peripherals. Do you think you can remember that you need a soft, lint-free cloth or should I remind you later?

✔ **Spare parts:** An assortment of screws, expansion card inserts, faceplaces, and cables should be kept on hand. If, for example, you need to remove a card and can't immediately replace it, you can cover its hole with an expansion card insert. You know the customer didn't save the one that came out of the PC, if one ever existed. You typically collect these parts as you work on more and more PCs.

Software Tools

You will definitely encounter questions that ask when, why, and what to expect from the software tools described in this section.

A PC's problem is not always apparent. Rarely do you arrive to find the power supply on fire, which would be a clear indication that the problem is actually the power supply. If you've worked with PCs long enough, you know that no problem is ever exactly what it seems. (Of course, the power supply or another FRM being on fire would definitely be an exception.) The problem often lies deep inside the computer, and you must employ something other than hardware tools.

When the problem is apparent, you may need to use diagnostic and trouble-shooting software. These tools are as essential to your tool kit as the Phillips screwdriver is. Whether they're a part of your travel tool kit is a policy matter for you or your employer. Using your software involves installing and uninstalling the software for each use. If your customer has a particular need or is having a repeating problem, you may want to encourage the customer to purchase a copy of the diagnostic software for his or her PC.

Luckily, some of these tools are included with the operating system, as are those discussed in the next section — "The domestic tools." Another group of software tools must be licensed (purchased) for use on one or more computers. This group is discussed in "The foreign tools," later in the chapter.

The domestic tools

Most of the items in this group of software diagnostic tools are usually included as a part of the operating system.

✔ **BIOS POST**: This effective diagnostic tool is built right into the PC and runs automatically every time the PC is powered on. If a serious hardware problem exists, most likely the POST finds it and reports it to you. Check out Chapter 5 for more information on this process.

✔ **POST card:** (Not the kind Aunt Sally sends to you from Iowa and the other exotic places she visits.) This piece of hardware (an expansion card) is a dedicated circuit card that interprets the POST error codes written to address 80h. (The "h" means hexadecimal — see Chapter 2 for more information on this and other numbering systems used in the PC.) A POST card saves you the trouble of counting beeps and decoding them. Chapter 5 has more information on POST beep codes and their meanings.

✔ **MSD.EXE:** (also known as Microsoft Diagnostics): This DOS utility, which should probably be carried with you, creates and reports a brief inventory of your PC. This inventory is useful for seeing a system's configuration, including the BIOS, disks, memory, and system resource assignments, such as IRQs (interrupt requests) and I/O (input/output) addresses to LPT and serial ports. It was included with MS-DOS and Windows versions through Windows 95, but it is no longer distributed.

MSD.EXE will run under Windows 95. Although it is on the Windows 95 release CD and can be copied to the system, it isn't included in a normal Windows 95 installation. Run MSD.EXE in DOS mode, not in a DOS window, under Windows 95.

✔ **SCANDISK.EXE:** This program, installed as a part of all Windows versions, checks and reports hard disk problems, including file system corruption and hard disk read errors. If a PC is not shut down properly, this utility will run automatically when the PC is next restarted.

✔ **MEM.EXE:** This DOS utility is distributed with Windows 9*x* versions. It provides details about the memory configuration and usage on a PC.

✔ **DEFRAG.EXE:** This DOS and Windows utility rearranges data clusters on the disk to improve disk I/O efficiency.

✔ **SYSEDIT.EXE:** This Windows tool is used to view or edit INI, AUTOEXEC. BAT, CONFIG.SYS, and other system files.

✔ **Windows Device Manager:** This tool is useful on Windows 9*x* and 2000 systems for a problem caused by a resource conflict, IRQ, DMA channel, or I/O address. The Properties feature shows the device driver, resource settings, and much more for a specific hardware device. See Chapters 20 and 21 for more information.

The foreign tools

Three types of software tools can be used to help troubleshoot, diagnose, or repair PC problems:

✔ **Anti-virus:** Due to the increase in e-mail, Web, and other Internet access, PCs need immunity against computer viruses. A variety of anti-virus software packages are on the market. Having an anti-virus program available on a floppy disk can help you solve a customer problem caused by a virus before it spreads to other system users.

✔ **Diagnostic and troubleshooting:** A number of diagnostics packages are available, such as QAPlus (www.diagsoft.com), AMIDiag (www.megatrends.com), and those listed in "Loop-back plugs" earlier in the chapter, that perform troubleshooting, system tune-ups, hardware diagnostics, and system status reporting. Often these packages include other features such as file encryption, file compression, undelete, and other file utilities.

> ✔ **Uninstaller/Cleaning:** TheWindows environment uses the first-in-stays-here mode of file management. Windows programs leave behind more junk than NASA, which is why uninstall and file cleanup software are essential tools. Although you may never be called upon to clean up a customer's files, you may need to remove conflicting or out-of-date DLLs or the like. For an extensive list of this type of software, visit CNET's Windows File Cleanup Utilities page at `http://winfiles.cnet.com/apps/98/file-cleanup.html`.

Working with a Multimeter

The A+ Core Hardware exam expects you to know how to use, when to use, and what to measure with a multimeter. Expect questions in the trouble-shooting area that ask which settings to use when measuring volts, amps, and ohms. If you don't have much experience with a multimeter, get one and read the booklet that comes with it or ask a more experienced PC service technician to explain it to you.

Most PC technicians carry a multimeter in their travel tool kit. A multimeter is a voltmeter, an ammeter, and sometimes an ohmmeter all rolled into one. It measures electrical resistance, voltage, and current. Most multimeters used by field technicians are battery powered, but some higher-end models use AC power.

The A+ Core Hardware exam expects you to know how to use a multimeter to identify, troubleshoot, and isolate common FRM electrical problems. This section includes some laboratories to give you some practice using the multimeter.

Using other meters to get by

A multimeter combines the testing capability of several other devices. In fact, a multimeter is also referred to as a *volt-ohm-meter (VOM)* or a *multitester*. If you prefer, you can use separate devices to test for volts, amps, and ohms. You should know at least what these devices are and what each measures (if you can remember the name, you should know what they do). Don't sweat the technical definitions. Here is a description of each of these devices:

> ✔ **Voltmeter:** This device measures a circuit's potential difference (volts). Virtually every multimeter, digital or analog, measures voltage. You may run into the abbreviation DVM (digital voltmeter) in product documenta-tion. If you do, DMM (digital multimeter) works just as well.

> ✔ **Ammeter**: This device measures a circuit's current (amps). Some low-end multimeters may not measure amps, but PC repair technicians rarely measure amps anyway.
>
> ✔ **Ohmmeter**: This device measures resistance (ohms) and is a common feature on nearly all multimeters.

Sorting out multimeters

A *multimeter* is a mass-produced piece of electronic test equipment that is used to measure the properties of AC and DC electrical power circuits. The range of capabilities available on multimeters is quite wide, and even the simplest (and cheapest) have features you will never, or at least rarely, use.

The two major categories of multimeters are digital and analog.

Digital multimeters

A digital multimeter does not typically include a computer. The term digital means that the output numbers that represent the results of a measurement are displayed on an LCD (liquid crystal diode) screen. In other words, the results are displayed as digits, as illustrated in Figure 3-2 earlier in the chapter and in Figure 3-5. There are handheld and desktop models, but most PC technicians prefer the handheld model for its portability.

Analog multimeters

An analog multimeter, which performs the same functions as a digital multimeter, displays its results on a scaled dial that uses a needle to indicate the value measured, as illustrated in Figure 3-6. Analog multimeters are preferred by some technicians because they are usually less expensive than digital multimeters, so if you lose one, it won't be too difficult to replace. An economical digital multimeter costs around $20 and an analog version around $14. One drawback to a switched range analog multimeter is that it can be difficult for most beginners to read accurately.

Switching or ranging: What's your pleasure?

Digital multimeters are available in two different functional types:

> ✔ **Switched range**: As illustrated in Figure 3-2, this type of multimeter has a large central dial that must be set to the value appropriate to the measurement you are performing. For example, if you set the dial to a 20 VDC (volts direct current), then the highest value that will be measured is 20 volts. This is the setting you would use for most PC power supply systems, although on some of the newest systems, you may have occasion

to use the 2 VDC setting to measure 1.3 volt circuits. The AC settings are used to measure alternating current — the power type that comes from the wall outlet. You probably won't use all of the settings available on your switched range multimeter. See Chapter 2 for more information on AC and DC power and Chapter 10 for information on the power supply FRM.

✔ **Autoranging**: On this type of multimeter, the central dial positions are used to indicate the quantity, such as volts and amps, that you want to measure. If you set the dial to the *V* setting, it will automatically set its range to the source being measured to display both the measurement value and type, such as 5.5 V to indicate volts DC. A drawback to an autoranging multimeter is that its level of convenience carries a higher price.

A multimeter has two probes: a red (positive) probe and a black (negative) probe. When you test a device, place the red probe on the *hot point,* or high point, of the current and place the black probe on the *ground,* or low point. The voltage of the circuit is calculated as the difference in the readings of these two points.

Never, repeat, never connect a multimeter to the main (building) electrical supply line, which carries 20 kilowatts or more of power. This is very bad for your multimeter and it won't do you much good, either.

Using a multimeter

On a PC, a multimeters are used to measure voltage (volts) and resistance (ohms) between two points. Volts and ohms are always measured between two points. Typically, current (amps) is not measured on a PC because the circuit must be altered to do so. If you really need to know the amps of a circuit, it's easier to measure the volts and amps and then calculate the amps using Ohm's law ($I = V/R$), where I is the amps (current), V is the volts, and R is the ohms (resistance).

You can actually make four measurements on a PC using a multimeter:

✔ **Amps:** Measure the strength of an electrical current

✔ **Farads:** Measure the capacitance of an electrical device (See Chapters 10 and 13 for more information on farads.)

✔ **Ohms:** Measure the resistance in an electrical medium

✔ **Voltage:** Measures the electrical potential of a circuit

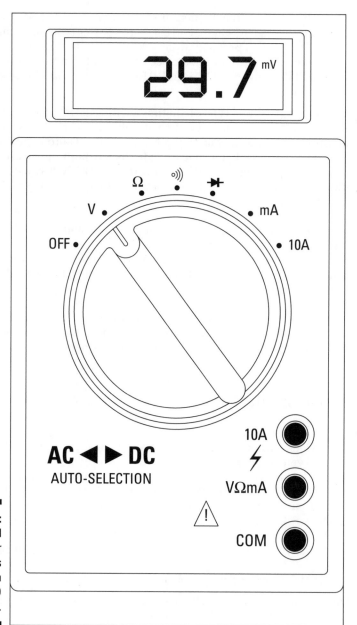

Figure 3-5:
A digital multimeter displays its results on an LCD display.

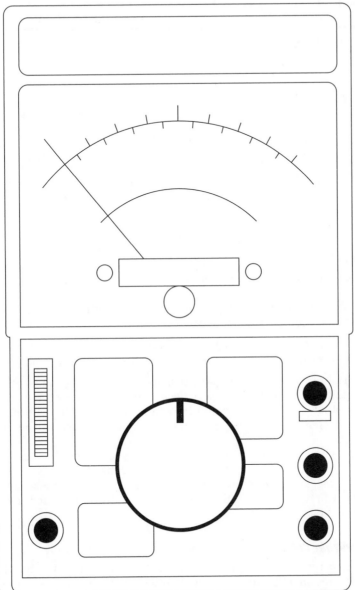

Figure 3-6:
An analog
multimeter.

Why you measure for an electrical property is something that you should understand. Table 3-1 lists the type of problems that can be identified in some systems and the property that is measured.

Table 3-1	Troubleshooting with a Multimeter	
Component/System	*Property*	*Potential Faults*
Power supply connectors	Volts	Defective power supply, cables, or connectors
Cable connections	Ohms	Broken or defective cable
Cable shielding	Ohms	Broken or defective cable sheath or insulation
Electrical FRMs	Volts or Ohms	Improper electrical operation to specifications

Probing for power

When preparing a multimeter for use, you must set three things:

✔ **The type of current you're measuring:** AC or DC (also known as VDC — voltage direct current).

✔ **What you're measuring:** Set the appropriate indicator or dial to voltage (volts), current (amps), or resistance or continuity (ohms).

✔ **The range of values expected:** If you're measuring voltage from the power supply, the voltage range is 3V to 12V, and for the AC wall plug's output, the range is around 105V to 125V. You can find Autorange multimeters that sense the incoming power and set the range automatically.

Lab 3-1 gives you some general experience using the multimeter. Lab 3-2 shows you how to check the continuity on a cable. If you have a DVM that doesn't measure continuity, skip Lab 3-2. The purpose of these labs is to enable you to understand the process of using the multimeter and not the actual results.

Measuring volts

Voltage is the easiest and most common measurement that is made with a multimeter on a PC. Here are the general steps to follow when measuring voltage:

1. **Set the dial to measure DC voltage.**

2. **Choose the voltage range. Typically, this will be 20V or lower based on what you are measuring.**

3. **Hold the black (negative) probe to a grounding point on the circuit.**

4. **Touch the red (positive) probe to a hot point on the circuit.**

Lab 3-1 applies these steps to the task of measuring the volts coming from the power supply.

Lab 3-1	Measuring Volts on a Power Supply Connector

1. **Turn off the PC, but leave it connected to the wall outlet.**

2. **Turn on the multimeter and set it to measure DC current voltages less than 20V.**

3. **Open the computer case and remove the cover.**

4. **Locate an unused power supply connector or remove one from a floppy disk, hard disk, or CD-ROM drive.**

   Remember to put on your ESD wrist strap and connect it to either a static ground mat or the PC case.

5. **Turn on the PC.**

6. **Touch the black probe to one of the black wires (it doesn't matter which one) in the power connector.**

7. **While holding the black probe on the black wire, touch the red probe to the connector's yellow wire. The multimeter should display a reading of +12V. It will probably be somewhere in the range of +11.5 to +12.6V, which is fine.**

   If you get another reading, such as something around 5V, you probably have the probes reversed. Verify which wires you are touching with the probes. If you are on the right wires, you may have detected a problem with your power supply.

8. **Now touch the red probe to the power connector's red wire while still holding the black probe to the black wire. The multimeter should now show a reading of +5V(+4.8V to +5.2V).**

Measuring resistance

The amount of resistance, or *continuity,* a circuit has to allow an efficient flow of electricity is measured in ohms. The general steps to measure resistance are

✔ Be sure the circuit (power connector, trace, or cable) has no power running through it. If the circuit to be tested is inside the PC, turn off the PC's power supply. You could damage your multimeter if you test a circuit that has power running through it.

✔ Set the multimeter to test ohms and set an appropriate range.

✔ Touch the multimeter's probes to two metal points on the circuit. If you get a zero value, set the range higher or lower.

Lab 3-2   Checking Continuity on a Cable

1. **Set the multimeter to measure resistance (ohms).**

   See your multimeter's manual for how to set this.

2. **Use the cable from a modem (a null modem cable) or from any external serial device.**

   Disconnect the cable from any devices on either end.

3. **Place either probe on Pin 2 of one of the cable's connectors and the other probe on Pin 2 of the connector at the other end of the cable.**

   If you're unable to make a good contact at the female end of the cable (the end with the holes), use a short bit of wire or a straightened paper clip to extend the probe into the hole.

   The multimeter should give a reading, buzz, or beep to indicate continuity in the cable. If you do not get buzzed or beeped, either no continuity exists in the cable, or you have not made a good connection. Try a few more times and if you still get no reading — chances are there is no continuity and you have discovered a bad cable. Before you chuck it out, try testing all of the remaining pins, using the cable's pinout for which pins are connected to each other. Chapter 11 has more information on connectors and their pinouts.

A paper clip is an excellent tool in the right cases. In addition to extending cable pins for continuity testing, you can use it to open a stuck CD-ROM drive (see Chapter 9).

Prep Test

1 **When servicing a PC, on which of the following do you attach the grounding wrist strap to prevent ESD?**

A ○ To the chassis inside the case

B ○ To the static shielding bag that came with the computer

C ○ To a static ground mat

D ○ To the chassis, but only if a ground mat is not available

2 **What procedure is used to measure continuity between two points with a multimeter?**

A ○ Set the meter to ohms and test the circuit with power to it.

B ○ Set the meter to ohms and test the circuit without power to it.

C ○ Set the meter to amps and test the circuit with power to it.

D ○ Set the meter to amps and test the circuit without power to it.

3 **In which of the following situations do you not use a multimeter?**

A ○ When measuring DC volts

B ○ When measuring RAM

C ○ When measuring resistance

D ○ When measuring AC volts

4 **The Windows software tool used to view and edit INI files**

A ○ File Manager

B ○ Sysview

C ○ Regedit

D ○ Sysedit

5 **An IC is best removed using**

A ○ Needle-nose pliers

B ○ A Phillips screwdriver

C ○ An IC chip tool

D ○ An expansion card slot filler

6 **The screwdriver that is made especially for screws with an internal, faceted, star-like hole is a**

A ○ Phillips screwdriver

B ○ Torx screwdriver

C ○ Nut driver

D ○ Tweaker

7 The Windows software tool that's used to find and repair hard drive problems is

A ○ MSD.EXE

B ○ MEM.EXE

C ○ DEFRAG.EXE

D ○ SCANDISK.EXE

8 The type of software that's used to remove orphaned or unwanted files is

A ○ Uninstaller

B ○ Diagnostics

C ○ Troubleshooting

D ○ Anti-virus

9 A multimeter is typically used to measure which of the following? (Choose three.)

A ❑ resistance

B ❑ voltage

C ❑ current

D ❑ potential

10 If you use a screwdriver set with interchangeable tips, be sure that the tips are

A ○ Magnetic

B ○ Carbon steel

C ○ Nonmagnetic

D ○ Insulated

Answers

1 **D.** To the chassis, but only if a ground mat is not available. The best place to attach an ESD wrist strap and grounding cord is to a static ground mat. If a mat isn't available, attach the wrist strap to the chassis frame with the computer plugged into a wall outlet. *See "ESD wrist strap."*

2 **B.** Set the meter to ohms and test the circuit without power to it. Continuity is measured in ohms. With power running through a cable, you're testing current or power. Without the power, you're testing continuity. *Review "Working with a Multimeter."*

3 **B.** When measuring RAM. RAM is measured in bytes or bits. A multimeter is used to test for voltage, power, resistance, and continuity. *Look at "Working with a multimeter."*

4 **D.** Sysedit. SYSEDIT.EXE is used to view or manually edit Windows 95 configuration and system files. *See "The domestic tools."*

5 **C.** IC chip tool. Although a slotted screwdriver also works well, IC chip tools are specifically made for this task. *See "Tools you can safely leave at the shop."*

6 **B.** Torx screwdriver. The Torx screwdriver is considered to be tamper-proof and less likely to be damaged. It's used in Apple and Compaq cases. *Review "Screwdrivers."*

7 **D.** SCANDISK.EXE. SCANDISK is a Windows tool that finds and repairs problems with the hard disk and the folders and files stored on it. *Look up "The domestic tools."*

8 **A.** Uninstaller. An uninstaller program, also known as cleanup program, identifies system files left behind by removed applications, temporary files, and unwanted Internet files for possible removal. *Check out "The foreign tools."*

9 **A, B, C.** Multimeters typically measure ohms, volts, and amps. *See "Working with a multimeter."*

10 **C.** Nonmagnetic. Magnetic tips can cause damage when in contact with sensitive components on the motherboard and disk drives. *Look at "Screwdrivers."*

Part II

Keeping the Smoke in the Box

It's another cow box mutilation, Sheriff. Look how cleanly the case has been severed. And if my hunch is right, you won't find the motherboard within a thousand miles of here.

In this part . . .

Most of the PC service technician's world exists inside the PC case in the form of the motherboard, processor, memory, BIOS, bus structures, the power supply, and disk drives. In a way, this is the techie part of a techie job. Almost half of the Core Hardware exam and one third of the OS Technologies exam relate to the components found inside the case. So, this part of the book should be a first stop in your preparation for the test.

Chapter 4

The Motherboard

- -

Exam Objectives

▶ Defining the function and purpose of the motherboard

▶ Identifying motherboard form factors

▶ Explaining the function of a chipset

▶ Describing the operation of cache memory

▶ Upgrading the motherboard

- -

*T*he A+ exam tests your knowledge of the central role played by the motherboard. The motherboard is by far the most important electronic circuit in the computer. It acts as the gatekeeper to the CPU — all outside devices wishing to interact with the CPU must pass through the motherboard. It is all-powerful. It is all-knowing. Ignore that man behind the curtain!

At least 30 percent of the Core Hardware exam contains questions about the motherboard, its bus structures, CMOS, BIOS, chipsets, and the compatibility of the system components on the motherboard. Another 30 percent relate to CPUs, memory, installation, and troubleshooting.

You need to know about data and address buses, processor capabilities and compatibilities, the contents of the CMOS and how they are updated, and the role of the system ROM and BIOS in booting the system.

I can hear you asking, "Is that all?!" It's only natural that an exam with "Core" in its name tests you on the core components and issues of the PC. In the PC, nothing is more "core" than the motherboard, processor, and memory. Because so much of the A+ Core Hardware exam deals with these areas, I chose to spread out the review on motherboards, processors, BIOS and CMOS, bus structures, and memory systems over a few chapters. This arrangement should help prevent a brain boil-over while you're studying.

Quick Assessment

Defining the function and purpose of the motherboard

1 A main printed circuit board that houses many of the essential parts of a PC is more commonly called the _____.

Identifying motherboard form factors

2 A _____ defines the size, shape, and mounting of a motherboard.

3 The three most common motherboard form factors are _____, _____, and _____.

4 The most popular motherboard form factor is the _____.

Explaining the function of the chipset

5 The motherboard feature that includes I/O and bus structure controllers is the _____.

Describing the operation of cache memory

6 _____ is fast memory that is used as a data buffer between the CPU and RAM.

7 _____ is typically located outside the CPU.

8 The _____ sets the limit for amount of memory a PC can cache.

9 Three major considerations for upgrading the motherboard are _____, _____, and _____.

10 An important factor in choosing a replacement motherboard is the _____ of the CPU.

Answers

1 *Motherboard (or systemboard or mainboard).* See "By any other name, it's still mother."

2 *Form Factor.* Review "Motherboard Sizes, Shapes, and Styles."

3 *AT, Baby AT, and ATX.* Take a look at "Motherboard form factors."

4 *ATX.* Check out "The ATX form factor."

5 *Chipset.* Peruse "Stacking Up the Chipsets."

6 *Cache memory.* See "Caching In on a Good Thing."

7 *L2 (Level 2) or external cache memory.* Review "Caching levels inside and outside the CPU."

8 *Chipset.* Check out "Counting your cache."

9 *CPU, form factor, and documentation.* Take a look at "Upgrading the Motherboard."

10 *Mounting,* or *slot,* or *socket.* See "Upgrading the Motherboard."

Understanding the Motherboard

This section prepares you to meet the exam objective of identifying popular motherboards and their components, architecture, and compatibilities. I can't over emphasize the importance of knowing this material for the exam. Not only does it have its own domain in the exam blueprint, but it also has seeped into all parts of the test.

Most experts, and at least one writer, have theories on the importance of the motherboard. You've probably seen many references to the motherboard that characterize it in human anatomy terms. It has been called the heart, backbone, spine, soul, and brain of the computer. However, it is much more than one single organ.

Every essential component directly or indirectly involved with making the PC function properly is either on, attached, or connected to the motherboard. For all intents and purposes, the motherboard *is* the computer. A computer without a printer, a CD-ROM, or a monitor is still a computer. However, a computer without a motherboard is simply an empty metal box that just sits there giving very bad response time.

The primary components of the PC attach or plug into the motherboard, which creates the functionality of the PC. The major components included on or connected to the motherboard include the CPU, memory, expansion cards, disk drives, keyboard, mouse, and monitor. You know — all of the really important parts of the PC.

By any other name, it's still mother

The motherboard is often referred to as a *systemboard* (although, at one time there was a distinction between the two). A systemboard integrated video, audio, graphics, and other device support into the board's architecture, whereas a motherboard did not. IBM has always called its motherboard a systemboard. Apple Computer calls its motherboard a logic board, while others refer to theirs as a planar board. These terms are still around today, but for the most part, they are interchangeable because most motherboards are now systemboards and vice versa. I tend to favor the term motherboard, but from time to time I will call it a systemboard for variety.

Families, form factors, and other relatives

The motherboard of a PC is a large printed circuit board that is home to many of the most essential parts of the computer, including the microprocessor, chipset, cache, memory sockets, expansion bus, parallel and serial ports, mouse and keyboard connectors, and IDE, EIDE, or SCSI controllers. The motherboard binds the PC's operational components together. Even devices, such as printers, hard drives, and CD-ROMs, are either connected to or controlled by the devices or controllers on the motherboard.

A wide variety of shapes, sizes, and types of motherboards is available. Regardless of the age of a PC, it is safe to say that at least one manufacturer still produces a motherboard to fit it. Manufacturers attempt to set their motherboards apart from the others and increase their value by incorporating more or fewer controllers, expansion buses, processor sockets, external connectors, and memory slots. For consumers, a very wide range of motherboards with a deep list of features is available to fit into an even wider range of PCs. However, if you don't do your homework before buying a new motherboard, this wide range of selection can be bad news, and you can end up with lower-quality components than you desire.

Motherboards and systemboards are manufactured under a number of competing standards, each of which was designed to solve a particular design, engineering, or marketing problem. Motherboards come in every size — from very small to very large. Some styles even divide the motherboard into several interconnecting pieces. The good news is that you only need to know about a few motherboard form factors and what differentiates them for the A+ Core Hardware exam.

Motherboard families

A motherboard can be categorized into a variety of families or types, depending on its design and function. Motherboards can be integrated or nonintegrated, and they can be a motherboard style or a backplane style.

A *motherboard-style mainboard* aggregates a PC's primary components on a single printed circuit board (PCB). The single circuit board is what makes it motherboard style. A *backplane mainboard* has a number of card slots into which *daughterboards,* such as processors and memory circuit cards, are inserted to add capabilities.

The two types of backplane mainboards are passive and active. A *passive backplane* board provides only a bus structure and some data buffering to interconnect the daughterboards. An *active backplane* adds a bit of intelligence to assist the daughterboards.

An integrated motherboard incorporates most of the circuitry that would normally be added through expansion cards, including video, disk controllers, and others. The downside of this simplicity is that if one of the circuits goes bad, the whole board may be affected. The opposite style is a nonintegrated motherboard, which is the traditional style of motherboard that requires the circuitry for major subsystems, such as video, disk controllers, audio, and others, to be added through expansion cards. The upside is that if a card goes bad, only that card needs to be replaced.

As illustrated in Figure 4-1, integrated motherboards, which integrate the most significant components of the computer on a single circuit board, are quickly becoming the standard. This type of motherboard includes the CPU and its associated support chips, memory, device controllers, and expansion slots that give peripheral devices access to the computer's internal bus.

Motherboard form factors

The shape, packaging, and to a certain extent, the function of a motherboard are defined by its *form factor*. Many different form factors are available — some that are generally accepted in the industry and some that are open to interpretation by manufacturers. However, the exam blueprint for the A+ Core Hardware exam lists only the three most commonly used motherboard form factors:

- ✔ **AT:** This motherboard is patterned after the original IBM PC AT motherboard.
- ✔ **Baby AT:** This motherboard is a smaller version of the AT form factor motherboard.
- ✔ **ATX:** Similar in size to the Baby AT, the ATX adds additional features and is the most commonly used form in today's PCs. The ATX motherboard allows for easier installation of full-length expansion cards and cables and is easier to cool.

More information on each of these form factors is included later in the chapter in "Motherboard Sizes, Shapes, and Styles."

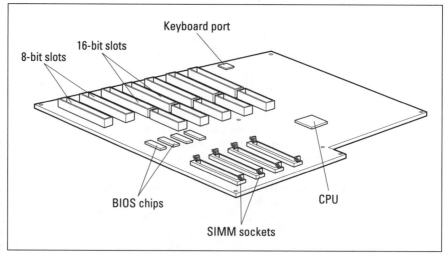

Figure 4-1:
The primary components of a typical motherboard.

Keyboard port

16-bit slots

8-bit slots

BIOS chips

CPU

SIMM sockets

The components on the motherboard

The motherboard consists of layers of components added to the basic circuit board, similar to the layers of a pizza. Using the pizza analogy, think of the motherboard as the crust, and the components, which add its functionality, as the toppings. For the A+ Core Hardware exam, you need to know not only what makes up the crust but each of the ingredients as well. In this chapter, I cover the details of the motherboard and the chipset, but the other major components of the motherboard has its own chapter (which should be a clue as to the importance of these topics).

In addition to the motherboard, processor, and CMOS, you need to know each of the following toppings, I mean components, listed in Table 4-1. These components are typically found inside the system unit and considered, after they are installed, a part of the motherboard's sphere of control.

Table 4-1	Motherboard Components You Must Know for the A+ Exam
Component	*Where You Can Find It in This Book*
BIOS and CMOS	Chapter 5 — "BIOS Ins and Outs"
Bus architectures	Chapter 6 — "Bus Structures"
Cache memory	See "Caching In on a Good Thing" later in this chapter
Microprocessors	Chapter 7 — "Microprocessors"
Memory	Chapter 8 — "Memory Systems"
Storage devices	Chapter 9 — "Storage Systems"
Power supply	Chapter 10 — "Power"
I/O ports	Chapter 11 — "Serial, Parallel, and Other Ports"

Riding the Bus

Part of understanding the operation of the motherboard is understanding its bus structure. Most of the motherboard exam questions are about bus architectures. This section provides you with a brief overview of this area, but check out Chapter 6 for a much deeper review of this important part of the test.

The CPU moves data values and signals around the computer on a network of very small wires that interconnect it to all the other components on the motherboard. This network is called the *bus*.

The lines used to move data around inside the computer form the internal bus. The lines used to communicate with peripherals and other devices attached to the motherboard form the external bus. Think of the internal bus as being a hallway in a large building, such as a very large hospital (the ones with the colored lines on the floor) or the Pentagon. In this example, the external buses would be the hallways that lead directly to outside doors.

You can find four primary types of bus structures on most motherboards:

- ✔ **Address:** The components on the motherboard pass memory addresses to one another over the address bus.
- ✔ **Control:** Used by the CPU to send out signals to coordinate and manage the activities of the motherboard components.
- ✔ **Data:** Because the primary job of the computer is to process data, logically the data must be transferred between peripherals, memory, and the CPU. Obviously, the data bus can be a very busy hallway.
- ✔ **Power:** The power bus is the river of life for the motherboard's components, providing each with the electrical power it needs to operate.

The number of wires in a bus controls the number of bits that can be transferred over the bus. For example, a 32-bit bus must have 32 wires.

Motherboard Sizes, Shapes, and Styles

Although the blueprint of the A+ Core Hardware exam lists only the AT, Baby AT, and ATX form factors, don't be surprised if references to other form factors show up on the exam. For that reason, you should at least review the form factors listed in Table 4-2 to familiarize yourself with the various form factors that have been produced.

Table 4-2	Motherboard Form Factors		
Form Factor	*Width (in inches)*	*Length (in inches)*	*Design Type*
IBM PC	8.5	13	Motherboard
IBM PC XT	8.5	13	Motherboard
AT	12	11–13	Motherboard
Baby AT	8.5	10–13	Motherboard

Form Factor	Width (in inches)	Length (in inches)	Design Type
LPX	9	11–13	Backplane
Micro-AT	8.5	8.5	Motherboard
ATX	12	9.6	Motherboard
Mini-ATX	11.2	8.2	Motherboard
Mini-LPX	8–9	10–11	Backplane
Micro-ATX	9.6	9.6	Motherboard
NLX	8–9	10–13.6	Backplane
Flex-ATX	9	7.5	Motherboard

Essentially, a *form factor* defines a motherboard's size, shape, and how it is mounted to the case. However, form factors now include the size, shape, and function of the system case; the type, placement, and size of the power supply; the system's power requirements; the location and type of external connectors; and the case's airflow and cooling systems.

Remember that the motherboard, power supply, and system case can each have a form factor. Typically, in a single PC, they all have the same form factor, but some power supplies and cases can handle a variety of mother-board form factors. See Chapter 10 for more information about power supply and case form factors.

The AT form factor

After the early success of its PC and PC XT models, IBM introduced its 16-bit PC AT (which allegedly stood for "Advanced Technology"), which added enough additional circuitry to increase the size of its motherboard (and case). The size, shape, and mounting placements of the AT's case were the standard that clone manufacturers used for their XT-upgrade motherboards. The popularity of the PC AT and its form factor established it as the first real motherboard form factor standard. The AT form factor motherboard, shown in Figure 4-2, is nearly square at 12 inches x 11–13 inches.

The Baby AT form factor

Following the success of the IBM PC AT, clone manufacturers began releasing their own 16-bit PCs. Higher integration technology reduced the space required by support chipsets and circuitry, which allowed the motherboard to be reduced as much as 3.5 inches in width and 2 inches in height. This new style board became known as the Baby AT, shown in Figure 4-3. Because the Baby AT fit the AT form factor mountings, it quickly became very popular and surpassed the AT as the form factor of choice. Most of the computer cases manufactured between 1984 and 1996 were Baby AT form factors.

The ATX form factor

The ATX form factor is the one you'll see most often on the job, and it is the default form factor of the A+ Core Hardware exam. Don't expect to see too many questions directly about the design and features of any of the mother-board form factors, but expect to see questions that require you to have an understanding of the motherboard, its design, and its components.

The ATX form factor is generally based on the smaller Baby AT motherboard size. However, size is about the only thing they have in common. The ATX form rotates the motherboard's orientation by 90 degrees and incorporates a new set of mounting locations and power connections. The I/O ports on an ATX motherboard are in a two-row block on the back of the PC.

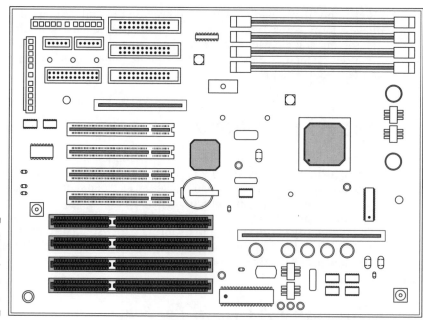

Figure 4-2: An AT form factor mother-board.

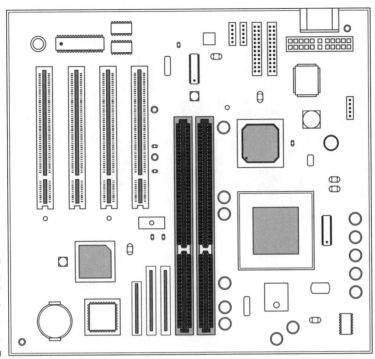

Figure 4-3:
A Baby AT
form factor
mother-
board.

The ATX form factor resulted from the lessons learned from the Baby AT and other small motherboards. The ATX mounts the CPU and RAM away from its expansion slots and closer to the power supply's cooling fan, as shown in Figure 4-4. This arrangement improves the amount of airflow available to cool the CPU and RAM chips. Originally, the ATX power supply fan pulled air into the case, flowing it over the CPU and out of the case's vents. However, this resulted in dust and other airborne particles (such as chalk dust, metal filings, and more) being pulled into the case. Newer ATX designs vent the case by pulling hot air away from the CPU and RAM and passing it out of the case. The ATX design also supports an additional case fan, which are recommended for PCs with 3-D video accelerators, multiple hard drives, and other high-heat-producing adapter cards.

The ATX design also incorporates a number of features into the power system. The motherboard can control the power on and off functions of the power supply, a feature called *soft switching*. The ATX form provides *split voltage* (a range of voltages, usually 12v, 5v, and 3.3v) to the motherboard, which eliminates the need for a voltage regulator included on earlier form factor motherboards.

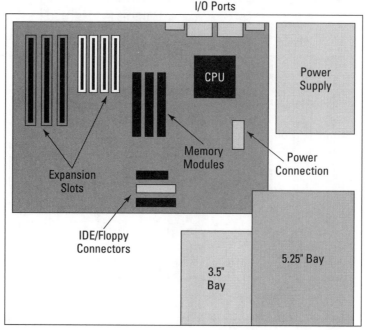

I/O Ports

CPU

Power Supply

Memory Modules

Power Connection

Expansion Slots

IDE/Floppy Connectors

3.5" Bay

5.25" Bay

Figure 4-4: The standard ATX layout.

The ATX form factor locates the I/O ports in a two-row block on the rear of the board, as shown in Figure 4-5. The top row includes a PS/2-type keyboard or mouse connector, a parallel port, and a blank slot that can be used for a second parallel port. The bottom row includes a second PS/2-type keyboard or mouse connector, two serial ports, and a series of blank ports that might be used for sound or video card connectors. The defined size of the connector area on an ATX motherboard is small (6.25 inches x 1.75 inches), which helps eliminate the clutter of cables found near the rear panel of a Baby AT motherboard.

Expect to see references to the ATX and the Baby AT form factors on the Core Hardware exam. In most instances, the reference will be to attaching devices, such as expansion cards and power supplies.

Stacking Up the Chipsets

The bus structures and interfaces supported by the motherboard and CPU are controlled by functions included on the chipset. The *chipset* is a group of chips that together help the processor and other peripheral devices plugged into the motherboard communicate with each other. The chipset controls the bits (data, instructions, and control signals) that flow between the CPU and system memory over the motherboard's buses. The chipset also manages data transfers between the CPU, memory, and peripheral devices. It also supports the expansion bus and any power management features of the system. However, the chipset contains only enough instructions to issue control commands to device drivers, which are what actually control the peripheral device.

Chipsets are integrated into the motherboard and usually cannot be upgraded without changing the entire motherboard. A PC's chipset is matched to the motherboard and the CPU as a set. Some chipsets support more than one processor, but in general, a given chipset is matched to a single processor type. Along this line, you will commonly see the chipset referred to by the CPU's mounting on the motherboard, for example, Socket 7 chipsets, Socket 370 chipsets, or Slot A chipsets. See Chapter 7 for more information on processors and their mountings.

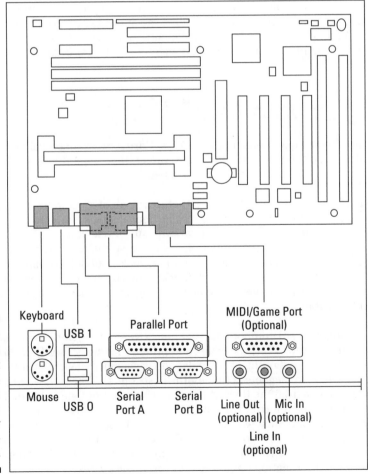

Figure 4-5: The placement of the I/O ports on an ATX form factor motherboard.

Keyboard

USB 1

Parallel Port

MIDI/Game Port (Optional)

Mouse

USB 0

Serial Port A

Serial Port B

Line Out (optional)

Mic In (optional)

Line In (optional)

At one time, a chipset consisted of several smaller single-purpose controller chips. Each separate controller, which could be one or more chips, managed a single function, such as controlling the cache memory, handling interrupts, or managing the data bus. Today's chipset combines this set of controller functions into one or two larger, multifunction chips. *VLSI (very large scale integration)* has allowed these many chips to be combined into one or two chips.

Chipsets, especially two-chip chipsets, are divided into a North Bridge (the larger chip) and a South Bridge (the smaller chip). The North Bridge provides support and control for main memory, cache memory, and the PCI bus controllers. The South Bridge provides control for peripheral devices and those controllers that are not essential to the PC's basic functions, such as the serial port controller.

The chipsets are not the only controller sets on the motherboard. The most prominent controller sets are the keyboard controller and a superset of input/output device controllers called the Super I/O controller. The Super I/O chip combines controllers that are common to all systems. Controller chips are also found on many high-end devices and adapter cards.

Caching In on a Good Thing

Expect to see questions on the A+ Core Hardware exam on cache memory, which is a motherboard component. Understand what it exists, why it is, its limitations, and how and when it is used.

One of the mysteries of the PC is that nearly all of its components, including the processor, the memory, the motherboard data buses, and the hard drive, operate at different speeds and data transfer rates. You may think that these parts could be coordinated better, but because they are the products of competition, they cannot. No single company makes all of the components that go into a PC (although Intel certainly is trying). Each of the competing companies is trying to develop the fastest, biggest, and best computer component possible.

Two motherboard components that must overcome their differences and work together are the CPU (processor) and primary memory (RAM). RAM works in nanoseconds (billionths of seconds) and is seemingly faster than the CPU, which works in megahertz (millionths of seconds). However, when the CPU requests data from the RAM, it takes a fair amount of time to locate the data and then transfer it over the data bus to the CPU. No matter how fast the RAM may be, the CPU must wait while all of this is happening, and this is bad! One of the underlying design goals of the PC is to prevent the CPU from being idle as much as possible. This is where cache memory comes in. (See Chapters 7 and 8 for more information on processors and memory, respectively.)

Thanks for the cache memories

Cache memory is an extremely fast memory type that acts as a buffer between RAM and the CPU. It holds frequently requested data and instructions so that they are immediately available to the CPU when needed. Yes, it is a bit more complicated than that; but for the A+ exams, just remember that cache memory and the caching process hold data and instructions from a slower resource or process so that they are ready when needed by a faster device or process.

A *cache* is a buffer that is used to mitigate the speed differences between devices. Today's PCs commonly include cache memory between the RAM and the CPU and perhaps between the hard drive and RAM, as well. Caching is used in two ways on the PC:

- **Cache memory:** This is a relatively small and very fast memory storage located between the PC's primary memory (RAM) and its processor (CPU); it is used to hold data and instructions retrieved from RAM to provide faster access to the CPU.

- **Disk cache:** This cache buffer is used to speed up the transfer of data and programs from the hard drive into RAM. Disk cache, which is either in RAM or some additional memory on the disk controller, holds large blocks of frequently accessed data.

Cache memory, the one I focus on because it is the one on the test, is usually a small amount of Static Random Access Memory or SRAM. (See Chapter 8 for more information on this and other types of memory.) SRAM is made up of transistors that don't need to be frequently refreshed like DRAM, which is made up of capacitors. (But you already knew that.)

SRAM is very fast, with access speeds of 2ns (nanoseconds) or faster. This is much faster than DRAM, which has access speeds around 50ns. Because of its speed, SRAM cache memory can transfer data to the CPU at a much faster rate than it would take to transfer the same data from main memory. Another contributing factor to the speed of the cache is its proximity to the CPU, which eliminates most of the latency (delay) involved with transfers from RAM.

SRAM isn't used for primary memory in a PC for very good practical and economic reasons. SRAM can cost six times more than DRAM and requires a lot more space on the motherboard to store the same amount of data as DRAM.

Caching in operation

The CPU interacts with RAM through a series of *wait states,* during which the CPU pauses for a few cycles to allow time for the data it has requested to be located and transferred from RAM to its registers. If the data is not already in

RAM, which means it must be fetched from the hard drive, additional CPU wait states are required. Cache memory attempts to eliminate CPU wait states by eliminating any CPU idleness.

Caching involves more than a little gambling. The operations of cache memory are based on *the principle of locality of reference,* which assumes that the next data to be requested is very likely located immediately following the last data requested. Caching copies the data just beyond the last data requested into cache memory, assuming that it will be the data that the CPU will ask for next. As iffy as this may sound, PC caching systems are surprisingly successful about 90 to 95 percent of the time.

If a PC did not have cache memory, all requests for data and instructions by the CPU would be served from RAM. Only the data requested would be supplied with no anticipation of what the CPU would be asking for next. This is similar to having go all the way to the supermarket for a single can of your favorite drink every time you want a cold one. Without caching, the CPU would get bogged down in memory requests, just as you would spend all of your time running to the store every time you got thirsty.

Adding cache memory is a lot like buying an ice chest — it saves you a lot of time because it gives you a place to store your beverages, so you won't have to go to the store as often. Because caching anticipates the CPU's next request, the whole system speeds up. With a hit ratio of 90 to 95 percent, caching saves a tremendous amount of wait cycles for the CPU, just like the ice chest saves you a few trips.

Caching levels inside and outside the CPU

Cache memory is located in two general locations: inside the processor (internal cache) and on the motherboard (external cache):

- ✔ **Internal cache:** Also known as *primary cache,* internal cache is located inside the CPU chip, also called *on the die.*
- ✔ **External cache:** Also called *secondary cache,* external cache is located on the motherboard outside the CPU. This is the cache referred to on PC specifications.

Cache is also commonly referred to by its level or proximity to the CPU. Cache is designated in two levels:

- ✔ **Level 1 (L1) cache:** Level 1 cache is often used interchangeably with internal cache and rightly so. L1 cache is placed internally on the processor chip and is, of course, the cache memory closest to the CPU.

✔ **Level 2 (L2) cache:** L2 cache is normally placed on the motherboard very close to the CPU; but because it is not inside the CPU, it is designated as the second level of cache. Although L2 cache is commonly considered the same as external cache, L2 cache can also be included on the CPU, just a little behind L1 cache.

Level 1 is not higher in ranking than Level 2 cache. The levels of cache work together, and data are located on either level, depending on the rules and policies of the caching system. Level 1 cache cannot be increased without changing the CPU. On the other hand, L2 cache can be upgraded on most motherboards. L2 cache modules plug into special cache module mounts or cache memory expansion sockets on the motherboard.

Counting your cache

When it comes to cache memory, more is better. However, there are limits and exceptions to how much cache a system and its chipset will support. Adding more cache to a PC will likely increase its overall speed, but it may also decrease its performance. Should you add too much cache, simply keeping the cache filled from RAM can eat up the CPU cycles you were hoping to save.

If one ice chest provides enough drink cache to eliminate some trips to the store, it makes sense that two chests will save twice as many trips. There is some logic to this, but your savings are dependent on your ability to carry two chests' worth of drinks on each trip. If you are unable to carry enough to fill both ice chests on a single trip, you will need to make a second trip, and that seriously eats into your time savings. Adding too much L2 cache to some PCs can affect the system's performance in this same way. The first 256K of L2 cache should improve the performance of a PC, but an additional 256K of L2 may, in fact, reduce its performance.

Most Pentium class PCs include enough cache memory to cache (buffer) 64MB of RAM, which emerged as the standard sizing for L2 cache on most newer systems. The PC's chipset sets the limit of how much RAM it can cache, and an upper limit of 64MB is common. What this means is that regardless of how much RAM you add to the PC, no more than 64MB will be cached, and this can affect the PC's performance. Before upgrading cache memory, read the documentation of the motherboard and chipset.

Upgrading the Motherboard

If your PC isn't quite as fast or as powerful as you'd like, you can either get a new PC or upgrade its motherboard and/or its components. Depending on the upgrade you wish to make, upgrading the motherboard or the components on the motherboard typically costs less than a brand new PC. Buying a new PC is not a part of the A+ exams, but upgrading the motherboard is, so I focus on that.

The three major considerations when looking to upgrade a motherboard are the CPU, the form factor, and documentation. Yes, there are other things to consider, but if you get these three right, the rest should generally fall into place.

Here is a list of the criteria to be considered when evaluating the upgrade of a PC:

- ✔ **CPU:** The CPU that can be used to upgrade the PC depends on the motherboard, its form factor, and its chipset. The CPU can be upgraded on nearly all Pentium motherboards. However, the CPU socket on the motherboard controls which CPU can be used to upgrade the system. Some upgrades are just not practical. For example, trying to replace a Pentium 75MHz processor with a Pentium III Xeon will likely also involve replacing the motherboard, chipset, and perhaps the power supply and more. However, stepping up to the next level of processor can be relatively effortless, provided the new processor is within the motherboard's specification. Some processors, such as the Pentium Pro and Pentium II processors, have unique motherboard configurations and aren't typically compatible with other Pentium-based motherboards. See Chapter 7 for more information on processors.

- ✔ **Sockets and slots:** Replacement motherboards usually have at least one ZIF (zero insertion force) socket. The most common socket style on newer computers is the Socket 7 mounting. Processors with SEC (Single-Edge Connector) packaging require either a Slot 1 or Slot 2 connection. You must consider the mounting of the CPU when considering an upgrade. See Chapter 7 for more information on processors and their mountings.

- ✔ **Bus speed:** The bus speeds supported by a motherboard and chipset must be matched to the processor. In addition to the processor, most motherboard components, especially the cache memory, are matched to the motherboard's speed.

- ✔ **Cache memory:** Virtually all Pentium motherboards have between 256K and 512K of Level 2 cache memory on the board; and some, such as the Pentium Pro and higher processors, include L2 cache on the CPU chip. Additional L2 cache can be added to the motherboard, but remember that it must be matched to the motherboard's bus speed.

- ✔ **Memory modules**: Depending on the vintage of your PC, it may use DIP (dual inline packaging), SIMM (single inline memory module), or DIMM (dual inline memory module) for its memory. Before you start cramming memory modules into open slots, verify the total amount of memory the motherboard supports and the memory technology the processor and chipset support. See Chapter 8 for more information on memory modules and technologies.

✓ **Expansion bus:** Before you run out and buy a new motherboard, it is important to consider the expansion cards and adapters installed on the current motherboard. Unless the new motherboard will replace some of the cards with built-in connectors, the current expansion cards will need compatible slots on the new motherboard.

✓ **BIOS:** When choosing a new motherboard, pick one with a BIOS that features flash ROM, Plug and Play (PnP), ATA and Fast ATA, and the newer power management standards, such as APM (Advanced Power Management) or SMM (System Management Mode).

✓ **Chipset:** The chipset is matched to the processor and the motherboard. Typically, this is included as a part of the motherboard and cannot usually be replaced.

✓ **Form factor:** If you aren't changing the PC's case, you are limited to the form factor of the case or those that will fit into it. An ATX case will take some of the later form factors, but you should check with the case manufacturer on this. If the PC is older, in which case (no pun intended), it is likely a Baby AT form factor.

✓ **Power supply**: Remember that the power supply shares the form factor with the case and motherboard. Typically, the power supply is included with a new PC case, but contrary to common belief, it is not always so.

✓ **Built-in controllers and interfaces:** Depending on your preferences, you may want more or fewer built-in controllers and plugs on the motherboard. Consider the connections and adapter cards on the current motherboard in making this choice.

✓ **Documentation:** To paraphrase the current cliché, the motherboard with the most documentation wins. Remember that documentation available on the Internet counts.

Here's a tip on expansion slots on generic motherboards: Make sure that none of the expansion slots when occupied block access to a memory socket, the ROM BIOS, password-clear jumper, or CMOS battery. This consideration may save you some hassle later during maintenance or repair.

Prep Test

1 Which of the following is not a common name for the primary printed circuit board in a PC?

A ○ Mainboard
B ○ Motherboard
C ○ Planar board
D ○ Systemboard

2 Which of the following are common motherboard form factors? (Choose three.)

A ❏ Mother AT
B ❏ AT
C ❏ ATX
D ❏ Baby AT

3 Which of the following motherboard form factors is nearly square?

A ○ Mother AT
B ○ AT
C ○ ATX
D ○ Baby AT

4 Which of the following FRMs does not get its size and shape specified in a form factor standard?

A ○ Power supply
B ○ System case
C ○ Memory
D ○ Motherboard

5 The feature used to resolve the speed differences of the CPU and RAM is

A ○ Disk cache
B ○ Main memory
C ○ Cache memory
D ○ Data bus

6 Which computer component contains the circuitry necessary for all components or devices to communicate with each other?

A ○ Motherboard
B ○ Adapter board
C ○ Hard drive
D ○ Expansion bus

7 **Which statement best describes the purpose of the motherboard?**

A ○ Supplies DC power to the peripheral devices
B ○ Interconnects the primary components of the PC
C ○ Executes all instructions of the PC
D ○ Stores and processes the data of the PC

8 **The principle of locality reference says that**

A ○ The next data to be requested is the one before last
B ○ The hard drive should not be next to the CPU
C ○ The next data to be requested is the last one
D ○ The next data to be requested is located immediately following the last one

9 **Level 1 cache is located where?**

A ○ On the motherboard
B ○ On an adapter card
C ○ On the CPU
D ○ On the ROM BIOS

10 **Cache memory is what type of memory?**

A ○ DRAM
B ○ SRAM
C ○ Virtual memory
D ○ There is no standard memory type used for cache.

Answers

1 **C.** Okay, so this is a trick question. Planar board is an older term that was once used for passive backplane boards. Don't expect to see planar on the exam. *See "By any other name, it's still mother."*

2 **B, C, D.** Now, don't go thinking that all the questions on the A+ exams are this easy. Mother AT is obviously not a form factor, but it's all easy and obvious when you know the material. *Review "Motherboard form factors."*

3 **B.** The AT motherboard is 12 inches wide x 11–13 inches tall. *Look it up in "AT form factor."*

4 **C.** Typically the form factor includes the size and shape and fit, I might add, of the case, power supply, and motherboard. *See "Motherboard Sizes, Shapes, and Styles."*

5 **C.** Cache memory holds the data that the CPU is likely to use next, which speeds up the transfer to the CPU, hopefully eliminating CPU wait states. *Review "Caching In on a Good Thing."*

6 **A.** The bus structures are located on the motherboard/systemboard. *Check out "Understanding the Motherboard."*

7 **B.** The motherboard is the platform that interconnects all of the primary components of the PC. *Take a look at "Understanding the Motherboard."*

8 **D.** The caching system uses the principle that the next data is likely the data located immediately after the last one requested. *See "Caching in operation."*

9 **C.** Level 1, also known as internal, cache is located on the CPU, which is also called on the die. *Look over "Caching levels inside and outside the CPU."*

10 **B.** Cache memory is usually a small amount of SRAM. *Review "Thanks for the cache memories."*

Chapter 5

BIOS Ins and Outs

● ●

Exam Objectives

▶ Reviewing BIOS basic terms, concepts, and actions

▶ Listing the actions of the boot process

▶ Defining the purpose and usage of the CMOS

▶ Upgrading the system BIOS

▶ Troubleshooting boot and BIOS problems

● ●

*B*efore computers got their first operating systems, programmers had to write their own input and output routines in order to get input in and output out. They had to include a routine in each program to read the input and create the output. At some point in the computer's evolution, some smart programmer type figured out that because every program needs to get input and produce output, creating standardized versions of these functions and including them as a part of the system's software would be an excellent idea. This concept has advanced to the point where the computer even has specialized instructions that tell it which peripheral devices are attached and if they're operating properly so that the PC can look for the appropriate input and output device drivers it needs. These instructions form the PC's Basic Input/Output System, or as it's more commonly known, the BIOS.

If you look over the test objectives of the Core Hardware exam, you find the system BIOS and associated topics are listed multiple times in three of the five domains of the test. The BIOS, boot process, CMOS, and other system startup and input/output topics and activities are important to the PC repair professional, not only for the A+ exams, but on the job as well. The BIOS holds the key to the system's efficient operations; it can be the best diagnostics tool in your toolkit — not to mention that it starts up the PC every time you power it up.

So, if you start the PC but ignore the process that brings the PC up to its operating state, you may want to pay attention to the valuable and critical process that takes place because you need to know and understand it for the A+ exam.

Quick Assessment

Reviewing BIOS basic terms, concepts, and actions

1 BIOS refers to _____.

2 The address of the first instruction of the BIOS is called the _____.

Listing the actions of the boot process

3 The type of startup performed when a PC is off is a(n) _____.

4 The type of startup performed when a PC is on is a(n) _____.

5 The process that is used to test and verify the PC's hardware during startup is called the _____.

Defining the purpose and usage of the CMOS

6 CMOS refers to _____.

7 The PC's system configuration is stored in the _____ memory.

8 Removing the _____ will reset the user and supervisor passwords.

Upgrading the system BIOS

9 Upgrading the ROM BIOS under software control is called _____.

Trouble-shooting boot and BIOS problems

10 Errors that occur before the monitor is available are signaled with a _____.

Answers

1   *Basic Input/Output System.* See "Getting to Know the BIOS."

2   *Jump address.* Review "Booting Up the System."

3   *Cold boot.* Check out "Starting cold and running warm."

4   *Warm boot.* Take a look at "Starting cold and running warm."

5   *POST (Power On Self-Test).* See "Running the POST process."

6   *Complementary Metal Oxide Semiconductor.* Review "Verifying the hardware."

7   *CMOS memory.* Look over "Setting the BIOS configuration."

8   *CMOS battery.* Check out "Security and passwords."

9   *Flashing.* Take a look at "Updating the BIOS."

10   *Beep code.* See "Running the POST process."

Getting to Know the BIOS

The *BIOS (Basic Input/Output System)* is a collection of software utilities and programs that can be invoked by the operating system or application software to perform a variety of hardware-related tasks. Although many operating systems now contain their own device-oriented programs to improve performance, the BIOS contains a program for just about every activity associated with accessing hardware, including programs for starting the system, testing the hardware, reading and writing to and from storage devices, and moving data between devices.

It boils down to this: The BIOS is the opening act of the PC. It ensures that the hardware is alive, well, and ready for the operating system and then gets the operating system up and running. If you're like most PC users, you probably give the system BIOS of your PC very little notice each time it does its magic when you power it up. That is, until there's a problem and then you'd probably like to shoot the messenger.

The BIOS performs three primary functions, all vital to the usefulness and function of the computer:

- ✓ It boots the PC.
- ✓ It verifies the configuration data that tells it the internal and peripheral devices that are supposed to be connected to the PC.
- ✓ It provides the interface between the hardware (the attached devices) and the software (such as the operating system, device drivers, and application software).

Booting the PC

The instructions that start up the PC and load the operating system into memory and keep it running are part of the group of instructions that are collectively referred to as the *system BIOS*. The process of starting up the computer and loading the operating system is commonly called *booting the computer,* or simply the *boot sequence.* Booting and boot do not refer to any part of kicking or stomping, but are derivatives of the phrase "pulling oneself up by one's own bootstraps," or being able to self-start. When the computer boots, the BIOS is in charge.

When the PC is powered on, the BIOS supplies the PC with its first set of instructions. The instructions supplied by the BIOS are what the PC executes during its power on or boot up sequences until it is able to fetch and execute instructions on its own.

Verifying the hardware

The configuration of a PC is stored in a special type of nonvolatile memory, called *Complementary Metal-Oxide Semiconductor,* or *CMOS* (pronounced "sea-moss"), which requires very little power to hold onto its contents. CMOS is the technology used in nearly all memory and processor chips today. However, in early PCs, it was used only to store the configuration data of the PC. So, although it's used throughout the PC's circuits, CMOS is synonymous with the storage of the PC's configuration data.

CMOS runs on about 1 millionth of an amp of electrical current. This efficiency allows it to store configuration data for a long time, perhaps even years, powered only from low voltage dry cell or lithium batteries. The CMOS battery is located on the motherboard; in older systems it's located in a battery pack attached to the sidewall of the system case.

When the system starts the boot sequence, the BIOS starts a program called the Power-On Self-Test, or POST, that verifies the data in the CMOS to the physical devices it can detect on the system. More on this later in the chapter in the "Running the POST process" section.

Getting input in and output out

After the PC is up and running, its peripheral devices communicate with the system through their device drivers. The system BIOS allows your old PC AT software to run on your Pentium III PC. The BIOS interacts with the hardware to carry out the actions demanded of it. After the PC is booted, the BIOS becomes part of a four-layer software operating environment that allows software to run on a variety of PC platforms without too much trouble. Figure 5-1 shows the four layers of the PC's operating environment.

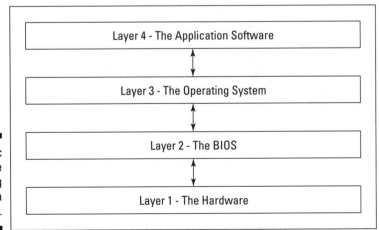

Figure 5-1:
The operating layers of a PC.

The application layer (for example, a word processing application) interacts with the operating system, such as Windows, to process its inputs and outputs. The operating system, which can't possibly be created to be exactly compatible with every configuration of PC, interacts with the BIOS, which in turn interacts with the PC's hardware. The BIOS allows the operating system and the application to be created for a general class of hardware because it's specifically created to work with certain types and configurations of hardware. The layers use a standard interface, supplied by the BIOS, to interact with the layer below (or above) it.

BIOS Chipology

An essential part of studying the BIOS is studying the chips (as in integrated circuits made from silicon "chips") on which it is stored and delivered to the PC. You don't need to become an electronics engineer to take the A+ Core Hardware exam, but it sure wouldn't hurt you to know these common chip terms:

- ✔ **Read Only Memory (ROM):** Although not solely a BIOS chip, ROM chips are permanently loaded with instructions during the manufacturing processes. The instructions written to a ROM chip, which cannot be changed under any circumstance, are called *firmware*. No longer a common vehicle for the system BIOS, on earlier PCs, the BIOS was stored on a ROM chip (Figure 5–2).

- ✔ **Programmable Read Only Memory (PROM):** A PROM is essentially a blank ROM chip that can be programmed with data or instructions. A PROM burner (also called a PROM programmer), a special device used to write to the PROM, enables you to store any data you want. The PROM burner induces high voltage (12 volts compared to the 5 volts used for normal PROM operations) to load the data to the chip. The higher voltage burns a memory location to turn its preexisting binary 1 into a 0, if needed. This process is irreversible so what you burn is what you get (WYBIWYG). After you burn that zero into the PROM, there's no going back. For that reason, you may hear PROM memory referred to as One Time Programmable Memory.

- ✔ **Erasable Programmable Read Only Memory (EPROM):** An *EPROM* (pronounced "e-prom," which isn't a dance attended over the Internet) is a variation of the original PROM with the added feature of data that can be erased so that the chip can be reprogrammed. Unlike the PROM, you can reuse the EPROM instead of discarding it when its contents are no longer valid. The EPROM has a small quartz crystal window on the top of the chip through which ultraviolet (UV) rays can access the chip's circuitry. The UV light causes a chemical reaction that erases the

EPROM by turning the 0's back into 1's again. To prevent accidental erasure of the EPROM chip, a label tape is normally placed over the quartz crystal window. Figure 5-3 shows an EPROM chip. The downside of an EPROM is that it must be removed from the system to be reprogrammed, which is not always possible.

✓ **Electronically Erasable Programmable Read Only Memory (EEPROM):**
An EEPROM (pronounced "e-e-prom") is the common BIOS chip on newer systems. An EEPROM chip can be reprogrammed like the EPROM, but unlike the EPROM it doesn't need to be removed from the motherboard. An EEPROM can be updated through specialized software that is usually downloaded from the BIOS or chip manufacturer's Web site. This process is known as *flashing,* which is why this chip is also commonly called *flash ROM.* Because they're easy to upgrade, EEPROM chips are also used in a variety of other things, such as cars, modems, cameras, and telephones.

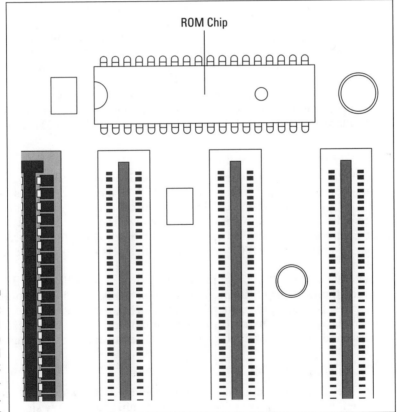

Figure 5-2:
A ROM
BIOS chip
mounted
on a PC
mother-
board.

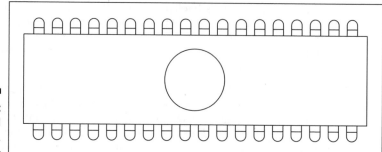

Figure 5-3: An EPROM chip.

Starting up the BIOS

When you power up your PC, the processor is eager to go, but unfortunately its memory is empty and the processor has nothing to do. So, there must be a mechanism included on the system to provide the first instructions to be executed into RAM. Because this chapter is about the BIOS, you shouldn't be surprised that the BIOS contains that mechanism. Getting the processor its first instructions is a fairly simple arrangement. Each time the PC starts up, the processor needs to execute the same set of instructions to start the ball rolling. Because the processor can't execute any instructions to find these instructions, they must be available in the same place every time. This first set of instructions (that loads the BIOS into memory) is hard-wired to a fixed, standard location, called the *jump address,* on the BIOS ROM chip.

Taking the high memory road

The BIOS program is loaded to the last 64KB of the first megabyte of RAM (memory addresses F000h to FFFFh), aka *high memory area,* as shown in Figure 5-4. Processor and BIOS manufacturers established this location as a standard so that the processor always knows the exact location of the BIOS in memory. The processor gets its first instructions from this location and begins executing the BIOS program, which starts the boot sequence.

Several different BIOS programs exist in a PC. Besides the main BIOS program, there are also BIOS programs to control many of the peripheral devices. For example, most video cards have their own BIOS programs that provide additional instructions used for controlling the video display. Hard disks and many SCSI adapters also have their own BIOS programs.

Shadowing the ROM

In older 16-bit computers, a technique called *ROM shadowing* is used to speed up the boot process because ROM chips have a very slow access speed (150 nanoseconds). *ROM shadowing* copies ROM (BIOS) data into RAM and associates the actual location in RAM with the address of the BIOS on the

ROM. The slow-witted processor thinks it's reading the BIOS from the oh-so-slow ROM, when really it's reading from the oh-so-much-faster-RAM. What a hoot, huh! I discuss RAM and system memory in detail in Chapter 8.

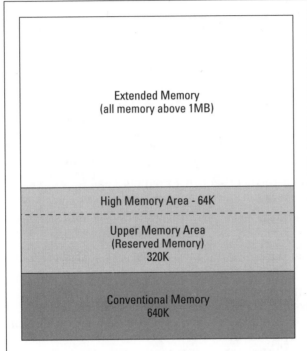

Figure 5-4:
The standard DOS memory allocation.

Booting Up the System

What the BIOS actually does during its boot sequence varies slightly from manufacturer to manufacturer, but here are the steps performed during the boot sequence:

1. When the PC is powered on, the internal power supply initializes.

   The power supply doesn't immediately provide power to the rest of the computer. First, it determines whether it can supply the proper voltages that the PC's components require. The power supply sends out a POWER GOOD signal when it determines that it can supply reliable power to the rest of the PC. When the chipset receives this signal, it issues a SYSTEM RESET signal to the processor.

2. When the processor receives the SYSTEM RESET signal, it accesses the jump address for the start of the BIOS boot program at its hard-wired preset address and loads it into RAM.

The *jump address* contains the actual address of the BIOS boot program on the ROM BIOS chip. The jump address is typically located at address FFFF0 (hexadecimal) or 1,048,560 (decimal), which is at end of the first megabyte of system memory. For more information on hexadecimal and other number systems used in the PC, see Chapter 2.

3. With the primary part of the BIOS now loaded to RAM, the POST process begins.

If any fatal errors happen during the POST process (problems that prevent the PC from operating normally), the appropriate error beep codes sound or perhaps an error message displays, and the boot process stops. At this point in the boot process only the system speaker (because it's technically part of the motherboard) can notify the user of errors.

4. If all is well, the boot sequence continues and the system BIOS loads the device BIOS of the video adapter (if there is one) and loads it to memory.

As your PC boots, the video adapter's information displays on the monitor.

5. Any other device-specific BIOS routines, such as those for the hard disks or SCSI devices, are loaded.

Information, usually including the manufacturer and the BIOS version, displays. The BIOS begins a series of tests on the system, including a run-up count of the amount of memory detected on the system. Because the display is now available, any errors found in this process are displayed on the monitor as an error message instead of a beep code played through the system speaker.

6. The system determines if the devices listed in the CMOS configuration data are present and functioning, including tests for device speeds and access modes.

7. The serial and parallel ports are assigned their identities (COM1, COM2, LPT1, and so on), and a message is displayed for each device found, configured, and tested.

If the BIOS program supports Plug and Play (PnP), any PnP devices detected are configured. Although it usually goes by much too fast to read, the BIOS displays a message for each device it finds and configures.

8. The configuration is confirmed.

The BIOS displays a summary screen that details the computer as the BIOS sees it. This summary screen signals that the system is verified and ready for use.

9. The BIOS looks in the CMOS data to determine which disk drive to use for the operating system. If the boot device is the hard disk, the BIOS looks for the master boot record. If the boot device is a floppy disk or a CD-ROM, it looks at the first sector of the disk for the operating system's boot program. If the boot program is not found on the first device listed, the next device indicated is searched, and then the third, and so on until the boot program is found.

If no boot device is found, the boot sequences stops and an error message ("No boot device available") is displayed.

Starting cold and running warm

One of the first objectives of the A+ Core Hardware exam is to identify the basic terms, concepts, and functions of a PC's boot processes. This includes the actions and the sequence of the actions involved in starting the computer from a power-off status (cold boot) or restarting a PC that's already running (warm boot). A *cold boot* starts when the PC's power is switched on and a *warm boot* is performed whenever the PC is restarted or reset with the power already on. One of the most common ways to start the warm boot is by using the official keystrokes of the PC repair technicians' secret club — Ctrl+Alt+Delete — but then you already knew that.

A cold boot is the whole BIOS enchilada. It causes the BIOS to guide the PC's boot sequence through a series of steps that verify the computer's integrity. The exact steps vary slightly, depending on just about everything about or in your PC (manufacturer, BIOS, and hardware configuration). A warm boot does not run the POST and reestablishes the operating system and drivers on the PC.

Expect one or two questions on the cold boot process and the sequence of its actions in the "Installation, Configuration, and Upgrading" Core Hardware exam domain. You may also see two or three boot sequence or POST questions in the "Diagnosing and Troubleshooting" domain as well.

Running the POST process

Any questions on the boot sequence you encounter will most likely be about the POST process. The POST is a hardware diagnostic routine built into the BIOS that checks the PC's hardware to make sure that everything that's supposed to be there is present, and that everything is working properly. The POST process ensures that the system is ready to begin the boot sequence.

If the POST process detects errors, it generates a signal to indicate where in the process the error occurred and which device had the error. Not all POST errors are fatal; the POST process generally continues past nonfatal problems. If a fatal error is detected, (such as "no memory is found") the POST process signals its error code and halts the boot process immediately. If the POST detects an error before the device drivers for the monitor are loaded, then it must signal an error the only way it can: using sounds, actually beeps, issued through the PC's system speaker.

The meaning of a beep code depends on the manufacturer of the BIOS. Each BIOS maker has its own set of beep codes, which can also vary from one version to the next — similar to having a different Morse code scheme for every ham radio. Well, maybe not really *that* bad!

Just about all BIOS programs will sound a single beep right before displaying the BIOS startup screen. As long as the boot sequence continues, the beep doesn't indicate a problem. BIOS beep codes can be used to troubleshoot hardware failures occurring in the POST procedure.

Decoding POST messages

After the POST and boot sequence have advanced to the point at which they have use of the video to display messages, they can display a numerical error message to indicate a failure that occurred during the POST or boot sequence. For example, a POST message code in the 300 series indicates that a keyboard error was detected during the POST.

For the exam, know the major groups of numerical error codes such as those listed in Table 5-1, which lists the major groups of the POST hardware diagnostics messages commonly used on PC systems. Each of the different BIOS systems uses many of the codes listed, but no single BIOS uses all of these codes. I include only those codes that you may encounter on the test. Many more exist, especially in the IBM system world. One of the problems of these error codes is that the list continues to grow without much being deleted.

Table 5-1	POST Hardware Diagnostic Message Groups
Code	*Description*
1xx	Motherboard errors
2xx	Main memory errors
3xx	Keyboard errors
5xx	Color monitor errors

Code	Description
6xx	Floppy disk controller errors
14xx	Printer errors
17xx	Hard disk controller errors
86xx	Mouse error

Floppy disk controller POST error messages are in the 600 range and keyboard errors cause POST errors in the 300 range.

Other boot errors that occur can appear to be POST errors when in fact they are more commonly caused by a new or recent addition to the system. For example, after a new hard disk is installed, the system may boot to a blank screen if the new slave hard disk drive is not configured in the CMOS correctly or configured as a master. A new hard disk that has not been partitioned or formatted will likely cause a no operating system error.

Other devices can also cause boot time errors. An improperly installed motherboard may indicate many other device problems, and newly installed RAM can cause parity and other fatal memory errors to show up at POST time if the RAM is the wrong speed or uses a different data width.

BIOS startup screen

Immediately after the BIOS loads the video and other device-specific BIOS programs, it displays its startup screen. Although this display varies by manufacturer, it generally contains the following information:

- **Version:** The BIOS manufacturer and the BIOS program's version number and version date.
- **Startup program keys:** The keyboard key or keys used to access the BIOS setup program. Typically, these are the Delete (Del) key or a Function (F1 or F2) keys, but could also be a key combination, such as Ctrl+Esc.
- **Logos:** A logo from one or more of the following: the BIOS manufacturer, the PC manufacturer, or the motherboard manufacturer.
- **Energy Star:** If the BIOS supports the Energy Star standard, aka the Green standard, an Energy Star logo is displayed. Virtually all newer computers display this logo, but only those pre-Pentiums with an upgraded BIOS display it.

> ✔ **Serial number:** The BIOS program's serial number appears either at the end of the display or at the bottom of the screen. The serial number of the BIOS is specific to the combination of the motherboard, chipset, and program version.

For more information on system BIOS than you ever thought you'd need, visit Wim Bervoets' excellent BIOS Web site (www.ping.be/bios/).

System configuration summary

After the BIOS completes its work but before it starts loading the operating system into memory, it displays a summary of the system configuration. What's displayed depends of the manufacturer and version of the BIOS. Typically, the following information is displayed:

> ✔ **Processor:** The type of microprocessor, such as Pentium, Pentium Pro, and so on.

> ✔ **Coprocessor:** If a math coprocessor or floating point unit (FPU) is installed on the system, it is indicated as "Installed." Virtually every processor since the 386DX (with the exception of SX models of the 386 and 486 processors) has an integrated FPU and is indicated as "Integrated."

> ✔ **Clock speed:** Measures the clock speed of the processor in MHz. This information may be displayed on the same line as the processor type.

> ✔ **Floppy disk drives:** Indicates whether the system has any disk drives, the size, and capacity of each floppy disk.

> ✔ **Hard disk, CD-ROM, and DVD drives:** If the system includes ATA disk drives or ATAPI optical or tape drives, the BIOS displays the drive types detected, including the primary master and slave drives and any secondary slaves and masters found, including the manufacturer, capacity, and access modes of each drive.

> ✔ **Memory size:** Indicates the amount of memory in base, extended, and cache memory. The base memory (conventional memory) size is always 640KB. Displays the amount of extended memory on the system minus the amount set aside for the BIOS. The BIOS doesn't report the amount of memory reserved for the high-memory area that contains the BIOS itself. The cache size is displayed separately.

> ✔ **Memory type:** The type and configuration of the physical memory is displayed, including the number of memory banks or modules installed and the memory technology in use. For example, the display may indicate "EDO DRAM at Bank 1" or "FP: 0 was detected."

- ✔ **Video type:** Unless your computer is more than 10 years old, the display type is usually "VGA/EGA," which really doesn't tell you anything except that the video adapter was detected.

- ✔ **Serial ports:** The system resource addresses (usually 3F8h and 2F8h) of any serial or COM ports detected.

- ✔ **Parallel ports:** The system resource address (usually 378h) of the parallel port is displayed.

- ✔ **Plug and Play (PnP) devices:** If any PnP adapter cards are detected by the BIOS, a description of each may be displayed.

Booting up the softer side

Chapter 19 discusses the sequence of events that follow the hardware boot sequence to load the operating system, device drivers, and other system software that make the PC ready for the user.

Be sure you learn the sequence of the system files loaded to start the Windows operating system running from a cold boot.

Setting the BIOS configuration

Usually a PC is shipped from the factory with all the peripheral devices it will ever have already installed and its system configuration already complete and stored in CMOS. If a PC needs upgrading or new peripherals installed, you can view and alter the configuration as necessary. The BIOS setup and configuration data is accessed through one of the startup programs. This program, called the *setup,* is available for only a very short time during the system boot sequence and you can access it through a specific key or combination of keys.

Always create a backup of the BIOS settings each time the BIOS configuration changes and for every new PC added to the network. To make a backup of the BIOS settings, simply write them down on paper and keep it in a safe place.

Setup program

To gain access to the BIOS setup program, press a key designated by the BIOS, which is displayed during the initial boot process. Figure 5-5 shows the information displayed during the boot sequence. Notice that it shows that the F1 function key is used to access the setup program. Table 5-2 lists the keystrokes used to access the setup program for most of the popular BIOS programs.

```
PhoenixBIOS 4.0 Release 6.0
Copyright 1985-1998 Phoenix Technologies Ltd.  All Rights Reserved
Copyright 1996-1998 Intel Corporation.
404CL0X0.15A.0006.P02


Intel® Celeron(tm) processor 333 Mhz
128MB System RAM

Legacy Keyboard . . . Detected
Legacy Mouse . . . . . Detected

Fixed Disk 0: QUANTUM FIREBALL EX10.2A-(PM)
ATAPI CD-ROM: MATSHITA CR-588-(SM)
ATAPI Removable Drive: IOMEGA ZIP 100-(SS) ATAPI

Press <F1> to enter SETUP
```

Figure 5-5:
A sample
BIOS
startup
screen.

Table 5-2	BIOS Setup Program Access Keys
BIOS	*Keys*
AMI	Del (Delete)
Award	Del or Ctrl+Alt+Esc
Compaq	F10
IBM Aptiva	F1
Phoenix BIOS	F1 or F2

The setup program manages the hardware configuration stored in CMOS memory. The settings included in the configuration, although somewhat standardized, vary with the BIOS. Pressing the startup program access key starts the program used to display and modify the system setup data. The setup program menus are the first things displayed.

Standard configuration menu

On nearly all newer PCs, the configuration data is managed and maintained on two levels:

  ✔ **The standard configuration.** Includes the system clock and basic data on the hard drives, floppy drive, and video adapter.

✔ **The advanced setup.** The standard configuration menu may also list the processor type, memory type and speed, and the amount and type of memory.

Here's a list of the basic standard settings and parameters you normally find on the standard configuration menu:

✔ **System date:** Sets the MM/DD/YY date for the system. On Windows 98 and 2000, this BIOS setting can be adjusted from the built-in Date/Time Properties feature.

✔ **System time:** Displays the time in the 24-hour clock format (11:00 PM displays as 23:00). Like the system date, this setting can be adjusted from the Date/Time Properties feature of Windows.

✔ **IDE primary and secondary masters:** The parameters of the hard drives configured as the primary master or secondary master, if any, are configured in these entries. On most BIOS systems, the default setting is commonly "Auto," which refers to autodetection.

✔ **IDE primary and secondary slaves:** The parameters of the hard disk drives configured as the primary slave or secondary slave, if any, are configured in these entries. On most BIOS systems, the default setting is commonly "Auto," which refers to autodetection.

✔ **Floppy disk drives A and B:** Listed separately, because there is commonly no B floppy drive installed, the type of disk drive in the system is indicated in this entry. The default for the A drive is typically the 1.44 MB drive and "Not Installed" for the B drive. The choices are typically

- **1.44 MB:** The normal everyday 3.5-inch floppy disk drive.

- **1.2 MB:** Although rarely used anymore, the normal 5.25-inch floppy disk drive.

- **2.88 MB:** The high-density 3.5-inch floppy disk drive, called the Big Floppy. Rare, but shows up on some of the latest systems.

- **720 KB:** The low-density 3.5-inch floppy disk drive.

- **360 KB:** The dinosaur of floppy disk drives, the low-density 5.25-inch disk drive.

- **None or Not Installed:** No floppy drive is installed in the A or B positions.

✔ **Video display:** This setting defines the display standard in use and is usually VGA/EGA indicating that the PC is using a VGA or SVGA card.

✔ **Halt on:** Some BIOS programs enable you to set which errors you want the BIOS to stop (halt) during the POST and boot sequence. The choices range from all errors (a good choice), to no errors (a bad choice), and many "All but the. . ." settings (it depends) that prevent errors on certain devices from stopping the boot.

The truly cautious and wise PC repair technician creates a complete backup of the PC's hard disk before messing with the PC's BIOS or its setup configuration, especially the advanced settings.

Advanced setup menu

The settings in the advanced features or advanced setup menu are specific to the motherboard, processor, and chipset. Typically, access to these settings is a menu choice listed on the startup programs menu page.

You should know the kinds of things that are included under the advanced settings, but don't spend a lot of time memorizing them. Just understand the basic differences between the standard configuration and the advanced settings. To really lock this in, boot your own PC and access the startup program and the CMOS configuration data. Review the standard and the advanced settings and make a mental note of the types of settings included in each.

Plug and Play options

The startup program should also include special menus for PnP. If a PnP menu is available, a general PnP option may be listed in the advanced features. You can set this option on or off to match the operating system.

You can't simply count on the operating system to handle PnP devices. Some operating systems such as Windows NT and 2000 don't directly support PnP, which means that the BIOS must deal with any PnP device configurations.

Extended System Configuration Data (ESCD)

If the BIOS does support PnP, the startup program stores *Extended System Configuration Data (ESCD)* in CMOS. ESCD defines the system resource assignments of PnP devices. ESCD also serves as a communications link between the BIOS and the operating system for the PnP devices.

Other startup menus

Depending on the BIOS, you may find other menus listed on the setup program's menu page. These menus typically focus on one particular aspect of the system's configuration. Some of the menus you may find are:

- **Power management:** This menu contains options used to control the system when it is automatically powered down through power conservation settings.

- **Integrated peripherals:** This menu defines the configuration of the devices that are integrated into the motherboard, such as serial and parallel ports, audio, and USB ports.

Security and passwords

The ability to set the user and supervisor password for the BIOS and the CMOS data is included on a separate menu or in the advanced features menu on older systems.

If the user password is set, the computer isn't allowed to boot until the proper password is entered. The supervisor password protects the BIOS program's settings and the system configuration. Without the supervisor password, a user can't access the BIOS settings, but the system will boot. If you choose to set either of these passwords, you put yourself in the situation of really needing to remember them, but there are second chances.

If you forget the user password and remember the supervisor password, you can enter the BIOS setup data and clear or change the user password. If you forget both passwords, you're stuck. Your only recourse is to open the computer and use the password-clear jumper (see Figure 5-6) located on the motherboard near the CMOS chip and its battery. You can also clear the CMOS settings, including all advanced settings that you may have changed and the passwords, by removing the CMOS battery, shown in Figure 5-7. That's one reason that you want to keep a backup copy of the system setup written down and kept in a safe place.

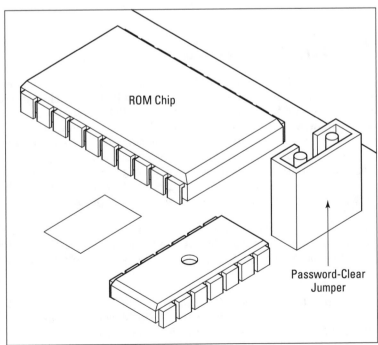

Figure 5-6:
The Password-Clear jumper on a PC mother-board.

ROM Chip

Password-Clear Jumper

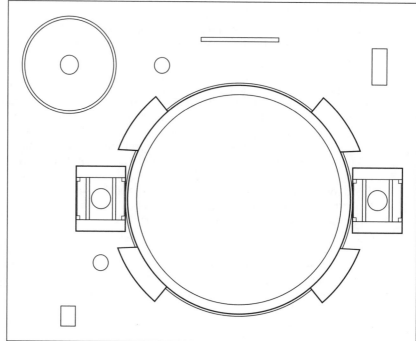

Figure 5-7:
The CMOS battery on a PC mother-board.

Updating the BIOS

Upgrading the BIOS on most older PCs (those with the BIOS loaded on a ROM chip), required you to physically remove the BIOS ROM chip and replace it with the new ROM chip containing the new BIOS version — something that was not always easy or possible to do. This really cramped your style if you wanted to upgrade the processor or chipset, which usually requires a BIOS upgrade. This process could introduce a wide range of problems into the PC, including ESD, bent pins on the chips, damage to the motherboard from clumsy fingers, and more. For many people, it was easier to simply upgrade to a new PC and avoid the anxiety and potential problems.

For the Core Hardware exam, you should know when a system BIOS should be updated and how the update is done. You should also know what problems to expect if the BIOS upgrade process is interrupted and how the BIOS is recovered.

Fortunately, the EEPROM has replaced the PROM and is the BIOS ROM of choice. This is fortunate because the EEPROM can be updated in place on the board through a process called *flashing*. Flashing allows you to upgrade the contents of the EEPROM under the control of a software utility program. Yes, there are still motherboards around that require the BIOS ROM to be physically replaced in order to upgrade it, but they are rare and virtually all new systems include flash BIOS. For the A+ exam, you should be aware of both approaches to upgrading the BIOS, but focus on flashing.

The BIOS manufacturers that produce flash BIOS provide software utilities to control the flashing process. The flash utility is easily obtained from the manufacturer's Web site or by mail. Depending on the manufacturer, the flash utility contains routines to verify the BIOS version to the motherboard and chipset and to prevent the BIOS from receiving the wrong version. The flash software runs on a PC after it has booted. Be sure you follow the manufacturer's instructions to the letter.

Flashing dangers

Flashing, for all its benefits, carries a few risks as well. When you begin flashing a BIOS ROM, you absolutely must complete the process. Remember that the flash process is replacing the contents of the EEPROM. If the process is interrupted, you'll likely end up with a corrupted and unusable BIOS. If the flashing process is interrupted — for example, somebody trips over the power cord, a power failure occurs, the flash software has a bug, or the PC is accidentally knocked off the table — depending on where you are in the flashing process, the probability of a having a corrupted BIOS chip is high.

Flashing the wrong BIOS version is another way to corrupt the BIOS ROM. Flashing can be unforgiving and many flash utilities will load whatever BIOS version you give it without question. The software provided to flash your BIOS may not include security features to prevent this from happening. The flashing utilities from the larger BIOS companies (such as Award and AMI) include features that check the version of the flash file against the model of motherboard and let you know of any mismatch. A corrupted BIOS leaves you in a real Catch-22 situation. To flash your BIOS ROM you must boot the PC and you can't boot the PC with a corrupted BIOS.

In spite of the dangers, the whole process of flashing the BIOS usually takes only a few seconds and the risks are actually low. But you should take no chances. Avoid flashing your BIOS in an electrical storm; be sure your computer is protected against power surges or brownouts by a uninterruptible power supply (UPS); and check twice that you are flashing your BIOS with the current version.

Preventing accidental flashing

After you flash your BIOS, you still may have the flash utility on your PC and that means there is a chance of accidental flashing. If this were to happen and you replace the BIOS with the same complete version, there should be no harm. However, if the accidental flashing operation is interrupted, or your current BIOS is replaced by an older or incompatible version either inadvertently or maliciously, the effect is the same as no BIOS at all — a PC that won't boot.

Most motherboards that support flash BIOS include a jumper block that can be set to disallow flash updates. To flash the BIOS ROM, the flashing security jumper has to be in the correct position. If you plan to flash your BIOS, open the system case and check the position of this jumper. After you flash the BIOS, reset this jumper and you're prevented from accidentally flashing it again. Another very good reason to use the flashing security jumper is to prevent access from computer viruses that attempt to change the flash BIOS code.

The BIOS savior

The boot block is a 4KB emergency boot program included with the BIOS. The flashing recovery mode allows you to recover from an incorrect or corrupted BIOS. The boot block will restore the BIOS from a special floppy disk or CD-ROM, available from the BIOS manufacturer. If the motherboard supports it, this feature may need to be enabled through a jumper.

More BIOS Resources

The links provided below lead to excellent references for anyone who needs a complete overview of BIOS features and functions, as well as useful insight into system BIOS setup, upgrades, and optimization.

- **BIOS Optimization Guide** (www.rojakpot.com/Speed_Demonz/ BIOS_Guide/). Adrian Wong's definitive BIOS upgrade and optimization Web site.

- **PC Guide System BIOS** (www.pcguide.com/ref/mbsys/bios/). Charles Kozierok's excellent Web site has a wealth of information on not only PC BIOS, but anything and everything PC.

- **PC Mechanic's BIOS Guide** (www.pcmech.com/bios/). This Web site features David Risley's BIOS Guide that includes tutorials on a variety of BIOS topics.

- **The BIOS Companion** (www.electrocution.com/biosc.htm). This Web site features excerpts from the book *The BIOS Companion* by Phil Croucher that includes sections on the BIOS and flashing.

- **Smart Computing** (www.smartcomputing.com). This is the Web site for a print magazine that features articles on a wide range of PC topics in plain English. Search on BIOS to find a number of articles.

Prep Test

1 What does the acronym BIOS stand for?

- **A** ○ Binary Input Output System
- **B** ○ Basic Independent Operating System
- **C** ○ Basic Input Output System
- **D** ○ It has no specific meaning.

2 Starting the PC when it's powered off causes which type of boot cycle to be performed?

- **A** ○ cold boot
- **B** ○ warm boot
- **C** ○ dead boot
- **D** ○ restart

3 The hardware configuration and chipset features of a PC are stored in which type of memory?

- **A** ○ ECC
- **B** ○ DRAM
- **C** ○ CMOS
- **D** ○ EDO

4 Which of the following ROM types can be reprogrammed under software control?

- **A** ○ ROM
- **B** ○ PROM
- **C** ○ EPROM
- **D** ○ EEPROM

5 Using a software utility to upgrade the BIOS is called

- **A** ○ flashing
- **B** ○ strobing
- **C** ○ burning
- **D** ○ upgrading

6 The BIOS is loaded into which area of system memory?

- **A** ○ Conventional
- **B** ○ Upper memory block
- **C** ○ Extended memory
- **D** ○ High memory area

7 **What event signals the end of the boot sequence?**

A ○ POWER GOOD signal

B ○ The operating system is running

C ○ A single beep code

D ○ The POST process ends

8 **POST error messages in the 3xx series indicate an error with which FRM?**

A ○ Motherboard

B ○ Keyboard

C ○ Floppy disk controller

D ○ Hard disk controller

9 **What is the purpose of the boot block?**

A ○ Prevent the system from rebooting during flashing

B ○ Reboot the system when the power supply is dead

C ○ Restore the BIOS if it becomes corrupted

D ○ Restore the supervisor and user passwords

10 **Which of the following actions is not performed during the boot sequence?**

A ○ A backup copy is made of the CMOS configuration data

B ○ POST process

C ○ Serial and parallel ports are assigned their port identities

D ○ The configuration summary screen is displayed

Answers

1 **C.** The BIOS is the basic input/output interface between the operating system and the hardware. *See "Getting to Know the BIOS."*

2 **A.** The "cold" refers to fact that the system is not powered on or warm. *Review "Starting cold and running warm."*

3 **C.** The CMOS memory holds all of the BIOS related hardware and advanced feature settings. *Check out "Setting the BIOS configuration."*

4 **D.** Electronically Erasable Programmable Read Only Memory (EEPROM) can be reprogrammed using special software utilities. *Take a look at "BIOS Chipology."*

5 **A.** Flashing is the process used to upgrade a BIOS by replacing the contents of the BIOS ROM with a newer version. *Peruse "Updating the BIOS."*

6 **D.** The last 64K of the first megabyte of memory is reserved for the BIOS program. *Look over "Taking the high memory road."*

7 **B.** The last step of the boot sequence is to load the operating system and turn control over to it. The BIOS remains in RAM to handle interactions with the hardware. *See "Booting Up the System."*

8 **B.** The 300 series indicates a boot error with the keyboard. The specific error depends on the BIOS manufacturer and how they have assigned the error codes. *Review "Decoding POST messages."*

9 **C.** On those systems equipped to do so, the boot block provides a safety net that allows the BIOS to be restored from a floppy disk or a CD-ROM. *Check out "The BIOS savior."*

10 **A.** No, a backup copy of the CMOS is not made, but this is something you should do yourself on paper every time you make any changes to the BIOS configuration settings. *Take a look at "Booting Up the System."*

Chapter 6

Bus Structures

· ·

Exam Objectives

▶ Identifying PC motherboard expansion buses

▶ Explaining the function of Plug and Play (PnP)

▶ Defining the PC Card (PCMCIA) interface

▶ Configuring IRQs, DMAs, I/O addresses, and logical devices

· ·

*I*nterfacing with the system is one area of the A+ exams that's very detail oriented and precise. In many of the exam domains, a general knowledge of basic concepts is usually sufficient, but that's not the case with the topics in this chapter, and rightly so.

As a PC repair technician, much of your job is adding new or replacing old hardware, which involves installing new adapter cards and cabling in customer PCs. To do these tasks, you must thoroughly understand the bus structures, IRQs, DMA functions, and input/output addressing associated with each particular motherboard. A solid understanding of how these technologies function is what gives you the confidence to plug a new high-priced video card into the appropriate expansion slot and set it up correctly with the operating system. Without a doubt, installing, configuring, and cabling new peripherals and adapter cards is the most techie part of being a PC technician.

Although its specific domain will have only around ten questions, as much as 40 percent of both A+ tests may have questions relating to this chapter's topics. So, this is one chapter you may want to look at a little more carefully, especially if you don't do this type of work very much. I really condense a lot of facts and concepts into this chapter to help you prepare for the questions that I bet trip up most of the people who fail the exams.

Quick Assessment

Identifying PC mother-board expansion buses

1 The two general types of bus structures on every motherboard are _____ and _____.

2 The system bus provides four different system necessities: _____, _____, _____, and _____.

3 The ISA architecture provides a(n) _____-bit bus.

4 _____ was the first 32-bit architecture.

Explaining the function of Plug and Play

5 _____ is a configuration standard that allows the BIOS and operating system to automatically configure expansion boards and device adapters.

Defining the PC Card (PCMCIA) interface

6 The Type II PC Card is primarily used to add _____ or _____ to portable computers.

Configuring IRQs, DMAs, I/O addresses, and logical devices

7 _____ are the resources used to interface, communicate, and control individual device adapters and controllers.

8 A(n) _____ channel allows a device to bypass the processor to access memory directly.

9 A(n) _____ is a signal from a device to the processor that a service or special action is needed.

10 The default IRQ for COM1 is _____.

11 The default I/O address for LPT1 is _____.

Answers

1   *Internal, external.* See "Bus structures basics."

2   *Power, control signals, addresses, and data.* Review "Understanding the internal bus."

3   *16.* Study "Plugging into the expansion bus."

4   *MCA (Micro-Channel Architecture).* Review "Plugging into the expansion bus."

5   *Plug and Play.* Review "Fun with Plug and Play."

6   *Modems or NICs (network interface cards).* Take a look at "Upgrading notebooks and portables."

7   *System resources.* See "Working with System Resources."

8   *DMA (direct memory access).* Review "Accessing memory directly with DMA."

9   *Interrupt.* Study "Requesting an interrupt, or how to get IRQed."

10   *IRQ 4.* Take a look at "Using input/output (I/O) addresses."

11   *378h.* See "Using input/output (I/O) addresses."

Bus Structure Basics

Although you may see a question on the Core Hardware exam that involves the definition of a bus, most of this first section is background information for the real techie stuff that follows. If you look at the bottom of any PC motherboard, you will see an interconnecting maze of pathways that are used to transport data, addresses, and instructions around the system. Each of these pathways is a *bus*, which is a group of tiny, very thin wires that carry signals from one part of the motherboard to another.

Two general types of bus structures are on every motherboard:

- **Internal bus:** Interconnects main memory, the CPU, and all other components on the motherboard
- **External (expansion) bus:** Connects the outside world of peripherals to the motherboard

When I compare a bus to a multilane highway, I'm referring to the size (meaning its width or capacity) of the bus. The width of a bus determines the amount of data and how large an address it can transmit. The width of a bus is stated in bits. Just like a 4-lane highway has a capacity for 4 vehicles a time, a 16-bit bus is capable of transmitting 16 bits of data at a time, and a 32-bit bus can transmit 32 bits of data. Obviously, the wider a bus is in bits, the more data it can carry.

The speed at which data moves on a bus is controlled by its clock speed, which is measured in megahertz (MHz). If the speed limit on the highway is faster, more cars and trucks per hour can move over it. Likewise, higher bus speeds are able to transmit more data per second. Think of it this way: If a bus (a passenger bus) needs to carry 300 people from point A to point B, but has a carrying capacity of only 66 people at a time, it obviously must make several trips. The faster the bus goes in making its outbound and inbound trips, the sooner all the people get to beautiful downtown point B. Another solution would be to get a bigger bus. A faster bus (the computer kind) allows more data to be transferred faster, which in turn makes the operating system and applications run faster. For the exam, you must understand the compatibilities, capabilities, and limitations of the various bus architectures detailed in this chapter.

Understanding the internal bus

You should have a good understanding of general bus architectures for the Core Hardware exam. You may not be asked any specific questions from this area, but it will sure help you understand some of the questions you will be asked.

Don't worry about the difference between the specific system bus structures of a 386 processor and those of the latest Pentium technology. Concentrate on the various bus architectures used in device I/O (chipsets and expansion cards), which is where you, the repair technician, most likely come into contact with the bus.

The internal bus, also known as the system bus, is that maze of wires on the motherboard. It provides the internal components of the computer with four different necessities:

- ✔ **Power:** Power comes to the motherboard straight from the power supply. The motherboard uses the *system bus* to distribute power to components mounted on or plugged into it.

- ✔ **Control signals:** The control unit within the CPU sends out control signals to coordinate the activities of the system. These signals are carried on the internal *control bus*.

- ✔ **Addresses:** PC components pass data and instructions between one another using memory location addresses to reference the location of the data or instructions in memory. Addresses are transmitted on the internal *address bus*.

- ✔ **Data:** Data and instructions are transferred between components on the internal *data bus*.

PC buses carry data, instructions, or the addresses of data or instructions. Just as a passenger bus stops at different places to pick up or drop off people, a PC bus deposits or collects addresses or data at the different components (CPU, memory, and so on) to which it is connected. The address carried on the address bus references the source or destination location of the data or instructions carried on the data bus.

In a way, the contents of the address and data buses are like a letter going through the postal service mail. The envelope (the letter's address bus) has the address of the letter's destination, and the message inside of the envelope (the letter's data bus) is its data.

On Pentium motherboards, the system chipset is the communications controller between all the components that interact with the system bus. The system chipset coordinates with each component or device to ensure that each device properly interacts with every other one. See Chapter 4 for more information on motherboards and chipsets.

Defining the external (expansion) bus

For the exam, you need to know what each of the expansion bus features is and how each is used, and you need to understand how and why each is applied. Not only will this understanding help you on the test, but it will also help you later in this chapter.

In the context of the PC, when most people refer to "the bus," they are referring to the data bus and, without knowing it, the address bus. The external bus must connect and coordinate with these two internal bus workhorses.

Earlier in this chapter, I list the external bus as one of the general bus structures of the PC. This bus, also called the *expansion bus,* allows peripheral devices to communicate with the motherboard and its components, almost as if they were a part of the motherboard itself. To add a new device to the PC, the device's adapter card is plugged into the expansion bus via a compatible expansion slot on the motherboard. After it's plugged in, the device is able to communicate with the CPU and other system components.

The expansion slot for any of the supported expansion bus architectures comprises a certain number of small metal spring connectors that line each side of the connector slot. The slot connectors match up with the tabs on the card's edge connectors, as shown in Figure 6-1. Like pins in a serial or parallel cable, each connection between the slot and card form a channel that services a particular need of the expansion card. Some channels carry power, some connect to the address and data buses, and others are used for system resources, such as the *clock signal, IRQ, I/O address,* and *DMA* interfaces. Here is a brief description of each of these system resources:

- ✔ **Clock signal:** This connection provides the card with the signal of the bus clock so that it can synchronize its communications with the buses of the motherboard.

- ✔ **Interrupt request (IRQ):** A request that tells the CPU to interrupt what it's doing to take care of the special needs of the device sending the IRQ. Devices are assigned IRQ numbers so that the CPU knows which device is the rude one. When you install a new device that requires services from the CPU, it is assigned an IRQ number, which enables the CPU to know which device is nagging it and requesting service. On occasion, devices may share an IRQ, provided both devices do not attempt to interact with the CPU at the same time.

- ✔ **Direct memory access (DMA):** DMA channels allow certain devices to bypass the processor and access main memory directly. DMA devices have the intelligence to handle their own data transfers to memory. Some bus architectures allow more DMA channels than others, but two devices can't share a DMA channel.

✔ **Input/Output (I/O) address:** This system resource is assigned to a device via its expansion slot. The I/O address, also called an *I/O port* or *hardware port,* allows the CPU to send commands directly to the device by writing them to an assigned area in memory that the device checks frequently. The I/O address is a one-way-only line that works like a reverse IRQ. The CPU uses the I/O address to send a command to the device. If the device responds, it uses the data bus or DMA channel to do so. Only one device can be assigned to an I/O address.

✔ **Bus mastering:** Another feature attached to expansion slots and expansion cards that allows one device to interact directly with another is *bus mastering.* Usually, the expansion card plugged into a slot has a bus master processor on the card that directs this activity. Most modern motherboards, especially those with the PCI bus (see "Plugging into the expansion bus" later in the chapter), support bus mastering because it improves performance.

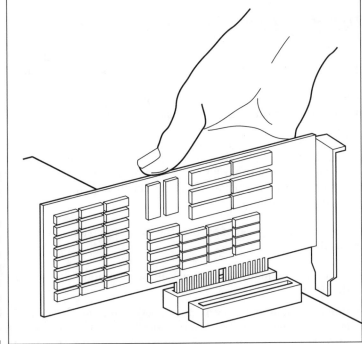

Figure 6-1:
The connectors on an expansion card are aligned to those in the expansion slot.

Fun with Plug and Play

Plug and Play (PnP) is a configuration standard that allows the system BIOS and the operating system to configure expansion boards and other devices automatically so that the user or PC technician won't have to worry about setting DIP switches, jumpers, and system resources (IRQ, I/O addresses, DMA, and so on). In effect, you just plug in the device or adapter card and play with it.

In order to use PnP on a system, four requirements must be met:

✔ The system BIOS must support PnP.

✔ The motherboard and its chipset must support PnP.

✔ The operating system running on the PC must support PnP.

✔ The bus of the expansion slot used must be compatible with PnP.

All versions of Windows from Windows 95 on, including Windows 2000, fully support PnP, although Windows NT only partially supports it. PnP is compatible with ISA, EISA, MCA, PC Card (PCMCIA), and PCI devices and adapters. All PCI devices are PnP, but not all PnP devices are PCI devices.

Plugging into the expansion bus

For the exam, you need to know what differentiates one expansion bus architecture from another and which are the most commonly used types.

One bit of terminology adjustment is in order here: An expansion bus architecture is the same as an expansion slot type.

A variety of expansion architectures have been used in PCs over the years, including 8-bit, ISA, EISA, MCA, VLB, and PCI. When you open the PC's case and look at the motherboard, the expansion slots you likely see are ISA, AGP, and PCI, as illustrated in Figure 6-2. A motherboard can often support several types of expansion slots.

Here's a brief description of each of the expansion slot architectures that has been used in PCs:

✔ **8-bit bus:** Not many of these left around, so don't worry about it for the exam.

✔ **Industry Standard Architecture (ISA):** Pronounced "ice-ah," ISA was introduced with the IBM AT and called the AT bus in its early days; it provided a 16-bit data bus. As shown in Figure 6-3, the ISA bus is characterized by adding an additional short slot to a slot on the 8-bit bus to create the 16-bit connector. ISA added eight additional IRQs and doubled the number of DMA channels. ISA expansion cards were designated to the appropriate IRQ or DMA numbers through jumpers and DIP switches. The ISA architecture also separated the bus clock from the CPU clock to allow the slower data bus to operate at its own speeds. ISA slots are found on 286, 386, 486, and some Pentium PCs.

✔ **Micro-Channel Architecture (MCA):** Introduced with the IBM PS/2, MCA was the first 32-bit option and featured bus mastering and a 10 MHz bus clock for expansion cards. The MCA expansion slot is about the same size as the ISA slot, but has about twice as many channels. MCA cards are also configured to their IRQ and DMA assignments by software, which is an improvement over the jumpers and DIPs of the ISA architecture.

✔ **Extended ISA (EISA):** Pronounced "ee-sah," this architecture was developed by a group of companies to overcome the limitations of ISA and compete with MCA. In effect, EISA takes the best parts of MCA and builds on them. It has a 32-bit data bus, uses software setup, has more I/O addresses available, and ignores IRQs and DMA channels. EISA uses only an 8 MHz bus clock to be backward compatible to ISA boards. (A device that is backward compatible supports all of its previous versions.) In this case, EISA supports ISA expansion boards along with its own.

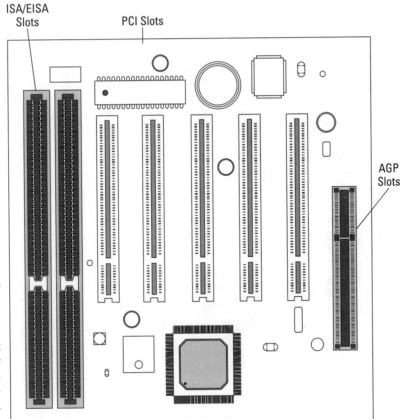

ISA/EISA Slots

PCI Slots

AGP Slots

Figure 6-2:
The expansion slots most commonly found on a mother-board.

✔ **VESA Local Bus (VLB or VL-bus):** VLB was used first on 486 systems and grew out of the need for the data bus to run at the same clock speed as the CPU. VLB was developed by the Video Electronics Standards Association (VESA) to place a port more or less directly on the system bus with what was called a bus slot or a processor direct slot.

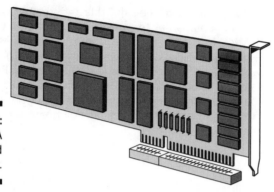

Figure 6-3:
The ISA
16-bit card
and slot.

✔ **Peripheral Component Interconnect (PCI) bus:** Introduced with the Pentium PC, PCI is a local bus architecture that supports either a 32- or 64-bit bus, which allows it to be used with both 486 and Pentium computers. The PCI bus is also processor independent because of a special bridging circuit contained on PCI boards. Its bus speed is 33 MHz, giving it much higher throughput than earlier cards. The PCI architecture and expansion slot, shown in Figure 6-4, also support ISA and EISA cards. PCI cards are also PnP, which means they automatically configure themselves to the appropriate IRQ, DMA, and I/O port addresses.

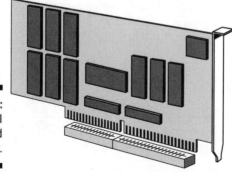

Figure 6-4:
The PCI
card and
slot.

For the exam, remember the bus width in bits for each bus structure, especially the ones that are 32 or more bits. Table 6-1 summarizes the basic characteristics of the bus structures discussed earlier.

Table 6-1	**Bus Architecture Characteristics**		
Bus	*Bus Width (bits)*	*Bus Speed (MHz)*	*How Configured*
8-bit	8	8	Jumpers and DIP switches
ISA	16	8	Jumpers and DIP switches
MCA	32	10	Software
EISA	32	8	Software
VL-Bus	32	Processor speed (up to 40 MHz)	Jumpers and DIP switches
PCI	32/64	Processor speed (up to 33 MHz)	PnP

Upgrading notebooks and portables

The *PC Card,* or its original name *PCMCIA (Personal Computer Memory Card International Association) bus,* is used to add external devices to a notebook or hand-held computer. PC cards, which are about the size of a credit card, are used to add memory, modems, network interface cards, and even hard disk drives to portable computers. These cards slide into slots that are usually on the side of a notebook computer. The three standards for PC Cards are:

- ✔ **Type I:** Cards that are 3.3mm thick and used for memory additions. Type I cards have a single row of connectors.

- ✔ **Type II:** Cards that are 5mm thick and used primarily to add modems or network interface cards (NICs). Type II cards have two rows of connectors.

- ✔ **Type III:** Cards that are up to 10.5mm thick and used to add an external hard disk to a notebook computer. Type III cards have four rows of connectors.

Plan on seeing a test question on the type of devices supported by the PC Card (PCMCIA) types. See Chapter 15 for more information on portable systems and PC Cards.

You can hot-swap PC Cards, which means you can remove or insert them with the system's power on.

Using SCSI

The *Small Computers System Interface* (*SCSI*, pronounced "skuzzy") is an interface and not technically an architecture. It is used to connect a wide variety of internal and external devices, such as CD-ROM drives, printers, and scanners. You can connect up to eight different SCSI devices in a daisy-chain fashion to the host adapter card installed in a SCSI slot. SCSI is actually a technology used for interfacing multiple devices through a single connection on the motherboard. SCSI adapter cards can themselves be PCI, VL-Bus, EISA, or ISA. Chapter 9 includes a more in-depth discussion on the SCSI interface and its various technologies.

Bus interfacing

Most of the later PC systems (486 and later) support multiple bus interfaces. On these systems, some provisions must be made to interconnect the different bus architectures and allow their devices to communicate with one another. This objective is accomplished using a *bridge,* which connects two dissimilar systems. This term means the same thing in networking, as well. The most common bridge is the PCI-ISA bridge supplied by the chipset in virtually all Pentium systems. To see the interface bridges on your PC, use the Windows Device Manager and access the System Devices tab illustrated in Figure 6-5. The Windows Device Manager displays a list of the controllers and bridges supplied by the chipset.

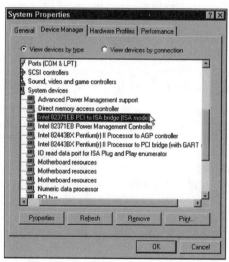

Figure 6-5:
The
Windows
Device
Manager's
System
Devices tab
shows the
device
bridges
included on
the chipset.

Working with System Resources

In the realm of PC configuration, the term *system resources* refers to the mechanisms used to interface, communicate, and control individual device adapters and controllers, along with the serial, parallel, and mouse ports. For the most part, the CPU and the peripheral devices on a PC use the elements of the system resources as a set of communications channels. Any device, including the motherboard, expansion cards, and peripherals, that wants to communicate with the CPU must use one or more of the system resource components: the IRQ (interrupt requests), I/O (input/output) ports (also known as I/O addresses), and DMA (direct memory access) channels.

Unfortunately, a bit of memorization is required in this area for the Core Hardware exam. You need to know which IRQs are used with which devices (see "Requesting an interrupt, or how to get IRQed") and which devices are assigned to which I/O addresses (see "Using input/output (I/O) addresses"). You must also be familiar with the use and common assignments of DMA channels. (See "Accessing memory directly with DMA.") In other words, you must know the relationships of the primary system resources and the physical and logical devices (see "Naming the logical devices") to which they are assigned.

Requesting an interrupt, or how to get IRQed

An *interrupt* is a request from a device (other than the CPU) to the CPU for a service, action, or special action. If you've ever dined at one of the large coffee shop chains, you've probably seen a form of interrupt processing in use. Usually, above the kitchen service window is a sign with a bank of numbers that can be individually lighted. When the very busy server has an order ready, the cook lights up the server's number on the sign. When the server is able to interrupt what he or she is doing, he or she serves that order to the customer. The server number that alerts the server to the order is much like the interrupt requests used in PC interrupt processing. When a device needs the CPU to perform a task, such as transferring data from memory, issuing an I/O, and so on, it sends a signal to the CPU using the IRQ line it is assigned. Each device is assigned a specific IRQ number (much like the food server) so that the processor knows the device to which it needs to respond.

Interrupt requests are sent to a special system component, called an *interrupt controller,* which is either a separate chip on the motherboard or is incorporated into the chipset. The interrupt controller receives and verifies requests and passes them on to the processor. Two interrupt controllers have been on PCs since the 286, each managing eight IRQ lines with each IRQ tied directly to a particular device. The two interrupt controllers are linked, or *cascaded,* through IRQ 2, which is set aside for this purpose.

Conflicting interrupts

For the exam, understand the ramification of IRQ conflicts and how to avoid them.

An IRQ is assigned to one specific device, and although two devices can share an IRQ, it just doesn't work to have them active at the same time. If two devices are assigned the same interrupt, the processor could become confused and send its response to the wrong device at the wrong time, causing untold horrors to happen. Assigning two active devices to the same IRQ creates an *IRQ conflict,* a serious system no-no.

An IRQ conflict can cause both devices to perform sporadically (in the best case) or not work at all (in the worst case). Similar devices can share IRQs, but they can't be used at the same time. IRQs are assigned by the system BIOS during POST and the boot process. Reassigning an IRQ or changing the assigned IRQ of a device is done differently depending on the adapter card and perhaps the operating system. On most earlier PCs (those running DOS and Windows 3.*x*), a device IRQ can be set through a jumper on its adapter card or the use of proprietary installation software. On Windows 9*x* and 2000 PCs, a device's IRQ assignment can be managed through the Device Manager. Lab 6-1 lists the steps you use to access IRQ settings on a Windows PC, a topic you are likely to see on both of the A+ exams.

Lab 6-1   Accessing IRQs in the Windows Device Manager

1. **Right-click the My Computer icon on the Desktop to display a shortcut menu.**

2. **Choose Properties from the menu to display the System Properties box.**

   Or

1. **From the Start⇨Settings Menu, open the Control Panel.**

2. **Click to open the System icon.**

3. **Choose the Device Manager tab, click the Computer level icon, and then choose Properties.**

4. **From the System Resources display, choose the View Resources tab and click the Interrupt request (IRQ) option to display the IRQ settings, shown in Figure 6-6.**

Using the Windows Device Manager, IRQ settings are changed or assigned in the properties of the individual device.

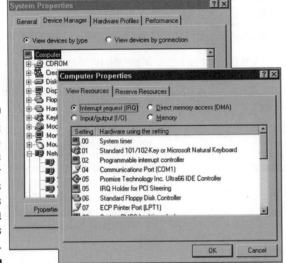

Figure 6-6:
The
Windows
Computer
Properties
window lists
the IRQ
assignments
of a PC.

Assigning IRQs

For the exam, study Table 6-2 carefully. You should know the IRQ assignments for devices standard to all PCs.

Table 6-2	Default IRQ Assignments	
IRQ#	**Default Use**	**Description**
0	System timer	Reserved interrupt for the internal system timer.
1	Keyboard controller	Reserved interrupt for the keyboard controller.
2	Bridge to IRQs 8–15	In cascaded interrupt systems, IRQ 2 is used as a link to IRQs 8–15, which means it's not available for general use; if needed by an older system, it's replaced by IRQ 9 (see "Requesting an interrupt, or how to get IRQed" for information on cascaded interrupts). You may also see IRQ 2 assigned to programmable interrupt control.

(continued)

Table 6-2 *(continued)*

IRQ#	Default Use	Description
3	COM2 and COM4	Many modems are preconfigured for COM2 on IRQ 3. It's also used as the default interrupt for COM4, should a system have four serial ports in use.
4	COM1	Normally used by the serial mouse. It's also the default interrupt for COM3.
5	Sound card	Often the default IRQ for network interface cards. Used on some older systems for the hard disk drive and is the default interrupt for LPT2 (the second parallel port). Most sound cards are preset to IRQ 5.
6	Floppy disk controller	Reserved for the floppy disk controller (FDC).
7	LPT1	This interrupt is normally used for the first parallel port.
8	Real-time clock	Reserved for the real-time clock timer, which is used by software to track events to "real world" time. (IRQs 8–15 are not available on an 8-bit system.)
9	None	A popular choice for network interface cards, but it's generally available for any use. It does replace IRQ 2 in cascading interrupt systems, so it should not be used if IRQ 2 is in use. Hardware MPEG 2 cards and SCSI host adapters can also use it.
10	None	This IRQ has no specific default settings, but it is commonly used for video cards and modems.
11	None	No default assignment, but is it used by some SCSI host adapters, PCI video cards, IDE sound cards, and USB controllers.

IRQ#	Default Use	Description
12	Motherboard mouse (PS/2) connector	On motherboards supporting a PS/2 mouse (mini-DIN connection on the motherboard), this IRQ is reserved for the PS/2 mouse. A PS/2 mouse on this interrupt frees up IRQ 4 (and COM1) for other uses. Some video cards may also use this IRQ.
13	Math coprocessor or floating point unit (FPU)	Reserved for the integrated floating point unit (386DX and later) or a math coprocessor (386SX and earlier).
14	Primary IDE adapter	Reserved for the primary IDE controller, which controls the first two IDE (ATA) disk drives. On PCs with no IDE devices, it can be reassigned in the BIOS setup for other uses.
15	Secondary IDE adapter	Reserved for a secondary IDE controller, if present. Can be reassigned in BIOS, if needed.

Using input/output (I/O) addresses

For the exam, remember the starting I/O address for devices common to all PCs. Every device must have a unique address, without exception, so you won't find trick questions in this area.

Every device in the PC uses *input/output addresses* (which are also known as I/O addresses, I/O ports, or I/O port addresses). The address in the I/O address points to the location in memory that's assigned to a specific device to use for exchanging information between itself and the rest of the PC. The I/O address is a device's internal post office box number.

Virtually every device in the PC has an I/O address assigned to it along with a segment of memory to hold messages and data. The size of the memory segment varies with the amount of data a device needs to pass on to other devices, but in general, the memory segment assigned to a device ranges from 1 to 32 bytes, with 4, 8, or 16 bytes being common. These areas of memory allow a device to do its work without worrying about what other devices or the processor may be doing.

For example, when a modem receives data, it wants to pass the data along to the PC for processing, but where can the data be put? The modem writes the data to the I/O address of the COM port to which the modem is attached, and when the CPU is ready to process this data, it knows right where to look. This process of using I/O addresses to complete input/output operations is called *memory-mapped I/O*.

I/O addresses are expressed in hexadecimal and written as 3F8h. The lower-case "h" indicates it's a hexadecimal address (see Chapter 2 for more information on hexadecimal numbers). When working with I/O addresses, it's not important to determine the size of the memory segment assigned or even decipher the hex address itself. Just remember these addresses are in hexadecimal and ignore the *h*.

For the exam, memorize only the starting addresses of devices that are common to all PCs, such as the keyboard, LPT1, and COM1.

Table 6-3 lists many, but not all, of the common I/O address assignments used in PC systems.

Table 6-3	Common I/O Address Assignments
I/O Address Range	*Device or Port Commonly Assigned*
000-00Fh	DMA channels 0–3 controller
020-021h	IRQ 0–7 interrupt controller
060h, 061h	Keyboard
0F8-0FFh	Math coprocessor
130-14Fh	SCSI host adapter
170-177h	Secondary hard disk controller
1F0-1F7h	Primary hard disk controller
200-207h	Game port
220-22Fh	Sound cards
278-27Fh	LPT2 or LPT3
2E8-2EFh	COM4
2F8-2FFh	COM2
300-30Fh	Network cards
3B0-3BBh	VGA video adapter

I/O Address Range	Device or Port Commonly Assigned
3C0-3DFh	VGA video adapter
378-37Fh	LPT1 or LPT2
3E8-3EFh	COM3
3F0-3F7h	Floppy disk controller
3F8-3FFh	COM1

You can view I/O address assignments on a PC using the Windows Device Manager's Computer Properties dialog box, as shown in Figure 6-7.

Figure 6-7:
The
Windows
Computer
Properties
window lists
the I/O
address
assignments
of a PC.

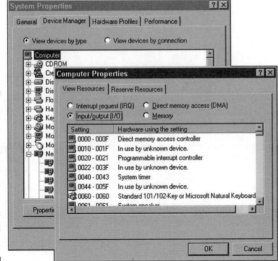

Accessing memory directly with DMA

There are no questions on the A+ Core Hardware exam regarding the default assignment of DMA channels. Concentrate your studies on what a DMA channel is and does.

A *direct memory access* (DMA) channel allows a device to bypass the processor to directly access memory. Those devices with a DMA channel assignment gain the advantage of faster data transfers that do not have to pass through the CPU. Not every device on the PC needs or uses DMA channels. DMA use is common in some disk drives, tape drives, and sound cards. Most operating systems handle DMA assignments through PnP configuration. One drawback to using DMA is that while the DMA device is working faster, the CPU may be put on hold, slowing everything else until the DMA data transfer is complete.

A DMA channel can be assigned to only one hardware device. If two devices are assigned to the same DMA channel, both devices will have problems or the PC may crash. Sound cards seem to have the most trouble with DMA conflicts, primarily because they are hard to preset to a particular DMA channel. Most other DMA devices are more flexible and will take whatever DMA channel is available.

The best way to avoid DMA conflicts initiated by the sound card is to install it before other devices that require DMA channels, such as a scanner or a CD-ROM drive.

Table 6-4 lists common DMA channel usage. However, if you look at the assignments on your PC, you may find the same devices assigned to different channels, which is common.

Table 6-4	DMA Channel Assignments
DMA Channel	*Assignment*
0	DRAM refresh
1	Sound card
2	Floppy disk drive
3	ECP or EPP parallel port
4	DMA controller
5	Sound card
6	Available
7	ISA IDE Hard Drive Controller

DMA channel assignments are set using the preset assignments of a device's adapter card, DIP switches, or jumpers on the device adapter card, the assignments made during PnP configuration, or through the BIOS setup utility.

You can view DMA channel assignments in the Windows Device Manager's Computer Properties dialog box, as shown in Figure 6-8.

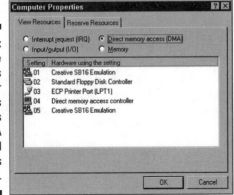

To view DMA channel assignments, follow these steps:

1. **Select My Computer from the Desktop.**

2. **Use the right mouse button to display the shortcut menu and choose Properties.**

3. **Choose the Device Manager tab.**

4. **Highlight Computer at the top of the device hierarchy shown, and click Properties.**

5. **Choose Direct Memory Access (DMA) to display the channel assignments on your system.**

You can also use these steps to view the status of the other system resources: IRQ, I/O address, and memory assignments.

Naming the logical devices

Many devices are assigned both a physical address and a logical name. Logical device names are assigned to serial ports (which are given the logical names COM1 to COM4) and parallel ports (LPT1 and LPT2). Logical names eliminate the need for software to track what could be the moving target of I/O addresses, not to mention the physical layout of the different mother-board form factors in use.

Logical device names are assigned during the POST process by the system BIOS. The BIOS searches the I/O addresses for devices in a preset order and assigns them a logical name in numerical order each time the system boots.

Table 6-5 lists the default assignments for COM and LPT ports.

Of the tables shown in this chapter, the following table may be the best one to review right before the exam. It's brief and holds most of the information about logical devices you should memorize for the test.

Unfortunately, to see logical device assignments on a Windows system, you must view each device separately. From the Device Manager dialog box, select the logical device from the device hierarchy and choose the Resources tab to see the device's system resource assignments, as shown in Figure 6-9. This window is also good for tracking down any resource conflicts a device may have.

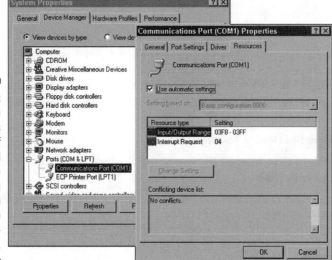

Figure 6-9:
The
Properties
window of
a logical
device
showing
its system
resource
assign-
ments.

Table 6-5	Logical Device Name Assignments	
Port	*I/O Address*	*Default IRQ*
COM1	3F8-3FFh	4
COM2	2F8-2FFh	3
COM3	3E8-3EFh	4
COM4	2E8-2EFh	3
LPT1	378-37Fh	7
LPT2	278-27Fh	5

One way to remember at least one IRQ assignment is to add the 1 from COM1 to the 3 from COM3 to get the 4 from IRQ4. Yes, this memory aid is fairly complicated, and perhaps convoluted, but it worked for me.

Prep Test

1 The default I/O address for COM1 is

A ○ 2F8-2FFh

B ○ 3F8-3FFh

C ○ 378-37Fh

D ○ 3F0-3F7H

2 The first 32-bit bus was

A ○ PCI

B ○ EISA

C ○ MCA

D ○ VESA

3 A PC has a sound card that locks up whenever the parallel tape backup unit is used on the system. What is most likely the problem?

A ○ A DMA channel conflict

B ○ An IRQ conflict

C ○ The sound card is installed in an incompatible bus slot

D ○ There is no system problem other than a defective sound card

4 To automatically configure a PnP device, a system must have all the following except

A ○ A PnP BIOS

B ○ PnP hardware devices

C ○ A PnP OS

D ○ A PCI system bus

5 COM1 normally uses which IRQ?

A ○ IRQ 2

B ○ IRQ 3

C ○ IRQ 4

D ○ IRQ 5

6 The CPU uses an IRQ to

A ○ Control devices attached to the system

B ○ Generate a log file containing interrupt requests

C ○ Identify a peripheral and find the software that controls it

D ○ Protect the system from hardware device failures

7 **What IRQ is often used for LPT1?**

A ○ IRQ 2

B ○ IRQ 10

C ○ IRQ 7

D ○ IRQ 5

8 **What should you do about an IRQ conflict?**

A ○ Reassign the device IRQ settings using the best appropriate method

B ○ Nothing, as long as the I/O addresses of the devices aren't in conflict

C ○ Nothing, as long as the devices are never used at the same time

D ○ Always refer to the devices by their logical device names

9 **Bus clock speed refers to**

A ○ The external speed of the CPU

B ○ The internal speed of the CPU

C ○ The speed of the hard drive

D ○ The speed at which data on the bus moves

10 **A PC Card hard drive fits in which type of slot?**

A ○ Type I

B ○ Type II

C ○ Type III

D ○ Type IV

Answers

1 **B.** *See "Using input/output (I/O) addresses."*

2 **C.** Micro-Channel Architecture was the first 32-bit expansion bus architecture. *Review "Plugging into the expansion bus."*

3 **B.** When two devices directly affect how the other one works, it most likely is a system resource conflict, and very likely an IRQ conflict. *Check out "Conflicting interrupts."*

4 **D.** PnP devices are available in just about every bus architecture. All PCI devices are PnP, but not all PnP devices are PCI. *See "Fun with plug and play."*

5 **C.** IRQ 4 is the default IRQ assignment for COM1. *Review "Assigning IRQs."*

6 **A.** Interrupts and IRQs (interrupt requests) are used by the processor to communicate and control the activities of peripheral devices. *Look at "Requesting an interrupt, or how to get IRQed."*

7 **C.** LPT1 (the first parallel port) is virtually always assigned IRQ 7. *See "Assigning IRQs."*

8 **A.** IRQ assignments can be made, depending on the device and operating system through a jumper on the card, installation software for the device, or through the operating system (Windows 95). *Check out "Conflicting interrupts."*

9 **D.** The bus clock controls the transfer rate of data on the data bus. *Review "Bus structures basics."*

10 **C.** Type I PCMCIA (PC Card) cards are used to install RAM; Type II cards are used to install a modem or network card; and Type III cards are used to install disk drives. *Take a look at "Upgrading notebooks and portables."*

Chapter 7

Microprocessors

● ●

Exam Objectives

▶ Identifying popular microprocessors

▶ Distinguishing CPU chips by their basic characteristics

● ●

*T*he A+ Core Hardware exam tests your knowledge of the central role played by the system's microprocessor, which has become essential knowledge for the professional PC repairperson. There was a time when replacing the CPU was nearly as complicated as replacing a house, and I don't mean the kind of house that has wheels. But today's motherboards feature sockets and slots into which several types and versions of microprocessors can be interchanged. You still have to watch out for compatibility issues, but it's not uncommon for customers to want you to upgrade their PC instead of replace it.

At least 10 percent of the Core Hardware exam is questions about processors, their characteristics, and their compatibilities. For each popular CPU (starting with the Pentium chip), you need to know its general characteristics, including physical size, voltage, its caching abilities, the socket or slot it uses to mount to the motherboard, and details like the number of pins on its packaging.

For an exam with two parts named Core Hardware and OS Technologies, you should expect to be tested on the core technologies of the PC and, trust me, the CPU is a core technology. About the only thing more core is perhaps the motherboard.

You need to memorize a bit in the CPU content area. The good news is that the processors before the Pentium and its clones have been eliminated from the exams. You won't need to worry about when the math coprocessor was integrated into the CPU and the data bus width of the 286 or 486. Pentium-class processors, which include all brands and not just Intel, have steadily progressed along a natural evolutionary path with only a few exceptions. The differences between them aren't really so great.

Quick Assessment

Distinguishing CPU chips by their basic characteristics

1 The processor unit that performs numerical calculations and logical comparisons is the _____.

2 The three primary bus structures on most motherboards are _____, _____, and _____.

3 The _____ is a processor packaging that mounts into a single slot on the motherboard.

4 The Pentium processor generates about _____ degrees Fahrenheit.

5 MMX is short for _____.

6 The socket that mounts Celeron chips with 370 pins is the _____.

7 The slot style that mounts the Pentium II Xeon processor is the _____.

8 The Pentium processor requires _____ volts.

Distinguishing between popular CPU chips

9 The data bus on the Celeron processor is _____ bits wide.

10 The K6 processor is manufactured by _____.

Answers

1 *ALU (Arithmetic and Logic Unit).* Take a look at "Examining the microprocessor."

2 *Address, control, and data.* Review "On the CPU bus."

3 *SEC (Single Edge Connector) or SECC (Single Edge Connector Cartridge).* Review "CPU packaging."

4 *185.* See "Keeping the processor cool."

5 *Multimedia extensions.* Read "Extending out to multimedia."

6 *Socket 370.* See "Socket to it."

7 *Slot 2.* Check out "Slot types."

8 *5.* Study the table in "Intel processors."

9 *64.* Review "Intel processors."

10 *AMD.* Take a look at "AMD processors."

Looking at Microprocessors

Everything a computer can do for you — that is, all of its magic — is performed by its microprocessor. The *microprocessor* performs all the arithmetic, logic, and computing actions of a PC. You may see your PC as a word processor, a computer game, a World Wide Web browser, your e-mail, or any of the other tasks you perform on your PC. In fact, each of these is software made up of thousands of instructions that the CPU executes one at a time to create the actions you see and use. The *processor,* which is short for both microprocessor and *central processing unit (CPU),* is used interchangeably for the electronic circuitry that uses digital logic to perform the instructions of your software.

Technically speaking, a microprocessor is an integrated circuit that contains millions of transistors interconnected by small aluminum wires. Its processing capabilities control and direct the activities of the PC by interacting with the other electronic components on the motherboard, such as the main memory, bus structures, cache memory, and device interfaces.

One of the objectives of the exam is to measure how well you can identify a CPU by its basic characteristics. The idea is that if you're given a key characteristic of a microprocessor, you should be able to identify the processor. For example, if a question asks which CPU has additional instructions for multimedia support, you would choose "Pentium MMX." Or, if a question asks which processors have MMX capabilities, you would choose the Pentium Pro as the MMX choice.

You need to know about microprocessors in detail for the exam. I mean, little nitpicky stuff such as clock speeds, bus widths, features included or supported, mountings, packaging, manufacturer, and evolution. The subject of processors is an area where test writers can't resist getting specific. In many areas of the test, a sound, solid, experienced, and general knowledge of a subject can be enough to get you by, but not here. You need to know this stuff in detail.

Examining the microprocessor

As I detail in this section, a microprocessor has several parts. Don't memorize the following list of components; just study it for background and general knowledge.

Microprocessor anatomy

The microprocessor is a multifunction integrated circuit made up of several parts that work together to execute the instructions passed to the CPU. The primary parts of the microprocessor, as shown in Figure 7-1, are:

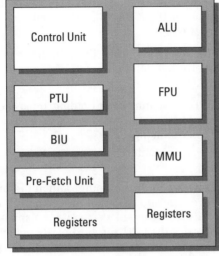

Figure 7-1:
The primary
parts of a
PC micro-
processor.

- ✔ **Arithmetic and Logic Unit (ALU):** The ALU performs the numerical cal- culations (except those done by the FPU) and comparative logic func- tions, including all add, subtract, divide, multiply, equal to, greater than, less than, and other arithmetic and logic operations.

- ✔ **Bus Interface Unit (BIU):** The BIU supervises the transfer of data over the bus system between devices and the CPU and serves as the interface point for the CPU and the external bus for the CU.

- ✔ **Control Unit (CU):** It may sound obvious, but the control unit *controls* the processor's functions by telling the other parts of the CPU how to operate, what data to use, and where to put the results.

- ✔ **Decode Unit:** Most program instructions are combinations of simpler instructions. The decode unit decodes incoming instructions into indi- vidual CPU commands.

- ✔ **Floating Point Unit (FPU):** The FPU handles the floating point operations for the ALU and CU. *Floating point* operations involve arithmetic on numbers with decimal places and higher math operations such as trigonometry and logarithms. The FPU also may be called the math coprocessor, the Numerical Processing Unit (NPU), or the Numerical Data Processor (NDP).

- ✔ **Memory Management Unit (MMU):** The MMU handles the addressing and cataloging of where data is stored in RAM and cache memory. Any data that the CPU needs from memory is requested from the MMU. The MMU manages memory segmentation and paging allocations and translates all logical addressing into physical addressing. (See Chapter 8 for more information on memory addressing.)

- ✔ **Pre-Fetch Unit:** The Pre-Fetch Unit preloads the CPU's instruction registers with instructions whenever the BIU is idle, which allows the CPU to look ahead at future instructions.

- ✔ **Protection Test Unit (PTU):** Works with the CPU to monitor that functions are carried out correctly. If it detects something done improperly, it generates an error signal.

- ✔ **Registers:** Built into the CPU are a number of holding areas and buffers used to temporarily hold data, addresses, and instructions being passed around between the CPU's components.

On the CPU bus

The *bus,* as it relates to the pathways on the computer and in the processor, carries the various signals, addresses, and data that move about the PC between its components. The bus is a group of electronic transmission lines that interconnect the components of the CPU, motherboard, and expansion cards. Bus structures have different sizes, ranging from 16 to 64 bits on modern microprocessors, which determine the amount of data that can be transmitted. Just as an 8-lane highway carries more traffic than a two-lane road, a 64-bit bus carries more data than a 16-bit bus.

A PC has several distinct bus structures, the most important of which are:

- ✔ **Data bus:** Carries data to and from the CPU, main memory, and peripheral devices. The width (in bits) determines the amount of data that can be transmitted at a time.

- ✔ **Address bus:** Carries addresses of data and instructions between memory and the CPU. The width (in bits) determines the size of the address (represented as a binary number) that can be passed over the address bus.

- ✔ **Control bus:** Carries control information, such as the status of the devices, between the CPU and other devices. The information passed over the control bus provides data that indicates that data is ready to be read, a device is waiting to use the bus, and the type of operation a device is requesting (read, write, interrupt).

Chapter 6 is dedicated to the bus structures on a PC.

CPU packaging

The actual microprocessor and its associate electronic circuits are packaged in a protective outer packaging. When you look at a processor, it's the packaging you see and not the microprocessor itself. Typically, the processor's packaging is ceramic or plastic.

The outer covering of the processor protects its core (also called the die) that contains the microchip and the wiring that connects the chip to the processor's mounting pins. A variety of packaging types have been used on processors. Here are the ones you should know for the A+ Core Hardware exam:

✔ **Pin Grid Array (PGA):** Common among early processors, the mounting pins are located on the bottom of the chip in concentric squares. Figure 7-2 shows the difference between this package and other packages. The earliest chips were packaged in the Ceramic PGA (CPGA). Later chips, including some current ones, use the Plastic PGA (PPGA). The early Pentium chips used a variation that staggered the pin pattern (in order to cram more pins onto the package) called the Staggered PGA (SPGA). The Pentium III features a variation of the PGA package with its Slot 370-like Flip Chip-Pin Graphics Assembly (FC-PGA).

✔ **Plastic Ball Grid Array (PBGA):** The primary difference between this packaging technology and the PGA is that the PBGA doesn't have mounting pins projecting from the bottom of the chip, which eliminates the threat of bent pins on the bottom of the processor. Otherwise, these package styles look similar.

✔ **Single Edge Connector (SEC):** You may find a few variations on the name of this packaging technology, including the Single Edge Contact Cartridge (SECC) and others. They all boil down to a packaging style that is mounted perpendicular to the motherboard into a single slot, much like expansion cards and memory modules. The Pentium II was the first processor to sport this new packaging style. This style made cooling the processor easier.

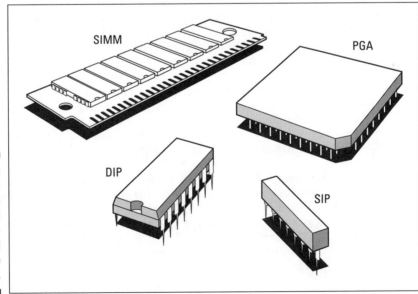

Figure 7-2:
A comparison of the more popular pin-mounted chip packages.

Keeping the processor cool

Before the Intel 486, microprocessors were cooled primarily by the airflow inside the case created by a system fan in the power supply. This process was called *radiant cooling*. Any heat radiated by the processor was cooled by air being sucked by the fan into the system case. Beginning with the 486, processors are cooled with a *processor cooling fan* or a *heatsink* or both, attached directly to the surface of the processor. In addition, the system fan was reversed to extract the heated air from inside the computer case and force it out.

With the Pentium processors came heat and cooling problems for the PC. The Pentium chip runs much hotter than earlier CPUs and requires special heat dissipation and cooling. You need to know a few things about the heat problems and cooling requirements of the Pentium chips for the exam.

The Pentium processor operates at 185 degrees Fahrenheit (85 degrees Celsius). The Pentium III processor operates about 100 degrees Celsius (which is about 212 degrees Fahrenheit) or at the boiling point for water. The PC's cooling system is designed to keep the processor operating near its optimal temperature. Therefore, you want to keep the PC's case closed to ensure that its cooling system is operating efficiently. The form factor for the case, motherboard, and power supply designed to support a particular processor is designed to provide cooling to keep the processor at or near its designed operating temperature. At temperatures above its normal operating temperature, a processor begins to perform poorly, shut down, or become permanently damaged. Heatsinks and fans are designed to draw the heat up and out of the processor's packaging and carry it away on the tines of the heatsink and the airflow of the fan.

On Pentium and Pentium Pro processors, heatsinks and fans are clipped directly on the processor, attached with a dielectric gel, also called *thermal grease*. Later Pentium models, like the Celeron, the Pentium II, and the Pentium III (all of which have SEC packaging), have mounting points to attach fans and heatsinks directly to the processor.

In addition to the air flow system of the PC, the Pentium processor also uses special motherboard configurations to help cool it. This may include a fan or a heatsink, or both, mounted directly on top of the processor. The fan sucks the heat away from the chip and up into the PC's air flow to be blown away. A heatsink is a device that looks something like a bed of nails that wicks the heat into its tines where the air flow cools it. If a processor has both, the fan sits on top of the heatsink.

Thermal grease (also known as heatsink jelly, heatsink compound, thermal gunk, thermal compound, or thermal goo) improves the heat conductivity between the processor and its heatsink. It eliminates any gaps between the two, working like a denture adhesive, allowing the CPU's heat to transfer to the heatsink more efficiently.

Because most thermal grease is mercury based, avoid getting it on your skin, and definitely don't use it for denture cream.

Comparing sockets and slots

Two general types of mountings are used to mount processors to the mother-board: sockets and slots. Most processors are available in only one mounting style, disregarding ceramic versus plastic, and others, such as the Celeron, are available in either a PGA type or a SEC type package.

Socket to it

There have been a variety of socket types used for PC microprocessors. For the exam, pay close attention to those used for Pentium-class processors. Here are ten of the most commonly used socket types:

- ✔ **Socket 4:** Mounts the 273-pin PGA package of the Pentium 60 and Pentium 66 processors.

- ✔ **Socket 5:** Mounts the 320-pin staggered pin grid array (SPGA) of early 3v Pentium processors.

- ✔ **Socket 7:** A socket type still in use that mounts the 321-pin SPGA of the later release Pentium processors and the chips of AMD, Cyrix, and IDT (see "Competing processors").

- ✔ **Super 7 Sockets:** An extension of the Socket 7 design used for the AMD K6 processors.

- ✔ **Socket 8:** A 386-pin SPGA ZIF-socket for the Pentium Pro processor.

- ✔ **Socket 370:** Designed for the Celeron processor in a plastic pin grid array (PPGA) packaging. Its name comes from the number of pins it supports.

Yes, there were socket types before and after the Socket 4 that weren't used for Pentium-class processors. Sockets 0 through 3, and 6 were used to mount various package forms of the 486 processor.

Slot types

Slot type connections use a single slot mounting on the motherboard that mounts the processor in the same manner used for memory modules or expansion cards. The packaging technologies that mount in slot connectors are: Single Edge Processor Package (SEPP); Single Edge Connector Cartridge (SECC); and similar names all involving the words "single edge."

Four types of slot mountings are used to attach microprocessors to motherboards:

✔ **Slot 1:** Technically called the SC-242 (Slot Connector — 242 pins) connector. It is a proprietary Intel connector used for Celeron, Pentium II, and Pentium III processors.

✔ **Slot 2:** Technically the SC-330 connector, the Slot 2 connector is an Intel mounting for its Pentium II Xeon and Pentium III Xeon chips. This slot style enhances the ability of multiple processors installed in the same PC to work together.

✔ **Slot A:** AMD Athlon processors use this slot style, which is physically the same as a Slot 1 connector. However, it uses different pin assignments, making it unusable by Intel processors.

✔ **Slot M:** Designed to hold the 64-bit Intel Itanium processor.

Intel processors

Most of the PCs you work on as PC repair technician have processors from Intel Corporation, and because Intel is one of the companies that helped develop A+ exams, you can expect most of the processor questions relate to Intel processors.

For the exam, about the only thing you need to remember specific to Intel is the numbering and naming schemes it has used for its CPUs, and how that contrasts to the processors of other manufacturers. You won't be asked to identify the manufacturer of a CPU, but knowing Intel's evolution may help you to identify bad choices in a question.

Based on A+ Core exam objectives, you need to know the type of mounting, voltages, clock speed, and bus width for each of the popular (meaning Intel) microprocessors. Table 7-1 includes information for the CPUs you need to know for the test. The order of the processors in the table is important as it indicates their evolution, although the later processors do overlap a bit.

Table 7-1			Microprocessor Characteristics			
CPU	**Package**	**Voltage**	**Speed (MHz)**	**Data Bus (bits)**	**Memory (MB)**	**Cache (K)**
Pentium	PGA	5	60–200	64	4096	16
Pentium	PGA	5	166–233	64	4096	32 MMX
Pentium	PGA	1.5	150–200	64	64,000	1,000 Pro
Celeron	PGA, SEC	1.5	266, 600	64	4096	128
Pentium II	SEC	1.5	233–450	64	64,000	512

CPU	Package	Voltage	Speed (MHz)	Data Bus (bits)	Memory (MB)	Cache (K)
Pentium II Xeon	SEC	1.5	400–450	64	64,000	512–1,000
Pentium III	SEC, FC-PGA	1.5	450–933	64	64,000	256
Pentium III Xeon	SEC	1.5	500–933	64	64,000	256

Here are brief descriptions for each of the processors included in Table 7-1:

✓ **Pentium:** This processor features 32-bit multitasking using RISC design techniques and a superscalar architecture that executes two instructions in the same clock cycle. The Pentium expanded the internal bus to 64-bits and high-speed internal cache.

✓ **Pentium Pro:** The Pentium Pro was developed as a network server processor specially designed to support 32-bit network operating systems, such as Windows NT, and to be used in configurations of one, two, or four processors, with 1 megabit of advanced second level (L2) cache.

✓ **Pentium II:** The Pentium II is the Pentium Pro with MMX technology added. The P–II, as it is commonly referred to, is excellent for multimedia work that requires support for full-motion video and 3D images.

✓ **Celeron:** Developed for use in desktop and portable computers, the Celeron is a low-cost version of the Pentium II.

✓ **Pentium III:** Although recently surpassed by the Pentium IV, the Pentium III has been the highest-powered processor in the Intel arsenal. It features 9.5 million transistors, a 32K L1 cache, 512K of L2 cache, and clock speeds of 450MHz to 1GHz.

✓ **Xeon:** The Xeon processors, both Pentium II and Pentium III, are successors to the Pentium Pro as a network server processor that is capable of addressing and caching up to 64GB of memory with its 36-bit memory address bus. Xeon processors can be configured with 4 to 8 CPUs in one server.

Extending out to multimedia

MMX (short for multimedia extensions) technology has added three features to the Pentium processor:

✓ Fifty-seven new instructions to improve video, audio, and graphics capabilities

  ✔ SIMD (Single Instruction Multiple Data) technology, in which one instruction can control several data items

  ✔ Cache doubled to 32K

For some really detailed information on Intel processors, visit Intel's processor press guides site at `www.intel.com/pressroom/kits/processors/`. You also may want to visit Intel's interactive microprocessor museum at `www.intel.com/intel/museum/25anniv/`.

Cyrix processors

Cyrix, which is now owned by VIA Technologies, produced a family of Pentium clone processors that was designated as the 6x86-P series. The "P" in the name indicates that its performance rating is the equivalent to an Intel Pentium model. For example, the 6x86-P200 is said to have the performance equivalent of a Pentium 200MHz processor. Cyrix produced models ranging from its 6x86-P120 to the 6x86-P200. The 6x86-P series had overheating problems as well as some incompatibility issues, which prompted Cyrix to produce a low-power, low-temperature version, the 6x86L.

Also known as the MII, the Cyrix 6x86MX processor contains an MMX instruction set. The 6x86 MX has a "P" rating of P-166 to P-433. The VIA Cyrix III microprocessor is the equivalent of the Intel Pentium II Celeron processor.

AMD processors

Intel didn't have much competition until Advanced Micro Devices (AMD) released its own 75 MHz 5x86 microprocessor. The AMD 5x86 processor was compatible with 486 motherboards, but had similar power to the early Pentium processors. AMD's next line, the K6, which included 3DNow, AMD's own multimedia commands, was designed to compete with the Pentium MMX, but outperformed it in speed and price. A newer model of the AMD K6 line is the K6-2+, which added more L2 cache and advanced power control features to the processor chip. The K6-III processor features 256K of L2 cache and clock speeds from 400MHz to 600MHz. The K6-III+ adds 1MB of cache to the processor chip.

AMD currently produces a pair of very powerful processors in its 1GHz Athlon and the 700 MHz Duron processors. The Athlon supports Intel's MMX and AMD's 3DNow, as well as improved FPU functions. It has 256KB of L2 cache and 128KB of L1 cache on the chip and has the power to decode more instructions simultaneously than the Pentium III. The Athlon is plug compatible with the Slot 1 connector, but it is designed for AMD's Slot A bus, which runs at bus speeds of 200MHz to 400MHz. The AMD Duron processor is designed for general computing, including business, home user, and portable applications.

Prep Test

1 Which of the following processors doesn't include MMX instructions?

A ○ Pentium

B ○ Pentium Pro

C ○ Pentium II

D ○ Celeron

2 The processor unit that supervises the processor's functions and directs the actions of the other units of the processor is the

A ○ ALU

B ○ BIU

C ○ CU

D ○ MMU

3 MMX stands for

A ○ Multimegahertz

B ○ Multimedia extensions

C ○ Maximum megahertz

D ○ Multisession extension

4 The purpose of the CPU's registers is

A ○ To store configuration information when the computer is first powered on

B ○ To hold the jump address

C ○ To temporarily hold data, addresses, and instructions for the other CPU units

D ○ To provide an interface to the hard drives

5 Which CPU packaging form was used for nearly all processors before the Pentium II?

A ○ Pin Grid Array

B ○ Plastic Ball Grid Array

C ○ Single Edge Connector

D ○ Flip Chip — PGA

6 What is the CPU packaging type used for the Pentium II and Pentium III?

A ○ Pin Grid Array

B ○ Plastic Ball Grid Array

C ○ Single Edge Connector

D ○ Flip Chip — PGA

7 **The main chip found on the motherboard that executes instructions is the**

   A ○ Math coprocessor

   B ○ CMOS memory

   C ○ Microprocessor

   D ○ ROM chip

8 **What are the three primary bus structures on a PC motherboard?**

   A ○ Address, Instruction, and Information

   B ○ Control, Location, and Data

   C ○ Memory, Interface, Command

   D ○ Address, Data, Control

9 **Which of the following is used to keep a Pentium processor cool?**

   A ○ Liquid nitrogen

   B ○ A fan

   C ○ A heatsink

   D ○ No special equipment is needed

   E ○ B and C

   F ○ A and B

10 **How much memory is the Pentium II capable of addressing?**

   A ○ 4MB

   B ○ 16MB

   C ○ 4GB

   D ○ 64GB

Answers

Microprocessors

1 B. The Pentium Pro was designed for use in network servers and did not include MMX capabilities. *See "Looking at Microprocessors."*

2 C. The control units control the activities in and around the CPU. *Review "Microprocessor anatomy."*

3 B. Fifty-seven new instructions are added to Pentium MMX processors to handle multimedia activities. *Look up "Extending out to multimedia."*

4 C. The CPU's registers are temporary storage and buffers that are used by the units of the CPU, like the CU and ALU, to move data between units. *Check out "Microprocessor anatomy."*

5 A. The PGA (Pin Grid Array) remains a very popular CPU processor packaging form. The Celeron processor is available in both the PGA and the SEC (Single Edge Connector) packages. *Review "CPU packaging."*

6 C. The SEC packaging provides a better cooling system for the high-end Pentium chips as well as reduces the space required on the motherboard for its circuitry. *Check out "CPU packaging."*

7 C. If you answered anything else, go back and read *"Looking at Microprocessors."*

8 D. The data bus carries, well, data; the address bus carries, well . . . I think you get it. *See "On the CPU bus."*

9 E. Sometimes both a fan and a heatsink are used. See *"Keeping the processor cool."*

10 D. Just because a processor claims it can address a humongous amount of RAM, it doesn't mean that the motherboard or chipset can make it all available. *Review "Intel processors."*

Chapter 8

Memory Systems

● ●

Exam Objectives

▶ Identifying the terminology, location, and physical characteristics of memory

▶ Differentiating parity and non-parity memory

▶ Defining DOS/Windows memory management

● ●

About 15 percent of the A+ Core Hardware exam deals with questions on the motherboard and memory systems. Of that percentage, you can count on about half pertaining to different types of memory, how it's packaged, how it's installed, and the rest.

It's difficult to say how much of the remaining 85 percent of the test touches on memory and subjects like parity, error checking, and other topics I include in this chapter. But these issues are woven throughout the test, just like they are in real on-the-job life.

The OS Technology Exam also includes questions on memory, but they relate more to the structure and allocation of memory as it relates to memory management in the Windows environment. I touch on memory management in this chapter; the information you need to know for the OS exam is in Chapter 19.

Every professional PC repairperson must have a good understanding of memory systems, how they work, how they're configured, how to avoid problems, and how to identify, isolate, and solve problems.

You should at least review this chapter to make sure that you're familiar with the concepts and terminology of a rapidly changing technology — especially if you're one of the old duffers who, like me, are still clinging to their AT waiting for the overdrive chip to come out.

Quick Assessment

1 Memory packaged in the _____ form is installed directly on the motherboard.

2 _____ DRAM is the most common type in use.

3 _____, which is much faster and more expensive than DRAM, is used for memory caching.

4 Memory that loses its contents when its power source is lost is _____.

5 The three package types of DRAM memory are _____, _____, and _____.

6 _____ involves the use of an additional bit for each 8 bits of data.

7 _____ can detect and correct 1-bit errors in data.

8 The first 640K of system memory is called _____.

9 The upper 384K of the first megabyte of memory is _____.

10 All memory above 1MB is called _____.

Answers

1   *DIP.* See "Taking a DIP."

2   *EDO.* Review "DRAM technologies."

3   *SRAM.* Check out "Static RAM (SRAM)."

4   *Volatile.* Look at "Refreshing Your Memory: Memory Basics."

5   *DIP, SIMM, DIMM.* See "DRAM packages."

6   *Parity.* Review "Understanding parity."

7   *ECC or Error Correction Code.* See "Correcting parity errors."

8   *conventional memory.* Take a look at "Logical Memory Layout."

9   *expanded or upper memory area.* Check out "Upper memory area."

10   *extended memory.* Study "Extended memory."

Refreshing Your Memory: Memory Basics

You can look at memory in two ways:

- ✔ As the physical chips and modules that plug into the motherboard
- ✔ As the scratch pad space that holds the data and instructions in use

For purposes of the A+ exams, you need to know something about both, including the names, purposes, and uses of the various types and packages of memory. You also need to know something about memory configuration, and a bit more about the troubleshooting processes (troubleshooting in general is one of the major focuses of the A+ exams).

Memory systems are complex and offer a depth of material — the kind of stuff engineers get misty-eyed over. For such a physically small thing, memory is a large subject. But not here! I give no lengthy diatribes on why parity memory is better or the like. I give you just the facts along with a small amount of background information to help you understand the exam's questions — which is a trick in itself sometimes.

The PC has two basic levels of memory:

- ✔ **RAM (Random Access Memory):** Holds the instructions and data in use by the operating system and software applications before and after they pass to the CPU. RAM is volatile; to hold its contents, it must have a steady power source. Should the power stream be broken, anything stored in RAM is erased. No power — no data; pretty straightforward.

- ✔ **ROM (Read-Only Memory):** Is nonvolatile and retains its contents through even the darkest power outage. For more information on ROM, see Chapter 5.

RAM is by far the faster of the two types of memory. In fact, RAM is often used to shadow the BIOS ROM to improve its performance during the boot process. If you're asked what copying the contents of the BIOS ROM into RAM for faster access to the instructions by the CPU is called — the answer is *shadowing*.

When *volatile* memory loses its power source, it also loses its contents. Most types of RAM, especially DRAM, is volatile and that's why when you turn off the PC's power (or trip over the power cord), everything in RAM is lost. *Nonvolatile* memory, like ROM and other types, do not lose their contents when their power source is lost.

Random Access Memory (RAM)

RAM is the primary memory of the PC and is generally installed directly on the motherboard in a variety of package types, which I deal with later. Many types of RAM exist, and the ones you'll need to know something about for the Core Hardware exam are:

- DRAM (Dynamic Random Access Memory)
- EDO RAM (Extended Data Output RAM)
- RIMM (Rambus Inline Memory Module)
- SRAM (Static RAM)

In addition to the types of RAM used in primary memory, you should also need to know about two of the types of RAM used on video cards:

- VRAM (Video RAM)
- WRAM (Windows Accelerator Card RAM)

You need a solid understanding of RAM, its packaging forms, and its technologies for the exam. Many questions assume you know what the types of RAM are, where they're installed, and their characteristics. For example, you may be asked which is the fastest of the RAM types (SRAM), or how DIMM memories are installed (in vertical sockets on the motherboard).

Dynamic RAM (DRAM)

DRAM (pronounced "dee-ram," but not in the same context as "dee-bears," "dee-blackhawks," or "dee-bulls") is the RAM everyone talks about. It's the most commonly used type of memory. It's not a complex circuit compared to some and, as a result, is not expensive. However, its design also requires that it be refreshed regularly or it loses its contents. This need for constant refreshing gives DRAM its dynamic tag.

DRAM must be refreshed every two milliseconds. A special refresh logic circuit reads and then rewrites the contents of each DRAM address, whether it's in use or not.

DRAM is also the slowest of the memories, clocking in with access speeds around 50 nanoseconds (ns) or higher (remember that higher here means slower). Older DRAM had an access speed of around 120 ns.

DRAM technologies

REMEMBER

DRAM comes in a variety of popular technologies. The following lists the characteristics of each of the DRAM technologies:

- **Extended Data Out (EDO):** This is the most common type of DRAM. It's common in most Pentium and later PCs, except those with memory buses over 75MHz.

- **Fast Page Mode (FPM):** This type of DRAM is occasionally called non-EDO RAM. It's generally compatible with motherboards with memory buses with speeds under 66MHz.

- **Burst Extended Data Out (BEDO):** This DRAM is EDO memory with pipelining technology added for faster access times. BEDO allows much higher bus speeds than EDO.

- **Synchronous DRAM (SDRAM):** Like its SRAM cousins (see the next section), SDRAM is tied to the system clock and reads or writes memory in burst mode.

- **Rambus DRAM (RDRAM):** Rambus is a proprietary DRAM technology developed by Rambus, Inc. (www.rambus.com) that has memory speeds of up to 3.2Gbps. RDRAM comes on a module that is very similar to a DIMM, called a RIMM (Rambus Inline Memory Module).

- **Synchronous Link DRAM (SLDRAM):** This is an enhanced version of SDRAM memory that uses a multiplexed bus to transfer data to and from the chips rather than fixed pin settings. SLDRAM has transfer rates as high as 3GBps range. Unlike RDRAM, this is an open technology.

- **Video RAM (VRAM):** This specialized DRAM is used on video cards and not for main memory. VRAM applies dual porting, which means that it can be written to and read from at the same time. This allows the processor and the refresh circuitry for the monitor to access VRAM at the same time. Another type of video RAM is *Windows RAM* (WRAM), also called *Windows Accelerator RAM,* which has essentially the same properties as VRAM.

You will definitely see the DRAM technologies on the A+ exams. Familiarize yourself with the general descriptions provided here, which should be enough for FPM, EDO, burst EDO, RDRAM, and SDRAM. VRAM and WRAM are covered in more detail in Chapter 13.

DRAM packages

DRAM memory comes in three package forms:

- DIP (Dual In-line Package)
- SIMM (Single Inline Memory Module)
- DIMM (Dual Inline Memory Module)

SIMM and DIMM packages are like mini-expansion boards that have either surface-mounted SOJ (Small Outline J-lead) or TSOP (Thin, Small Outline Package) DRAM soldered on one (SIMM) or two (DIMM) sides of a circuit card. Figure 8-1 shows the basic forms of a DIP and a memory module (a SIMM is shown).

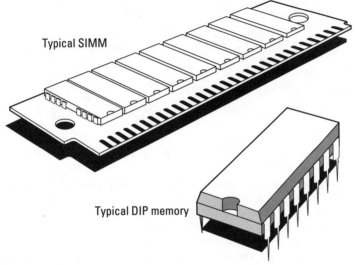

Figure 8-1: The two basic package forms of DRAM: A DIP chip and a memory module (SIMM).

Typical SIMM

Typical DIP memory

Taking a DIP

This package form of DRAM memory chips is used to install memory directly on a motherboard. The DIP form is a through-hole electronic component, which means it installs through the holes of a socket directly into a circuit board's surface. Figure 8-2 shows how DIP memories are installed on a motherboard. See "Installing memory" later in this section.

SIMMing right along

The memory standard on middle-aged PCs (486s and early Pentiums) is the Single Inline Memory Module (SIMM). The edge connector on a SIMM module has either 30 pins or 72 pins. A SIMM's memory capacity ranges from 1MB to 16MB in either a one-sided or two-sided style, with chips soldered to one or two sides of the board. Figure 8-3 shows a typical SIMM.

As shown in Figure 8-4, a SIMM is installed on the motherboard in a special vertical socket that has clips that hold the module tightly in place and to maximize the amount of memory installed in a minimal space. Because the Pentium processor uses a 64-bit path to memory, 32-bit SIMMs must be installed in pairs. As shown in Figure 8-4, each SIMM bank has two sockets. You must completely fill a SIMM bank before moving on to another bank.

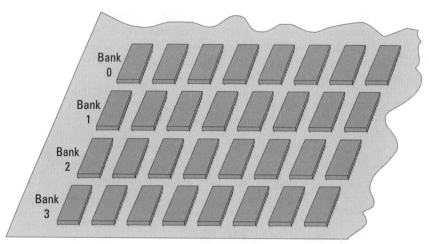

Figure 8-2:
DIP DRAM
chips are
installed in
rows (called
banks)
directly on
the PC's
mother-
board.

Moving up to DIMM

The Dual Inline Memory Module (DIMM) is the memory standard on most newer and larger PCs. Because its 64-bit memory matches the 64-bit data path of the Pentium processor, you only need to install one DIMM module at a time. In comparison to the SIMM, a DIMM has 168 contact pins as opposed to the 30 and 72 pins of the SIMM. A DIMM looks just like a SIMM, except that it's slightly larger, has memory chips on both sides, and about twice as many contacts on its edge connector.

DIMMs come in different voltages: 3.3V and 5.0V, and as buffered or unbuffered, which yields four possible combinations. A smaller version of the DIMM is Small Outline DIMM (SODIMM). The SODIMM is a smaller package module used primarily in laptop computers.

On the RIMM

Where SIMM and DIMM are generic names for a type of memory module, RIMM is a trademarked name for the Direct Rambus memory module. A RIMM looks like a DIMM, but has 184 pins on its edge connector. RIMM memories transfer data in 16-bit chunks. A RIMM is packaged inside an aluminum sheath, called a heat spreader. The heat spreader covers the entire assembly to protect against overheating. Figure 8-5 shows the parts of a RIMM module.

Figure 8-3:
A typical
SIMM.

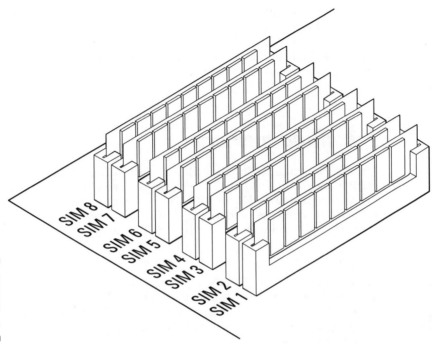

Figure 8-4:
SIMM
sockets full
of SIMMs.

SIM 8
SIM 7
SIM 6
SIM 5
SIM 4
SIM 3
SIM 2
SIM 1

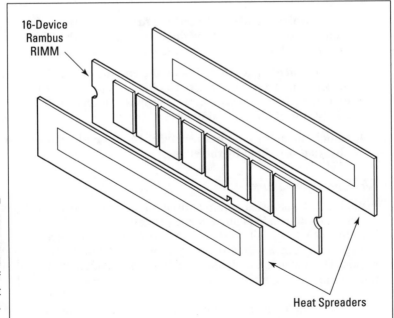

16-Device
Rambus
RIMM

Figure 8-5:
RIMM
modules are
packaged
inside of
a heat
spreader.

Heat Spreaders

A smaller version of the RIMM, the SORIMM (Small Outline RIMM) is very much like the SODIMM, with the exception of the Rambus technology.

If you want more information on memory than your brain can possibly hold, visit Kingston Technologies' "Ultimate Memory Guide" at `www.kingston.com/tools/umg`.

Installing memory

The installation procedures for DIP memory and SIMMs and DIMMs are quite different. If you're a working PC repairperson, you have most likely had an occasion to install a SIMM or DIMM. However, chances are that you have managed to avoid the need to install a DIP memory chip. You do need to have some idea of the processes used to install memory in a PC.

But, first . . .

You do have your ESD (Electrostatic Discharge) protection on, don't you? You should take steps to protect the PC and especially memory chips or modules. It doesn't take very much of an ESD to severely damage the memory you're installing. Always perform these steps before installing memory in the PC (or for any other operation inside the case):

1. **Turn off the PC and disconnect the AC power cord.**

2. **RTFM, which stands for "Read the *fabulous* manual. (Hungry Minds is a family company)." Follow the instructions in the PC's owner's manual on how to locate the memory expansion sockets.**

3. **Before touching anything inside the case or opening the memory's package, make sure you first touch an unpainted, grounded metal object, such as a chassis wall or support, to discharge any static electricity stored on your body or clothing.**

4. **Handle memory modules carefully. Don't bend or flex them and always grasp them by the edges.**

Working in the bank

Installing DIP memories requires three things: patience, small fingers, and patience. As shown in Figure 8-6, the process involves aligning the pins of the DIP chip into its socket one side at a time (while avoiding any bent pins) and then pressing down with a steady, gentle pressure until the chip seats in the socket. The socket on a DIP chip is a pass-through mounting that allows the pins of the DIP to contact the memory circuitry beneath the socket.

You must completely fill a bank of memory before you begin to install chips in another bank. The width in bits of each memory chip is combined to match the width of the processor's data bus to the memory area. The width of this bus determines the number of chips that constitutes a bank.

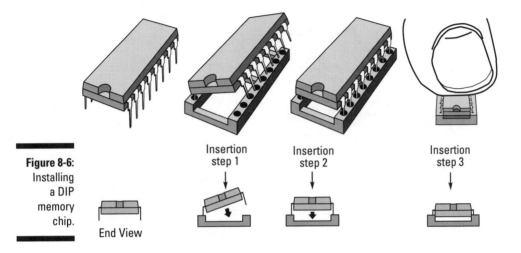

Figure 8-6:
Installing
a DIP
memory
chip.

Insertion
step 1

Insertion
step 2

Insertion
step 3

End View

Putting in the SIMMs

Figure 8-7 shows the process used to install a SIMM. The module is aligned to the socket at about a 45-degree angle. As it is lifted to a vertical position and seated into the socket, the clamping clips on the ends of the socket grab the module and hold it in place.

To remove a SIMM, release the clamping clips and push the module to a 45-degree angle and then lift it out.

Dropping in a DIMM

A DIMM is installed by inserting the module into an available memory socket. A DIMM is keyed to match the socket, so it will only go in one way. After the DIMM is aligned to the socket slot, firmly press down on the module until it seats in the socket slot and locks into place with a snap.

To remove a DIMM, nearly all DIMM sockets have ejector tabs. Press down on the ejector tabs and the module pops up and out of the socket slot. Carefully lift the module out of the socket.

Putting in a RIMM

A RIMM is installed in special RIMM connectors. Check the motherboard's documentation to see whether a pair of RIMM connectors exists on the board. Most likely they're the connectors you couldn't identify. Both slots of a RIMM connector set must be occupied by two RIMM modules or a single RIMM module and what is called a C-RIMM (Continuity RIMM). A C-RIMM doesn't contain any memory; it's only a pass-through module that completes the memory channel.

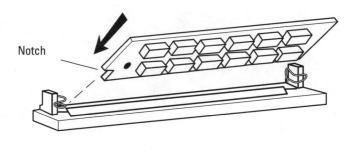

Notch

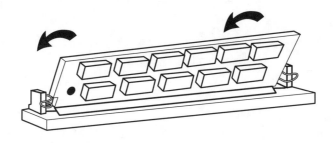

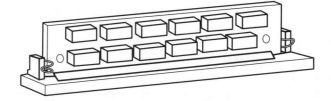

Figure 8-7:
Installing a
SIMM.

You install RIMM modules almost exactly like a DIMM — press down until the locking clips snap onto the module. To remove the module, press the ejector tabs outward, which pops the module out of the socket.

Hot swapping flash memory

Notebook and palmtop computers can have flash memory added with a PC Card. A PC Card looks a little like a credit card (see Figure 8-8) and slips into a slot usually located on the side of the notebook's base. One feature of PC Cards is *hot swapping,* which allows you to remove and replace the card while the system is running. Chapter 15 covers portable systems and PC Cards in more detail.

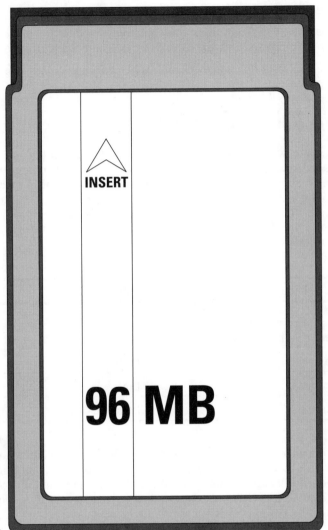

INSERT

96 MB

Figure 8-8:
A PC
Card flash
memory
module.

The Personal Computer Memory Card International Association (PCMCIA) is the standards authority on PC Cards. This organization has developed three primary standards for PC Cards that define the cards' size and use. PC Cards are 85.6 millimeters (mm) by 54 mm (or about 3.4 inches by 2.1 inches). The thickness of the card is set by the three card type standards. See Chapter 15 for more information, but briefly the three standard types of PC Cards are:

✔ **Type I:** Up to 3.3 mm thick and used primarily for adding memory

✔ **Type II:** Up to 5.5 mm thick and commonly used for I/O devices, such as data/fax modems, network interface cards, and mass storage devices

✔ **Type III:** Up to 10.5 mm thick and used for rotating mass storage drives

Static RAM (SRAM)

SRAM is static, which means it is able to retain its data and doesn't need to be refreshed. As long as it has a power stream, it holds its charge and contents. SRAM also has very fast access times, in the range of 15 to 20 ns (comparing to the 50 ns to 120 ns of DRAM). SRAM is physically two pins longer in package size than DIP DRAM and because it's a more complex technology, it costs a lot more. Table 8-1 contrasts SRAM to DRAM in terms of their general characteristics.

Table 8-1	DRAM versus SRAM
DRAM	*SRAM*
Slow and must be constantly refreshed	Fast and doesn't require refreshing
Simple	Complex
Inexpensive	Expensive
Physically small	Physically large

SRAM is packaged as either a single DIP chip or as a COAST (Cache On A Stick) module in a variety of increments. The type of SRAM and the amount a motherboard will support, like everything else, depends on the motherboard. SRAM is available as either synchronous or asynchronous. Synchronous SRAM uses the system clock to coordinate its signals with the CPU, and asynchronous doesn't. Because of its greater cost and bigger size, SRAM is used primarily for Level 2 cache memory on the motherboard.

Memory caching enables the CPU to work more efficiently. Cache memory stores data and instructions and fetches them in anticipation of what the CPU will want next. When cache memory is correct, which is about 90 percent of the time, the CPU is able to get what it needs from the much faster SRAM instead of the slower DRAM. It is now common for a system to include between 128KB to 512KB of SRAM cache on the motherboard. Chapter 4 includes information on how caching works.

In spite of its constant thirst for power, DRAM works better for PC main memory because it's cheaper and needs less space. SRAM costs too much and takes too much space to be used for main memory. On the other hand, because of its speed and the fact that not that much memory is needed; SRAM is perfect for cache memory.

Ensuring Memory Integrity

In addition to all that you should know about memory for the A+ exams, one very important aspect of memory that's included in several domains is memory data integrity. It's one thing to store data in memory and quite another to be sure that what's there is still valid, especially if it hasn't been accessed in eons, or one or two hundred milliseconds, whichever comes first. As leaky as DRAM is, a mechanism has to exist to verify the integrity of the data.

Lucky for us, a mechanism does exist. In fact, two methods are used to ensure the integrity of data stored in memory: parity and Error Correction Code (ECC).

First, however, you need to know a little about the memory controller. The memory controller oversees the movement of data into and out of memory and, in doing so, determines the type of data integrity checking used. In both parity and ECC, the memory controller is key to the process. The memory controller generates the signals used to control the reading and writing of data from and to memory.

Understanding parity

Parity has been around for a very long time, or as long as the PC anyway. DRAM memory that implements parity checking has one additional bit for every 8 bits of data. This extra bit allows the system to verify the data format using two parity protocols — odd parity and even parity — that work very much the same. In a nutshell, if the system is using even parity, the extra bit is used as necessary to make the total number of positive (ones) bits an even number. In an odd parity world, the extra bit is used to create odd number totals. "Parity" is achieved when the total number of one bits in a byte adds up to either an even or odd number, depending on the parity technique in use.

When a character fails to have the appropriate number of bits, it causes a parity error. A parity error can be the first signal of a host of problems, ranging from one-time anomalies to faulty memory. Faulty memory can be the cause of repeated memory parity errors.

The limitation of the parity method for data integrity is that it can only detect an error. It has no mechanism to do anything about it. It doesn't know which of the bits are wrong and which are correct. When it detects a parity error, it only knows the count is wrong.

Some chips on the market use *fake parity.* Fake parity simply makes every bit count even or odd, depending on the method being used. In effect, this method is the same as no parity checking at all.

Nonparity memory

Nonparity memory systems don't perform data integrity checks. You can't use nonparity memory in a parity system. Doing so generates a parity error as soon as the system boots up. You can turn off parity checking on some systems in the BIOS setup. Parity memory works fine in a nonparity system — the extra bit is ignored.

You can just about count on being asked in one way or another about the difference between parity and nonparity memories. Parity memory contains an extra bit used to check the integrity of the data stored in each byte and nonparity memory does not.

Correcting parity errors

Error Correction Code (ECC) is a data integrity method used in place of parity memory on many systems. The difference between ECC memory and parity memory is that ECC can detect errors like parity memory, but it can also correct errors to a point. ECC memory can detect up to a 4-bit memory error, but it can only correct 1-bit errors. This isn't that big of a deal because a 4-bit error (that's not the same as a 50-cent error) is rare, and 1-bit errors are more common. Like the parity method does with all errors, when ECC sees a multiple-bit error, it reports it as a parity error. Believe me, if your memory has a 4-bit error, you want to know about it, and any attempt to fix it would be sheer guesswork anyway. Expect to see a question on the Core Hardware exam about the difference between ECC and parity memory systems.

Timing memory access

Memory access time is the time it takes for memory to make data available. This time is measured in nanoseconds (ns). Most of the memory around today has access times that range from 5 to 70 nanoseconds, with the higher number being the slower. This memory access speed is used as a rating of sorts for DRAM.

Of course, everyone prefers the fastest available access time, but that isn't always possible. Existing memory access time may limit the PC's capability of adding faster memory. Avoid mixing memory access speeds in the same computer, but if you must, use these precautions:

- ✔ **Use identical memory in a bank:** You should use the same type, speed, and technology of memory within a memory bank (a pair or group of memory module sockets). For example, never mix EDO and FPM memory within a bank of memory.

- ✔ **Put the slowest memory in the first bank:** Some systems use auto-detection to determine the speed of the memory installed on the system. If 60 ns memory is installed in bank 0 and 70 ns in bank 1, the system sets the former as the timing rate, causing problems for the 70 ns memory. Install the 70 ns memory in the first bank.

Real versus Virtual Memory

Physical memory, also called real memory, refers to the actual memory chips installed in the computer and used to store the programs and data actually in use by the computer. Larger programs or multitasking support can create a demand for memory that exceeds the amount of real memory available. On these occasions, it would be nice if the processor could borrow some additional memory for a while. To allow this borrowing, you can create some virtual memory. Virtual memory works much like a memory credit card in that it uses memory that doesn't really exist. It goes like this:

1. In a computer with 64MB of physical memory, the memory demand exists for 100MB of RAM.

2. The operating system creates a virtual memory space on the hard disk and assigns a virtual memory manager, which immediately opens a 36MB swap space (100 – 64) to handle the current excess demand.

3. The operating system smugly proceeds as if it now has 100MB of RAM, leaving the virtual memory manager to handle the swapping of inactive blocks in and out of RAM and the virtual memory swap space.

Virtual memory is the combination of installed physical memory and hard drive space that gives the appearance of more memory than is actually installed on the system. Virtual memory is the basis for multitasking in Windows 9*x*. Without virtual memory, you would not be able to run most of the software in use today. Windows 3.*x*, Windows 9*x*, and Windows 2000 Pro implement virtual memory in files called swap files.

Real Mode Versus Protected Mode

Before I dive into PC logical memory layout, I should review real-mode and protected-mode memory addressing. These two terms come up frequently in discussions of the memory space located above the conventional memory area (see "Logical Memory Layout"). In addition, and probably of more importance, these terms are on both of the A+ exams.

Among other more esoteric things, *real-mode* memory addressing means that the PC is emulating an 8086 processor and is limited to addressing only the first 1MB of RAM. This is the default mode for DOS applications.

The counterpart to real-mode is *protected-mode* memory addressing, in which a program is limited to its own memory space allocations, but it can access memory above the 1MB limit of real mode. It gets its name from the fact that programs in this mode are protected from other programs desiring its memory.

Just about every operating system other than DOS runs in protected mode, which can lead to some trouble. For example, if you boot your Windows system in MS-DOS mode, DOS can't access your protected-mode drivers. You need real-mode drivers for any of the peripherals you take for granted under Windows: CD-ROM, sound card, and so on. Loading these drivers to real mode may also run you out of memory quickly.

Logical Memory Layout

How Windows divides memory into logical divisions is something you should know for both tests. In fact, it may be the most important thing you should know about memory. The logical memory divisions of RAM are the subjects of direct and specific questions as well as referenced in questions in other domains. Spend the time to memorize the information included in this section.

Memory on the PC is broken into four basic divisions, as shown in Figure 8-9 and discussed in Table 8-2:

Table 8-2	Logical Memory Layout
Memory	*Description*
Conventional memory	The first 640K of system memory. Used by operating system kernels and standard DOS programs, device drivers, and TSRs.

Memory	Description
Upper memory area	The upper 384KB of the first megabyte of memory, located right above conventional memory. Reserved for the system BIOS and device drivers and special uses such as ROM shadowing. Also called expanded memory or reserved memory.
High memory area	The first 64K (less 16 bytes) of the second megabyte of memory. Although it's the first 64K of extended memory, it can be accessed in real mode.
Extended memory	Technically, this is all memory above 1MB, but in actuality it is any memory above the high memory area. Used by Windows for programs and data running in protected mode.

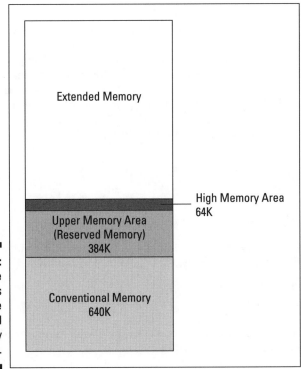

Figure 8-9:
The divisions of the logical memory layout.

Conventional memory

Conventional memory is used to run the operating system files, application programs, memory-resident routines, and device drivers. Conventional memory is the first 640K of system memory (refer to Figure 8-9). This fixed size is the result of two early developments:

- ✔ Early processors could not address more than 1MB of total RAM.
- ✔ IBM's decision to allocate the upper 384K of memory to BIOS and utilities, leaving 640K for the user and operating system.

Upper memory area

This is the upper 384K of the first megabyte of system memory. This area is typically allocated to special purposes such as the BIOS ROM, adapter ROMs, and video RAM.

It wasn't long before those developers who had grown tired of the 640K limitation began lusting after this space. So, it was redesignated as expanded memory, and special drivers were created to allow its use. The primary device driver used for this purpose is EMM386.EXE. This program frees up conventional memory by allowing unused portions of the reserved memory area to be used for DOS drivers and memory-resident programs.

The best way to implement EMM386 is by adding the following lines to the CONFIG.SYS file:

```
DEVICE=C:\DOS\EMM386.EXE
DOS=UMB
```

where UMB stands for upper memory blocks.

If you don't want to run EMS emulation, but you do want the ability to load drivers and TSRs to upper memory, the NOEMS option is added:

```
DEVICE=C:\DOS\EMM386.EXE NOEMS
DOS=UMB
```

Be sure you know and understand both of the previous examples of EMM386.SYS implementations for the tests.

High memory area

The high memory area (HMA) is the first 64K of the extended memory area. It's also the only part of extended memory that a program in real mode can access. This space is normally used by the operating system when the following specification is included in the CONFIG.SYS file:

```
DOS=HIGH
```

This statement tells the operating system (Windows) to load most of its code to the HMA instead of in conventional memory, freeing about 45K of conventional memory space for other functions.

Don't confuse high memory area with upper memory area. You will definitely see questions on the test that refer to both.

Extended memory

This one is pretty simple to understand: Extended memory is all the memory above the first megabyte. Every computer has an upper limit for extended memory that ranges from 16MB on the 286 to 4GB on a Pentium. It also can't be accessed, beyond its first 64K, in real mode.

Some people confuse extended memory with expanded memory. Expanded memory expands base memory to its full 1MB. Extended memory extends memory on up to the clouds.

Accessing higher memory areas

The HIMEM.SYS device driver is a memory manager that allows Windows 3.*x* and Windows 9*x*, EMM386.EXE, and other operating system utilities to see memory above 1MB. HIMEM.SYS creates Extended Memory Standard (XMS) memory.

Microsoft Windows 3.*x* and Windows 9*x must* have HIMEM.SYS or another XMS manager running in order to start up and run. Without this tool, Windows won't be able to detect extended memory. HIMEM.SYS converts extended memory into XMS memory. The program EMM386.EXE is an expanded/extended memory manager that allows the system to manipulate XMS memory.

To add expanded memory emulation, move some of the drivers and TSRs to upper memory, open up the extended memory frontier, include the following code in the CONFIG.SYS file:

```
DEVICE=HIMEM.SYS
DEVICE=EMM386.EXE NOEMS
DOS=HIGH
```

Windows 3.*x* and Windows 95 run on a DOS kernel. Including the statement DOS=HIGH reduces the size of the DOS kernel by approximately 39KB to 40KB, by shifting parts of the kernel into the high memory area.

All versions of Windows 3.*x* need HIMEM.SYS running to access extended memory. You could see a question about what must be running for Windows 3.*x* or Windows 9*x* to load. The answer is HIMEM.SYS.

Prep Test

1 The type of DRAM that is based on the Rambus technology is

- **A** ○ EDO DRAM
- **B** ○ SDRAM
- **C** ○ RDRAM
- **D** ○ VRAM

2 Which of the following are types of DRAM packaging?

- **A** ○ DIP
- **B** ○ SIMM
- **C** ○ DIMM
- **D** ○ RIMM
- **E** ○ All the above

3 SIMM modules must be install in pairs on a Pentium PC. Why?

- **A** ○ They are matched memory cells that cannot operate independently.
- **B** ○ It takes two 32-pin SIMMs to match the 64-bit data path of the Pentium.
- **C** ○ A Pentium requires a minimum amount of RAM to operate.
- **D** ○ It takes two SIMMS to equal one DIMM.

4 Parity memory validates the integrity of the data stored in RAM by

- **A** ○ Checking the header of each packet of data received
- **B** ○ Checking every eighth bit for errors
- **C** ○ Checking the RAM table in BIOS
- **D** ○ Counting the number of even or odd bits set to 1 in the data

5 BIOS programs are most often loaded to which area of memory?

- **A** ○ Conventional memory
- **B** ○ Upper memory
- **C** ○ Extended memory
- **D** ○ Virtual memory

6 Virtual memory is implemented on a Windows systems through what mechanism?

- **A** ○ RAM disk
- **B** ○ Upper memory area
- **C** ○ Swap files
- **D** ○ Mirror disks

7 **Which type of memory is most commonly used for L2 cache?**

A ○ DRAM

B ○ SRAM

C ○ SDRAM

D ○ PCMCIA

8 **All memory above 1MB is called**

A ○ Extended memory

B ○ Expanded memory

C ○ Upper memory

D ○ Base memory

9 **What is the first 640K of memory called?**

A ○ Upper memory

B ○ Extended memory

C ○ Conventional memory

D ○ Expanded memory

10 **The type of memory that is able to correct 1-bit parity errors is**

A ○ EDO

B ○ BEDO

C ○ Rambus

D ○ ECC

Answers

1 **C.** Rambus is a proprietary DRAM technology that is installed on RIMM modules. *See "DRAM technologies."*

2 **E.** All of these are DRAM packages. In fact, DIP is the packaging for SRAM as well. *Review "DRAM packages."*

3 **B.** SIMM assemblies must be installed in pairs because they only have a 32-bit data bus. On the other hand, a DIMM has a 64-bit path and can get by with a single module installed. *Check out "SIMMing right along."*

4 **D.** Parity checking involves using an additional bit with each 8 bits to set the total number of ones bits to either an even or odd number depending on the protocol in use. Take a look at "Understanding parity."

5 **B.** The upper memory area is used to hold BIOS programs and memory-resident drivers. *Study "Upper memory area."*

6 **C.** Windows creates virtual memory space in swap files. Without virtual memory, Windows would not be able to perform most of its multitasking. Look over *"Real versus Virtual Memory."*

7 **B.** SRAM, because it is larger in size and costs more is used primarily for cache memory on the motherboard. *Review "Static RAM (SRAM)."*

8 **A.** Memory above 1MB is called extended memory. *See "Extended memory."*

9 **C.** The first 640K of memory is conventional memory. *See "Conventional memory."*

10 **D.** Error correcting code (ECC) technology is able to identify 4-bit errors and correct 1-bit errors. *See "Real versus Virtual Memory."*

Chapter 9

Storage Systems

Exam Objectives

▶ Identifying basic terms, concepts, and functions of storage systems

▶ Formatting and partitioning hard drives

▶ Installing and configuring ATA (IDE) drives

▶ Installing and configuring SCSI devices

*S*everal different ways exist to store data with a PC. Some are familiar to everyone and some are not so well known. One of the problems with an industry-wide certification exam is that it expects you to know about all the various devices and FRMs (field replaceable modules) you may find in a customer's computer. I've attempted to cram as much as possible into this chapter for you, focusing on the storage devices you're likely to encounter on the A+ Core Hardware exam.

Remember that the exams won't necessarily test you on the newest, latest, or greatest up-to-the-minute technologies available at the time you take the test. The A+ exams are written against a generic set of objectives that attempts to include the PC components you are likely to encounter as a working PC repair professional. So, don't spend your time reading the latest issues of PC magazines to bone up on the newest revelations in storage devices. Your time will be spent wisely if you expand your knowledge of the storage devices in general and focus on the topics included in this chapter.

It's assumed that you understand how bits are organized into bytes and that bytes and words are used to store both text and numeric data. It's also assumed that you know that data stored in memory is temporary and to store data permanently, you must use permanent storage media, such as a hard drive. These are the assumptions of the A+ Core Hardware exam as well. If those assumptions are correct and you know this much, you're off to a good start.

Quick Assessment

Identifying basic terms, concepts, and functions of storage systems

1 ATA and IDE stand for _____ and _____, respectively.

2 A hard drive cluster is a collection of _____.

3 _____ and _____ are the two primary data encoding schemes used to translate data into flux transitions on disk media.

Formatting and partitioning hard drives

4 A(n) _____ should never be low-level formatted.

Installing and configuring ATA (IDE) drives

5 You can connect _____ hard drives to a single ATA IDE cable.

6 RAID level _____ provides for disk striping without parity.

7 The two general translation modes used on ATA IDE disk drives are _____ and _____.

8 LBA refers to _____.

9 The interface used with CD-ROM, DVD, and tape drives is the _____.

Installing and configuring SCSI devices

10 You must install _____ at the beginning and end of the SCSI chain.

Answers

1 *AT Attachment and Integrated Drive Electronics.* Review "IDE technology."

2 *Sectors.* Look at "Organizing data on disk."

3 *FM, RLL.* See "Reading and writing to a disk."

4 *IDE disk drive.* Check out "IDE technology."

5 *Two.* See "IDE technology."

6 *0 (zero).* Review "Raid!?!."

7 *PIO and DMA.* See "IDE protocols and modes."

8 *Logical block addressing.* Check out "Moving bigger blocks of data."

9 *ATAPI.* Look at "CD and DVD interfaces."

10 *Terminating resistor pack, or terminators.* Look at "SCSI technology."

Understanding the Basic Terms

You may not always think of the floppy disk as a removable storage system, but it is — along with CD-ROMs, DVDs, optical disks, and tape cartridges. Removable storage, also known as removable media, allows for expansion of the permanent storage space whenever it's needed and the ability to store the media and its data outside of and away from the PC.

Hard drive technologies

Five types of hard drive technologies have been used in PCs over the years:

- ST506
- ESDI (Enhanced Small Device Interface)
- IDE (Integrated Drive Electronics)
- EIDE (Enhanced Integrated Drive Electronics)
- SCSI (Small Computer System Interface)

ST506 and ESDI are outdated hard drive technologies, along with the AT computer in which they were used. Most of the PCs in use today use either an IDE/EIDE or a SCSI hard drive.

The A+ Core Hardware exam includes questions on IDE, EIDE, and SCSI (including RAID) drive technologies. Focus your review on hard drive storage in these technology types.

ST506/ESDI technologies

These systems were the first hard drive technologies. Besides being big and slow, they were complex to install and replace. Their cabling had to be installed in a certain sequence and with the twist at a certain connector, and then a set of jumpers was used to indicate their drive select setting.

As I contrast in the next section, these devices had to be *low-level formatted* (the process of creating the disk's cylinders and checking for bad surface media), then *high-level formatted* (preparing the device for files), and finally the operating system was installed. It's not important that you remember what low-level formatting is for the A+ Core Hardware test beyond the fact that it is essentially not done on any of the drive technologies after the ST506 and ESDI drives. It's also *not* important that you know what ESDI stands for.

IDE technology

IDE (Integrated Drive Electronics) gets its name from the fact that its controller board is integrated into the disk drive assembly itself, which contrasts to earlier technologies that used a controller board mounted in one of the motherboard's expansion slots. IDE was originally developed as an inexpensive alternative to the expensive SCSI technology (see "SCSI technology" later in this chapter). IDE is one of the most popular disk drive interfaces in use.

IDE is a simple interface technology compared to its predecessors. The IDE interface is used to connect hard drives, CD-ROMs, DVDs, and tape drives to a PC. With the interface controller built into the disk drive itself, only a pass-through board is needed to connect the device to the motherboard. The interface card that's plugged into the motherboard for an IDE disk drive is often a multifunction card supporting the floppy drives, game ports, serial ports, and more. Most of the newest motherboard designs (see Chapter 4) incorporate one or two IDE/EIDE controllers into the motherboard, which eliminates the need for the pass-through card.

Be aware that IDE, or the interface that is called IDE, is really the *ATA (AT Attachment)* interface. In fact, the standard that defines the IDE interface for CD-ROMs, DVDs, and tape drives is called *ATAPI (ATA Packet Interface)*.

You should also know that IDE uses a 40-pin connector to connect the drive to the pass-through card or to the motherboard via a 40-wire ribbon cable. That cable should never be more than 18 inches long (to protect the integrity of the data signal passing through it). An IDE interface supports up to two 504MB drives.

IDE drives are low-level formatted at the factory. A *low-level format* is one that scans the disk storage media for defects and sets aside sectors with defects so that they aren't used for data, preventing later problems. IDE drives should never be low-level formatted by a user or a technician. Only a *high-level format,* such as that performed by the DOS/Windows command FORMAT or the Windows Explorer Format function, shown in Figure 9-1, is used to prepare the disk partitions for use by the operating system and to store data. (See "Formatting the disk" later in this chapter.)

IDE protocols and modes

The ATA IDE interface standard defines a variety of features and translation modes that are used to interact with the disk drive and the internal systems of the PC. Here are the two you should be aware of for the A+ Core Hardware exam:

✔ **PIO (programmed input/output) modes:** This is the standard protocol used to transfer data over an ATA IDE interface. Five different PIO rates or modes exist, each with a different maximum data transfer rate, expressed in megabytes per second (MBps). Transfer rates range from 3.3 MBps (Mode 0) to 11.1 MBps (Mode 3) to 16.6 MBps (Mode 4). Modes 0, 1 (5.2 MBps), and Mode 2 (8.3 MBps) are supported by all ATA IDE standards. Modes 3 and 4 are supported only by the ATA-2 (see "ATA-2 (EIDE) technology" later in this chapter).

✔ **DMA (direct memory access) modes:** This data transfer protocol, which is also called *bus mastering,* allows the hard drive's built-in controller to control the transfer of data into the PC's main memory without involving the CPU, as is the case with a PIO transfer. Don't confuse this with the DMA function of the same name, used with the ISA (industry standard architecture) bus structure usually included in the system chipset. The IDE DMA requires a PCI bus and works independently of any other DMA functions of the PC. IDE DMA is defined in a series of modes that each support a different maximum data transfer rate that range from the 2.1 MBps of the Single Word 0 mode to the 13.3 MBps of the Multiword 1 mode to the 33.3 MBps of the Multiword 3 or DMA-33 mode. All ATA IDE standards support DMA modes with speeds up to 4.2 MBps (Multiword 0), but DMA modes with speeds of 13.3 and above are supported only by ATA-2 and above standards (see "Moving ultra fast" later in this section).

A drive typically uses either PIO or DMA and rarely both. In fact, using both would be very inefficient because both the CPU and the disk controller vie to move data to and from RAM.

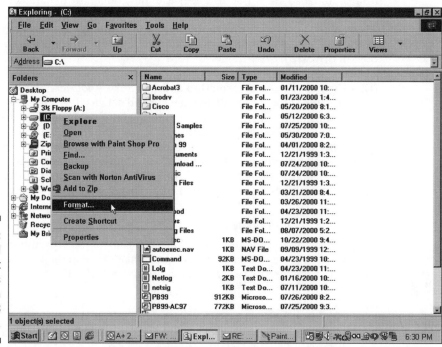

Figure 9-1:
A high-level format function is available in Windows 98 Explorer.

ATA-2 (EIDE) technology

If your computer and those on which you work are relatively new (1995 or later), it's likely that the interface in use is EIDE (Enhanced IDE) or what is more correctly called ATA-2. This interface enhanced the original ATA IDE standard to take advantage of the fact that newer BIOS systems could handle disk drives much larger than 504 MB, to which the ATA IDE standard was limited. This ability to work with larger drives was possible because of translation modes that allowed the BIOS to talk to the hardware differently than it talked with software.

ATA-2 is an ANSI (American National Standards Institute) standard, which makes it a real and official standard. The many variations of the ATA-2 standard, such as EIDE, Fast ATA, and Fast ATA-2, are really nothing more than marketing names rather than variations of the standard. So, for the A+ Core Hardware and Operating System Technologies exams, remember that ATA-2 and EIDE are interchangeable.

The ATA-2 standard, which is also backward compatible to ATA IDE drives, defines a number of features that provide for larger disk volumes and faster data transfers. In addition to adding additional and faster PIO and DMA modes (see "IDE protocols and modes" earlier in this chapter), ATA-2 also includes the ability to *block transfer* data, which groups a number of data reads and writes into a single interrupt, and support for logical block addressing (LBA).

Moving bigger blocks of data

Logical block addressing (LBA) is an enhanced feature that extends the capability of the device to address larger data blocks than was possible in standard ATA IDE drives that used traditional *cylinder/head/sector (CHS)* addressing or the *ECHS (extended CHS)*. ECHS translation, which is also called *large mode* by some BIOS systems, is the translation mode that helped to break the 504MB barrier for some IDE drives.

Instead of the standard CHS type of addressing, LBA uniquely identifies each sector on the disk with a sector number. CHS addressing is much like standard postal addressing schemes that use a street address, city, and state to locate a particular dwelling. LBA is more like the "Plus Four" zip code scheme used in the U.S., which attempts to uniquely number each delivery point within a zip code. LBA assigns each sector a unique number which is used to locate, read from, and write to it. Most of the BIOS systems sold since 1995 include support for LBA, as well as ECHS, or Large mode, address translation.

Moving ultra fast

The ATA interface standard continues to be improved with additional error correction, self-monitoring and reporting capabilities, and faster speeds.

For example, the ATA-3 interface includes logic called S.M.A.R.T., which stands for *Self Monitoring Analysis and Reporting Technology*. This gives the disk drive the ability to send information to the PC's operating system when its operation is degrading for any reason.

ATA-4 defines the variation of the ATA-2 standard that is called the *Ultra ATA interface*. Like the other ATAs, Ultra ATA has a few aliases: Ultra DMA or *UDMA,* ATA-33, DMA-33. Ultra ATA adds one new DMA mode that supports a data transfer speed of 33 MBps per second. It also includes special error detection and correcting code that helps maintain the integrity of the data as it moves at high-speed over the standard ATA IDE 40-wire ribbon cable, which has yet to be upgraded.

ATA-5 and ATA-6 have added DMA data transfer speeds of up to 66.6 MBps and 100 MBps, respectively.

Storing data on tape

Tape is primarily a backup medium today, and many larger systems, especially network servers, have either an internal or external tape drive. This is a good use of the medium, its serial nature, and its relative compact size. Some problems exist with using tape, but they are avoidable with proper care and diligence. You should rotate tapes regularly, store them in a cool dry place, and replace them at least once a year.

Tape drives are used primarily for backing up large databases and hard drives. Because of the tape's streaming capabilities, it's perfect for recording data so that it can be restored later. Data on a tape cartridge is stored in a serial format, and a tape drive rarely offers any form of random data retrieval or restoration. Data is written to the tape in the same way that music is recorded on an audiocassette and with the same limitations. If you want to play the third song on an audiotape, you have to fast forward over or listen to the first two songs on the tape. The same is true of data written to the tape. If you want to restore the third file on the tape, you must skip over the first two files before you can start.

Identifying tape media

You can attach a tape drive to the PC as either an internal or an external device. Whether you eat up a slot in your case for one depends on how much data you back up and how often. Tape cartridges come with either 4mm or 8mm tape. Several types of tape media and drives can be used with a PC system. Table 9-1 lists the most common types found in PCs.

For the Core Hardware exam, remember that DAT and DLT are by far the most common forms of tape drive used on desktop PC systems. The other types listed in Table 9-1 are more common on local area network servers and larger PCs.

Table 9-1	Common Tape Drive Systems Used in PCs		
Drive Type	**Media Size**	**Capacity**	**Compatible Media**
DAT (digital audio tape) Cartridge	4mm	1GB — 20GB	DDS (digital data storage) standard media
DLT (digital linear tape)	.5 inch	10GB — 50GB	Quantum, Super DLT
Exabyte	8mm	2.5GB — 60GB	Exabyte proprietar media
QIC (quarter-inch cartridge)	.25 inch	40MB — 20GB	DC-2000, QIC, QIC-wide, QIC-EX, and Travan (the most popular)
Redwood	.5-inch	10GB — 50GB	StorageTek proprietary

Most tape drives are installed on the IDE/EIDE interface along with other storage media. Most of the larger capacity drives also have a models for the SCSI interface.

Storing tape media

Should a hard drive failure or another catastrophe strike your computer and you were to lose all of your stored data or programs (especially the ones for which you don't have the CDs), having a recent backup could save you time, money, and blood pressure. Chapter 17 discusses the various types of backups you can create and when, but in this chapter the important thing is where to store the tapes that hold all your valuable data. How data is written to a tape is discussed earlier in the chapter in the section, "Storing data on tape."

Common sense tells you not to leave tape cartridges lying around the computer room. Leaving them on or near any form of electromagnetic field, such as on top of the monitor or UPS (see Chapter 10) is also a bad idea. The best place to store your tape cartridges is in a cool and dry place. It can't hurt if they are in a fireproof location as well, for obvious reasons. You may want to store highly-sensitive data offsite in a safe deposit box or with a data storage or archival company.

Floppy disks and drives

Unless you have been repairing computers in Elbonia for about ten years, I'm confident that you know what a floppy disk is and how it's used. You may even know that the most popular size of floppy disk is 3.5 inches. There have been larger sizes of floppy disks used in the past, but I'll bet that maybe you haven't even seen anything bigger than a 3.5 inch floppy disk anyway.

A floppy disk is perfect for transporting files of around 1MB in size between computers that aren't directly or indirectly connected by a local or wide area network (a technique known as *sneaker net*). Multiple floppy disks can also be used to record large files or backups. However, there are some dangers involved in using a floppy disk in many computers, not the least of which are computer viruses, which I discuss in Chapter 17. I cover the organization used on a floppy disk in the section, "Organizing data on disk," later in this chapter.

CD-ROM and DVD technologies

CD-ROM (Compact Disc-Read-Only Memory) and DVD (Digital Versatile Disc or Digital Video Disc) are optical storage technologies that use a laser to read data from (and in some cases, store data to) its media. For purposes of the A+ Core Hardware test, it isn't important to know all of the ins and outs of how CD-ROM and DVD drives read or write data to their media. The Core Hardware exam deals with these devices as forms of storage units that are installed in a PC or may need troubleshooting and diagnostics at some point. So don't waste a lot of time dissecting CD-ROM or DVD drives to learn their inner workings or how their media are constructed.

CD-ROM drives

A CD-ROM has the capability of storing up to 650MB of data. Its data is recorded in reverse of the old vinyl phonograph records — you remember those, they sell them at yard sales a lot. Data on a CD-ROM is recorded in one long continuous strand beginning on the inside edge and winding to the outside edge. It's common today for a PC to have a CD-ROM drive that also records data to the CD. These drives as a group are called CD-R (Recordable) or CD-RW (Read/Write) depending on whether they can be written to once (CD-R) or written to like a floppy disk a limited number of times (CD-RW).

CD-ROM drives are available in a wide range of transfer speeds. In fact, the transfer speed of a CD-ROM drive sets its type. CD-ROM types are stated as "X" factors. Each increment of the X is worth 150K in transfer speed. For example, a 1X CD-ROM has a transfer speed of 150K, an 8X CD-ROM has a transfer rate of 1200K, and a 24X CD-ROM has a transfer rate of 3600K. Just in case you're curious, 1X represents the speed of a CD-A (Audio).

In the storage scheme of things, the CD-ROM is the slowest of the devices found on the average PC. Of course, RAM is the fastest, followed by the hard drive, and poking along in last is the CD-ROM. This usually isn't a problem because users don't use the CD-ROM for its speed. The CD-ROM is valuable to its users for the content of its discs.

DVD drives

DVD is actually a family of optical disc storage technologies. In general, DVD uses an optical disc (meaning it uses a laser to read or write the disc) that is the same size of a CD, but that's where the similarities end. A DVD is double-sided which means that at minimum it should hold at least twice as much data as a CD. In fact, depending on the format used to record its data, a DVD-ROM, the kind used with a PC, can hold from 4.7GB to 17GB, or roughly the equivalent of 7 to 26 CD-ROMs. Two added features of a DVD drive are that it reads CD-ROMs and, because DVD-ROM and DVD-Video have the same format, it will play DVD-Video movies on your PC.

CD and DVD interfaces

For the most part, internal CD-ROM and DVD drives use the ATA IDE interface as defined in the ATAPI (ATA Packet Interface) standard. Nearly all external CD and DVD drives use the SCSI interface, but a growing number of internal drives also use a SCSI interface. Most SCSI drives, but not all, come with their own host adapter cards, just in case the CD or DVD is the only SCSI device installed. Before installing a SCSI drive, verify that the PC already has a SCSI host adapter installed.

SCSI technology

The *Small Computer Systems Interface (SCSI)* is a collection of interface standards that covers a wide range of peripheral devices, including hard drives, tape drives, CD-ROMs, and disk arrays (RAID). SCSI is pronounced *skuzzy*. It rhymes with fuzzy and not *scoozy*, which would sound like the Italian word for *pardon me*. SCSI is not as common in small office and home PCs primarily because its components cost more and these PCs don't need the flexibility and high-end performance of this interface. ATA IDE is by far the most common interface in those environments.

SCSI is actually not an interface. It is more like a system bus structure on which many SCSI devices can connect to a single SCSI controller by sharing a common interface, called the *SCSI bus* or *SCSI chain* (see Figure 9-2). Each device connected to the SCSI bus is assigned a unique device number. These numbers are configured to the device with jumpers, DIP switches, or rotary dials located on the device. Most BIOS systems that support Plug and Play include a feature called *SCSI Configured Automatically* or *SCAM* that sets SCSI device IDs automatically by software. In order for this to work, the BIOS, the host adapter, and the peripheral device must all support the SCAM.

When the SCSI controller (which counts as one of the numbered devices) wants to communicate with one of the devices on the bus, it sends a message encoded with the unit's device number. Any reply to the SCSI controller includes the sender's number. Like IDE/EIDE devices, SCSI devices also have their controllers built in and are able to control their own data access and capture activities, as well as interpret requests from the PC that are passed to it from the SCSI controller.

SCSI devices are connected in what is called a daisy chain, which means that each device is connected in series with the next device on the bus. That is, of course, unless the device is the last device, in which case it uses a DIP switch setting or a resistor block to terminate the bus. Internal SCSI devices attach to a ribbon cable that can connect multiple devices. The ribbon cable is connected to a single port that provides service to all of the devices attached to the cable. The internal SCSI cable serves as the common bus media for all internal devices. External devices usually have two ports, one each for the incoming cable and another to connect to the next device in line or for the terminator, if it is the last device on the bus. Figure 9-2 shows the SCSI bus. As shown, the devices on each end of a SCSI chain terminate the bus.

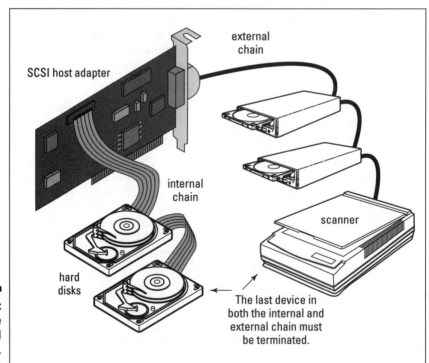

Figure 9-2:
An example
of a SCSI
bus system.

Meeting the SCSI clan

Just as World War I was not given a number until World War II began, the original SCSI interface is now SCSI-1. This implementation of the SCSI standard has a 5MB transfer rate, uses either a Centronics 50-pin or a DB-25 connector, and has an 8-bit bus. Major improvements have been made to the original SCSI-1 interface in the succeeding versions: SCSI-2 and SCSI-3.

SCSI-1

The original SCSI standard, developed in 1986, defined the basic specifications of the SCSI bus structure, including its commands, transfer modes, and cabling. SCSI-1 supported 8 devices on an 8-bit bus that supported up to 5MBps of data transfer. SCSI-1 was not universally accepted and devices from different manufacturers were not always compatible.

SCSI-2

The extensive advancements in SCSI-2 solved many of the problems of SCSI-1. SCSI-2 established the foundation of the SCSI bus on which all future enhancements have been built. SCSI-2, which is also called *Fast-Wide SCSI,* defines two separate protocols:

 ✔ **Fast SCSI:** Features data transfer speeds of up to 10MBps over the SCSI-1 8-bit cabling.

 ✔ **Wide SCSI:** Provides for 16-bit and 32-bit SCSI bus structures.

It's important to note that these two protocols can be used together to create a Fast and Wide SCSI bus. SCSI-2 also increased the number of devices that could be supported on the bus to 16. SCSI-2 is also backward compatible with SCSI-1 devices, but the SCSI-1 devices can only operate at their original speeds.

SCSI-3

Also known as Ultra SCSI, SCSI-3 defines data transfer speeds up to 20MBps over an 8-bit bus or higher speeds over the Wide SCSI bus. Table 9-2 details the various SCSI specifications, including the newer Ultra SCSI and its variations.

Table 9-2	SCSI Specifications			
SCSI Type	**Bus Width**	**Maximum Devices**	**Transfer Speed (MBps)**	**Connector Size (Pins)**
SCSI-1	8	8	5	25
SCSI-2	8	8	5	50
Fast SCSI	8	8	10	50

continued

Table 9-2 *(continued)*

SCSI Type	Bus Width	Maximum Devices	Transfer Speed (MBps)	Connector Size (Pins)
Wide SCSI/ Fast Wide SCSI	8	16	20	68
Ultra SCSI	8	8	20	50
Wide Ultra SCSI	16	16	40	68
Ultra2 SCSI	8	8	40	50
Wide Ultra2 SCSI	16	16	80	68
Ultra3 SCSI/ Ultra160	16	16	160	68
Ultra320	16	16	320	68

For more information about SCSI specifications, visit the Web site of the SCSI Trade Association (SCSITA) at www.scsita.org.

Serial SCSI or FireWire technology

An alternative bus interface that is associate with SCSI-3 is *Serial SCSI*, better known as *FireWire*, which defines a high-speed serial bus structure that can connect up to 63 devices. FireWire is also called IEEE 1394, i.Link, and HPSB (High Performance Software Bus). It is capable of data transfer speeds of 100Mbps in its original specification and up to 3200 Mbps in the newer IEEE 1394b specification. FireWire supports hot swapping (the addition or removal of peripheral devices without restarting the PC), multiple data speeds over the same bus, and isochronous data transfers (time dependent data transfers, such as telephony voice, and real-time video transmissions), which makes it an excellent bus for the transfer of multimedia content.

Watching your As and Bs and Ps and Qs

Skim the following information on SCSI cabling. I've not seen a question from this area, but that doesn't mean one won't appear.

SCSI systems connect to the host adapter in a daisy-chain fashion. This means that the devices are connected in series one to the other in a kind of high-tech conga line. SCSI devices installed as internal devices use a 50-pin ribbon cable very much like the floppy disk cable without the twist. External SCSI devices may require one or more of a series of 50-pin and 68-pin cables, depending on the standard in use. For example, a SCSI-2 device requires an A-cable (50-pin) and a B-cable (68-pin). The B-cable should not be confused with the SCSI-3 P-cable (68-pin) that must be used with a Q-cable (68-pin), and so it goes. When installing a SCSI device, read the manual carefully before you start connecting stuff.

All SCSI devices should be powered on before the PC to allow the SCSI host adapter (usually inside the system) to detect and interrogate each of the devices on the SCSI bus.

RAID!?!

Though not specifically listed in the blueprint of the Core Hardware exam, you should have some understanding of RAID technology in case it's included in a situational question or as an answer option.

A *Redundant Array of Independent Disks (RAID)* is a storage technology that uses two or more hard drives in combination for high availability, fault tolerance (error recovery), and performance. RAID disk drives are used frequently on servers but generally aren't necessary for a personal computer.

One of the fundamental concepts of RAID drives is *data striping*. In this process, data files are subdivided and written to several disks. This technique allows the processor to read or write data faster than a single disk can supply or accept it. While the first data segment transfers from the first disk, the second disk is locating the next segment, and so on.

Another common feature of RAID systems is data mirroring. This feature involves writing duplicate data segments or files to more than one disk to guard against losing the data should a hard drive fail.

Ten different RAID levels exist — 0 through 7, 10, and 53, each more complicated than its predecessor. The RAID levels you should know for the A+ Core Hardware exam are:

- ✔ **RAID 0 — Data Striping:** Interleaves data across multiple drives. Doesn't include mirroring, redundancy, or any other protection against device failure. RAID 0 is not fault tolerant.

- ✔ **RAID 1 — Data Mirroring:** Provides fault tolerance by completely duplicating data on two independent drives. This provides a failover disk in the event that one of the mirrored disks should fail.

- ✔ **RAID 3 — Parallel Transfer with Parity:** Provides fault tolerance by transferring data to and from three or more hard drives with data striped across the drives and the parity bits, which are used to reconstruct the data in the event of a drive failure and stored on a separate and dedicated drive.

- ✔ **RAID 5 — Data Striping with Parity:** Provides fault tolerance by employing essentially the same application as RAID 3. However, RAID 5 stores the parity bits from two drives on a third drive to provide for data stripe error correction. This is the most popular RAID technology implemented.

Working with Disk Storage

You'll find questions that are about disk storage directly or include disk storage indirectly scattered throughout the A+ exams. It's hard to predict how many questions you can expect on the exam versions you'll see, but my guess is between three and five on the Core Hardware exam and perhaps fewer on the Operating Systems Technologies exam. So because each question is worth so much, you should study this disk storage thoroughly.

Organizing data on disk

Just as you need an organization scheme to file documents in a file cabinet so you can find them later, the disk also needs one. If you aren't interested in finding the data later for some reason, then you really don't need to worry about organization. This is called the FISH file-organization technique — First In Stays Here. But if you do care, you need some organization scheme.

Even before you can get your data organized, the PC and disk drive must have an organization technique that helps them place and find data stored on the media. The following are the building blocks of disk media organization and some basic disk storage terms you absolutely should know for the exam:

- **Tracks:** A track is a concentric circular area of the disk that is discrete to all other tracks (see Figure 9-3). A length of a track is one circumference of the disk. On a hard drive, there may be 1,000 or more tracks. When data is written to the disk, it begins with the outermost track first.

- **Sectors:** A sector, shown in Figure 9-3, is a single segment of a disk created by cross-sectioning divisions that intersect all the tracks. In addition to dividing each track into manageable pieces, sectors provide addressing references. Data can be addressed by its track and sector numbers, much like directions to a building located at the intersection of two major streets.

- **Clusters:** Groups of sectors used by operating systems to track data on the disk. There are normally about 64 sectors to a cluster, but the size of the disk drive determines the actual number of sectors in a cluster.

- **Cylinders:** This addressable feature is unique to hard drives. A cylinder is a logical grouping of the same track on each disk surface in a disk unit. All of the tracks with the same track number on all of the hard drive's surfaces form a cylinder. For example, if a hard drive has four platters, it has eight surfaces and eight track 52s, as shown in Figure 9-4. All eight of the track 52s make up cylinder 52. This feature allows data to be written to each platter on the same track, eliminating the need to move the read/write heads.

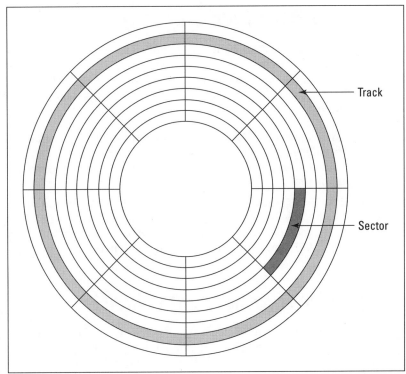

Figure 9-3:
A disk platter divided into tracks and sectors.

Track

Sector

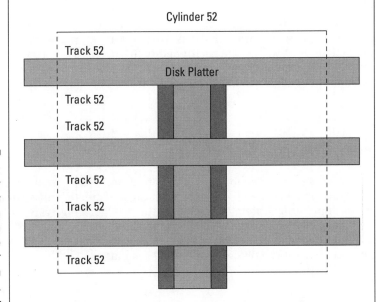

Figure 9-4:
A cylinder logically groups the tracks with the same number from each disk.

Cylinder 52

Track 52

Disk Platter

Track 52

Track 52

Track 52

Track 52

Track 52

Reading and writing to a disk

Before data can be read from a disk, it must be written to the disk through a process called *flux transition,* which means that the storage media is altered with an electromagnet to either a positive or a negative charge. Primarily, two different encoding schemes have been used to convert data into flux transitions:

- ✔ **FM (Frequency Modulation) and MFM (Modified Frequency Modulation):** Some of the first widely used encoding methods. These schemes simply recorded a 1 or a 0 as different polarities on the recording media.

- ✔ **RLL (Run Length Limited):** Allows for higher track and data density by spacing one-bits farther apart and specially encoding each byte. RLL introduced data compression techniques, and most current disk drives (IDE, SCSI, and so on) use a form of RLL encoding.

Interleaving data on a disk

You probably won't see a question on the A+ Core Hardware exam about interleaving; it's no longer used in most newer disk drives because of increased speeds and efficiencies. But be careful not to confuse interleave with interlace, which is a video display technique. *Interleave* relates to PC hard drives, and *interlace* relates to PC monitors. Be sure of the question before answering.

Interleaving is a technique that allows the read/write head to use the rotation of the disk to its advantage. If a disk drive has an interleave ratio of 3:1 (or 3 minus 1), it writes one sector and then skips two before writing the next. Likewise, an interleave of 2:1 means that it writes to every other sector (2 minus 1 equals 1). An interleave of 1:1 is the same has having no interleaving at all.

Formatting the disk

The processes included in this section are described in generic terms. The particular process used to format, partition, and create a file system in the various operating systems included on the A+ Operating Systems Technologies exam, such as Windows 9*x,* Windows NT, Windows 2000, OS/2, and others, is something you will need to know. Chapters 19, 20, and 21 cover these actions for the different operating systems.

A disk drive undergoes two levels of formatting before it's installed in the PC. The low-level format shouldn't concern most PC repair technicians because it's done at the factory during manufacturing. Low-level formatting accomplishes two major things:

- ✔ Builds the sector identification on a disk that is used by the drive to find sectors during read or write operations
- ✔ Physically scans the disk media for defects and records the location of any unusable areas found

During the procedure to install an operating system on a disk, the disk is prepared by performing a high-level format of the disk. The command used to perform a high-level format varies from one operating system to the next, but in general the process is about the same. For example, in the Windows 9*x* installation, the high-level format (performed from the Windows Explorer, as shown in Figure 9-1) creates a separate FAT table that's used by the operating system to track disk clusters.

Different operating systems use different file systems to manage disk storage. A high-level format creates the operating system's file system and management tables and files. Table 9-3 lists the file systems used by the operating systems you find on the A+ exams.

Table 9-3	File Systems
Operating Systems	**_Primary File System_**
DOS	File Allocation Table (FAT) aka FAT16
OS/2	High Performance File System (HPFS)
Windows 3.*x*	Virtual File Allocation Table (VFAT)
Windows 9*x*	FAT32
Windows NT and 2000	NT File System (NTFS)

The Windows file systems

Focus on the primary file system supported by each operating system. But, just so you have some knowledge of what each is about, review the following items:

- ✔ **FAT:** A table used by DOS and early releases of Windows 3.*x* to place and locate files on a disk. It also tracks the pieces of fragmented files.
- ✔ **VFAT:** The 32-bit file system used in Windows for Workgroups and older releases of Windows 95. VFAT served as an interface between applications and the physical FAT. I think its most outstanding feature was that it supported long filenames.

✔ **FAT32:** The file system used in Windows 95 (OEM Service Release (OSR) 2) and Windows 98. It supports larger disk capacities (up to two terabytes), and because it uses a smaller cluster size, it produces more efficient storage utilization. Windows 2000 supports FAT32 with disk volumes of up to 32GB.

✔ **HPFS:** The file system supported by IBM's OS/2 operating system. It supports disk drives as large as 2TB and individual files as large as 2GB and 256-byte filenames. HPFS coexists on a system with an existing FAT file system.

✔ **NTFS:** Introduced with the Windows NT operating system and supported under Windows 2000 as NTFS 5.0, which is not completely backward compatible. Windows NT and 2000 also support FAT32 and the legacy FAT file systems as well. NTFS features transaction logs to help recover from disk failures, has the capability to set permissions at the directory or individual file level, and enables files to span several physical disks.

✔ **CDFS and UDF:** Windows 98 and 2000 also support two CD-ROM and optical disk file systems, the CDFS (CD File System), and the UDF (Universal Disk Format). UDF is slowly replacing CDFS as the standard optical disk file system.

Partitioning the hard drive

For the test, you should know the reason for partitioning the hard drive, something about the partitions themselves, and that FDISK is the command used in both Windows and DOS. The FDISK utility is used to partition the hard drive into logical subdivisions, which are seen by the operating system as separate logical (as opposed to physical) hard drives.

Specialized software utilities exist that can be used to format and partition hard drives, such as Partition Magic from Power Quest (www.powerquest.com) or Partition Commander from V Communications (www.v-com.com). These tools provide a graphical interface that provides disk volume and partition information beyond the basic data provided by the FDISK command.

You partition the hard drive to do the following:

✔ Divide the disk into logical subdrives that are addressed as separate drives; for example, C, D, and E

✔ Create separate areas of the disk to hold multiple operating systems, such as Windows and Linux, in their own partitions

✔ Separate programs from data into separate partitions to ease the backup process

Hard drives are divided into primary and extended partitions. Typically, the *primary partition* is the one used to boot the system. Any other partitions on the drive are *extended partitions* and can be used for another operating system or subdivided further (up to 23 more times). A hard drive can be divided into a maximum of four primary partitions, but some systems, such as DOS, require that only one primary partition be active or visible at a time.

The two types of partitions, primary and extended, can be allocated to be system and boot partitions as well. A *system partition* is the disk volume that contains the files needed to boot an operating system on a particular type of hardware. On most systems, the "active" partition is the system partition. The *boot partition* holds the operating system's executable and support files. The boot partition can be the same, and frequently is, the same as the system partition, which in turn can be the primary partition.

Partitioning disks can improve disk efficiency. Under DOS and Windows, cluster sizes are automatically assigned in proportion to the disk size. The bigger the disk, the bigger the clusters, and large clusters can result in slack space (wasted disk space). Reducing the size of the disk through partitioning reduces the cluster size as well. A wide range of software tools is available to help partition a hard drive effectively.

In DOS, Windows 3.*x*, and early releases of Windows 95, a hard drive over 2GB in size must be divided into partitions each smaller than 2GB if you want to use the entire disk. Windows 95 OSR2 and Windows 98, which implement FAT32, can create a primary partition of 8GB. Windows 2000 supports any FAT32 partition of any size.

After a hard drive is partitioned, the first sector on cylinder 0 (the outermost track) is reserved for the master boot record that contains the partition table. All partition types have a partition table that's used to track its contents. However, the partition table in the master boot record contains the mapping for all partitions on all drives. The master boot record uses the partition table to locate and use the active primary partition to boot the system.

Compressing the disk

This section is provided strictly for background material. You may run into a question or two that include the term *disk compression* either in its scenario or as a wrong answer. Don't fret too much about the ins and outs of disk compression. The cost per megabyte for disk space is low enough that most people just get a bigger disk, rather than put up with the overhead of disk compression.

A number of third-party disk compression utilities are available for use with PC hard drive systems. DOS and Windows 3.*x* use a routine called DBLSpace. Windows 9*x* includes a disk compression utility called DriveSpace that works by creating a new uncompressed logical drive, called the host drive, where it stores the CVF (Compressed Volume File), a form of VFAT for the compressed drive. The uncompressed drive also contains files that should not or cannot be compressed, such as system files. Any unused space is available to the user.

Installing and Configuring Storage Devices

The process used to install and configure a floppy disk, hard drive, CD-ROM, DVD, or tape drive is basically the same. Only a few subtle and specific tasks differentiate these tasks. The task on which the A+ Core Hardware exam focuses is aligning and attaching a device's cabling. As you review the procedures used for each device in the following sections, pay particular attention to how the cabling is aligned and installed for each device.

Installing floppy disk drives

The three things you must consider when installing a floppy disk drive in a PC are

- ✓ **Media:** Which diskette sizes has the user been using to back up data or install software? Don't do the customer a favor and upgrade the system to a 3½-inch floppy drive when all of his files are on 5¼-inch floppies.

- ✓ **Physical size:** Three package sizes (also called form factors) for floppy disk drives exist: full-height, half-height, and combination half-height. A full-height drive, which is big, bulky, and takes about two expansion slots, is common in older PCs. The half-height drive is half as tall as a full-height drive and is the size of one expansion slot on a PC case. This drive is the *de facto* standard in use today. The third form combines both a 3½-inch and a 5½-inch drive into a single half-height drive.

- ✓ **Capacity:** Floppy disks range in their storage capacity. Depending on how many sides and the media density of the disk, 5¼-inch floppy disks hold between 360K to 1.2MB. Depending on the same variables, 3½-inch disks hold from 720K to 1.4MB.

Installing a floppy disk drive

To install a floppy disk drive in a computer, you must install the floppy disk drive controller card in the motherboard. Three types of floppy disk controller interfaces are used in PCs:

✔ **Standalone cards:** Usually not a single purpose card, floppy controller cards install into an expansion slot on the motherboard. For example, many floppy controller cards also include a game port, a serial port or two, a parallel port, and, of course, the disk interface.

✔ **Disk controller cards:** It has been common for a single card to provide the interface for the hard drive and the floppy disk since the days of the 286. This practice reduces the number of expansion slots needed to install what are considered system necessities.

✔ **Built-in controllers:** On systems sold in the past four years, the motherboard typically includes an interface adapter that is supported through its chipset for a floppy disk.

Cabling the floppy disk drive

The common floppy disk cable is a 34-wire ribbon cable that is usually light blue in color with one edge painted either red or blue. Usually three connectors are on the cable, as shown in Figure 9-5. The three connectors connect to the controller card and up to two floppy disk drives.

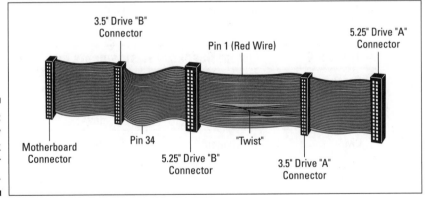

Figure 9-5:
A floppy disk connector cable.

3.5" Drive "B" Connector

Pin 1 (Red Wire)

5.25" Drive "A" Connector

Motherboard Connector

Pin 34

5.25" Drive "B" Connector

"Twist"

3.5" Drive "A" Connector

To be sure you have the floppy cable installed correctly, you can use two tricks: 1) remember "Big Red is Number One," and 2) in most cases, the red edge should point toward the AC power cord. I apologize for the sports metaphor, but it works for me.

A floppy cable is installed in a specific way. In addition to worrying about the alignment of the cable and getting Pin 1 installed on the controller card (Pin 1 is either marked with a "1" or a white dot on the controller card connector), you must also make sure that you use the correct connector with the proper disk drive. Some computer manufacturers go one step further to make this even easier. For example, Compaq uses a keyed cable connector for its floppy and IDE drives that can be connected in only one way.

As shown in Figure 9-5, two two-connector sets for floppy disk drives are on the cable. The first set of connectors, in the middle of the cable, is for the B floppy disk drive. After the twist in the cable, that is, at the end of the cable, are the A floppy disk connectors.

The floppy drive is connected to the power supply via a special 4-pin flat power connector (usually a Berg connector). Most power supplies provide at least two of these connectors. See Chapter 10 for more information on connecting internal devices to the power supply.

Configuring the floppy disk drive

Fortunately, the drive cable takes care of any configuration problems you may have, unless you're installing a used drive. The drive select jumpers that assign an identity to the drive are usually set to DS2, or drive select 2, at the factory. The twist in the cable near the A: connector tricks the system into thinking that the drive connected after the twist is DS1, or drive select 1.

A key part of configuring any storage device, including a floppy disk drive, is ensuring that the proper system resource settings (IRQ, DMA, and I/O ports) are used and that no conflicts exist with other devices. Table 9-4 includes the system resource settings used for a floppy disk drive.

Table 9-4	System Resource Assignments for Floppy Disks	
Resource Type	*Resource Assigned*	*Comment*
IRQ	IRQ6	Default setting for floppy disk drives
DMA	Channel 2	Default setting for floppy disk controller (FDC)
I/O Address	03F0 — 03F7	Default for FDC (excludes address 03F6)

See Chapter 6 for more information on system resource assignments and their importance.

Terminating the relationship

The last floppy drive (usually A) must be terminated at one end. This is especially true of older full-height and some half-height drives. Those drives have a terminating resistor plugged into the end of the cable to absorb all signals and prevent signal echoes from bouncing back down the line and crashing into new incoming data.

Again, technology is taking care of you, because all 3.5-inch drives have a pre-installed, non-configurable terminating resistor. With 3.5-inch drives, each drive shares the role of termination. If you have only one drive on the chain, it terminates itself. If you mix 5.25-inch and 3.5-inch drives on the same chain, the terminator on the 5.25-inch drive should be removed unless it's the end. Terminating resistors look like 16-pin memory DIP chips.

Installing ATA hard drives

 You do not low-level format an IDE/EIDE or SCSI drive. If you did low-level one of these drives, you may render it totally useless by wiping out its sector translation information.

Mounting the disk drive

As I describe in the section, "Configuring the floppy disk drive" earlier in the chapter, hard drives share two physical sizing characteristics with floppy disks, the overall physical dimensions of the disk drive itself and the size of the drive bay into which it can be mounted. Many of the newer system case form factors now include both externally accessible drive bays into which hard drives can be mounted as well as internal drive bays that are not accessible without opening the system case.

Hard drives have two form factors: 5.25-inch and 3.5-inch. The larger form factor usually fits into the standard half-height drive bay on most system cases without other mounting hardware. The 3.5-inch drive form usually must be installed in a tray to accommodate the oversize half-height bay. If a case includes an internal drive bay, it is usually a smaller bay that is just right for the smaller form factor.

Orienting the cable

You can expect one or two questions on the number of drives supported by ATA or IDE (2) and ATA-2 or EIDE (4) and how the cables are aligned. Two cables must be attached to the disk drive: a data cable and a power cable. The power cable is attached to the power supply and is a keyed 5-pin cable that attaches directly to the drive in a matching connector port. Chapter 16 also has information on installing these drive types.

ATA drives are connected to either an adapter card or to the motherboard with a 40-pin ribbon cable that must also be aligned to pin 1. The alignment is performed the same as for the floppy ribbon cable. Only two ATA IDE drives can be installed in a system, with one the master and the other the slave. Up to four ATA-2 or EIDE drives can be installed in a system with two drives on each of the two cables. One of the cables is designated as the primary and the other as the secondary interfaces. There is a master and a slave on each interface, and you will see references to primary master, primary slave, secondary master, and secondary slave on the exam.

Configuring a hard drive

ATA drives must be designated either as a master or a slave. The *master* is the primary disk drive from which the system is normally booted. The slaves are not. Regardless of whether you install two IDE or four EIDE drives, one drive on each cable should be designated as the master. You must set any other drives as slaves. This is done with jumpers on each drive controller. This step is important because two masters will fight each other to the death, and two slaves will stand around lost, waiting for instructions. The result in either case is no disk access. Read the manuals for the drives carefully to locate and set the jumpers appropriately.

Hard drives themselves are not directly configured with system resource assignments during their installation. However, the interface (IDE, SCSI) or its host adapter does. Table 9-5 lists the system resources used by the IDE and SCSI interfaces on a PC.

Table 9-5	System Resource Assignments for Hard Drives	
Resource Type	**Resource Assigned**	**Comment**
DMA		Not used for IDE or SCSI interfaces
IRQ	IRQ14	Reserved for the primary IDE controller (first two IDE (ATA) drives)
IRQ	IRQ15	Reserved for the secondary IDE controller (second two IDE (ATA) drives)
I/O Address	1F0—1F7	Primary HDC (hard drive controller)
I/O Address	170—177	Secondary HDC
I/O Address	370	IDE Controller

See Chapter 6 for more information on system resource assignments and their importance.

Installing and configuring optical drives

CD-ROM and DVD drives are installed using the same process as hard drives and typically occupy a half-height bay on the front panel of a PC so that the user has access to the disk tray and drive controls. These drives are typically ATAPI devices and install on an ATA IDE data connection to a proprietary adapter card, to a multipurpose adapter card, or directly to the motherboard IDE connectors.

Internal CD-ROM or DVD drives should also be connected to the PC's sound card, assuming it has one installed. A thin three-wire cable is usually included with the CD or DVD drive that is used to interconnect these two devices. Check the documentation for your sound card to determine where a particular brand of CD or DVD drive should be connected. The power connector used is one of the same 5-pin Molex connectors used for a hard drive. See Chapter 10 for more information on connecting internal devices to the power supply.

When installing an IDE CD-ROM drive to a system that has an IDE hard drive installed, you must configure the CD-ROM as a slave. See the drive manual for the correct setting. If no IDE hard drive exists, the CD-ROM can be set to be the master, but some CD-ROMs run only as slaves.

CD-ROM and DVD drives are configured to the interface and are not directly assigned system resources. For a list of the system resources assigned to the IDE (ATA) interface, refer to Table 9-5.

To operate a PC's CD-ROM drive in a DOS environment, its device driver must load from the CONFIG.SYS file during the boot process. If the CD-ROM drive is to be installed internally, you have the choice of either an IDE or SCSI. The IDE is less expensive, but the SCSI offers greater future expandability. Anyway, give the customer the choice.

Installing and configuring a SCSI hard drive

SCSI devices, although mentioned here and there on the previous edition of the A+ exams, take on new importance on the latest A+ Core Hardware exam. You can expect to see a question or two about the idiosyncrasies of how a SCSI bus chain is installed and configured — a lot differently than the relatively simple process used for ATA devices.

Configuring the SCSI adapter

Many SCSI host adapters are configured via a block of DIP switches located on the adapter card. For example, an Adaptec SCSI host adapter is configured by setting its switches to the settings listed in Table 9-6. Some SCSI adapters are Plug and Play and do not require physical configurations on the card before installation.

Table 9-6	Sample Switch Settings for Configuring a SCSI Host Adapter	
Switch	*On/Off*	*Setting Represented*
1	On	Plug and Play disabled
	Off	Plug and Play enabled
2	Off	Together with Switches 3 and 4 sets default I/O address
3	Off	
4	Off	
2	On	Together with Switches 3 and 4, sets alternative I/O address
3	On	
4	On	
5	Off	Disables FDC defaults
6	Off	Together with Switches 7 and 8, sets BIOS default address
7	Off	
8	Off	

Driving Miss SCSI

Most SCSI host adapters require a device driver to be installed. On a Windows system, the device driver for a SCSI adapter can usually be located in the list of supported SCSI host adapters to have it automatically installed and configured on the system.

Lab 9-1 lists the general steps used to install the device driver for a SCSI host adapter on a Windows NT or 2000 system.

Lab 9-1   Installing a SCSI Host Adapter Device Driver

1. **Log on to the system as the administrator or a user with administrator privileges.**

2. **Open the Control Panel by choosing Start➪Settings➪Control Panel.**

3. **Activate the SCSI Adapters window from the SCSI Adapters icon.**

4. **Click the Drivers tab.**

5. **Ensure that a driver for the SCSI Adapter is not already installed. If the proper driver is already installed, it doesn't need to be reinstalled.**

6. **Click the Add button and then select the driver from the Driver list. Make sure the driver is available on the Windows system media or on the hard drive.**

7. **Close the windows when completed and restart the system.**

Problems of the cabling kind

Because so many devices, from 1 to 16, can be attached to a SCSI bus, the cabling that connects them can be the primary source of problems on the chain. One problem is the cable can be too long. SCSI-1 chains cannot be more than 6 meters long, which is about 19 feet according to the trusty conversion calculator at Metric USA (www.metricusa.com). Not 6 meters for the internal bus and 6 meters for the external bus, but 6 meters altogether for both. And to get downright technical, the cables inside any external SCSI devices count too!

SCSI-2 and SCSI-3 bus chains (because they're fast and wide) are limited to only 3 meters, or just under 10 feet and have the same rules of inclusion as SCSI-1. One other limitation is that a SCSI cable in any SCSI chain should not be less than 6 inches (approximately 0.15239999939 meters) as a general rule.

Terminating the bus

You can use two types of termination to terminate a SCSI bus: passive and active. *Passive termination* can be used only with a SCSI-1 system because this system does not include voltage regulation and passive termination can cause problems on longer chains. *Active termination*, which does regulated voltage at the termination point, should be used whenever possible, and you should never mix active and passive termination on the same system.

On an external chain, the termination is a plug or cap that is attached to the open port on the last device on the chain. Internal chains are terminated through a jumper or a resistor block. Knowing how a SCSI chain is terminated isn't important, but absolutely remember that the SCSI chain is terminated at each end, internal and external. By the way, the last device on the internal SCSI chain should usually be a disk drive.

Avoiding conflict

Each SCSI device must be assigned an ID number. As I indicate earlier in this chapter, the number is assigned through a jumper or a DIP switch block. Because the SCSI bus, depending on the standard in use, supports 8 to 16 devices, including the host adapter, the numbers range from 0 to 7 and 8 to 15. Device ID 7 is reserved for the SCSI host adapter. You can assign the other devices any of the other numbers, but slower devices such as CD-ROMs should be assigned a higher SCSI ID. This gives them lots of time to process data on the SCSI bus. A SCSI hard drive used to boot the system is assigned SCSI ID 0.

SCSI devices are accessed in a priority scheme. Device ID 7 has the highest priority, as it should, followed by devices 6 through 0 and then devices 15 through 8, if they are in use and supported.

If you have both an ATA IDE disk drive and a SCSI disk drive on a system, the IDE drive should be the boot drive. The SCSI host adapter is set to 7; the boot hard drive is set to 0.

Troubleshooting problems of the SCSI kind

When problems show up on a SCSI bus, especially after you have added or removed a SCSI device either internally or externally, use the steps in Lab 9-2 to try to pinpoint the problem:

Lab 9-2	Troubleshooting SCSI Device Problems

1. **Determine the total length of both internal and external (including any cable inside external devices) to verify that you haven't exceeded the maximum length for the interface type you're using.**

2. **Verify that each SCSI device has been assigned a unique address.**

3. **Only the last device on both the internal and external chains should be terminated.**

4. **Check all cables and connectors for defects and fit.**

5. **Verify that any new devices added to the system are not providing termination power. (Only the adapter card should provide termination power for a system terminated with active termination.)**

6. **Check the settings of the host adapter.**

7. **Verify that the terminators aren't damaged.**

Prep Test

1 Which RAID level provides for disk striping with parity?

A ○ 0

B ○ 1

C ○ 4

D ○ 5

2 When should high-level formatting be done on an IDE hard drive?

A ○ By the manufacturer at the factory

B ○ Before it's partitioned with FDISK

C ○ After it has been partitioned with FDISK

D ○ IDE drives should never be high-level formatted

3 Which of the following are ATA IDE data transfer modes? (Choose two.)

A ❑ PIO

B ❑ IRQ

C ❑ DMA

D ❑ ISA

4 Which of the following is not an addressing scheme used by ATA and ATA-2 devices?

A ○ LBA

B ○ CHS

C ○ WKRP

D ○ ECHS

5 Which of the following is not a commonly used tape drive system type?

A ○ ATA

B ○ DLT

C ○ QIC

D ○ DAT

6 DVD and CD-ROM drives use an IDE interface as defined in which standard?

A ○ MAPI

B ○ CDAPI

C ○ ATAPI

D ○ ATARI

7 The encoding scheme used on virtually all current disk drives is

A ○ DMC

B ○ RLL

C ○ FM

D ○ MFM

8 A hard drive cluster is made up of

A ○ Cylinders

B ○ Tracks

C ○ Sectors

D ○ Hard drives

9 When installing IDE/EIDE disk drives, at least one drive must be assigned as the

A ○ Slave

B ○ Host

C ○ Controller

D ○ Master

10 How many devices can be attached to a SCSI-2 chain?

A ○ Two

B ○ Sixteen

C ○ Eighteen

D ○ Eight

Answers

1 **D.** RAID 5 provides data striping at the character level and implements stripe error correction. *See "RAID!?!."*

2 **C.** IDE disk drives never need low-level formatting, but they should be high-level formatted after being partitioned to load the operating system to the drive. *Review "IDE technology."*

3 **A, C.** Although DMA is the transfer mode most commonly used in PCs over the past few years, PIO devices are still in use. *See "IDE protocols and modes."*

4 **C.** Although one of my favorite TV shows features fictional radio station *WKRP in Cincinnati* and not an addressing scheme used by ATA devices. *Look at "Moving bigger blocks of data."*

5 **A.** ATA is a storage device interface standard and not a form of tape drive. *Review "Identifying tape media."*

6 **C.** ATAPI (AT Attachment Packet Interface) is the standard that defines the interface used for CD-ROM, DVD-ROM, and some tape drives. *See "CD and DVD interfaces."*

7 **B.** RLL allows for higher track and data density by spacing bits further apart and encoding each byte. *Review "Reading and writing to a disk."*

8 **C.** Clusters are groups of sectors. Normally about 64 sectors are in a cluster, but the size of the disk drive determines the actual number of sectors in a cluster. *Look at "Organizing data on disk."*

9 **D.** When installing IDE/EIDE drives, you must designate one (or more if using an EIDE interface) of the drives as the master. Designate the other drive on each cable as a slave. *See "Installing ATA hard drives."*

10 **C.** Up to eight devices can connect to a SCSI-1 bus, and a SCSI-2 bus supports up to 16. *Review "Meeting the SCSI clan."*

Chapter 10

Power

Exam Objectives

▶ Recognizing PC power supply terms, concepts, and functions

▶ Explaining PC power supply safety procedures

▶ Detecting common PC power supply problems

*O*ne of my favorite you-never-can-tell stories is the "Case of the Fibbing Sibling." Anyone who has had the pleasure of being a brother or a sister (or parent, for that matter) has experienced the "Not me's." This happens when your loving sibling has done something worthy of parental consternation and when asked about it says, "Not me!" This translates to mean that *you,* the innocent bystander, must have done it.

This story reminds me of a power supply that was also the fibbing sibling. A brand-new computer gave a POST disk drive error right out of the box. A new disk drive was sent for and installed. When the system was rebooted, it had the same error. The hard disk cables were replaced, but to no avail. The motherboard was replaced, and the system finally booted. However, a few days later the problem returned. Eventually, with no other parts to swap, the power supply was replaced. End of problem.

The power supply has one of the highest failure rates of any PC component. In spite of this, it's often the last component suspected for a problem. A faulty power supply can cause untold damage to the computer and, as the preceding story relates, can send the PC repairperson on a wild goose chase.

Quick Assessment

Recognizing PC power supply terms, concepts, and functions

1 The PC power supply converts _____ power into _____ power.

2 The power supply also contains the main cooling _____ of the PC.

3 The PC power supply generates five voltages: _____, _____, _____, _____, and _____.

4 The PC power supply's output is measured in _____.

Explaining PC power supply safety procedures

5 A(n) _____ happens when disturbances create a temporary high-voltage burst that travels down the power line.

6 _____ are small variations in the voltage of the power line.

7 A(n) _____ reduces power problems by absorbing spikes and smoothing line noise.

8 UPS stands for _____.

9 A Green Star device reduces its power consumption by _____ in sleep mode.

Detecting common PC power supply problems

10 During the POST processing, an error code of 021 indicates a(n) _____ error.

Answers

1   *AC, DC.* See "Power to the 'Puter" and "Internal power."

2   *Fan.* Study "Cooling it."

3   *+5V, –5V, +12V, –12V, +3.3V.* See "Converting power."

4   *Watts.* Review "Overloading the power supply."

5   *Power surge.* Look at "The paradox of external power."

6   *Line noise.* Review "The paradox of external power."

7   *Surge suppressor.* Check out "Suppressing the surge."

8   *Uninterruptible power supply.* Take a gander at "Hedging your bet."

9   *99 percent.* See "Saving the planet."

10 *Power supply, or Power Good signal.* Review "Diagnosing POST problems."

Power to the 'Puter

In spite of the power supply's importance, you won't find many questions on the A+ exam specifically about it. When you boil it down, all it does is supply power and help cool the case. However, expect questions on system and processor voltages, the cooling system, surge suppressors, UPSs (Uninterruptible Power Supplies), and why they are needed. Two basic facts of computer power are that much of the computer runs on either 5 or 12 volts of direct current (DC) power internally, and the electrical outlet on the wall supplies alternating current (AC) at about 110 to 115 volts. The PC's power supply bridges these obviously incompatible worlds by converting raging AC power from the wall into the docile DC power used by the computer.

Obviously, the computer can't run without a power supply, which supplies power to all the components in the computer. It also regulates incoming power voltage to eliminate the spikes and electrical noise common to most electrical systems. It is also the main part of the cooling system.

To the PC power supply, two types of power exist: external and internal.

The paradox of external power

External power, which comes from your home or office wall outlet, is the power everyone tends to take for granted — as long as it's there, it's fine. You may be surprised at the number of problems external power can have: line noise, spikes, surges, brownouts, and blackouts, among the major ones. Most of these problems go unnoticed, because they are usually small enough that the computer's power supply can deal with them (all except a blackout, of course). But, these power problems can lead to reliability problems in your computer.

When you plug your PC directly into the wall socket, you are subjecting the PC to several problems. Some of these problems your computer can handle, but over time, even unnoticed problems can take their toll and result in major damage. You should know for the test the kinds of problems that the PC can experience from external power. These problems are

- ✔ **Line noise:** Consists of small variations in the voltage of the power line. A small amount of line noise is normal in just about every system, and all but the very cheapest power supplies can handle it. If you have the PC plugged into its own circuit (unshared line), you should have little trouble from line noise. However, if your computer shares an extension cord with the pop machine or its circuit with a megaton air conditioner, line noise is a certainty, and it will soon cause some major problems. What will usually happen is that the line noise eventually burns out the power-regulating circuits in a PC's power supply. After that, any line noise on the power line could pass through the power supply unscathed straight to the motherboard or disk drives and the other unsuspecting internal components of the PC.

✔ **Power surges:** A power spike, which is called an overvoltage event by the power company, happens when disturbances, such as distant lightning strikes or other anomalies in the electrical supply grid, create a voltage spike that travels down the line and to your wall plugs. The surge lasts only a few thousandths of a second, but that's plenty of time for the voltage to increase to 1,000 volts or higher. High voltage spikes can degrade a PC's power supply. Multiple surges over time can destroy it.

✔ **Brownouts:** Called an undervoltage event by the power company, a brownout is the opposite of a power surge (overvoltage event) and happens when a sudden dip occurs in the power line voltage. A brownout doesn't typically last too long, but it can. In most cases, the power level drops below normal levels for a time and then returns to normal. Brownouts are extremely common during periods of heavy load on the electrical system, such as hot afternoons or cold mornings. The reduced voltage level causes many devices to run slower than normal or malfunction in other ways. Low voltage for an extended time can do just as much damage as spikes.

✔ **Blackouts:** A blackout occurs when the power fails completely. The problems caused by a blackout are usually more frustrating than damaging, but the fluctuation of power surrounding a blackout can harm your system. If you're in the middle of a long document (that you hadn't yet saved), or were defragmenting or fixing other hard disk problems (and the allocation tables weren't completely rebuilt) when the power goes out — you very likely have problems. More often, though, the damage occurs when the power returns suddenly, usually in the form of a huge spike.

✔ **Lightning strikes:** This is the big spike, and it can deliver a million volts or more. I don't need to tell you what would happen if one were to hit your home or office directly. However, a strike even in the vicinity can result in a very high voltage spike. I have witnessed what a lightning strike can do to a building. Everything plugged in was completed destroyed or melted down: computers, copiers, fax machines, telephones, and more.

Internal power

The PC runs on DC. The computer's power supply converts AC power into the various DC voltages and signals used by the PC's components and circuits. The computer power supply, like that shown in Figure 10-1, is a switching power supply. It reduces the 110V incoming voltage to the 3.3V, 5V, and 12V charges used by the PC by switching the power charge off and on. In a very simplified explanation, you get 20 watts from a 100-watt signal by leaving the PC on 20 percent of the time and off 80 percent of the time. In this way, only the amount of power needed is generated.

The PC power supply functions only when it has demand. It has to know how much power to produce from the switching process used to generate its DC voltages. A power supply without some demand will not function properly and may even damage itself. Never "test" a power supply without connecting it to at least one 12V line — for example, a disk drive.

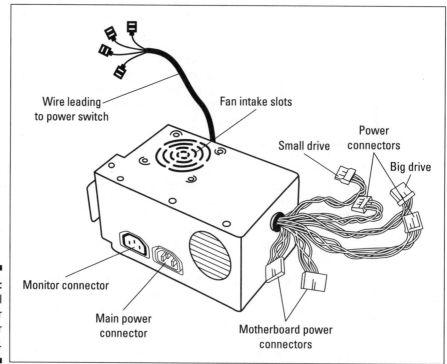

Wire leading to power switch

Fan intake slots

Power connectors

Small drive

Big drive

Monitor connector

Main power connector

Motherboard power connectors

Figure 10-1:
A personal computer power supply.

Protecting against Power Evils

There are certainly ways you can fight back against the evils of external power. In fact, several levels of protection exist, ranging from none to too much, that you can use to protect your computer system from power problems. It's all in how much you want to spend, with costs ranging up to several hundred dollars or more.

For the A+ Core Hardware exam, be very familiar with the benefits and limitations of the various types of power protection devices described in this section. The exam has few trick questions, but one that you might look for is, "Which of these devices provide surge suppression?" The answer is that almost every one of these devices provides surge suppression. So, don't be tempted to quickly choose "surge suppressor." Consider the other answers as well.

Two types of damage can be done to the PC by electrical forces: catastrophic and degradation. *Catastrophic damage* is when the device is destroyed all at once in a single event. *Degradation* is when a device is damaged over a period of instances and begins to fail or has intermittent problems.

In the following section, I discuss some of the ways you can practice safe power.

Never, never, never, cut the grounding pin off a PC power plug cord. This is like looking the power monster in the face and smugly daring it to bite you.

Suppressing the surge

Most users plug their computers into a power strip or surge suppressor. These devices, which provide protective levels ranging from psychological to pretty good, are generally available. At the psychological level is the less-than-ten-dollars power strip, which is not much more than a fancy extension cord. At the pretty-good level are full surge suppressors that include line conditioning. You will see the following line so often in the discussion on power protection that you will think it is my mantra, but typically, the more you pay, the better the protection.

The primary component of a surge suppressor is a Metal Oxide Varistor (MOV). The MOV protects the computer by taking the hit from voltage spikes. The problem with MOV is that one big spike or an accumulation of small surges over time can knock it out. Some surge suppressors have a light to indicate that the MOV is still all right.

A surge suppressor reduces power problems by absorbing spikes and surges and by smoothing out line noise (this is called line conditioning). Surge suppressors at the high end of the cost range offer more protection, but some protection is always better than none. Unfortunately, how much protection you have really depends on how much you pay.

Know the following two main features when choosing a surge suppressor for the test:

- ✔ **Clamping voltage.** The voltage at which the suppressor begins to protect the computer.

- ✔ **Clamping speed.** The time lapse before the protection begins, or how much time elapses between detection and protection.

Not all surge suppressors include line conditioning. Check the box and any literature carefully when buying one.

Here are some other things to look for (familiarize yourself with the units of measures — Joules, decibels, and watts — used in the following descriptions):

- ✔ **Energy Absorption:** Surge suppressors are rated in Joules, which measures their capability to absorb energy. The higher the rating, the better the protection: 200 Joules is basic protection, 400 is good protection, and 600 is superior protection. You need to be familiar with Joules for the test.

- ✔ **Line Conditioning:** The line conditioning capability of a surge suppressor is measured in decibels. The more decibels of noise reduction, the better the line conditioning.

- ✔ **Protection Indicators:** If you have a surge suppressor, you're familiar with the LED that indicates you are protected. Unfortunately, how reliable the indicator is depends on how much you paid. Less-expensive units will absorb enough power over time to degrade them. However, one thing is for sure — if the LED is out, get a new suppressor. You have no way of knowing whether you're protected if a suppressor has no indicator.

- ✔ **Levels of Protection:** Surge suppressors have three levels of protection that indicate the maximum number of watts the suppressor allows to pass through to anything plugged into it. The standard ratings are 330 (best), 400 (better), and 500 (good).

Underwriters Laboratories (UL) has established a standard (UL 1449) for surge suppressors. A suppressor with UL approval has met this standard and should protect your system.

Conditioning the line

Line conditioners filter the power stream to eliminate line noise. Because they're usually expensive, few PC users use a true line conditioner, preferring to purchase this capability in other devices, such as a surge suppressor.

Protecting the back door

A connection to the computer that most people forget when securing the power is the telephone cord connected to the internal modem. In the event of an electrical storm or lightning strike, power can surge up the telephone lines just as mean, fast, and nasty as on the power lines. When installing a surge protector, be sure it has phone-line protection. Another way to get this protection is to install a separate phone/modem isolator, an inexpensive device you can buy at any electronics or computer store. This may not be on the test, but you should know it anyway.

Hedging your bet

An uninterruptible power supply (UPS) tries to live up to its name by providing a constant (uninterrupted) power stream to the computer. Under normal conditions, a surge protector can also handle brownout conditions. When the power drops below a certain level or is disrupted completely, the UPS kicks in and provides power for a certain number of minutes, or even hours in some cases. Expect a question or two on UPSs.

All UPS units have two sets of circuits. One side is the AC circuit that, in effect, is an expensive surge suppressor. The other side is the battery and DC to AC conversion. Yes, that's right — DC to AC conversion. The batteries store a DC charge that must be converted to AC because that's what the PC expects. Two types of UPS units are available and differ in the following ways:

- ✔ **Standby UPS.** Operates normally from its AC side. When the power drops, it switches over to its battery backup side.

- ✔ **In-line UPS.** Operates normally from its DC or battery backup side. The AC side is only used in the event of a problem with the battery-powered circuits.

UPS units are often confused with a standby power supply (SPS), or battery backup, which supplies power only when none is available and has no power-conditioning capabilities.

Never plug a laser printer into a conventional PC UPS. Laser printers draw a tremendous amount of power at startup and use power in "gulps" during their fusing processes, and few UPS units can handle the demand. Laser printers also inject noise back into the UPS or surge suppressor.

Saving the planet

The A+ Core Hardware exam tests you on environmental issues surrounding the PC and its peripherals, including the hazards and safeguards.

To reduce the amount of electricity consumed by computers, the U.S. Environmental Protection Agency (EPA) established guidelines for energy efficiency under a program called U.S. Green Star, also known as Energy Star. On Green Star systems, the power supply works with the computer's components and some peripherals to reduce the power they use when idle.

Green Star devices have a standby program that puts them into sleep mode after the device has been idle for a certain period. In sleep mode, the device reduces 99 percent of its power consumption and uses no more than 30 watts of power.

The Power Supply

This section concentrates on the first exam objective listed at the beginning of the chapter: recognizing PC power supply terms, concepts, and functions. This section covers a few questions you should expect on the test.

The power supply is a black or silver box with a fan inside and cables coming out of it. It's located either at the back of a desktop case or at the top of a tower or mini-tower case. The power supply is distinctive because of its big yellow warning label with scary-looking symbols and warnings. The purpose of this label is to warn you not to try to fix a power supply.

A caution sticker (you'll know it — it says "Caution") on an electric or electronic device in a PC alerts you to possible equipment damage. A warning label (says "Warning" and has lightning bolts, a skull and crossbones, or the like) alerts you to possible electrocution, which could hurt you.

Just to quench your curiosity, inside the power supply, one part in particular should keep you out: a 1,000-microfarad capacitor. Capacitors store electricity, even when the power is off. This particular capacitor performs line conditioning by absorbing any power coming in above the normal level and using it to replace power below normal levels. If you were to touch the capacitor, it would shock you — potentially with bodily harm or worse. Because you can buy a new power supply in the range of $25 to $80, I'm not sure it's worth risking your life to open up the power supply to try to fix it. A good quality power supply should last for years, providing the computer with stable electrical current, assuming that it has been protected adequately. On the other hand, a low quality, faulty, or overloaded power supply can cause all kinds of problems in a system. A bad power supply can cause hard disk drives to develop bad sectors and affect memory to cause what seem like software bugs — problems that are usually hard to pin on the power supply.

Anatomy of the power supply

Be familiar with the parts of the power supply for the exam.

The features you can access on the outside of the power supply are incredibly standard even between form factors. The primary power supply components are

- ✔ **Power cord:** I think you know what this is.

- ✔ **Passthrough connectors:** Located on the back of the power supply. In the past, these connectors were used primarily to plug a monitor into the power supply, which enables you to turn the monitor on and off with the computer's power switch. This feature has all but disappeared from PCs, because it's no longer necessary to plug the monitor into the power supply.

- ✔ **Power switch:** On older PCs, this switch extended through the case wall from the power supply on a back corner of the PC. More recently, the power switch is now on the front of the case. In the newer ATX power supply, the power switch works differently altogether. Instead of a physical on/off switch connected directly to the power supply, the switch is now electronic. You don't so much turn on or off the computer as you request the motherboard to do it.

- ✔ **110V/220V Selector switch:** Allows you to select between the two voltages. If a power supply has one, be sure that it's set correctly. This switch comes in handy when you jaunt over to Europe with your PC.

When a monitor is plugged into the power supply's passthrough connector, the monitor is not being powered by the PC's internal power supply. It's called a passthrough plug because it passes the AC power through. You have only gained the convenience of turning the monitor on and off with the PC.

Cooling it

The power supply also contains the main cooling fan that controls airflow through the PC case. The power supply fan is the most important part of a PC's cooling system. Air is forced to flow through the computer case and over the motherboard and electronic components, which generate heat as they work. Any interruption to the airflow can cause sensitive components to degrade or fail. The power supply fan should be kept clean and clear.

Only with the case closed and intact does the PC cooling system function at its optimum level.

If a power supply's wattage rating is sufficient to supply the computer's electrical requirements, the fan should be adequate to handle the computer's cooling needs, although Pentium-class processors require additional cooling or heatsinks of their own.

As I cover in more detail later in this chapter, two popular form factors for power supplies exist: the Baby AT and the ATX. I bring up form factors here only because these two types of power supplies cool the system differently. A form factor defines the size, shape, and fit of the components of a particular case, motherboard, and power supply combination.

✔ The Baby AT, which has been the standard until the past year or two, cools the system by pulling air out of the case and blowing it out through the fan. You can feel the air blowing out of the fan on this type of power supply. If you've ever opened up an old PC AT computer that has been in use for a while without the case being opened, you know firsthand one of the primary problems with this type of cooling. Room dust, smoke, chalk in school settings, and all else is sucked into the computer to accumulate on grills, wires, components, and so on. This buildup can affect the cooling system's capability of cooling the motherboard and drives by restricting the airflow. Buildup also can possibly short out the motherboard or other components.

✔ The ATX form of power supply sucks air into the case. This method helps keep the case clean by pressurizing the inside of the case. The power supply is situated on the board so that air blows straight over the processor and RAM. This was originally intended to eliminate the need for a CPU fan, but nearly all Pentium-class processors include their own fans and heatsinks.

In either case, all expansion slot filler slides should be in place and the case should be in place and intact to allow the cooling system to do its job.

Overloading the power supply

A PC's power supply directly controls its expandability. Every power supply has a maximum power demand that it can support, expressed in watts. When you upgrade a PC by adding an additional drive, replacing the motherboard, or installing a new processor, the responsibility falls on the power supply to produce the power the PC now demands. I mentioned earlier in this chapter the problems that come with an overloaded power supply.

Power supplies are rated in watts capacity, which should not be confused with watts used. A 250-watt power supply has the capacity to convert up to 250 watts of power, but if its system only demands 100 watts, then it only converts 100 watts. You can't burn up a system with a high wattage power supply; it doesn't work that way. However, it does run up your electric bill.

Converting power

What the power supply does is simple: It converts AC to DC. Any number of devices exist to help convert currents one way or another, for example, the power converter I plug into my van's dashboard so my kids can watch video-tapes as we motor along. Another type allows my portable CD player to plug into the wall when the batteries are dead. Another lets my notebook PC run from an AC supply, while it charges the batteries. If only it were as simple for the desktop PC as it is for the notebook PC. The PC power supply must provide a variety of voltages at different strengths and manage some power-related signals for the motherboard.

Standard voltages

Know this stuff for the test. The power supply provides the following voltages to the motherboard and drives:

- ✔ **+5V:** The standard voltage of motherboards with all processors below 100 MHz (early Pentium, 486, 386, and so on) and many peripheral boards.

- ✔ **+12V:** Used primarily for disk drive motors and similar devices. Modern motherboards also pass this voltage to ISA bus expansion slots.

- ✔ **–5V and –12V:** Included in most power supplies for compatibility with older systems. Most modern motherboards don't use either of these voltages. Power supplies that produce these values do so at very low (less than 1 amp) amperage. Check the label on your power supply.

> ✔ **+3.3V:** The standard voltage level for motherboards for 100 MHz processors and above (Pentium, Pentium Pro, and equivalent chips run at 3.3V (some use even lower voltages internally). Upgraded motherboards must convert the 5V signal from the power supply into 3.3V for the processor, requiring a voltage regulator on the motherboard. Newer power supplies provide the 3.3V power for the CPU directly.

Concentrate on which voltages are used with which types of devices, especially the voltage of all Pentium-class processors, listed in Table 10-1. For example, disk drives use the +12V lines, the Pentium processor uses 3.3V, and the other lines (+/–5V and –12V lines) are primarily used for backward compatibility.

Processor voltages

Processors actually have two levels of power that they use. The first, which is called *external voltage,* or *I/O voltage* is the voltage used to power the devices mounted to motherboards compatible with a certain processor. The second level of power for a processor is its *internal voltage.* The internal voltage is important in the sense that the higher this number, the more heat the processor generates. As you study the voltages listed in Table 10-1 for the Pentium-class processors, you'll notice a trend of smaller internal voltage levels.

Table 10-1		Processor Voltage Levels	
Processor	**Version**	**External**	**Internal**
80486DX4	Intel	3.3	3.3
AMD & Cyrix 5x86		3.45	3.45
Pentium	60–66	5	5
Pentium	75–200	3.3/3.5	3.3/3.5
Pentium MMX		3.3	2.8
6x86		3.3	3.3
AMD K5		3.52	3.52
Pentium Pro	150	3.1	3.1
Pentium Pro	166+	3.3	3.3
Pentium II		3.3	2.8
Pentium II	Celeron/Xeon	3.3	2.0
Pentium III		3.3	2.0
Pentium III	Xeon	3.3	1.65

Processor	Version	External	Internal
AMD Athlon		3.3	1.6
AMD K6-2	w/3DNow	3.3	2.2
AMD K6	166–200	3.3	2.9
6x86 MX		3.3	2.9

Fitting it in the box

Form factor refers to the shape and dimensions of a device. PC cases are designed to hold a particular power supply form factor. The power supply must match the designed form factor of the case as well as match its power to the motherboard. The form factor of a power supply is not often an issue except for upgrades and build-your-owns, because the power supply is usually purchased already installed in the case. The form factor of the case is usually more of an issue.

In general, the form factors of the motherboard are the same for the case and the power supply. The most common form factors used today are the Baby AT, the oldest standard that has been used for PCs until recently, and the ATX, the newest form factor.

The Baby AT is what most people think of as the standard desktop case and power supply. It will be around for quite some time, given the number of PCs in use with this form factor. Figure 10-2 shows the back of a Baby AT power supply. On the left side of the power supply is the power switch intended to extend through a hole in the system case.

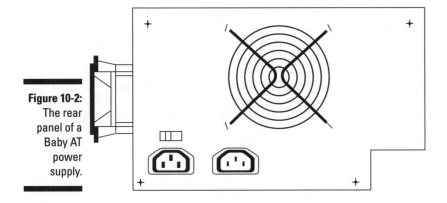

Figure 10-2:
The rear panel of a Baby AT power supply.

The ATX form factor has essentially replaced the Baby AT for new systems. The ATX power supply differs from the Baby AT power supply in three primary ways:

✔ ATX has additional voltage and power lines that are used to signal and control the power supply.

✔ The fan blows into the case instead of out like the Baby AT, which helps keep the case clean.

✔ The ATX power supply turns on and off with electronic signaling and not a physical power switch. It can also be switched on and off by software, such as a Windows shutdown.

Figure 10-3 shows the back of an ATX power supply.

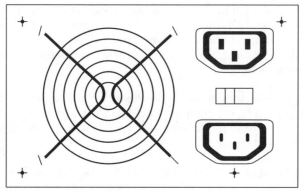

Figure 10-3:
The rear panel of an ATX power supply.

Connecting the Power

The Core Hardware exam includes power questions that relate to the motherboard, disk drives, and other devices. Some of these questions may appear to be about the device but will, in fact, be power and power connection questions. Review this section carefully.

The bundles of wire hanging out of the power supply are what the power supply is all about. They are the lines that carry juice to the various parts of the computer. Depending on the form factor, four or five bundles of wire come from the power supply.

Always be sure that the power supply is unplugged by removing its power cord from its back before you attach its connectors inside the PC.

Motherboard connectors

Don't expect to see any questions on the A+ Core Hardware exam on the specific pinouts (pin assignments) of power supply connectors. However, you may see questions dealing specifically with the power supply and the motherboard connections of specific form factors. The only form factors mentioned specifically in the test objectives are the Baby AT and the ATX; the ones I recommend you study.

You can definitely tell which form factor you have by the motherboard power connectors. The Baby AT power supply has two 6-wire connectors, and the ATX has a single 20-wire keyed connector.

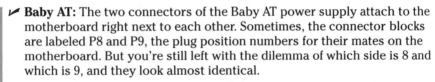

✔ **Baby AT:** The two connectors of the Baby AT power supply attach to the motherboard right next to each other. Sometimes, the connector blocks are labeled P8 and P9, the plug position numbers for their mates on the motherboard. But you're still left with the dilemma of which side is 8 and which is 9, and they look almost identical.

The P8 and P9 connectors are oriented correctly if all four of the black (ground) wires (two on each plug) are together in the middle. Any other orientation will likely damage the motherboard.

✔ **ATX:** The ATX power supply must be used with an ATX motherboard. Together, they eliminate any confusion with the power connection through a single 20-wire keyed connector. A keyed connector usually has a prong, lip, or finger that prevents it from being connected incorrectly. The ATX power supply also has power connectors for the front panel.

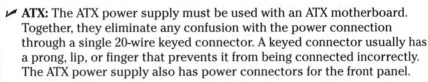

The ATX power supply is always on. Power is supplied to the motherboard even when the system power is off. Always disconnect the power cord from the back of the case before working on one.

Drive power connectors

Most power supplies have either three or four four-wire power connectors for internal drives. Two types and sizes of connectors exist and are easy to tell apart.

The larger power supply connector shown in Figure 10-4, which is also called a Molex connector, is used to connect almost all hard drives, CD-ROM and DVD drives, and 5¼-inch floppy drives.

Figure 10-4:
Some drives
use the
larger
(Molex)
power
supply
connector
and others
use the
smaller
(Berg)
power
supply
connector.

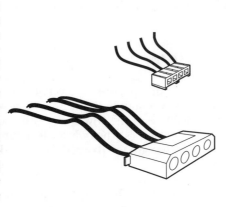

The smaller plug shown in Figure 10-4, which is also called a Berg connector, is used by 3½-inch floppy drives, some tape drives, and a few others. These connectors are keyed, so they can't be installed backwards, try as I might.

Troubleshooting the Power Supply

Although I don't recall any questions about troubleshooting the power supply on the tests, that doesn't mean there won't be any. At least review this section to remind yourself of the situations mentioned.

The power supply is obviously a very important component of the PC, but did you know that it's also the one most likely to fail? Day in and day out it suffers the slings and arrows of mean and nasty electrical power, sacrificing itself for the good of your computer. A recent study shows that, on average, the common workstation or desktop PC suffers over 120 power "events" every month. Not surprisingly, it can develop problems, if not a complex.

Three conditions exist in which you need to check out a power supply:

✔ After switching on the PC's power, nothing happens.

Solution: The first problem is the easiest to diagnose. After determining that the power cord is plugged into the power supply, the power cord is plugged into the surge suppressor, the surge suppressor switch is on and working properly, and power is available at the wall plug, you know that either the power switch is bad or the power supply itself has completely failed. In either case, you should replace the power supply.

Never stick anything into the fan to try to get it to rotate. This approach doesn't work, and it's way beyond dangerous.

✔ You've tried everything else to track down an intermittent problem to no avail. Although rarely thought of first, the power supply can be the real culprit in a power-related failure. However, determining the power-related part may prove difficult.

Solution: How can you tell whether the power supply is going bad? You can look for a number of symptoms: overheating, occasional boot failures or errors, frequent parity errors, noisy operation, or mild electrical shocks when you touch the case.

If you ever receive a shock (other than ESD) when you touch the case, you have power supply problems of the first magnitude — replace the power supply immediately!

✔ You're planning a big upgrade (new motherboard, new hard drive, DVD, and more), and you're worried that your power supply may be too weak to handle the new load.

Solution: When upgrading, remember that power supplies are rated by the wattage they produce. You can currently get from 100 to 600 watt units today. Unless you're building a super server with quad Pentium III Xeons and four or five internal SCSI drives, a power supply rated between 230 to 300 watts should work well for most average systems.

A quick and easy way to troubleshoot a computer power supply is to put your hand in front of the cooling fan. If it isn't blowing out air, chances are the power supply is bad, unless it's an ATX form factor case, in which case the system board may have a bad power switch.

To unplug or not to unplug

The exam may include a question on whether you should unplug the computer before working on it. My advice is as follows:

✔ If the ATX form factor is named or no form factor is mentioned specifically, the PC should be unplugged when you're working on it. ATX motherboards are hot — they have power going to them even when the power supply is powered off.

✔ Otherwise, if the Baby AT form factor is specified, the PC should be left plugged into the wall outlet to provide an earth ground. Somehow, I really doubt that you'll be asked for this information. Unplugging the PC when working on it and protecting it with good ESD devices are always good ideas.

Diagnosing POST problems

You may run into situational questions on the Core Hardware exam that require you to know which FRM (field replaceable module) is involved given a certain set of symptoms. Here are a few symptoms that indicate a power supply problem:

- ✔ The power light on the front panel is off.
- ✔ The power supply fan isn't operating.
- ✔ The computer sounds either a continuous beep or doesn't beep at all.
- ✔ The computer sounds a repeating short beep.
- ✔ The computer displays either a POST error in the 020–029 series (Power Good signal error) or a parity error.

Taking preventive measures

A number of actions can lengthen the life of a power supply. Many are environmental, some require equipment, and some are just plain common sense. They are:

- ✔ Run the computer in a cool, moderately humid environment. The cooler the air entering the fan, the better. The power supply produces heat like all other transformers. Use an air-conditioned room if possible.
- ✔ Either reduce the amount of dust and smoke in the air around the computer, or plan to clean it often. Blow the dust bunnies off the fan and power supply grills frequently using a can of compressed air. It can't hurt to do the same for the inside of the case every once in a while either.
- ✔ Use a surge protector, a UPS, or better yet, a true line conditioner.

Prep Test

1 A device that can supply backup power to a PC when the electricity fails and provides for line conditioning as well is called a(n)

A ○ SPS

B ○ UPS

C ○ Surge suppressor

D ○ Line conditioner

2 A device that protects a PC against overvoltage is called a(n)

A ○ UPS

B ○ Power conditioner

C ○ Surge suppressor

D ○ All the above

3 While you repair a PC, it should be

A ○ Plugged in

B ○ Unplugged

C ○ Turned on

D ○ Sober

4 A PC conforming to the Green Star standard reduces what percentage of its power consumption in Sleep mode?

A ○ 99

B ○ 90

C ○ 92

D ○ 96

5 What electronic component in the PC power supply absorbs most power spikes?

A ○ Resistors

B ○ Varistors

C ○ Coils

D ○ Capacitors

6 **What are two important factors to consider when selecting a surge suppressor?**

A ○ Switching rate and Joules dispersed

B ○ Switching speed and clamping speed

C ○ Clamping speed and clamping voltage

D ○ Joules dispersed and wattage

7 **Which of the following devices should not be connected to a UPS?**

A ○ A laser printer

B ○ A monitor

C ○ A PC power supply

D ○ You can connect any device to a UPS

8 **When the electrical power system fails completely, it's called a(n)**

A ○ Brownout

B ○ Blackout

C ○ Overvoltage

D ○ Undervoltage

9 **A power supply failure detected during the POST may be indicated with**

A ○ A constant beeping sound

B ○ No beep codes at all

C ○ An error code in the 020–029 range

D ○ All the above

10 **What are the two types of uninterruptible power supplies?**

A ○ Standby and interactive

B ○ In-line and out-line

C ○ Standby and in-line

D ○ In-line and interactive

Answers

1 **B.** A battery backup supplies only backup electricity. A surge suppressor provides line conditioning protection as does a true line conditioner. The uninterruptible power supply (UPS) does both. *See "Hedging your bet."*

2 **C.** Overvoltage is the same as a power surge or a spike. A surge suppressor absorbs the spike and prevents it from damaging your computer. *Review "Suppressing the surge."*

3 **B.** ATX form factor power supplies should be unplugged because they provide power to the motherboard even when the power supply itself is turned off. *Check out "To unplug or not to unplug."*

4 **A.** A device that conforms to the U.S. Green Star standard reduces its power consumption to less than 30 watts and reduces its overall consumption by 99 percent. *Try "Saving the planet."*

5 **D.** A capacitor is used to absorb a power spike and can be used to provide power to bring up an undervoltage condition. *Charge over to "The Power Supply."*

6 **C.** The clamping voltage is the voltage level at which the surge suppressor engages; the clamping speed is how soon after detection suppression begins. *Consider "Suppressing the surge."*

7 **A.** Laser printers draw a tremendous amount of power at startup, and few UPS units have enough power to handle the demand. *See "Hedging your bet."*

8 **B.** A blackout is the complete loss of power from the general electrical power supply system. *Review "The paradox of external power."*

9 **D.** All of these are indications that there may be a power supply failure. *Check out "Diagnosing POST problems."*

10 **C.** The standby UPS is like a big surge suppressor with a battery backup; the in-line UPS is a big self-charging battery that runs your computer with an emergency AC line, just in case. *Look at "Hedging your bet."*

Part III
Getting Data In, Out, and All About

The 5th Wave   By Rich Tennant

"It appears a server in Atlanta is about to go down, there's printer backup in Baltimore, and an accountant in Chicago is about to make level 3 of the game `Tomb Pirate`."

In this part . . .

You'll find that coverage on ports, connectors, printers, and other peripheral devices that you have to know for the A+ exam. Without peripherals and the means to connect them to the PC, there would be no interface to the PC for the user. In the latest versions of the Core Hardware and OS Technologies exams, the configuration and setup of the PCs ports, the use of the appropriate connectors, and how they are managed through the operating system are very important topics.

Chapter 11

Serial, Parallel, and Other Ports

• •

Exam Objectives

▶ Identifying common peripheral ports, cabling, and connectors

▶ Listing the system resource assignments of standard port types

▶ Explaining the troubleshooting procedures for the common port types

• •

*1*f you've ever spent hours trying to get a parallel port to accept a serial printer connected to a serial-to-parallel converter in hopes of salvaging a customer's old system printer, then you and I share a deep appreciation for the differences among input/output ports and their communications. Parallel ports are often used for printers, and the serial ports are where modems plug in. Although this isn't an altogether bad summarization of their differences, you need to know a bit more about the subtleties of these and a couple of other ports for the A+ Core Hardware exam.

You need to understand the ins and outs of each of the port types described in this chapter. Don't worry about the finite details of each port and its connectors, such as the electronic specifications or the exact pinout assignments of the connector. But you need to know the best use of each port type, the type of connector it uses, and the number of pins in or the shape of its connector. When it matters (I point out when it does), you should also know the standards that specify or define the usage of each connector or port type.

Review the information on ports in this chapter and in Chapters 12, 13, and 14 to gain some background and understanding of their function, the terminology, and their system resource assignments, such as COM and LPT ports, IRQs, and I/O address linkages.

Quick Assessment

Identifying common peripheral ports, cabling, and connectors

1 Serial data is transmitted _____ bit(s) at a time.

2 A(n) _____ cable is used to connect two computers directly via their serial ports.

3 Serial devices are controlled by a(n) _____.

4 The _____ standard covers bidirectional communications through a parallel port.

5 _____ ports are commonly used for printers on most PCs.

6 FireWire and i.Link are proprietary names for the _____ interface.

7 A(n) _____ port can support up to 127 devices.

8 COM1 is commonly assigned to IRQ _____.

Listing the system resource assignments of standard port types

9 LPT1 is typically assigned I/O address _____.

Explaining the trouble-shooting procedures for the common port types

10 Serial port problems are usually caused by _____ conflicts.

Answers

1   *One.* Check out "Understanding Serial Devices."

2   *Null modem.* Take a look at "Cabling the connection."

3   *UART* or *Universal Asynchronous Receiver/Transmitter.* Peek at "Is that UART?"

4   *IEEE 1284.* See "Keeping up to standard."

5   *Parallel.* Review "Looking at Parallel Devices."

6   *IEEE 1394.* Check out "There's fire in the wire: IEEE 1394."

7   *USB.* Look over "Connecting with USB."

8   *4.* See "Setting up a serial port."

9   *378h.* Take a look at "Troubleshooting a parallel port."

10   *System resource.* Review "Troubleshooting a serial port."

Defining Ports and Connectors

In the life of the PC repair technician, the really fun stuff, such as replacing the motherboard, upgrading the processor, or tracking down a transient error in memory, is only a small and diminishing part of the job. The real work involves the more mundane tasks like installing a new printer, connecting an external modem, rigging a nifty new mouse or keyboard, or adding the pizzazz of a digital camera. In spite of my feeble attempts to make these tasks sound exciting, they really boil down to not much more than connecting the device's cable and connector to one of a PC's ports. That's the stuff that fills your hours. That's why the A+ Core Hardware exam places some emphasis on knowing the different types of ports in use, the types of connectors used with them, and the proper way to put the two together.

Here is a checklist of what you need to know about ports and connectors for the test:

- ✔ The types of devices that use each port type
- ✔ The system resources used to configure serial and parallel ports
- ✔ The standards that define each of the common port types
- ✔ The connectors, meaning their sizes and shapes, and cabling used with each port type

Here are the port types you should know for the test:

- ✔ Serial
- ✔ Parallel
- ✔ USB
- ✔ IEEE 1394/FireWire

Understanding Serial Devices

Serial communications, which are conducted through serial ports, involve sending bits in a serial fashion, one bit a time. Serial means that the bits are sent in a series, a single-file stream. This contrasts to parallel, where several bits are sent at the same time side-by-side.

Serial and parallel devices, cables, ports, and communications are all based on the same basic premises:

- ✔ Serial data is transmitted one bit at a time.
- ✔ Parallel data is transmitted eight or more bits at a time.

These fundamental differences characterize all comparisons between these two communications modes. To transmit a single ASCII character via a serial port, eight separate one-bit transmissions are needed. On the other hand, a parallel port needs only one 8-bit wide transmission. In some ways, serial communications are like a single-lane country road, while a parallel transmission is like I-405 with eight lanes. Obviously, parallel communications can handle more data in less time.

Here are some things you may not know about serial ports and communications (and even if you already know it, this is still a good review for the test):

✔ A serial transmission moves less data than a parallel transmission for example, but it has more oomph and can travel a greater distance. A serial cable can be up to 50 feet long (compared to the standard 15-feet limit of a parallel cable). Beyond that distance, the data begins to lose its oomph and data errors can occur.

✔ Most serial devices are external devices that plug into the PC via a *serial port.* Serial ports are also called *COM ports,* or *RS-232 ports.*

RS-232 stands for IEEE (Institute of Electrical and Electronic Engineers, Inc.) "reference standard number two hundred thirty-two," and the term *COM* is used these days to mean serial port, although it's rumored to be an abbreviation for communications port.

✔ Serial ports are usually added to the PC via an expansion board, although newer computers now have one or two mounted on the motherboard as well.

If you look at the ports available on the back of the computer, serial ports are easy to recognize because they're always either a 9- or 25-pin male D-type connector. In contrast, a parallel port, which is similar in size and shape, is always a female connector regardless of how many pins it has. No gender jokes, please!

✔ Serial connectors are called DB-9 and DB-25. The *DB* stands for *data bus,* and the number is the number of pins in the connector. There are different configurations for serial connectors that use differing numbers of pins, but rarely are all the pins used. All serial connectors are DB type "D"-shaped connectors, but not all DB connectors are serial.

✔ PCs use only nine pins in a serial connection, which is why many PCs use the DB-9 connector in place of the DB-25 with its way-too-many and wasted pins. You will find the DB-25 plug on many older PCs, multipurpose adapter cards, and some modems, although it's becoming more and more rare.

✔ Nearly all PCs include the serial ports designated as COM1 and COM2, which are assigned to interrupt requests IRQ4 and IRQ3, respectively. Some PCs may also support COM3 and COM4 serial ports, which by default are also assigned to IRQ4 and IRQ3. On systems with all four serial ports, you may need to switch I/O port and IRQ assignments to accommodate them, especially if you plan to use them simultaneously.

✔ When serial ports are added to the PC via an expansion card (or cards), commonly COM1 uses a DB-9 connector and COM2 uses a DB-25 connector. However, no standard exists for this, so you may need to look at the card to see how the connections are labeled. It should come as no surprise that COM1 is labeled *COM1,* and COM2, well, you get it.

Setting up a serial port

Every PC technician needs to know and understand how serial devices and ports operate to ensure the proper installation of serial devices. For the A+ Core Hardware exam, you need to be familiar with serial communications terminology, its system resource assignments, and the purpose of a serial port's components.

Table 11-1 lists the system resource assignments for the common serial ports found on most PCs. Be sure you have these assignments engraved into your brain before the test.

Table 11-1	Serial Port System Resource Assignments	
Logical Device	*IRQ*	*I/O Address*
COM1	IRQ 4	3F8h
COM2	IRQ 3	2F8h
COM3	IRQ 4	3E8h
COM4	IRQ 3	2E8h

I don't have any cute little sayings to help you remember these assignments, so you just have to memorize them. However the *8h* part of the I/O address is the same for all COM ports, so all you need to do is remember that the odd-numbered ports (COM1 and COM3) have the odd I/O addresses (3F8h and 3E8h) and the even-numbered ports have the even I/O addresses (2F8h and 2E8h). In both cases, the IRQ is one more than the first number of the I/O port. I was right in the first place: It's probably much easier just to memorize them. Here are some of the key words in serial-speak that you may find lurking on the exam:

✔ **Data bits:** Indicates the number of bits used in the character coding scheme, or data word. Some systems use seven bits and others eight bits, with no other choices available.

✔ **Flow control (handshaking):** The embodiment of the protocol used to control the dialog of two serial devices. In general, flow control is used to manage the data flow by sending a character or signal to stop it.

Usually the flow control method used also has a means for restarting the data flow. See "DTE to DCE, over" for more details.

✔ **Parity:** Actually a group of five choices: even, odd, space, mark, or none. Parity is a way of checking whether the correct number of bits was sent and received. Most modems in use today do not use parity (a parity setting of none). Regardless of the setting, both devices in a serial communications must be set the same.

✔ **RTS/CTS (request-to-send/clear-to-send):** Sends signals to specific pins to stop and start the data flow. The CTS signal indicates that a device is ready to accept data, and the RTS signal indicates when a device is ready to send data.

✔ **Stop bits:** Used in certain serial communications to indicate the beginning and end of data words.

✔ **XON/XOFF:** One of the two most common forms of flow control, it sends control characters to stop the flow of data (XOFF) and restart it again (XON). This is the software method of flow control.

DTE to DCE, over

After a serial device such as a modem is connected to the PC, each takes on a designation as either the Data Terminal Equipment (DTE) or the Data Communications Equipment (DCE). When you connect a modem to a PC, the modem becomes the DCE and the PC is the DTE. These designations are used to determine which device initiates and controls the conversation between the two devices at various points in their interaction.

Table 11-2 lists the pin assignments of a serial connection.

Don't waste your time memorizing these pinouts. Instead, pay attention to what each pin is assigned to do and the role it would play in passing data back and forth to another device.

Table 11-2	Serial Connection Pin Assignments	
Pin Number	*Designation*	*Activity*
1	Carrier Detect (CD)	Indicates a connection is established.
2	Receive Data (RD)	All incoming data is received on this pin.
3	Transmit Data (TD)	All outgoing data is sent on this pin.

(continued)

Table 11-2 (continued)

Pin Number	Designation	Activity
4	Data Terminal Ready (DTR)	The host device (such as the PC) is ready to communicate.
5	Signal Ground	Not used on PC systems.
6	Data Set Ready (DSR)	The connected device (such as the modem) is able to communicate.
7	Request to Send (RTS)	Host device wants to communicate.
8	Clear to Send (CTS)	Connected device is ready to communicate.
9	Ring Indicator (RI)	The telephone is ringing.

The serial connector's pins are used to send signals to create what amounts to a conversation (the *handshaking*) between two serial devices. Picture that each pin is a light that's turned on to indicate the next of a sequence of events. Handshaking accomplishes the hardware flow control (the most common method) between the PC and the modem, as follows:

1. The DTE (Data Terminal Equipment), or PC, turns on the DTR (Data Terminal Ready) signal, indicating that it's good to go.

2. The DCE (Data Communications Equipment) acknowledges this message by turning on the DSR (Data Set Ready) that says, "Me too."

3. The DTE turns on its RTS (Request to Send) signal to let the DCE know it is ready to receive data.

4. The DCE acknowledges this request with a CTS (Clear To Send) that replies, "Here it comes!"

5. The data flows one bit at a time until one of the devices needs to stop it. This stopping is indicated by either the RTS or CTS being turned off. The flow starts again when the applicable indicator is turned back on.

Review the above steps until you have a good idea of what happens in a serial communications handshake. You're very likely to see a question that asks you about all or part of this sequence of events.

Cabling the connection

The cable used to connect a PC to a modem is called a serial cable, a modem cable, or a straight-through cable. In this cable, all the pins are connected one to one without any twists, crosses, or other fancy arrangements (that is, unless you need to use a 9- to 25-pin converter should the modem cable come with a 25-pin connector and the PC has a 9-pin serial port).

Although few serial port questions are on the A+ Core Hardware exam, there are some. And expect at least one with "null modem cable" as its answer. On occasion, two PCs are connected in a DTE-to-DTE arrangement. When this happens, the cable's pinout is changed to simulate the action of the modem by cross-connecting a number of the pins and creating what is called a null modem, or modem eliminator, cable. Both the modem cable and the null modem cable are generic, and you can purchase them at any electronics store.

Is that UART?

Serial devices are controlled by a *Universal Asynchronous Receiver/ Transmitter*, or *UART* for short. This specialized integrated circuit is found either on the device adapter card or on the motherboard (for those that have a serial port mounted on it). The UART chip controls all actions and functions of the serial port, including:

- ✔ Controlling all the connectors' pins and their associated signals
- ✔ Establishing the communication protocol
- ✔ Converting the parallel data bits of the data bus into a serial bit stream for transmission
- ✔ Converting the received serial bit stream into parallel data for transmission over the PC's internal data bus

It's probable that the UART will show up as a close-but-no-cigar answer on one or more questions, so be careful not to confuse it with the port itself. You may be asked something like, "Serial communications are controlled by what device?" And if you're not asked, you should be!

Troubleshooting a serial port

If you're having a serial port problem, the cause is most likely a system resource conflict. System resource conflicts include problems such as a serial device that fails intermittently or doesn't work at all, another device that stops working when the serial device is installed, or the PC locking up during the boot sequence.

The test requires that you know how to troubleshoot various situations, and you may encounter a question on troubleshooting a serial port. Don't worry;

there isn't that much to it. Here, let me help you out. To determine the source of the problem, check the following:

- ✔ **Inspect the port for bent pins.** Certain pins must be absolutely straight in order for the device to work properly.

- ✔ **Ensure that the cable is the appropriate cable for the device.** Some serial devices can't use a straight-through or null modem cable.

- ✔ **Check the Windows Device Manager for system resource conflicts.** An IRQ conflict is the most common error in this area. Remember, only one customer to an IRQ at a time.

- ✔ **Be sure that the serial cable is not more than 50 feet long.** Beyond this distance, you lose data integrity, which shows up any number of ways, none of which are good.

Looking at Parallel Devices

For the exam, know how parallel data is transmitted (eight bits at a time), the standard covering parallel port technologies (IEEE 1284 — see the section "Keeping up to standard"), and that parallel ports are used primarily for printers. This section provides you with additional background material.

There really isn't as much to know about parallel ports as there is to know about serial ports. Parallel data moves around much faster than serial data, which is why the internal bus structures of the PC use a parallel format. Parallel ports were originally designed specifically for printers. However, other devices have been adapted to them, including other types of output devices, input devices, and storage devices, all taking advantage of the bidirectional capabilities of IEEE 1284 parallel devices. These include some external CD-ROMs, external tape drives and Zip drives, as well as file transfer software over proprietary cabling.

Oh, and parallel cables shouldn't be more than 15 feet in length.

Keeping up to standard

You're definitely asked about the fact that IEEE 1284 is the standard for parallel ports, bidirectional parallel communications, and perhaps the ECP protocol.

In 1984, parallel port protocols were standardized by the IEEE (Institute of Electrical and Electronics Engineers). The standard, formally titled "IEEE Standard Signaling Method for a Bi-directional Parallel Peripheral Interface for Personal Computers," or IEEE 1284 as it's commonly known, incorporated the two parallel port standards that had been used up to that point with a new protocol, creating an all-encompassing port model. The standards included in IEEE 1284 are

- ✔ **Standard Parallel Port (SPP)** allows data to travel one-way only — from the computer to the printer.
- ✔ **Enhanced Parallel Port (EPP)** allows data to flow in both directions, but only in one way at a time. This lets the printer communicate to the processor or adapter that it's out of paper, its cover is open, and so on.
- ✔ **Enhanced Capabilities Port (ECP)** allows bidirectional simultaneous communications over a special cable, one that is IEEE 1284 compliant. Many bidirectional cables exist, but they may be EPP cables, which do not support ECP communications.

IEEE 1284 established the standard for bidirectional communications on the parallel port, and the ECP protocol allows for full-duplex (simultaneous communications in two directions) parallel communications.

Troubleshooting a parallel port

Trouble with a parallel port is usually in the device attached to it. Because a parallel port is virtually featureless, it either works or it doesn't (and it usually does). Problems are either in the connector (bent pins or blocked holes), the cable (wrong type — SPP, EPP, or ECP), or the device itself.

An outside chance exists that a problem may be a system resource conflict, but only if more than two parallel ports are on the PC. Remember that printers don't use IRQs or DMA channels, but other parallel port devices do. Check for system resource conflicts when troubleshooting non-printer parallel port problems.

Table 11-3 lists the common system resource assignments for parallel ports:

Table 11-3	Parallel Port System Resource Assignments		
Port	*IRQ*	*I/O Address*	*DMA Channel*
LPT1	IRQ 7	378h	DMA 3 (ECP capabilities)
LPT2	IRQ 5	278h	n/a

Making High-Speed Serial Connections

When the standard PC only had to support a printer and a modem as peripheral devices connected to its ports, a serial port or two and a parallel port or two were enough. But, in today's PC world, where there are scanners, portable hard disks, Zip and Jazz drives, and the no-PC-should-be-without-one force-feedback joysticks, not only would there not be enough serial and parallel ports, but even if there were, they wouldn't be fast enough to keep up.

There were attempts to include as many as eight serial ports on a single PC, but not every new device used a serial port. The next great interface was to be SCSI (Small Computer System Interface). But it was expensive, and a lack of an early standard hurt its chances. So, into the void came two new higher-speed serial data interconnection standards: USB (Universal Serial Bus) and the IEEE 1394 (FireWire).

Connecting with USB

The Universal Serial Bus (USB) is a newer hardware interface that supports low-speed devices such as keyboards, mice, and scanners, as well as higher-speed devices, such as a digital camera. USB, while still a serial interface, provides data transfer speeds of up to 1.5 MBps (12 MBps) for faster devices and a 1.5 MBps sub-channel speed for lower-speed devices. A newer version of the USB standard, USB 2.0, supports up to 480 Mbps for data transfer speeds.

USB uses a unique pair of connectors and ports, as shown in Figure 11-1. USB Type A connectors are used to connect devices directly to a PC or USB hub. You'll find USB Type A connectors on devices with permanently attached cables. USB Type B connectors are found on those devices that have a detachable cable. The cable uses a squarish Type B port on the device and connects to either a Type A or Type B socket (the cable usually has both on the other end) on the PC or hub.

The USB interface supports up to 127 devices on a system. These devices connect both to the PC directly or into one or more USB hubs, as shown in Figure 11-2. The fact that each USB port carries .5 amps of electrical power (which is enough to power most low-power devices, such as a mouse or keyboard) provides a great deal of flexibility for adding additional devices to the system regardless of its location. USB devices that require higher power usually use their own AC adapters.

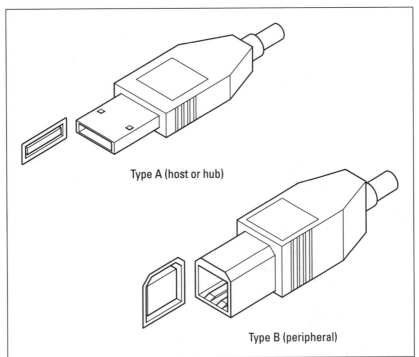

Type A (host or hub)

Type B (peripheral)

Figure 11-1:
USB
connectors
and ports.

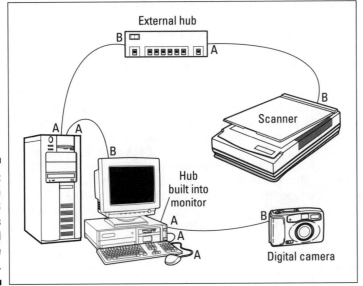

External hub

B

A

B

Scanner

A

A

B

Hub
built into
monitor

A

A

B

A

Digital camera

Figure 11-2:
Multiple
USB
devices
connected
to a single
PC.

The parts of a USB interface

A USB interface has three separate parts: the host, the hubs, and the peripheral devices.

- **USB host:** Just another way to say PC or computer. Your PC is the USB host device that carries the operating system, chipset, and BIOS that support the USB interface.

- **USB hubs:** USB interfaces can be built in a tiered fashion. A hub can be plugged into the host. Other hubs can be plugged into that hub, and USB devices can be plugged into each of the second tier hubs. As long as the whole bus has only 127 devices, including the hubs, there should be no problems.

- **USB devices:** In most cases, you will have only one or two USB devices plugged into your PC, and these will be directly connected to the PC itself.

Nearly all PCs sold today, whether desktop, tower, or notebook, feature at least one, and often two, USB ports.

How a USB bus works

When a USB device is plugged into a USB socket (hot-plugged or hot-swapped), the host, or the hub, detects a change in the voltage on the interface. The host then checks out the new device asking it to identify itself, a process called *enumeration* in USB-speak. The device identifies itself in terms of its type, who made it, what it does, and the amount of bandwidth it requires. The device is given an address code that identifies it uniquely from the other USB devices on the bus. Each device that is attached to the bus, even two of the exact same device, gets a unique address ID so that it can be referenced and addressed by the host.

After the device is assigned its ID, the operating system automatically loads the appropriate device driver or, if necessary, asks the user to provide the driver on a disk or CD-ROM. The good news is that unlike the serial and parallel ports, any resource conflicts are taken care of by the host, and there is no configuration of IRQs, I/O addresses, or DMA channels. When a device is unplugged from the system, the reverse takes place. Again, the host detects the voltage differences, retires the address ID, and notifies the operating system to unload the device driver. USB devices are the PC repairperson's dream, because other than plugging in and unplugging the devices, there is no other configuration or setup to do.

For more information on the Universal Serial Bus, visit the Official USB Homepage at www.usb.org.

There's fire in the wire: IEEE 1394

Another of the high-speed serial interface buses is defined in the IEEE 1394 standard. This standard is also known as the *i.Link* (Sony), *Lynx* (Texas Instruments), and the *FireWire* (Apple), which are proprietary, licensed versions of the IEEE 1394 standard, and the generic version is *High Performance Serial Bus (HPSB)*. The IEEE 1394 standard defines a serial bus protocol that provides data transfer speeds between 100 MBps to 400 MBps (around 12 MBps to 50 MBps) depending on how the standard is implemented. Newer definitions of the 1394 standard, under development by the 1394 Trade Association (www.1394ta.org), hope to provide data speeds in the range of 800 Mbps to 1.6 GBps. The IEEE 1394 connector looks something like a USB connector, except that it's just a bit larger and about halfway between rectangular and square — see Figure 11-3.

Figure 11-3:
The
IEEE 1394
connector
and plug.

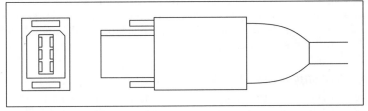

Defining the 1394 bus

The IEEE 1394 bus is similar to the USB interface (see "Connecting with USB" earlier in the chapter) in that it is a high-speed, Plug and Play bus that eliminates the need for devices to have their own power supplies. But, it goes USB one better by providing for *isochronous* (or real-time) data transfers, in which data is transferred within certain time constraints, such as multimedia data, where the audio and video must arrive together.

An IEEE 1394 port supports up to 63 external devices and is considered the link between PCs and consumer electronics. For example, through a 1394 port, a digital video camera can be used to both capture video content and then playback the video after it's been edited on the PC.

The primary difference between 1394 and USB is that 1394 is faster and, generally, more expensive. Therefore, 1394 is used mainly for those devices, such as a video camera, that require larger data transfers in a shorter time period, such as a digital video camera, whereas USB is used for the majority of other peripheral devices. But, another, and perhaps more dramatic, difference is that 1394 is a peer-to-peer interface that doesn't require a host system. Although heresy to PC repair professionals, a 1394 bus can exist quite well with no PC at all. A video camera can easily support and power several devices on a common interface, as shown in Figure 11-4.

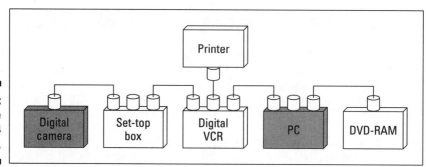

Figure 11-4:
A sample
IEEE 1394
bus.

Applications for 1394

Some applications that you may see for the 1394 standard involve connecting high-end peripheral devices to portable and desktop PCs. The devices that would use the 1394 connection to the PC are audio/visual and multimedia capture and playback devices, video conferencing, printers, scanners, external RAID storage devices, and consumer electronics like digital camcorders, VCRs, DVD units, and set-top boxes.

Software support for 1394

Most current operating systems, including Windows 98 and 2000, support IEEE 1394, but typically only if the device controller is an *OHCI (Open Host Controller Interface)* 1394 controller. Windows 2000 supports IEEE 1394 devices through its Serial Bus Protocol (SBP-2) drivers. On a Windows system, SCSI devices (see Chapter 9) can interface with 1394 devices through SBP-2 driver, which in this case would be called a *tailgate*. This allows a 1394 scanner to be supported by a SCSI driver on the system.

If you encounter a question on the Core Hardware exam that asks you to pick the fastest port from a list, typically an IEEE 1394 FireWire port is the fastest on a PC when compared to a USB, serial, or parallel port.

Working with Wireless Ports

Another kind of port you may find on a PC is one to which you'll never see a connection made, that is unless you have super powers and can see infrared light beams. This port, an *infrared (IR)* port, uses an invisible band from the lower end of the electromagnetic spectrum. IR light stops just short of the beginning of the visible light part of the spectrum. Infrared contrasts with ultraviolet (UV), which is another invisible band at the other, the high, end of the light spectrum. One use of UV light, besides tanning your body, is that it erases an EPROM after about 10 minutes of exposure.

Using this invisible beam, IR devices, which are also called *IrDA (Infrared Data Association)* devices, can be connected to a PC without the need of a physical cable. IrDA ports are common on notebook and other portable computers. IrDA is the trade organization for the infrared device industry that has established a number of standards defining and prescribing the use of the IR connection.

IR devices are line-of-sight devices, which means that they must have a clear, unobstructed path between their transmitters and receivers. IR devices are not new; IR is the wireless mode most often used by TV remotes and other wireless controllers. If anything is blocking the path, you must move either the obstruction or the controller to reopen the line of sight. Using an IR connection, a portable PC or a PDA (personal digital assistant) can connect to another PC, a keyboard, mouse, or a printer without the need for a physical cable connection. The IR connector on your PC or notebook is a small plastic window located usually on the front or side of the case. External IR connections can be attached to the PC via a serial port.

Here are some tips for working with IR devices:

✔ Two IR devices must have a clear, unobstructed line of sight between them.

✔ The devices you are trying to connect via IR must be at least 6 inches apart, but not more than 3 feet.

✔ The transmission pattern of the IR signal is a cone about 30 degrees wide. Make sure the devices are oriented to one another inside the transmission cone.

✔ Make sure that there are no competing IR devices in the vicinity that may interfere with the connection, such as a TV remote control.

Configuring PC Ports

If trouble should arise with any of a PC's ports, whether it's a serial, parallel, USB, IEEE 1394, or IrDA port, more than likely the problem is with the system resource settings. This typically happens when you add new devices to a PC that already supports a wide array or a large number of peripheral devices. Read the documentation that comes with your device and device drivers for the appropriate system resource settings.

Depending on the devices already installed on the PC and the system resources already in use, you need to be on the alert for resource conflicts (usually with IRQs). USB and IEEE 1394 devices are usually assigned to IRQ 11, but you can't count on that. An IrDA port is usually configured as either COM3 or COM4 and uses the default values typically assigned to those ports (refer to Table 11-1).

Prep Test

1 **A parallel port transmits data**

A ○ One data bit at a time

B ○ Four data bits at a time

C ○ One sector at a time

D ○ Eight data bits at a time

2 **A UART chip is used to control**

A ○ The Plug and Play BIOS

B ○ A parallel port

C ○ A serial port

D ○ The processor

3 **A serial port is almost always**

A ○ A female port

B ○ A male port

C ○ A DB-15 connector

D ○ A 36-pin connector

4 **An IrDA port requires which of the following conditions?**

A ○ Line of sight between transmitting and receiving devices

B ○ Digital phone lines

C ○ Clear radio frequency signals

D ○ Low humidity and a clean operating environment

5 **Equipment such as the PC and the printer are designated as**

A ○ DCE devices

B ○ DTE devices

C ○ XON devices

D ○ RTS devices

6 **The I/O address of COM1 is**

A ○ 2E8h

B ○ 3E8h

C ○ 2F8h

D ○ 3F8h

7 The two most common connectors used for serial ports are

A ○ Centronics 25- and 36-pin

B ○ DB-9 and DB-15

C ○ DB-9 and DB-25

D ○ Berg and Molex

8 Which of the following are IEEE 1394 type ports? (Choose two.)

A ❑ FireWire

B ❑ USB

C ❑ Flaming Geyser

D ❑ i.Link

9 Which of the following parallel port protocols allows bidirectional simultaneous communications?

A ○ ECP

B ○ SPP

C ○ EPP

D ○ TCP

10 The most common form of software flow control is

A ○ RTS/CTS

B ○ XON/XOFF

C ○ Stop bits

D ○ Handshaking

Answers

1 **D.** A parallel port carries an entire data character using parallel wires to carry each bit. *See "Looking at Parallel Devices."*

2 **C.** A UART (Universal Asynchronous Receive/Transmit) chip controls the functions and protocol of a serial port. *Review "Is that UART?"*

3 **B.** Serial ports are usually a male connector, whereas parallel ports are female connectors. *Check out "Understanding Serial Devices."*

4 **A.** Infrared (IR) devices require a clear, unobstructed line-of-sight between them. *Take a look at "Working with Wireless Ports."*

5 **B.** If the device could have been a terminal on a mainframe, it's Data Terminal Equipment (DTE). If it's used for communications purposes, like a modem, it's Data Communications Equipment (DCE). *Link up with "DTE to DCE, over."*

6 **D.** If you're having trouble remembering the I/O addresses for the IRQs and COM ports, just remember that COM1 comes first and gets the highest address (3F8). *Study "Setting up a serial port."*

7 **C.** These two connectors are very common on the PC, especially for serial ports. *See "Understanding Serial Devices."*

8 **A, D.** FireWire (Apple) and i.Link (Texas Instruments) are proprietary versions of the IEEE 1394 standard interface. *See "There's fire in the wire: IEEE 1394."*

9 **A.** SPP and EPP are parallel port standards that allow for one- and two-way communications, but both allow communications only one way at a time. TCP is either the stuff in the gasoline or the Internet protocol. *Review "Keeping up to standard."*

10 **B.** RTS/CTS is a hardware flow control method. Handshaking and flow control are synonymous terms, and stop bits are a part of the serial data transmission protocol. *Check out "Setting up a serial port."*

Chapter 12

Input Devices

Exam Objectives

▶ Identifying common input devices

▶ Defining input device terms, concepts, and functions

▶ Cleaning and caring for input devices

▶ Troubleshooting common symptoms and problems

*I*nput devices are included on the A+ Core Hardware exam primarily under installing, configuring, and upgrading field replaceable modules (FRMs). You may also run into preventive maintenance and troubleshooting questions about input devices. Don't expect to find many questions like "How many keys are on the keyboard?" or "How does a mouse work?" The keyboard and mouse, the major input devices, are essentially throwaway technology. It's a lot cheaper, in terms of both labor and parts, to simply replace a problem keyboard or mouse with a new module than to waste the time needed to repair one.

I can't quote statistics as proof (and I looked for them), but I bet that right after power problems ("It worked fine this morning before the power failure") and printer problems ("What does online mean?"), the most common service problem involves a keyboard ("I spilled my Mountain Dew on it and for some reason it stopped working"), or mouse ("The foot pedal doesn't seem to work anymore"). If I'm right, and I can't be too wrong on this, then as a certified PC repair technician, you need to understand how input devices work, connect, and fail. You especially need to know how to plug in the replacement unit.

Quick Assessment

Identifying common input devices

1 The _____ keyboard uses a capacitive membrane module.

2 The most commonly used PC keyboard format is the _____ keyboard.

3 The mouse type that uses captured digital images to detect movement is a(n) _____ mouse.

4 A(n) _____ mouse uses a ball and sensor mechanism to detect movement.

Defining input device terms, concepts, and functions

5 A(n) _____ mouse connects to a mini-DIN-6 connector.

6 The bus mouse attaches to its own _____.

7 The standard IRQ assigned to the mouse is _____.

Cleaning and caring for input devices

8 To remove paper bits and food crumbs from a keyboard, you turn it upside down and _____ it.

9 _____ and _____ are best for cleaning the ball of a mouse.

Trouble-shooting common symptoms and problems

10 A 300-range error code displayed during the boot sequence indicates a(n) _____ error.

Answers

1 *Capacitive.* Review "Capacitive keyboards."

2 *Enhanced.* Check out "Keyboards."

3 *Optical.* Click on "Sighting the optical mouse."

4 *Mechanical.* See "Rolling along with mechanical mice."

5 *PS/2.* Peruse "Connecting the mouse."

6 *Adapter or expansion card.* Review "Connecting the mouse."

7 *IRQ 12.* Check out "Driving Miss Mousey."

8 *Shake.* Review "Practicing keyboard preventive maintenance" for the common keyboard preventive maintenance actions.

9 *A swab, mild soap.* Take a look at "Taking good care of your mouse."

10 *Keyboard.* See "Solving boot sequence problems" for information on common keyboard errors during POST.

Keyboards

The A+ exam focuses on three areas of keyboards: connectors, preventive maintenance, and troubleshooting. If you're confident that you know how a keyboard works, skip to the section, "Connecting the keyboard," later in this chapter. Otherwise, review the following sections for background and terminology.

The obvious place to begin your review of input devices is with the most common input device of all — the keyboard (see Figure 12-1). The keyboard's role on a PC system should be fairly obvious. However, for those of you who have not given it much thought, the keyboard enables the user to communicate with the computer by using keystrokes.

Keyboard styles

The keyboard formats found on any DOS or Windows PC can be grouped into one of four categories:

- **XT:** 83 keys, 10 function keys, numeric keypad and cursor control keys combined, keyboard processor in keyboard. This keyboard, shown in Figure 12-1, is distinctive with its 10 function keys located on the left side.

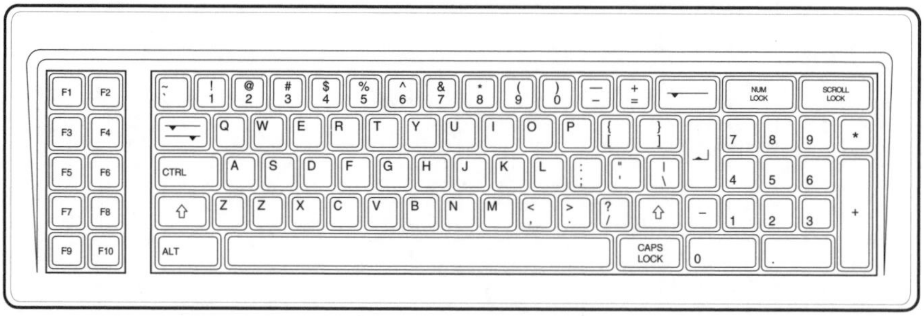

Figure 12-1:
The XT keyboard.

- **AT:** 84 keys, with the addition of the SysRq key, a larger Return key, and the keyboard processor moved to the system board. The 10 function keys are still located on the left side of the keyboard, as shown in Figure 12-2.

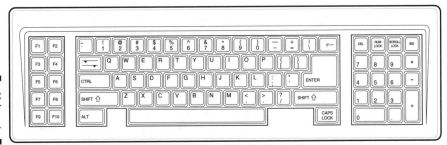

Figure 12-2:
The AT
keyboard.

✔ **Enhanced (also known as AT Enhanced):** 101 keys, including 12 function keys, separate cursor and screen control keys, and a numeric
keypad (see Figure 12-3). This style keyboard may even include buttons
for controlling a CD-ROM drive, the sound, and other built-in features of
the PC. Enhanced is still the most common keyboard type in use.

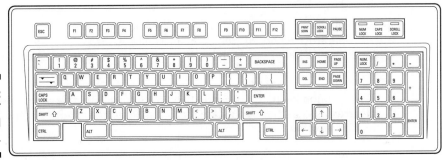

Figure 12-3:
The AT
Enhanced
keyboard.

✔ **Windows:** 104 keys, including keys to pop-up the Windows Start menu
and a key to show the pop-up shortcut menu.

✔ **Natural:** Enhanced keyboard with a built-in wristrest and an arched or
bowed keyboard shape; this keyboard may also separate into segments
(see Figure 12-4). The Microsoft Natural keyboard is probably the best
known of the natural style keyboards, but there are many "clones" on
the market as well.

✔ **Ergonomic:** Although the natural keyboards also claim to be
ergonomic, there are keyboards available that are truly ergonomic,
such as those from DataHand (`www.datahand.com`) and Kinesis
(`www.kinesis-ergo.com`).

REMEMBER

The enhanced keyboard (including ergonomics and naturals), also called the
AT enhanced or the 101-key keyboard, is the most popular type. The newer
keyboard styles are enhanced keyboards underneath their fancy cases.

Figure 12-4:
The natural style keyboard.

Keyboard basics

The keyboard is very simple to operate, and touch-typing aside, most people can operate a keyboard well enough. The keyboard is usually the primary input device for a PC, which is why people can become emotional when it breaks.

The common keyboard is a matrix of mechanical keys. Each key generates an electrical signal that's translated into a specific character or command value in the following way:

1. When you press a key, an electrical circuit closes and a *make code* signal is created.

2. When you release the key, the circuit reopens and a *break code* signal generates.

3. Using these codes, plus the location of the key on the keyboard grid, the keyboard microprocessor generates the *scan code.*

4. The keyboard driver, usually a part of the system BIOS, converts the scan code into the character assigned to that code, depending on the language configured to the keyboard.

Typecasting keyboards

Two types of key mechanisms are used in PC keyboards: *mechanical* and *capacitive.* Usually you know one from the other just by lifting it. As the name suggests, the mechanical is cheaper, bigger, heavier, and bulkier. The capacitive keyboard is sleeker, lighter, more reliable, and more expensive. Understand that the cost comparisons here are not like the difference

between a Yugo and a Mercedes, but more like the relative difference
between a plain hamburger and a deluxe cheeseburger.

Mechanical keyswitch keyboards

A mechanical keyboard is usually heavier than other keyboards and provides
a more positive tactile click to the key action. Although, as with most things,
age can play a part in how well the keys' action holds up. Each key is a separate electromechanical device called a keyswitch. Inside each keyswitch is a
spring to return the key after it's pressed. This spring can lose its bounce
with age and cause operating problems.

Capacitive keyboards

A capacitive keyboard, also called a *membrane keyboard,* is common on many
brand-name systems. It's more reliable and expensive than a mechanical keyboard, although it's very similar in appearance, construction, and operation.
It's much lighter than the mechanical keyboard as well. The one major exception is that in place of metallic contacts, it uses a capacitive membrane
module to generate its signals.

Connecting the keyboard

Connect a keyboard to the computer by plugging its connector, located at the
end of the cable attached to the keyboard, into a matching port on the PC.
You also can connect the keyboard through a wireless *infrared (IR)* system.
Chapter 11 contains more detailed information on the various connectors
used on the PC.

Physically connecting

Unless a keyboard is one of the new wireless breeds (see the section,
"Connections of the wireless kind," later in this chapter), it must be physi-
cally connected to the computer. This connection is made with one of three
connector types: a DIN-type 5-pin connector (shown in Figure 12-5); a mini-
DIN 6-pin, also known as a PS/2 connector (shown in Figure 12-6); or a
Universal Serial Bus (USB) connector (shown in Figure 12-7).

DIN connectors are also called DIN-5 and mini-DIN-6 connectors, representing
the number of pins they use. The mini-DIN connector gets its name due to its
smaller overall size. Some proprietary keyboards connect with the RJ-11 style
plug, but they are disappearing. DIN connectors have a notch or key slot that
prevents an incorrect connection.

The USB connector, shown in Figure 12-7, is becoming quite popular because
it supports a wider range of peripheral devices, not just keyboards and
mouse units. USB devices, which are plug and play interfaces, don't need to
be present when you boot the system.

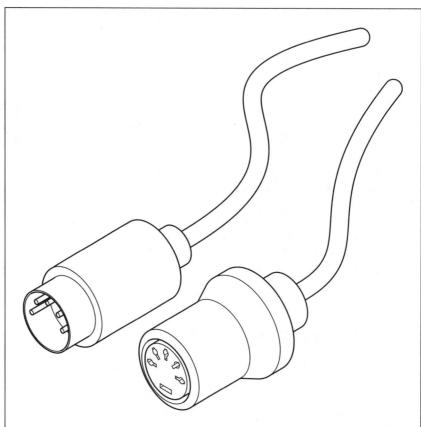

Figure 12-5:
The DIN-5
connector.

Connections of the wireless kind

That little red plastic window on the front of your desktop or notebook computer is actually a "port" through which a keyboard, mouse, or other specially equipped device can be attached. Systems with the little red window have a small infrared receiver built-in, but you can add one to the system through the standard keyboard and mouse (or touchpad) ports.

Wireless (IR) keyboards are considered "line of sight" devices, which means the keyboard must be directly in line (without obstruction) with the receiver to operate properly. However, many use a broadbeam technology that lets you use the keyboard with a wide range of operating angles, including facing away from the system unit. The operating range of most wireless systems is between 1 and 50 feet, but you can usually adjust the operating power to fit the distance at which you plan to use the keyboard.

Figure 12-6:
The mini-
DIN-6
connector.

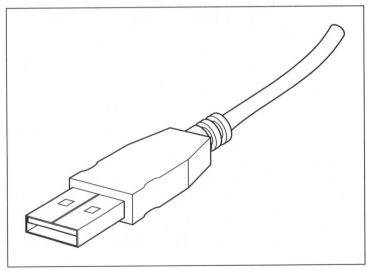

Figure 12-7:
The USB
connector.

Typically, a wireless keyboard has no on/off switch. It comes on when you press a key and puts itself "to sleep" after being idle for a predetermined period of time. That time frame is long enough so that the keyboard doesn't go to sleep between keystrokes, for most people anyway. The "sleep" function saves the life of the keyboard's batteries, which typically last for about a year.

Understanding device drivers

Keyboards, like all peripheral devices, require several types and layers of software to help them work. One of these software layers is the device driver, without which a peripheral device can't function. The more sophisticated the device, the more layers of software are required to make it work. Typically, a device's firmware serves as the device's BIOS. Just for the record, a *peripheral device* is any piece of hardware used for input, output, storage, or communications purposes.

As a rule, keyboards and other input devices are relatively unsophisticated and don't require much beyond the two fundamental layers: *firmware* and *device driver*.

✔ **Firmware:** Contains device interface information, such as IRQ (interrupt request), COM (serial) port assignments, and boot sequence support data, which is used to interact with the hardware, CPU, and the system BIOS (Basic Input/Output System). You find a device's firmware in one of three places:

- On a ROM (Read-Only Memory) chip located on a device controller card inserted into the motherboard

- As a part of the onboard integrated drive electronics located on the device itself

- Incorporated into the system chipset mounted on the motherboard

✔ **Device driver:** A device driver is software that communicates directly with a device and interacts with the PC's operating system. A keyboard's device driver is started during the system boot sequence by the BIOS and operating system. Chapter 5 discusses the interaction of device drivers and the system BIOS, and Part V contains additional information on the interaction of the Windows operating systems and device drivers.

The keyboard is typically assigned IRQ 1 and I/O address 060h. Anytime you see an IRQ, I/O address, or DMA channel assignment, remember it for the test.

Practicing safe keyboarding

Keyboards, especially mechanical ones, need to be cleaned periodically. You can clean a keyboard with the computer turned off by using the following steps:

1. **Turn the keyboard upside down and shake out any paper, potato chips, jujubes, cookie crumbs, paper clips, or the like.**

2. **Use an aerosol can of compressed air to dislodge any stubborn bits.**

3. **Wipe key tops with a soft cloth and an all-purpose cleaner.**

4. **Use a lint-free swab and the cleaner to clean between the keys.**

If soda pop or some other sticky stuff spills on your keyboard, you can rinse it with water, soak it in a sink or tub, or even put it through a dishwasher rinse cycle without using dishwasher or any other kind of soap. If you live out in the boondocks and have really gunky well water, use distilled water or Perrier or such to rinse the keyboard.

Be absolutely sure the keyboard is dry before reconnecting it to the computer and turning the power back on. Otherwise, any water left on the keyboard can at best cause phantom key connections or at worst, short out the keyboard membrane or switches. I don't recommend using a hairdryer or heat lamp to dry the keyboard, either. I guess a hairdryer is okay if you use only cold air, but a can of compressed air may be a better idea all around for blowing out any water in the mechanisms. In fact, I don't know that I'd actually wash the keyboard; if it's really that bad, perhaps a new keyboard is a better idea.

Troubleshooting the keyboard

It's true that both mechanical and capacitive keyboards can be repaired, but why bother? Replacing a keyboard is far less expensive than spending time troubleshooting and repairing it. Individual keyswitches may be replaced on a mechanical keyboard, but that should be the prudent limit.

To determine whether you have an electrical failure in the keyboard or on the system board, use the following steps:

1. **Turn off the computer.**

2. **Unplug the keyboard connector from the motherboard.**

3. **Turn on the computer.**

4. **Use a digital multimeter to check the voltages of the connector pins.**

    See Chapter 3 for more information on using a digital multimeter.

If any of the voltages are out of range (near +2 volts to +5.5 volts, depending on the pin), the problem is likely in the keyboard circuits of the motherboard. See the keyboard's documentation for the specific voltage and pinouts. Otherwise, the problem is probably in the keyboard.

As a professional PC repair technician, you should always listen carefully to the user's explanation of the problem and avoid jumping to conclusions whether you are servicing a keyboard or dealing with a motherboard malfunction. Don't assume that you know the problem or its solution ahead of time. Don't waste the customer's time or your energy troubleshooting a keyboard problem that would be solved less expensively with a new keyboard.

Solving boot sequence problems

Keyboard-related problems may occur during the POST (Power-On Self Test) process. As I explain in Chapter 5, the boot process has two means of indicating the source of the problem:

- ✔ **Early in the POST process:** Before the POST completes its system check phases, the video BIOS has not been loaded. As a result, only the system speaker is available to signal the operator. The POST produces a series of beeps of particular duration and sequence to the system BIOS installed on the PC, and the error is detected.

- ✔ **Later in the POST process:** After the video system is available for use by the POST or boot processes, the system can display error messages on the monitor. No standard exists for any of the error codes used by any of the BIOS systems. Each uses its own set of error codes, which, thankfully, are similar. In most cases, if a keyboard failure occurs, an error code in the range of 300 to 399 displays, indicating the keyboard error. The most common reason for a keyboard POST or boot error is a keystroke detected during the POST processing. This could be a stuck key, an accidentally-pressed key, someone leaning on the keyboard, or the corner of your *Scientific American* lying on the keyboard. The remedy is to simply clear the problem and reboot the computer.

Don't waste time memorizing POST error beep codes relating to keyboards or anything else. Each BIOS system has its own set of codes and some are quite lengthy. As far as keyboard problems go, knowing that the 300 series error codes relate to keyboard problems is enough. For a more inclusive list of the beep codes used by the most popular BIOS programs during POST, see Chapter 5.

The Mouse and Other Pointing Devices

Like the keyboard, a mouse can be found on nearly every PC in use and most definitely on every PC sold today. Some diehards still refuse to move to a Windows environment, clinging to their command line interfaces that don't have a mouse on their PCs. The time when you could get by without a mouse on your PC, if not gone altogether, is fading fast. Systems without a mouse or other type of pointing device will eventually go the way of the dinosaur.

You may encounter exam questions that cover one or more of these areas:

- ✔ Connecting the mouse to the computer
- ✔ The internal parts and operation of the mouse
- ✔ Device drivers (see Chapters 5, 20, and 21)
- ✔ Common preventive maintenance procedures

Rolling along with mechanical mice

Most mouse units in use today are the mechanical type, although optical units are making a comeback. The mechanical mouse uses a rubber ball, which moves as the user rotates the mouse. As the ball moves, it rotates a set of rollers, which in turn drive sensors that translate the ball's movement to move the screen pointer around the display. As the user moves his hand, the distance traveled and the speed of the ball is detected by the rollers and sensors, and the screen pointer moves a relative distance and speed accordingly.

An upside-down version of the traditional, mechanical mouse, called a *track-ball*, puts the ball on the top of the mouse. The user manipulates the ball with her fingers or thumb. However, any mouse questions you'll see on the Core Hardware exam deal with the standard mechanical mouse; so don't worry about trackballs for the test.

Taking good care of your mouse

If you have a mechanical mouse, you need to periodically clean its moving parts — the ball and rollers inside the ball housing. Cleaning should be part of routine maintenance because a dirty mouse can cause the screen pointer to move erratically or not at all.

In any case, use the following steps to clean the mouse:

1. **Open the ball access cover.**

   You can usually do this by either rotating or sliding the locking collar that holds the mouse ball in place. You can usually tell how to remove the cover by the large arrows stamped into it, showing the direction you need to push or twist.

2. **Clean the ball with a swab and a mild soap.**

   You may have heard that rubbing the mouse with a pencil eraser is a good way to clean it. Not! And neither is using anything that could react with the rubber to cause flat spots or make the mouse ball out-of-round, such as contact cleaner or alcohol, two commonly recommended cleaning solutions for the mouse housing.

3. **Blow into the ball housing.**

   I recommend using aerosol compressed air rather than your breath. Compressed air contains fewer germs and most likely less moisture as well. Replace the ball and reinstall the retaining ring, and you're back in business. Be sure to test the mouse immediately, and correct any problems that show up.

Sighting the optical mouse

The *optical mouse,* also known as the opto-mechanical mouse, uses either optical sensors and LEDs or a digital capture "eye" to sense the distance and speed of the mouse's movement. This type of mouse literally "sees" its movement over a surface and translates it into movement of the on-screen pointer.

Early optical mouse units required a special mouse pad, which was usually hard, shiny plastic or metal that had a grid of intersecting lines printed on it. As the mouse moved, an LED (light-emitting diode) reflecting off the shiny surface and grid lines were used to detect direction, speed, and distance. This mouse worked great, unless you lost the special mouse pad and couldn't use the mouse (or computer) at all.

The latest optical mouse works with a digital capture apparatus that literally takes around 2,000 pictures per second of the surface under the mouse to determine its movement. This means that any surface — the top of the desk, your jeans, the wall, the box it came in, and so on — can now be your mouse pad. A mouse pad is no longer needed, let alone a special optical mouse pad. Inside the optical mouse is a *digital signal processor (DSP)* that compares the captured images to detect even the slightest movement.

Unlike its predecessors, the new optical mouse, like Microsoft's IntelliEye Mouse, has no moving parts to pick up dust, dirt, jetsam, or flotsam that can impair its performance. This also means that you don't have to clean it.

Summarizing pointing devices

Table 12-1 lists other pointing devices that can be attached to the PC. For the test, you should at least be familiar with what they are.

Table 12-1	PC Pointing Devices
Device	*Use*
Joystick	Popular with flight and navigation games, and as a backup mouse
Trackball	In effect, an upside-down mouse where the ball is rotated to move the screen pointer
Touchpad	A reliable alternative to the mouse that can be integrated into the keyboard
Digitizing tablets	Used with drawing or CAD (computer-aided design) software to create line or vector graphics

Connecting the mouse

In case you've been on a remote desert island or in a deep dark cave for about ten years: A mouse is a pointing device commonly used on the PC. It's safe to say that every PC sold today comes with a mouse as standard equipment.

The mouse is available in five different units. These units differ in how they connect to the computer. The different units and their connectors are

- ✔ **Serial:** Connects via a 9- or 25-pin serial port usually with a DB-9 or DB-25 connector.

- ✔ **PS/2:** Connects with a mini-DIN 6-pin plug to a port usually mounted on the motherboard.

- ✔ **Combination:** Connects with either a mini-DIN (PS/2) 6-pin connector to a port on the motherboard or with a DB-9 or DB-25 connector through an adapter card to either a DB-9 or DB-25 serial port.

- ✔ **Bus:** Connects to its own adapter card. Bus mouse units usually connect with a mini-DIN-6 plug to an adapter added to the PC specifically to support the mouse.

- ✔ **USB (Universal Serial Bus):** A USB mouse is a hot-swappable device that can be added and removed from the PC without the need to restart the system. A USB mouse also shares the system resources of the USB port and does not require additional IRQ and I/O port resources.

✔ **Infrared:** If the PC has built-in IR support, in many ways the support of the mouse is provided directly from the motherboard and chipset. If the IR system is an add-on, it connects either via a serial or mini-DIN-6 port.

The most commonly used connector for a mouse is the PS/2. You should never connect a PS/2 mouse (or any other PS/2 device) to the PC while the PC is powered up. This could damage the port or the motherboard. And this is on the test, too!

Driving Miss Mousey

In the Windows 98 and 2000 world, most mouse units are plug and play and the operating system includes the proper device driver (see Chapter 20 for more information). However, on older systems such as Windows 3.x (where operating system services are supplied by MS-DOS) the device driver must be installed and the system configured to load the mouse unit each time it starts up.

Sight and Sound Inputs

You're not likely to be asked anything directly about sound or video capture devices. Just to be on the safe side, I cover them briefly. Most of the service issues with these systems involve system compatibility, which I detail in Chapter 6.

Multimedia and desktop publishing are less hardware issues than they are applications. Nevertheless, both are becoming standard functions of the PC. This standardization is evidenced by the MMX (multimedia extension) instructions and enhanced graphics support being added to processors and chipsets, and by the fact that virtually all PCs now come with speakers, extended RAM and cache memory, and graphics enhancement as standard features.

Capturing visual images

You can use three types of devices to capture images directly into the computer:

✔ **Scanners:** Available as either a flatbed scanner or as a handheld scanner and used to convert printed text and images into digital form for editing and manipulation.

> ✔ **Digital capture cards:** This type of adapter card is installed into an expansion card on the motherboard and connected to an analog video camera or digital video or still camera to capture still or motion images.
>
> ✔ **Digital cameras:** With the emergence of the handheld digital video and still cameras, the little camera that sits on top of your monitor and enables you to interact with sight and sound over the Internet is now called a *computer camera.* Most of the digital cameras, whether still or video, interface to a PC through either a serial or a USB port.

Video capture cards are assigned to an available IRQ and I/O address. Many also use and are assigned DMA channels, but no default settings exist for these devices. Don't worry, the exam has no trick questions about this.

Installing sound

You probably think of sound playback when you consider sound and the PC, but devices exist to capture sound as well. Sound capabilities, both input and output, are installed in a PC through a sound card, a special type of expansion card. Usually, a sound card has connection ports for microphones and speakers to enable it to capture sound and play it back.

Sound cards act like a modem of sorts, in that they are involved in the conversion of analog sound to digital data, and vice versa. Grossly simplified, sound capture involves grabbing a piece of the sound every so often to build a digitally reproducible facsimile of the original sound, also known as *sampling.* The sampled sound file is stored as a digital file on the computer, usually as a WAV or similar file type.

The sound card is generally assigned to IRQ 5 and I/O address 220h. A sound card can use up to three DMA channels. Channels 0, 1, and 3 for an 8-bit card, and channels 5, 6, and 7 for a 16-bit card.

Prep Test

1 **The keyboard and mouse are considered**

- **A** ○ Throwaway technology
- **B** ○ Shop-repairable items
- **C** ○ Factory-only repairable items
- **D** ○ Not repairable

2 **The technology used to detect movement on an optical mouse is**

- **A** ○ A low-grade laser beam
- **B** ○ A digital capture "eye"
- **C** ○ A video detection system that detects movement in the mouse ball
- **D** ○ Static electricity sensors

3 **Which mouse type is the most commonly used?**

- **A** ○ Trackball
- **B** ○ Mechanical mouse
- **C** ○ Touch pad
- **D** ○ Optical mouse

4 **What are the two types of keyboards in use today?**

- **A** ○ Standard and nonstandard
- **B** ○ Mechanical and optical
- **C** ○ Resistive and capacitive
- **D** ○ Mechanical keyswitch and capacitive

5 **Which of the following are connectors used by mouse units? (Choose two.)**

- **A** ❑ USB
- **B** ❑ Mini-DIN-6
- **C** ❑ DIN-5
- **D** ❑ Parallel

6 **What is the most commonly used PC keyboard format?**

- **A** ○ Ergonomic
- **B** ○ Natural
- **C** ○ XT
- **D** ○ Enhanced

7 **What type of mouse connects to either a serial port or a port mounted on the motherboard?**

A ○ Serial

B ○ PS/2

C ○ Bus

D ○ Combination

8 **A keyboard error code displayed during the boot sequence would be in what number series?**

A ○ 1700–1799

B ○ 300–399

C ○ 100–199

D ○ It may be a number from any series

9 **Device drivers provide**

A ○ Boot sequence support for peripheral devices

B ○ Operating support for peripheral devices

C ○ ROM-based interface instructions

D ○ User help information

10 **The joystick is**

A ○ A special tool used for RAM

B ○ The lever on a ZIF socket

C ○ A type of pointing device

D ○ A type of output device

Answers

1 **A.** The cost of repairing a keyboard or mouse for anything but the simplest problems can be more expensive than just replacing it with a new one. *See "Troubleshooting the keyboard."*

2 **B.** I don't think you'll actually see any questions about optical mouse units on the exam, but just connect the words optical and "eye" to be safe. *Check out "Sighting the optical mouse."*

3 **B.** Others may come and go, but the little mechanical mouse keeps on going, and going and going. *Review "Rolling along with mechanical mice."*

4 **D.** See "Typecasting keyboards."

5 **A & B.** The other types of connectors used are serial and infrared (IR), but, at least so far, the parallel port has not been used. *Review "Connecting the keyboard."*

6 **D.** The newer natural, ergonomic, and separating keyboards are essentially enhanced keyboards in new packages. *Take a look at "Keyboard styles."*

7 **D.** The combination mouse can be adapted to fit either type of connector, which allows it to work with just about any system. *See "Connecting the mouse."*

8 **B.** Any POST error code in the 300 to 399 range is a keyboard fault. Check with the BIOS manual for the specific error. *Look at "Solving boot sequence problems."*

9 **B.** Boot sequence support is provided by firmware. *See "Understanding device drivers."*

10 **C.** The joystick is very popular with flight-simulation games. *Review "Summarizing pointing devices."*

Chapter 13

Output Devices

Exam Objectives

▶ Identifying common output devices and their normal operation

▶ Identifying output device connectors

▶ Using preventive maintenance products

▶ Disposing of environmentally hazardous equipment

▶ Following safety procedures for high-voltage equipment

*U*nlike their input device cousins, which are adapted to gather data at their myriad sources, output devices are limited by sight and sound. As a result, the PC is designed to provide its users with things they can read, watch, or hear. Outputs that we can taste and touch will undoubtedly be out in the near future, don't you think, HAL? Output devices have only one purpose: to display (print or sound) the results of instructions and data entered by the user and processed by the PC.

On the common, everyday PC (one you are likely to repair) typically only two or three types of output devices exist: monitors, printers, and sound systems. Therefore, the A+ Core Hardware exam includes questions focused primarily on monitors and printers because virtually every PC has them. Sound is still somewhat new to the A+ world, but you may see a troubleshooting question or two on sound cards.

On the A+ Core Hardware exam, monitors and displays are included in three separate parts, but are primarily in the domains of "Installation, Configuration, and Upgrading" and "Diagnosing and Troubleshooting," with a slight mention in "Preventive Maintenance." I interpret the configuration part to include picking the right device for the customer's needs, setting the jumpers or DIP switches, and configuring software. Troubleshooting means isolating and repairing output device problems and the preventive issues surrounding proper disposal and cleaning of monitors.

This chapter also includes a quick review on PC sound devices. Printers are left for Chapter 14 because they now have their own domain on the A+ Core Hardware exam.

Quick Assessment

Identifying common output devices and their normal operation

1   The _____ is the primary component of the PC monitor.

2   A CRT paints its image using _____, which are tiny clusters of color dots.

3   The picture quality of a monitor is determined by its _____.

Identifying output device connectors

4   The VGA/SVGA standard connector has _____ pins.

5   A sound card typically uses IRQ _____.

Using preventive mainte- nance products

6   The monitor's glass builds up _____ and holds dust on its surface.

Disposing of environmen- tally hazardous equipment

7   A Green monitor is one that reduces its power by _____ in sleep mode.

Following safety procedures for high- voltage equipment

8   A CRT has a large _____ inside that holds an electrical charge.

9   You should not wear a(n) _____ when working inside a monitor.

10 A process called _____ eliminates most of the magnetization inside the CRT.

Answers

1 *CRT*. See "Looking Inside the Monitor."

2 *Pixels*. Check out "Looking Inside the Monitor."

3 *Resolution*. Review "Sizing up the display."

4 *15*. Look up "Making the connection."

5 *5*. Take a look at "Connecting to sound."

6 *Static electricity*. Charge to "Cleaning the monitor."

7 *99 percent*. Boldly go to "Saving the planet."

8 *Capacitor*. Mosey over to "Keeping the lid on."

9 *ESD grounding strap*. Zap to "Keeping the lid on."

10 *Degaussing*. Review "Exorcising the magnetic evils."

Looking Inside the Monitor

The PC's monitor is not an item that PC service technicians are often called on to fix, and rightly so. The A+ people recognize this fact and have included very few questions on the internal workings of the monitor. Study this section as background material for the terminology and concepts concerning monitors in general.

You don't need to know how the internal combustion engine works to put gas in a car. Likewise, you really don't need to know the inner workings of a CRT to install and configure a monitor, but you should have a general idea of how it works. After the system unit or perhaps the laser printer, the monitor represents the customer's next largest investment and is the only part of the system that actually holds its value. Your focus on the job and for the A+ Core Hardware exam should be the technologies that enable the monitor to work at its best.

The primary component in the PC monitor is the cathode ray tube (CRT). Although its name makes it sound a little like a demonic weapon from a science fiction movie, it's actually the technology used in virtually all computer monitors (and televisions) to produce the displayed image.

Lighting up the world

A monitor works by emitting an electron beam that moves back and forth, working from top to bottom and left to right one row at a time, and lighting up phosphor dots on the inside of the glass CRT tube. The dots are actually illuminated in patterns that create images on the CRT's display. It takes only a fraction of a second to create the image on the CRT. However, the brightness of the illuminated dots fades just as fast, requiring the entire display to be refreshed by repeating the laser and dot illumination process many times per second to keep the image on the CRT's screen.

On a color monitor, each dot carries one of three colors: red, green, or blue. Three dots (one of each color) are arranged together to create a *pixel* (short for *picture element*). Three electron beams illuminate a pixel's dots in varying degrees, and this mixture of color intensities produces different color shadings on the screen. When all the pixels on the screen are lit up, a picture forms in living color.

Speaking the language of the monitor

Here are a couple of monitor terms you may find in monitor-related questions on the exam:

✔ **Refresh rate:** This rate represents the time it takes the CRT's electron beam to paint the screen from top to bottom. Refresh rates are expressed as Hertz (Hz), which is one complete screen refresh cycle. Different monitors have different refresh rates. For example, VESA (Video Electronics Standards Association) has set the minimum refresh rate as 70 to 75 Hz for the Super Video Graphics Array (SVGA) monitor. See "Setting the refresh rate," later in this chapter.

✔ **Interlacing:** Interlaced monitors use two passes to draw the screen, drawing only the even count lines on the first pass and only the odd count lines on the second pass. An interlaced monitor usually has more screen flicker than a noninterlaced monitor, which draws the entire screen in each pass.

Inside the monitor is a controller board that performs the communication with the adapter card, directs the drawing of the CRT's display, and responds to the adjustment controls located on the monitor to adjust the display. The monitor's internal controller also determines the technology used in creating the display.

The names of the technologies that are used to control the illumination of the CRT's phosphor sound like a bad old movie title or a song by the Eagles: the *shadow mask* and the *aperture grill*.

Here's how they work:

✔ **Shadow mask:** A metal screen with thousands of very small holes. The mask is placed so that the holes are directly in line with the dots of each pixel. The shadow mask absorbs unwanted electrons and prevents the phosphor material between the pixels from being illuminated, which leaves a black border around each pixel.

✔ **Aperture grill:** Very thin vertical wires let more electrons through than the shadow mask, creating a deeper color display. Horizontal wires hold the vertical wires in place to keep the verticals from vibrating.

The Video Adapter Card

The video card, also called the graphics adapter, converts the graphic images from a software application or operating system into a series of instructions that tell the monitor's internal controller how to draw the image on the screen and the colors to use. Back when monitors displayed only monochrome, the video card was very simple in design, leaving most of the heavy work to the PC's CPU and RAM. However, graphics adapters now have their own onboard processor, called a graphic processing unit (GPU), and their own special video memory — all of which supports better and faster graphic images.

The video card and monitor must use the same graphics standard to work properly.

Connecting to adapter card standards

Here are the different video adapter card standards you will want to know:

✔ **Monochrome Display Adapter (MDA):** Does just what its name says — displays mostly text on a monochrome monitor. This digital adapter is still used for servers, process control, and monitoring systems where the display contains only text and a color display is not needed. Resolution is not an issue on MDA monitors. It works just like a dot matrix printer, using illuminated dots to form letters on each line of the display. A variation of the MDA that integrates graphics is the Hercules-based Monochrome Graphics Adapter (MGA).

✔ **Color Graphics Adapter (CGA):** This digital adapter was the first color adapter. It's capable of displaying four colors. CGA monitors support 320 x 200 (four colors) or 640 x 200 (two colors). In this case, as well as those that follow, as the number of colors increases, typically the resolution decreases. This trade-off must take place so that the video RAM is not exceeded. More on this later (see "Sizing up the display").

✔ **Enhanced Graphics Adapter (EGA):** This digital adapter supports 16 colors at a resolution of 640 x 350. Don't worry about this one for the exam. I only include it for continuity and comparison. EGA cards (and for the most part CGA) are obsolete.

✔ **Video Graphics Array (VGA):** VGA is the de facto standard for video adapters on Windows as well as several other operating systems (see Chapter 20). The VGA standard supports up to 640 x 480 with 16 colors or lower resolutions with 256 colors.

✔ **Super VGA (SVGA):** Most of the video standards that followed VGA and support resolutions and color depths higher than those of the VGA standard are grouped under the SVGA standard. The SVGA standard was developed by the VESA, which is made up of monitor and graphics card manufacturers and other companies interested in video standards. SVGA video cards support several resolutions, including 800 x 600; 1,024 x 768; 1,280 x 1,024; 1,600 x 1,200; and higher and up to 4 billion colors, although 16.7 million colors is more commonly used as the standard.

Table 13-1 lists the more popular video graphic adapter standards. Notice that as their resolutions increase, the number of simultaneous colors supported decreases.

Table 13-1	PC Video Adapter Standards	
Video Standard	*Resolutions*	*Colors*
VGA (Video Graphics Array)	640 x 480	16
	320 x 200	256
SVGA (Super VGA)	800 x 600	16
	1,024 x 768	256
	1,280 x 1,024	256
	1,600 x 1,200	256

Sizing up the display

The definitions of resolution — dot pitch, color depth, and aspect ratio — are very likely included in questions on the exam that relate to video cards, so review the following sections closely.

Resolution

The number of pixels available to be used to generate an image is key to the quality of the images produced — regardless of the technology used to light the pixels. The number of pixels available to produce an image is called *resolution*.

The more pixels available for use in creating the display, the higher the resolution, which results in a much better display. Resolution is stated as the number of pixels available horizontally on the screen by the number of rows of pixels available vertically on the screen. For example, 800 x 600 represents 800 pixels in each horizontal row and 600 vertical pixel rows (of 800 pixels each) on the screen. See Table 13-1 for a listing of the common resolutions supported on color monitors.

The resolution is important for two reasons: It determines the size and quality of the image displayed on the monitor and it is a major factor in determining the amount of video RAM that should be on the video card to support the display. Each pixel in a monitor's resolution requires a certain amount of data to encode exactly how the pixel should appear. For example, nearly 6MB of video RAM is required to generate a true color image using 1,600 x 1,200 resolution.

The size of the monitor's display (such as 15 inch, 17 inch, and so on) does have some bearing on the number of pixels available and the resolutions supported. A monitor using 640 x 480 resolution uses 307,200 pixels to create its display. The same monitor set to a resolution of 1,280 x 1,024 uses 1,310,720 pixels in the same display space. As the pixel count increases, the size of each pixel and the amount of space around it decreases. To demonstrate this, use Lab 13-1 to change the settings of your PC's monitor.

Lab 13-1   Setting the Display Resolution on a Windows PC

1. **Access the Display Properties window by right-clicking in an empty space of the Windows desktop and choosing Properties from the shortcut menu that appears.**

2. **Select the Settings tab to display the Screen Area and Colors boxes, as shown in Figure 13-1.**

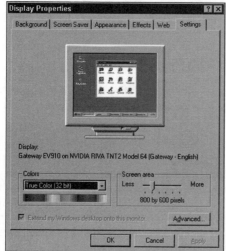

Figure 13-1:
The Settings
tab of the
Display
Properties
window.

3. **Move the slide selector from side to side to adjust the size of the Screen Area to a new setting.**

4. **From the pull-down list of Colors, choose a different color setting.**

5. **Click Apply to change the settings for your video system. The compatibility warning box (shown in Figure 13-2) appears giving you the option of restarting the system to make the change. The choice is yours, but the restart is typically not needed.**

6. **Another warning displays to let you know that the change may take a second or two (15 seconds is what it says). Click OK to proceed.**

7. **If you increase the resolution on your display, the images become smaller; if you decrease the resolution, they become larger.**

Figure 13-2:
The
compatibility
warning box
displays
when you
make video
settings
changes.

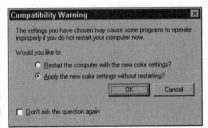

8. **Change the settings in the opposite direction to demonstrate the resolution range of your system.**

9. **Reset the settings back to your original settings, or if you found a new setting to your liking, keep it.**

One more thing about resolution. The higher the resolution, the smaller each pixel appears on the screen. If a user complains that his or her Windows icons are too small on his or her new monitor, lower the resolution.

Another setting that affects the performance of the video card and monitor is the refresh rate. Lab 13-2 details the steps used to set the refresh rate on your monitor or to check its setting.

Lab 13-2   Setting the Refresh Rate

1. **Follow the steps used in the preceding project to display the Display Properties Settings window.**

2. **Click the Advanced button to display the Properties window for the video adapter in your PC.**

3. **Select the adapter tab. The Refresh rate is selected from a list box that is located about in the middle of the window. On most Windows 9*x* or Windows 2000 PCs, the refresh rate is likely set to Optimal.**

Recovering from an Incorrect Refresh Rate

If you change the refresh rate and the result is a distorted or blurry image, reboot your PC into Windows Safe Mode and reset the refresh rate using the steps in the preceding project.

Dot pitch

The distance between pixels on the CRT is the *dot pitch*. Technically, the dot pitch is the distance in millimeters (mm) between dots of the same color in two adjacent pixels (for example, the distance between two adjacent green dots), but in effect, it is the distance between the pixels. Common dot pitch sizes on color monitors are in the range of .15mm to .30mm. (You will usually see the dot pitch expressed without the "mm" unit of measure.) The smaller the dot pitch, the better the picture quality. It also stands to reason that a smaller dot pitch makes room for more pixels, which gives the monitor a higher resolution.

Color depth

The number of colors that a video card or monitor can display is the *color depth*. It is also commonly called the *bit depth,* because the color depth is expressed as the number of bits used to define the colors of a particular video standard's color depth.

The color depth represents the number of individual colors that each pixel on the screen can display. It is always expressed as the number of bits used to describe each color in the color set. The common color depth settings are 8-bit, 16-bit, 24-bit, and 32-bit color. Figure 13-3 shows the settings available on a Windows 98 PC and its monitor.

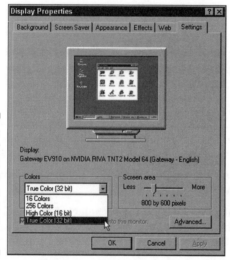

Figure 13-3:
The color
depth
settings
available
on a
Windows
PC.

The number of bits in the color depth determines the number of colors a video card or monitor can display. For example, 8-bit color uses 8-bits to number each of the colors. In binary numbers, the range of numbers available is 00000000 to 11111111, or the range of decimal numbers 0 to 255. In other words, an 8-bit color depth can display 256 colors.

The number of colors that a particular color depth supports is the largest binary number that can be displayed in its bit depth plus one. A 16-bit color depth can display 65,536 colors (or $2^{15}+ 1$), the 24-bit color depth has 16.7

million colors and 32-bit color supports over 4 *billion* colors. Depending on the PC, video card, and monitor, either 24-bit or 32-bit will be designated as the True Color setting.

The human eye can discern only around 16 million colors and has trouble distinguishing the color of adjacent pixels at about that level.

Aspect Ratio

The aspect ratio of a monitor describes the relative number of horizontal pixels to vertical pixels in the resolutions it supports. The standard aspect ratio for nearly all monitors and resolutions is 4:3 (read as 4 to 3). This is the aspect ratio of 640 x 480; 800 x 600;1,280 x 768; and several other resolutions. This number indicates the monitor's ability to display certain shapes and graphics, such as a circle, on the screen.

Sizing up the video memory

Most video cards come with 8MB to 32MB of video RAM, but there are high-end 3-D graphic cards that have as much as 64MB. Some people think that 64MB is far more than is needed, but others, especially the 3-D crowd, think that this may soon not be enough.

Table 13-2 shows the amounts of video RAM required by several common graphics settings.

Table 13-2	Common 2-D Video RAM Requirements	
Resolution	*Color Depth*	*Video RAM Required*
640 x 480	8-bit	307K
1,024 x 768	16-bit	1.57MB
1,024 x 768	24-bit	2.36MB
1,600 x 1,200	24-bit	5.76MB
1,600 x 1,200	32-bit	7.68MB

A 3-D video card requires more video RAM than a 2-D card, even when they use the same resolution and color depth. In addition to the 2-D (down and across), a third dimension of depth is added. 3-D graphic cards use three buffers to hold the graphics data: a front buffer, a back buffer, and a Z-buffer. For example, a 2-D video card with 4MB of video RAM can support a 1,600 x 1,200 16-bit display, but the same card can support a 3-D game only on an 800 x 600 16-bit setting. The Z-buffer consumes enough of the available RAM to require the resolution to be reduced.

The sizes of the front and back buffers are each the size required by the color depth. The Z-buffer uses 16-bits (or 2 bytes).

Looking at the Video RAMs

The memory (or RAM) on the video card is also called the frame buffer, because it holds graphic instructions about each scene or frame to be displayed on the monitor. The first form of video RAM was standard DRAM, the same kind of RAM found in early PCs. Because DRAM requires constant electrical refreshing to hold its contents, it didn't work well for video memory. For one reason, it could be accessed while it was being refreshed and the video system had to wait, which meant that its performance suffered. Since then, several memory technologies have been and are being used, each one increasingly more efficient and faster than the last.

The most common RAM technologies used with video cards are:

- **Dynamic Random Access Memory (DRAM):** The same DRAM used on early PCs.

- **Extended Data Output DRAM (EDO DRAM):** Provides a higher bandwidth and handles read/write cycles better than standard DRAM.

- **Video RAM (VRAM):** VRAM, not to be confused with the generic "VRAM," is a special type of DRAM that doesn't need to be refreshed quite as often. VRAM is *dual-ported,* which means it has two access portals, and the processor and RAMDAC (RAM digital to analog converter) can both be accessing it at the same time. As the saying goes, two doors are better than one, and dual-porting doubles the memory's speed.

- **Windows RAM (WRAM):** Called *Windows Accelerator Card RAM* on the A+ Core Hardware blueprint, WRAM is a dual-ported memory that runs a bit faster than VRAM.

- **Synchronous DRAM (SDRAM):** SDRAM is EDO DRAM that it is synchronized to the video card's processor and chipset. SDRAM is single-ported (one door) memory that is very common on video cards.

- **Double Data Rate SDRAM (DDR SDRAM):** DDR SDRAM has twice the data transfer speed of standard SDRAM. DDR memories are becoming more commonplace on video cards, especially on 3-D graphics accelerators.

- **Synchronous Graphics RAM (SGRAM):** An improvement on standard SDRAM adds features such as block writes and write-per-bit that support faster graphics performance. *Block write* is used to copy the contents of a color register into memory in a single clock cycle. *Write per bit* allows a single bit of a data block to be changed without the need to rewrite the entire data block. SGRAM, which is a single-ported memory, is found only on video cards with chipsets that support it.

✔ **Double Data Rate SGRAM (DDR SGRAM):** DDR does for SGRAM exactly what it did for SDRAM: doubles its data transfer rates.

✔ **Direct Rambus DRAM (RDRAM):** A newer general-purpose memory type that is used for the PC's main memory (as well as on video cards) that runs about 20 times faster than conventional DRAM. RDRAM includes bus mastering and dedicated channels between memory devices. *Bus mastering* allows the video card to take control of the PC's system bus and transfer data into and out of system RAM. This improves the performance of some video operations that use primary RAM for certain calculations, such as 3-D acceleration.

✔ **Unified Memory Architecture (UMA):** Many lower-cost systems intended for home use integrate graphics support and the video system into the motherboard. UMA is so named because it uses system RAM for video memory. This technology almost always produces inferior graphics performance.

See Chapter 8 for more information on RAM and memory technologies.

Interfacing with the video system

A large amount of data moves between the video card and the PC's CPU and RAM to create each frame of the video display. What you see on the monitor is actually a series of still images displayed very quickly. Each frame requires a great deal of information to be sent from the PC to the video card. The pathway that the video information data travels over must have more bandwidth than any other peripheral device interface on the PC. This is why either the PCI (Peripheral Components Interconnect) or the AGP (Accelerated Graphics Port) interfaces are used for most modern PC video systems. Yes, there are some ISA (Industry Standard Architecture) video cards still hanging around, but because the A+ exam doesn't care about them, neither should you.

Avoid the myth that the number of bits used on the video card's internal bus is also the number of bits used for the video card's interface. A 128-bit video card most likely uses a 32-bit interface. The width of the interface is 16 bits (ISA/EISA cards), 32 bits (VL-Bus, PCI, or AGP), or 64 bits (PCI).

The two most popular video system interfaces in use today are:

✔ **Peripheral Component Interconnect (PCI):** All Pentium-class motherboard chipsets support the PCI interface bus. PCI is commonly used for 2-D graphics cards, sound cards, network interface cards, and other expansion cards that attach directly to the motherboard. Of course, a PCI card slot is also required.

✔ **AGP (Accelerated Graphics Port):** The AGP interface was designed specifically for use as a video system interface. AGP runs twice as fast as the PCI interface and creates a high-speed link between the video card and the PC's processor. AGP also has a direct link to system RAM, which makes it possible for the video system to use system RAM for calculations and temporary storage. An AGP video card will only fit in an AGP slot.

Because of its faster transfer rates, AGP is quickly replacing the PCI interface as the interface of choice. In fact, AGP has evolved into several versions, each designated as a multiple of the original standard's speed. AGP 1X has a data transfer rate of 266 Mbps (compared to PCI's 133 Mbps), AGP 2X supports 533 Mbps, and AGP 4X transfers data at 1.07 Gbps (and no, I don't know what happened to AGP 3X). One reason for the increased speed is that AGP is a port and supports only one device (the video card), and PCI is a true bus structure over which the PC communicates with a number of devices.

Dealing with driver software

The software device driver is a major component of the modern video system. The device driver interacts between the video card's BIOS and any application software or operating system generating images to be displayed on the monitor. The driver software decides the most efficient way to use the features of the graphics processor and translates what an application wants to display into instructions that the video card can understand. A video card typically has a separate software routine in the device driver for each resolution or color depth combination.

Making the connection

Expect a question about the sizes of the different plugs used to connect the monitor to the system. The monitor connects to the system through a connector on the back of the adapter card or through a connector on the motherboard. Different plugs are used, each with a different number of pins. The number of pins on the connector is somewhat indicative of the adapter card's capabilities. Here are the different connectors for monitors:

✔ **15-pin:** The HD-15 connector (the HD means high-density) is the standard monitor connector on virtually all newer monitors and video cards, especially VGA and SVGA. The video card has the female connector into which the male plug of the monitor is attached. The HD-15 is a DB-style plug and connector.

- ✔ **9-pin:** Most older monitors, usually digital displays (CGA, EGA, and early VGA) use a 9-pin connector.

- ✔ **BNC connector:** Some very high-end monitors use a special cable that connects with a standard 15-pin connector at the video card and a 5-pin BNC connector at the monitor.

Monitor Power and Safety

Two areas of particular concern to the CompTIA that are strongly reflected in the A+ Core Hardware exam are safety and environmental issues of monitors. Count on seeing one or more questions on these issues on the Core Hardware exam.

Cleaning the monitor

Dust collects on the glass of the monitor and is held there by the static electricity that builds up over time. Never clean the monitor's glass with any liquid solution while it's powered on. A danger of personal and equipment damage exists. The static electricity built up on the screen can be conducted straight to you by the liquid cleaner when you wipe it off. If you want to use a spray cleaner, turn off the monitor, spray a cloth, and then wipe the monitor. You can also find antistatic wipes that are made just for this purpose.

Saving the planet

PC monitors contain high levels of lead. In fact, the average CRT contains from 5 to 8 pounds of lead, which can pose a threat if released into the environment. Many states now have laws stating that as long as the CRT's screen is still intact, the monitor can be safely recycled. Some public and many private recyclers are set up to handle the special requirements of PC monitor disposal.

In active mode, the monitor uses more power than the entire PC system. However, reducing the power consumption of monitors in their idle state is a focus of the United States Environmental Protection Agency (EPA) program called *Energy Star,* or *Green Star.* The purpose of this program is to certify PCs and monitors that use less than 30 watts in all power modes and reduce their power consumption by 99 percent in sleep or suspend mode. PCs that meet this standard can display the Energy Star logo.

Monitors meeting the Green standard must reduce their power consumption by 99 percent in suspend mode.

VESA's *Display Power Management System (DPMS)* protocol shuts down the parts of the monitor or motherboard that have been inactive for a certain period of time. PCs with both a motherboard and a monitor supporting the DPMS protocol significantly reduce the system's power consumption.

Protecting against electromagnetic evils

CRTs produce strong electrical and electromagnetic emissions, which are formidable and can wreak havoc on other electrical or magnetic systems. Debates are ongoing within the computing and health worlds regarding the possible threat of these emissions to humans. Some people believe that extended exposure can increase a person's risk of cancer, and others believe no risk at all exists. Everyone agrees that limiting your exposure to electromagnetic emissions can't hurt. So, it's not a good idea to hold a monitor up to your ear for extended periods.

Keeping the lid on

For the exam, memorize this section word for word. Even if you don't find this on the test, the information may just save your life.

You have no reason to open up a monitor to work on it. Chances are that you

- ✔ Don't have the foggiest idea what you're doing in there.
- ✔ Don't have the right tools or equipment to fix it.
- ✔ Will most likely kill yourself — the monitor holds 20,000 volts or more and *all* of it is still present even when the power is off.

If you must open the case to work on a monitor, *do not* wear an ESD grounding strap. Also, unplug the AC cord from the power source and use the buddy system (never work alone on a monitor). Do you get the impression that maybe you shouldn't work on monitors?

To be safe, send the monitor to the manufacturer or a repair company specializing in monitors or a salvage company to dispose of it properly.

Monitors use very high voltages and hold other hazards that can cause serious injury or even death, even when the power is off and disconnected. Never use a regular multimeter or other test equipment to measure the voltages on a monitor. Much like the PC's main power supply, some large *capacitors* inside the monitor hold some big nasty charges, and you don't want any part of them.

Exorcising the magnetic evils

Because preventive maintenance is an important part of the PC repair-person's job, the A+ Core Hardware exam requires you to know about monitor cleaning and preventive maintenance techniques. Chapter 17 covers this area in more detail.

The powerful electromagnetic forces in the monitor or any placed nearby can cause the internal components of the monitor to become magnetized. When this happens, the image resolution and color quality produced by the monitor can be distorted or faded, especially in the display's corners.

A process called *degaussing* eliminates most of the magnetization inside the CRT. Most color monitors have a built-in degaussing protocol that can usually be accessed from the monitor's front panel. A monitor should be degaussed fairly regularly, but be careful not to overdo it. Degaussing a circuit too much can damage it.

Adding Sound to the PC

You may see an exam question directly related to sound reproduction and capture technology, outside of the IRQ that's usually occupied by the sound card (IRQ5), or where the CD-ROM's audio cable connects (to the sound card).

Sound, beyond the little system speaker on the front of the system unit, is added through an adapter card in an expansion slot. Most newer computers come standard with a sound system (a sound card, a CD-ROM or DVD, and a set of speakers). For older systems, sound can be added to a PC with a multimedia upgrade kit (CD-ROM, sound card, microphone, and speakers) or as a single card and speakers.

Hearing all about the standards of sound

Essentially, three sound card standards have existed: the 8-bit AdLib, the higher-end SoundBlaster, and the General MIDI (musical instrument digital interface). Most sound cards in use today support both the SoundBlaster and General MIDI standards for recording and playback. The AdLib card has all but disappeared. Most sound cards are CD quality, which means that they capture and reproduce digital audio at the same resolution (CD-A) used for audio CDs.

For the test, remember that the two standards in use are the SoundBlaster and the MIDI standards.

A CD-ROM drive produces sound through a phone jack on its face, or sound can be piped through the sound card for broadcast to the PC's speakers. You can find an audio cable on the CD-ROM that connects to the sound card for this purpose.

Components of a PC Sound System

These components are common to PC sound systems:

✔ **Sound card:** The sound card combines all the inputs, outputs, and signal processors required to convert audio information into and from digital form into a single card. Sound cards are either ISA or PCI adapter cards or can be integrated directly on the motherboard through an audio chip.

✔ **Amplifier:** After the sound card has converted digital audio into an analog (audible) signal, the signal must be amplified before it can be played back on speakers. Most sound cards include a weak amplifier that is capable of driving a set of headphones or a set of small PC speakers. Some PC speakers include an amplifier in one or both of the speakers, which takes the burden off the sound card.

✔ **Speakers:** PC speakers are available as small passive systems that are powered from the sound card's headphone output or as active (amplified) 3-way surround-sound systems that rival many home theatres and somewhere in-between. Some computer monitors have speakers that are integrated into their bezels or that snap onto their sides. USB speaker systems do not require a separate sound card — all the sound processing is contained inside the speaker itself.

Turning on to sound cards

The sound card combines the components required to transfer sound into and out of a PC, including:

✔ **Analog input jacks:** Most sound cards have line-level and a mic-level inputs. *Line-level* inputs accept signals from electronic sources such as a CD player or directly from a musical instrument like a synthesizer. *Mic-level* inputs accept the signal from a microphone or an unamplified electric guitar.

✔ **Analog output jacks:** Nearly all sound cards have speaker out and line out analog output jacks. A small amplifier drives the *speaker out* jack and its output level is appropriate for a pair of headphones or PC speakers. The *line out* jack provides a line-level signal that can be used as an input to another sound device, like a stereo receiver.

- ✔ **Analog to Digital Converter (ADC):** The ADC converts analog audio data, such as a live voice or a musical instrument, into digital data that can be stored on a PC.

- ✔ **Digital I/O jack:** This jack, if present, allows digital devices to be directly connected to the PC and digital audio signals to be passed without being converted to analog.

- ✔ **Digital Signal Processor (DSP):** A feature once reserved for high-end sound cards, a digital signal processor (DSP) is now common on most newer sound cards. A DSP reduces the load on the PC's CPU for processing audio.

- ✔ **Digital to Analog Converter (DAC):** The DAC converts stored digital audio data into audible (analog) information that can be played back on speakers or headphones.

- ✔ **Game/MIDI port:** This dual-purpose connector, which is found on many sound cards, is used for game controllers such as joysticks and, through a special cable, can be connected to any external MIDI.

- ✔ **Synthesizer:** Many of the sounds that a sound card produces are generated on the card using a synthesizer chip.

Interfacing to the sound card

Sound cards are installed in expansion card slots on the motherboard using one of the following standard interfaces:

- ✔ **ISA (Industry Standard Architecture) bus:** ISA sound cards typically require some manual configuration to set their system resource settings, such as the I/O address, DMA, and IRQ. These values are set with either a series of jumpers or DIP switches on the card. Some cards also require a few commands to be entered into the AUTOEXEC.BAT and CONFIG SYS files.

- ✔ **PCI (Peripheral Component Interconnect):** PCI sound cards are typically Plug and Play and will be configured automatically by the BIOS or operating system, like Windows 9*x* or Widows 2000. In most cases, system resources, such as the IRQ and DMA, cannot be set manually.

Connecting to sound

For the exam, know which IRQ (interrupt request), DMA (direct memory access) channel, and I/O address are typically assigned to the sound card. You can learn more about IRQs, DMAs, and I/O addresses in Chapter 6.

SoundBlaster-compatible sound cards, the current standard, are normally configured to support

- ✔ DMA Channel 1
- ✔ IRQ 5
- ✔ I/O address 220

However, you may find that PCI sound cards can take as many as three DMA channels, if they are available.

Listening to sound files

A variety of audio file types can be stored and played on a PC. Audio file types typically go by their file extensions. Here are the most common audio file types:

- ✔ **AAC:** *AAC* is the compression standard expected to succeed MP3. *AAC (Advanced Audio Coding)* is another name for MPEG-2, which should not be confused with MP2.

- ✔ **AIFF:** *AIFF (Audio Interchange File Format)* is the Macintosh equivalent of the Windows' WAV format. This format can be played on a PC with the Windows Media Player.

- ✔ **AU:** *AU* is the UNIX audio file standard. Most Web browsers have built-in AU support, and newer versions of the Windows Media Player can play back AU files.

- ✔ **MID:** *MID* aren't really digital audio files; they contain MIDI data, which includes information such as the pitch and duration of each note.

- ✔ **MP3:** Short for MPEG-1 Layer 3, *MP3* is an audio compression standard developed by the Moving Pictures Experts Group (MPEG). MP3 compression has become popular because file sizes can be greatly reduced while retaining most of the original WAV file's sound quality.

- ✔ **RA or RAM:** Real Networks developed these file formats for streaming audio files. Real Audio files require a dedicated Real Audio player or browser plug-in for playback.

- ✔ **WAV:** *WAV* is the standard Windows audio file format with recording and playback support built into the Windows operating systems.

- ✔ **WMA:** *Windows Media Audio* is Microsoft's answer to Real Audio. WMA files can be played back on Windows Media Player and many other sound players.

Interfacing to a CD-ROM or DVD

CD audio is unique among PC audio formats because the CPU does not process the output from an audio CD. Instead both CD-ROM and DVD drives send their output directly to the sound card via a specialized cable. Although it may appear that the computer is processing CD audio because volume levels can be adjusted with a software mixer, all that is being controlled is the sound card's output level.

Cabling between a CD-ROM or DVD drive and a sound card is straightforward, especially if the drive shipped with its own audio cable (and most do). The analog output is always located at the rear of the drive, often to the left of the IDE or SCSI connector, and is typically well-marked, both on the card and in the documentation. Older drives and those that ship without an audio cable can be a bit more complicated, because there is no single standard for the cabling between a CD-ROM or DVD drive and a sound card. Different sound card and drive manufacturers often use proprietary connector types, creating a situation in which a "Panasonic to Sound Blaster" or "Sony to Pro Audio Spectrum" cable might be required. Fortunately, inexpensive (less than $10) universal cables are now available with multiple connectors that will fit almost any combination.

Prep Test

1 The sound card normally uses which IRQ?

A ○ IRQ 2

B ○ IRQ 5

C ○ IRQ 11

D ○ IRQ 9

2 To support a monitor with a resolution of 1,024 x 768 pixels and 65,000 (16-bit) colors, a video card with at least how many MB of video RAM is needed?

A ○ 2

B ○ 4

C ○ 8

D ○ 1

3 A customer calls you claiming that his or her floppy disk drive must be going bad because files are often missing or corrupted after they're saved to the floppy disk. When you arrive at the customer's site ready to troubleshoot the floppy disk drive, you discover a stack of floppy disks sitting on top of the monitor. What do you think may be the problem?

A ○ The customer is not actually saving the data to the disks.

B ○ The cause may be a bad box of disks, which the customer should throw out and replace with new disks.

C ○ The floppy drive is bad and you need to replace it.

D ○ Magnetic emissions from the CRT are possibly erasing the disks.

4 A monitor that uses two passes to draw the entire screen, drawing every other line on each pass, is what type of monitor?

A ○ Noninterlaced

B ○ Interlaced

C ○ Interleaved

D ○ Multiscan

5 Which of the following is not a type of video RAM?

A ○ WRAM

B ○ VRAM

C ○ SGRAM

D ○ ZRAM

6 **The audio wire that connects to the sound card is attached to**

A ○ The ground lead of the motherboard's power connection

B ○ The audio jumper on the motherboard

C ○ The CD-ROM drive

D ○ Nowhere, it is a never-used extra wire

7 **A monitor conforming to the Energy Star standard reduces its power by what percentage in sleep or suspend mode?**

A ○ 99

B ○ 80

C ○ 100

D ○ 96

8 **An ESD grounding strap should always be worn when working on the PC, except when working on a**

A ○ Memory board

B ○ CRT

C ○ Hard drive

D ○ Motherboard

9 **The distance between pixels on the CRT screen is measured as**

A ○ Resolution

B ○ Interlacing

C ○ Dot pitch

D ○ Dot triad

10 **Which of the following is not a type of video adapter card?**

A ○ CGA

B ○ VGA

C ○ LPGA

D ○ SVGA

Answers

1 **B.** A sound card that is SoundBlaster compatible, the current standard, supports DMA channel 1, IRQ 5, and I/O address 220. *See "Connecting to sound."*

2 **A.** This is calculated as $1,024 \times 768 \times 16 \times 8$. *Check out "Sizing up the video memory."*

3 **D.** The CRT produces electrical and magnetic emissions strong enough to corrupt the floppy disks. *Look at "Protecting against electromagnetic evils."*

4 **B.** An interlaced monitor uses two complete screen cycles to completely build the display or refresh the display. *Review "Looking Inside the Monitor."*

5 **D.** WRAM, VRAM, and SGRAM are all types of memories used on a video card. *See "Looking at the Video RAMs."*

6 **C.** The audio wire is actually a part of the CD-ROM assembly and is connected to the sound card to provide sound audio support. *Look up "Interfacing to a CD-ROM or DVD."*

7 **A.** The EPA Energy Star standard certifies equipment that reduces power consumption by 99 percent in sleep or suspend mode. *Check out "Saving the planet."*

8 **B.** Never work on the internal system of a monitor without proper equipment, but if you decide to do so, please don't wear an ESD wrist strap. *Zap over to "Keeping the lid on."*

9 **C.** Dot pitch is the distance between two dots of the same color in adjacent pixels. *Slide up to "Looking Inside the Monitor."*

10 **C.** LPGA may mean anything, but it definitely is not a video adapter card type. *Review "Connecting to adapter card standards."*

Chapter 14

Printers

• •

Exam Objectives

▶ Identifying printer ports, cabling, and connectors

▶ Explaining printer concepts, operations, and components

▶ Troubleshooting common printer problems

▶ Identifying common printer care procedures

• •

Although society cherishes the idea of a paperless society, it churns out more and more paper with thousands, even millions, of numbers, letters, and symbols to be interpreted as information. People thought that the computer would create a paperless society but, as near as I can tell, the opposite has happened. If anything, more paper is printed today than ever before, and computer printers are doing most of the printing. Printers come in a variety of models, but they all essentially perform the same task — printing information on paper.

Little doubt exists that the printer is a very important device to the PC system. It ranks right after the monitor in importance. Like the monitor, its importance is what makes its failure all the more disrupting. I can live without my sound card for a while, but when will you have my printer fixed?

In my experience, at least four in ten service calls involve a printer. Even if I'm wrong and the number is actually only 20 percent of the calls, of the ten major subsystems of the PC, the printer is still responsible for a disproportionate share of the problems, which is probably why the A+ Core Hardware exam has an entire domain devoted just to printers.

Quick Assessment

Identifying printer ports, cabling, and connectors

1 The most common connection type used for PC printers is _____.

2 The default I/O address of _____ is 378-37Fh.

3 A printer that includes a NIC is said to be _____.

Explaining printer concepts, operations, and components

4 Bidirectional parallel interfaces are defined in the _____ standard.

5 A(n) _____ printer uses an array of printwires to form and print a character.

6 Most laser printers use the _____ process or a derivative of it to print.

7 The _____ is used to uniformly charge the photosensitive drum.

8 The six steps of the laser printer process are _____, _____, _____, _____, _____, and _____.

Trouble-shooting common printer problems

9 Paper jams in a laser printer usually occur in the _____ area.

Identifying common printer care procedures

10 Laser printer toner consists of _____ -coated iron particles.

Answers

1 *Parallel.* See "Getting directly connected."

2 *LPT1.* Look at "Getting directly connected."

3 *Network-ready.* Check out "Connecting to a network."

4 *IEEE 1284.* Check out "Keeping up with standards."

5 *Dot matrix.* Review "Dot-matrix printers."

6 *EP (Electrophotographic).* Scan "Laser printers."

7 *Primary or main corona.* Look at "Inside the laser printer."

8 *Cleaning, conditioning, writing, developing, transferring, and fusing.* See "Printing with a laser printer."

9 *Paper pickup or paper feed.* Review "Troubleshooting Common Printer Problems."

10 *Plastic resin.* Take a look at "Inside the laser printer."

A Printer Is a Printer Is a Printer ...

Computer users get rather animated and emotional when their printers don't work. No matter what type of printer is involved, at some point it will all of a sudden just stop working. The true definition of a nanosecond is the length of time it takes the user to dial your number after the printer has not immediately spewed forth a document in perfect form. A significant portion of the exam is devoted to printers, their function, problems, and care. Although most of the questions are about laser printers, be ready for questions on dot matrix and inkjet (bubble jet) printers.

Some attributes that all printers share include the following:

- ✔ **They are peripheral devices.** However, attempts were made in the past to merge the printer into the computer or the monitor. (I still shudder over that one.)

- ✔ **They connect to the PC via a parallel, serial, network, USB, or IrDA interface.** The vast majority of printers attach either directly to a computer or to a network through a cable and a connector. When directly connected to a PC, the parallel connection is the most commonly used. However, when connecting to a network, the RJ-45 is used in most cases.

- ✔ **They all have some form of paper transport system to move the paper to and past the printing mechanism.** In every printer, some mechanism is used to push, pull, roll, or slide the paper through the printing process.

- ✔ **They have a printing or marking process.** Characters are formed on the paper in several ways. A key or a group of wires strikes an inked ribbon; an ink cartridge sprays heated ink; or a toner cartridge creates an image with an electrical charge, resulting in markings on the paper.

- ✔ **They have an engine.** Inside the printer resides the intelligence to accept information and commands from the PC and control the process of printing the information as directed.

Getting directly connected

Although some printers connect through a variety of port types, most PC printers connect to a PC through a parallel port, which is designated as LPT1, LPT2, or perhaps LPT3. Don't worry about what LPT stands for; if it ever had a meaning, it is long lost to the lore of the PC. My guess is that it was something like "line printer termination," but like I said, don't sweat it. LPT ports are designated and numbered according to their I/O addresses during the boot sequence by the system BIOS. See Chapter 11 for more information on connectors and port types, and Chapter 5 for more information on the boot sequence and BIOS.

Table 14-1 lists the IRQ and I/O address assignments typically assigned to the LPT ports. A PC printer interacts with the system through the memory area at the I/O address assigned to the LPT port to which it is connected. However, most PC printers don't actually use an IRQ, especially those attached to a PC running Windows 9x or later. Other parallel devices, such as an external tape, a storage drive, or cables associated with file transfer software, such as LapLink and others, do use interrupts and IRQs. There are no default DMA assignments made to the LPT ports, but DMA channel 3 is used by some types of LPT ports.

Table 14-1	LPT Port System Resources	
Parallel Port	*I/O Address*	*IRQ*
LPT1	378-37Fh	7
LPT2	278-27F	5
LPT3	3BC-3BFh	7 or 5

The most commonly used connectors used to connect printers directly to a PC are

✔ **25-pin DB (data bus) female connector:** The parallel port on the back of a PC is a 25-pin female connector into which the male connector counterpart on the printer cable (see Figure 14-1) is connected. Most computers today have only one LPT port, and it's usually mounted either on the motherboard or an expansion card.

✔ **36-pin Centronics:** This common connector, shown in Figure 14-1, is used at the printer end of the connecting cable. The PC end of the cable is a 25-pin male connector, as described in the previous bullet. The Centronics connector is also the standard connector for the HP-IB (Hewlett Packard Interface Bus). This general style of connector has become known as the Centronics connector because Centronics Corporation produced a large share of the printers used for the earliest PCs. Ampenol produced the original design. Other types of Centronics connectors are used on the PC, such as the 50-pin SCSI, but the 36-pin is the one used with printers.

✔ **USB:** Some of the latest printers now feature a USB connection in addition to the standard parallel connector. But, if the printer you're working on is a bit older, it can still be connected to the PC via a USB port using a USB to a parallel adapter cable. This cable has a Centronics connector on the printer end and a USB connector on the PC end. Why would you connect your printer via the USB port? You may want to free up your parallel port for another use, such as a scanner or a Zip drive, or you may want to connect the printer to a USB hub.

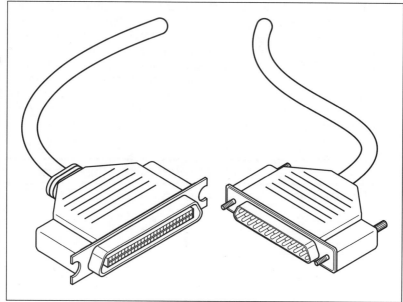

Figure 14-1:
The parallel
connector
(right)
and the
Centronics
connector
(left) are the
two most
common
connectors
used to
connect a
printer
to a PC.

✔ **IR (infrared) or IrDA (Infrared Data Association)**: Some adapters, such
as the one made by Extended Systems (www.extendedsystems.com),
can be used to connect a parallel printer to a PC through its IrDA connection, which frees the parallel port on the PC for other uses. A number
of handheld-size printers designed for use with notebooks and PDAs
that interface with an IrDA connection are also available, but these are
not covered on the exam.

A general rule for how long a parallel cable can be is that older Centronics
cables should not be more than 15 feet in length; between 9 and 12 feet is
best. Newer IEEE-1284 cables extend up to 30 feet in length, and 50-foot high-
end cables are available as well. Typically, if you need to be more than 10 feet
away from a printer, connect into a network.

Switching around

You can use a switchbox, either manual or automatic, to connect more than
one nonlaser printer or any other parallel device or devices to a single parallel port. You can also use them to allow multiple PCs to share a single printer.
A dial designates which PC or device is to be connected to the primary
device of the switchbox. The devices on the switchbox are called A/B
switches because the station designations are generically labeled alphabetically — A, B, C, and so on. An automatic switchbox senses activity on a line
and switches to it when its device connection becomes available.

Before you flood me with e-mails saying how successful you've been with your laser printer and your automatic switchbox, just remember that the following is just a caution. Because they are highly interactive with the printer, many laser printer device drivers (not all) have problems with switchboxes due to electrical noise. Taking the laser printer on- and off-line by changing the active location, either manually or automatically, can interrupt device driver commands and create electrical noise spikes that could possibly damage the laser printer or the PC's parallel port.

Keeping up with standards

Chapter 11, which covers parallel ports, includes a section on the IEEE 1284 parallel port and protocol standards. If you have not reviewed that chapter or the "Keeping up with standards" section, I strongly recommend that you make a point of studying it thoroughly. The IEEE 1284 standard, especially bidirectional communications on a parallel port, is definitely on the test.

Connecting to a network

As the cost of computing and printing continues to climb, sharing expensive resources, such as a high-end color laser printer, with several PCs by integrating the printer into the local area network (LAN) is a good idea. A printer that a home PC user is likely to buy typically does not include the components that make it network-ready. However, the printers usually found in business settings, which are usually shared over the network, can usually be purchased network-ready or can be adapted (as can the home printer) to connect to a network.

Printers that are network-ready have a network interface card (NIC) already installed into which an RJ-45 network connector can be inserted. Chapter 22 talks more about the process used to configure printers to the network, but it is becoming easier everyday. Operating systems are starting to recognize that nearly all computing environments include a printer, that there are literally hundreds of printers to choose from, and that including the printer drivers is a good thing.

If a printer is not network-ready, some network printer interface devices, such as Hewlett Packard's JetDirect, can be used to connect one or more printers to the network. These devices connect to the printer through its parallel port and provide a built-in NIC that connects to the network with a network connector (typically an RJ-45).

Figure 14-2 shows both a network-ready printer that is connected directly to the network and the use of a printer to network interface device to connect a printer that is not network-ready.

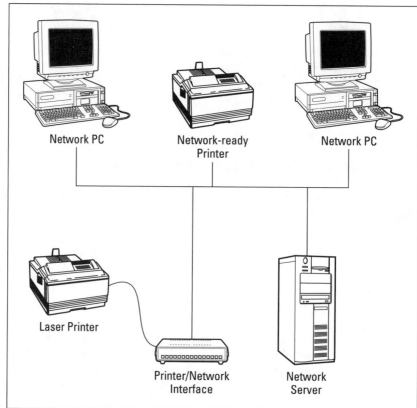

Figure 14-2:
Printers
can be
connected
into a
network and
shared by
many users.

A Plethora of Printers

You can connect many different types of printers to a PC. If you are one of the lucky few who always have the latest and greatest hardware, you probably have a distorted view of the kinds of computers that most users actually have — not the latest and greatest. Many dot-matrix, inkjet, bubble jet, and even some noisy, old daisy-wheel printers are still in use. Not everyone has a laser printer.

The printers that are listed in the objectives of the A+ Core Hardware exam (the ones you are supposed to know) are:

✔ **Dot-matrix:** These printers create characters by forming a group of hard-wire pins into the pattern of the letter, number, or special character and then striking the entire pin group through a ribbon, forming the character on paper.

> ✔ **Inkjet or bubble jet:** Inkjet printers are probably the most popular printer type in use. They produce a better-quality print without the noise of the dot-matrix printer and at a lower price than a laser printer. Inkjet printers produce an image by heating ink into steam and then "jetting" it onto the paper.

> ✔ **Laser:** These printers use a complex printing process to produce very high-quality documents. Laser printers are becoming more common on the desktop, especially with prices continuing to decline.

Dot-matrix printers

You may see questions on the exam about preventive care of dot-matrix printers, how they form characters and drive paper, and how their resolution is measured.

The dot-matrix printer is an impact printer that creates its printed characters using a matrix of very fine printwires that produce a pattern of dots. As the number of printwires used to create the character increases, so does its resolution and the quality of the printed image. Each pin, chosen from a matrix of pins, forms a dot on the page, and the pattern of dots creates the printed character. The resulting character is not as good as one created by a laser printer, but given the trade-off cost and flexibility, this is acceptable for many documents. Resolution is the number of dots that are printed in a square inch (dots-per-inch or dpi).

The most common numbers of printwires (pins) in the dot-matrix printer's printhead are 9, 18, and 24. A 24-pin printhead produces *near-letter quality* (NLQ) print. Printers with less than 24 pins are only capable of *draft quality* print, which produces characters with lots of wide-open spaces between the dots. If laser printer quality is Los Angeles, then draft quality is North Dakota.

To produce a character, the print mechanism extends all the printwires needed to create a character's pattern. Behind each printwire is a solenoid coil that causes the pin to extend and impact the inked ribbon. A spring then pulls each printwire back into the printhead. Because of the impact used to strike the ink of the ribbon onto the page, dot-matrix printers are commonly used in situations where forms or documents with many carbon copies are created.

The typical dot-matrix printer uses continuous form paper (in contrast to the cut sheet paper used in laser and inkjet printers). Much like a typewriter, dot-matrix printers use a platen (a large rubberized roller), under which the paper is fed. The platen provides spring tension to hold the paper in place and move it through the printer. When the platen motor rotates the platen, the paper is pushed up and past the printhead. If *typewriter* is a new term to you, visit Joanne and Ben Batchelor's History of the IBM typewriter site at www.etypewriters.com/history.htm.

Dot-matrix printers also support form tractors, or pin-feed tractors, which attach to the platen and are also driven by the platen motor. Form tractors provide a more consistent feed mechanism by using the pin-feed holes along the side of the paper to pull the paper and multiple part forms through the printer.

The speed of a dot-matrix printer is rated in characters per second (CPS). Common speed ratings for dot-matrix printers range from 32 to 72 CPS. The actual speed realized from the printer depends largely on its mode of operation. Dot-matrix printers operate in either font (normal text, numbers, and symbols) and dot-addressable (graphics and charts) modes.

The printhead in a dot-matrix printer can get extremely hot and should not be touched while in use. Be gentle when cleaning and handling the internal parts of a dot-matrix printer, particularly with the printhead and its print-wires (especially in aging dot-matrix printers). If you are too rough with the printhead, you can damage its tracking or its printwires.

Inkjet printers

Expect to see questions on the Core Hardware exam about inkjet printers, particularly about the way they form characters.

Inkjet, also known as bubble jet, printers are probably the most popular printer type in use. They are quiet and use an ink reservoir instead of a messy ribbon. The inkjet printer is a nonimpact printer, and except for the rush of the printhead moving back and forth, it makes very little noise. The ink reservoir is included in a disposable cartridge that also contains the printing mechanism. This means that each time the ink reservoir is replenished, a new print mechanism is also supplied.

Inkjet printers form characters by squirting ink using an elaborate ink-stream process, which utilizes as many as 50 tiny nozzles. The print quality of an inkjet printer is rated in dots per inch (dpi). The more dots in the image, the better the image. Inkjets range from 150 dpi to over 1400 dpi on photo-quality printers.

Inkjet printer speeds are rated in pages per minute (PPM) rather than characters per second (CPS) because the inkjet doesn't form each character separately. Rather, it prints one line at a time across the page. Each printed line contains only a portion of the print image oriented top to bottom. It takes several passes across the page to complete a complete line of text. Inkjet printer speeds range from 2 PPM to 9 PPM.

The paper feed mechanism of an inkjet printer is actually quite simple. A cut sheet of paper is fed from a stacked supply past the printhead by a series of rollers that also clamp the paper in place. The paper is advanced one print line at a time past the printhead, which moves back and forth across the paper. The finished page is stacked face-up above the original paper supply in a separate tray.

Laser printers

Laser printers are VIT (very important technology) on the A+ Core Hardware exam. Have a good understanding of general laser printer operations and the six steps of the laser printer's printing process.

Laser printers are considered page printers because they form and print all the text and graphics for one full sheet or page at a time. Three different printing processes are used in laser printers, each directly attributable to one or more manufacturer(s): EP, HP, and LED.

- ✔ **Electrophotographic (EP) process:** This process, which was the first laser printer technology, was developed by Xerox and Canon and is the technology used by all laser printers in one form or another. It uses a laser beam to produce an electrostatic charge and a dry toner to create the "printed" image.

- ✔ **Hewlett-Packard (HP) process:** The HP process is essentially the same as the EP process, with the exception of some minor operating procedures. It's similar enough to be considered the same process, yet different enough to get its own name.

- ✔ **Light-emitting diode (LED) process:** From outward appearances, you can't distinguish an LED printer from a laser printer. The difference boils down to the fact that an LED printer uses an array of about 2,500 light-emitting diodes instead of a laser to produce an electrostatic charge. An LED printer with a 600 dpi resolution has 600 LEDs per inch.

Inside the laser printer

Laser printers use toner to create the image on the printed page. Toner is a dry powder that consists of iron particles coated with a plastic resin that bonds to the paper during the print process. Toner is supplied to the printer in a removable cartridge that also contains many of the most important parts used in the printing process. The toner cartridge contains the photosensitive drum (a mechanism used to place a charge on the drum), a roller to develop the final image on the page, and, of course, the toner.

Plan on understanding just about everything there is to know about laser printers for the test, including the following list of major components. Expect questions about the overall laser printing process, as well as the role played by key components.

In addition to the toner cartridge, eight standard assemblies exist in a laser printer. These assemblies are

- ✔ **The drum:** The drum inside the toner cartridge is photosensitive, which means it reacts to light. The drum holds an electrostatic charge (except where it is exposed to light). The laser beam is reflected onto the surface of the drum to create a pattern of charged and not-so-charged spots, representing the image of the page to be printed.

- ✔ **High-voltage power supply:** The EP process uses very high voltage to charge the drum and transfer and hold the toner on the paper. The high-voltage power supply converts AC current into the higher voltages used by the printer.

- ✔ **DC power supply:** Like a computer, most of the electronic components in the laser printer use direct current. For example, logic circuits use +/–5V DC (volts direct current), and the paper transport motors use +24V DC. Also, like the computer's power supply, the laser printer DC power supply also contains the cooling system fan.

- ✔ **Paper transport:** Inside the laser printer are four types of rollers that move the paper through the printer. Each rubberized roller or set of rollers is driven by its own motor. The four roller types in the paper transport system are the feed roller (or the paper pickup roller), the registration roller, the fuser roller, and the exit roller.

If you're asked where most paper jams occur in a laser printer, the answer is the paper transport area.

- ✔ **Primary corona:** Also called the *main corona* or *the primary grid,* this device forms an electrical field that uniformly charges the photosensitive drum to –600V as a way to reset it prior to receiving the print image and toner.

- ✔ **Transfer corona:** This mechanism moves a page image from the drum to the paper. I cover how this happens a little later, but for now, know that the transfer corona charges the paper and the charge pulls the toner from the drum onto the paper. As the paper exits the transfer corona, a static charge eliminator strip reduces the charge on the paper so that it won't stick to the drum. Not all printers use a transfer corona; some use a transfer roller instead. When working on a printer with a transfer roller, be careful not to touch the roller with your bare hand or arm. The oils from your skin can spot the transfer roller and cause improperly charged paper, which shows up as defects in the printed image.

- ✔ **Fusing rollers:** The toner is melted permanently to the page by the fusing rollers that apply pressure and heat (between 165 and 180 degrees Celsius) to it. The fuser — not the laser — is what makes the printed pages hot.

✔ **Controller:** This is the motherboard of the laser printer, and it has similar architecture and components of a PC motherboard. The controller communicates with the PC, houses the memory in the printer, and forms the image printed on the page. Memory expansion is possible on virtually all laser printers. Adding memory allows the printer to reproduce larger documents or graphics in higher resolutions or to support additional soft fonts.

A printer that experiences frequent memory overflow errors has a bad memory board, a memory board that was installed incorrectly, or a memory board that needs additional memory. Diagnose this problem by eliminating these conditions in this order.

Printing with a laser printer

Six major steps are involved in printing a page on a laser printer. It's very important that you remember the sequence and activities of each step in the process. A catch phrase I've devised to help you remember the sequence is

California Cows Won't Dance The Fandango (CCWDTF)

The first letter in each word represents a step in the laser printing process: Cleaning, Conditioning, Writing, Developing, Transferring, and Fusing. (You may also see cleaning as the last step in other references, but on the exam, it's listed first.) Also be ready to list the steps in backward order. You'll need to develop your own shortcut for remembering the process backwards because I still have a headache from the last one.

Here is what goes on during each step of the EP laser printing process:

✔ **Cleaning:** Before a new page is printed, any remnants from the previous page are cleared away. The drum is swept free of any lingering toner with a rubber blade, and a fluorescent lamp removes any electrical charge remaining on the drum. Any toner removed in this step is not reused but is put into a used-toner compartment on the cartridge.

✔ **Conditioning:** The entire drum is uniformly charged to –600V by the primary corona wire (also known as the main corona) located inside the toner cartridge. This charge conditions the drum for the next step.

✔ **Writing:** The laser printer controller uses a laser beam and a series of mirrors to create the image of the page on the drum. The laser beam is turned on and off in accordance with the image to be created on the drum. At the spot where the laser's light contacts the photosensitive drum, the charge is reduced to about –100V. After the image has been transferred to the drum this way, the controller also starts the page sheet through the printer, stopping it at the registration rollers.

✔ **Developing:** The developing roller, located inside the toner cartridge, has a magnet inside of it that attracts the iron particles in the toner. As the developing roller rotates near the drum, the toner is attracted to the areas of the drum that have been exposed by the laser, creating the print image on the drum.

✔ **Transferring:** The back of the paper sheet (the one that has been waiting patiently at the registration rollers), is given a positive charge that attracts the negatively charged toner from the drum onto the paper as it passes. After this step, the paper has the image of the page on it, but the toner, which is held only by simple magnetism, is not yet bonded to it.

✔ **Fusing:** The fusing rollers apply heat and pressure to the toner, which melts and presses it into the paper to create a permanent bond. The fusing rollers are covered with Teflon and treated with a light silicon oil to keep the paper from sticking to them.

Preventive Maintenance and Supplies

Regularly performing preventive maintenance and taking proper care of a printer extends its life. Expect to see at least one question on the A+ Core Hardware exam regarding the cleaning, protection, and preventive maintenance of a printer — most likely a laser printer.

General printer housekeeping

Here are a number of common-sense and technical procedures that keep a printer working and reliable:

✔ Plug the printer into a surge protector or UPS (uninterruptible power supply). On a laser printer, first make sure that the UPS is capable of handling the power demands of the printer at startup; few conventional PC UPS units can.

Under the heading of *you heard it here first* (but you will again later): Never plug a laser printer into a conventional PC UPS. Laser printers draw a tremendous amount of power at startup, and few UPS units have enough power to handle the demand. If you use a UPS for your laser printer, be sure the UPS can handle the peak loading (peak power requirements) of the laser printer.

✔ Always use the type and weight of paper recommended for the printer to avoid print feed path jams. Some printers prefer laser paper that is finished on one side. Check the printer's documentation. Also check and remember the heaviest paper recommended for your printer (and never use anything heavier than that) to avoid paper jams and possible damage to the paper-handling mechanism of the printer.

 ✔ Clean dot-matrix printers regularly by vacuuming or blowing them out with compressed air. If you want to vacuum a laser printer, be sure you use only a vacuum and dust bag specially made for that task. The toner can really gum up a regular vacuum cleaner.

 ✔ Use a wire brush or rubber-conditioning product to clean and maintain the paper transport of an inkjet or laser printer. When trying to clear the paper path, never put anything inside a laser printer while it's running and always wait until the fusing area has cooled down before working in this area of a laser printer. Remember that it generates a great deal of heat to melt the toner to the paper and stays hot for some time afterward.

Keeping the laser clean, tidy, and operating

Laser printers have their own special needs when it comes to maintenance, which you should know, test, or no test. For the A+ Core Hardware test, you need to know about toner and the cleaning of the primary corona wire. The following list helps you properly address these special needs.

 ✔ The toner in a laser printer is really nasty stuff. If you have ever accidentally dropped a toner cartridge or ignorantly turned one over and shaken it, you know what I mean. If you ever have a toner spillage accident or see toner spilled inside the laser printer, don't use a regular vacuum to clean it up. Remember that toner is very fine particles of iron and plastic. The particles are so fine that they seep through the walls of most vacuum bags and get into the motor, where the plastic particles melt. Special types of vacuums and vacuum cleaner bags are made for working with toner.

 ✔ If you get toner on your skin, never use warm or hot water to clean it off. Warm water may cause the toner to fuse to your skin. First wipe off as much of the toner with a dry paper towel or soft cloth, then rinse with cold water, and finish by washing with soap and cold water.

 ✔ Usually packed with the toner cartridge is a cleaning brush or cotton swab that you can use to clean the transfer corona wire. You can clean the primary corona wire with a cotton swab as well. Be very careful not to break these wires while cleaning them.

 ✔ During the print process, the laser produces a gas called *ozone*. Most laser printers have an ozone filter that also captures toner and paper dust. Replace or clean this filter in accordance with the manufacturer's instructions in the printer's manual.

✔ Inside the laser printer are two or more mirrors that reflect the laser onto the drum. Using one of the ubiquitous, clean, lint-free cloths, periodically clean the laser mirrors — with the power off, of course. Never, I repeat, never look directly at the laser and never operate the printer with its cover off. Most printers will not power up with the cover open, anyway.

✔ The fuser cleaning pad and the fusing roller can also become dirty and leave unwanted toner blobs on the paper. Check these printer parts regularly and clean them as necessary.

Troubleshooting Common Printer Problems

The A+ Core Hardware exam may include situational questions that require you to choose the action that should be taken first or next in a set of given events. The troubleshooting sequence for a printer problem is fairly routine for most experienced PC service technicians, and you probably have your own. However, I suggest reviewing the following steps just to refresh your memory for the test.

The first real sign of a printer problem is that paper with printing on it isn't coming out of the printer. When this happens, look in four places:

✔ **Printer:** First check to see whether it's powered on and then check to see whether it's online. These suggestions may seem like bonehead stuff, but they are commonly the problem. Make sure that the printer has paper and that the feed tray, roller, or slide is in its proper position for operation. Check for a paper jam; if you find one, clear it, but also notice the point at which the jam occurred and check the rollers and paper feed mechanism carefully. Most paper jams happen in the paper pickup area, so look there first.

✔ **Cable:** If the printer seems to be all right, ensure that the cable is the proper type of cable. Nearly all laser printers and the newest inkjets and dot-matrix printers require an IEEE 1284 cable. If the cable is the right kind, then make sure that it's solidly connected at each end.

✔ **Port:** To check the port, use loopback plugs and diagnostic software. Believe it or not, after the printer itself, the parallel port has the next highest failure rate.

✔ **Software:** In the Windows environment, printers stall for just about any reason. If the printer status shows no problems, and you can't find any other problem, try restarting the system.

Beyond a printer not printing, the most common failure is a bad print image. Regularly cleaning the printer and its printing mechanism or printhead as directed by the printer's manuals helps to avoid this problem. As a professional PC repairperson, it is really worth your while to show customers how to clean these items themselves.

Setting Up a Printer in Windows

Expect to find a question or two about the procedure used to set up a printer on a Windows PC on the Operating Systems Technologies exam. Familiarize yourself with the process used by actually doing it a few times using different ways to access the Printer group on the Control Panel.

Before you can set a printer in a Windows environment, you must obtain the printer driver for that printer under the specific version of Windows that you operate. If you use Windows 3.*x*, then use a Windows 3.*x* printer driver; for Windows 95, use a printer driver designed for it. Typically, you can find the correct printer driver on the manufacturer's Web site.

Windows 9*x*, Windows NT, and Windows 2000 each carry a remarkable number of printer drivers with them. However, to be absolutely sure you have the latest driver for the PC's operating system, visit the manufacturer's Web site. Some printers come with a separate printer driver included on a floppy disk or CD-ROM.

Add new printers through the Printers function found on the Control Panel or on the Settings option of the Start Program menu. In either case, the Printers dialog box displays the Add Printer wizard icon (see Figure 14-3). Lab 14-1 details the steps to add a printer.

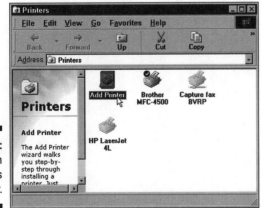

Figure 14-3:
Printers in
the Printers
folder.

Lab 14-1   Adding a New Printer

1. **From the Windows desktop, click the Start button to display the Start menu. Access the Settings menu and choose the Printers option.**

   Or double-click the My Computer icon to display the My Computer folder. Open the Control Panel and choose the Printers icon.

2. **With the Printer folder open, choose the Add Printer icon shown in Figure 14-3 to display the Add Printer dialog box (Windows 3.*x* or Windows 95) or start the Add Printer wizard (Windows 98 and Windows 2000).**

3. **If the printer you are adding is not included in the supported printers list, use the floppy disk or CD-ROM that came with the printer to supply the device driver by clicking the Have Disk button when appropriate.**

   After the printer driver loads, an icon for the new printer displays in the Printers folder.

Prep Test

1 The paper continuously jams in a laser printer. Where would you look first?

A ○ Pressure roller area

B ○ Transfer roller area

C ○ Fuser roller area

D ○ Paper pickup area

2 What happens in the conditioning phase of a laser printer?

A ○ The image is created on the drum.

B ○ The erasure lamps neutralize the drum.

C ○ The primary corona applies a uniform charge to the drum.

D ○ The paper is charged by the transfer corona.

3 The correct order of operations in the laser printing process is

A ○ Conditioning, cleaning, writing, developing, fusing, transferring

B ○ Cleaning, conditioning, writing, developing, transferring, fusing

C ○ Conditioning, cleaning, writing, developing, transferring, fusing

D ○ Cleaning, conditioning, writing, developing, fusing, transferring

4 On a system on which printing has been working well, the user gets an error message when he or she tries to print. No changes have been made to the system. After checking whether the printer is powered on, what do you check next?

A ○ Is the printer online?

B ○ Is the printer designated as the default printer?

C ○ Is the correct printer driver installed?

D ○ Will the printer print when attached to a different PC?

5 Reducing the negative charge on the areas of the drum that represent the image to be printed is done in which step of the laser printing process?

A ○ Transferring

B ○ Conditioning

C ○ Fusing

D ○ Writing

6 The toner is deposited onto the drum surface in which step of the printing process?

A ○ Writing

B ○ Conditioning

C ○ Developing

D ○ Transferring

7 Toner is bonded with the paper during which phase of the laser printing process?

A ○ Writing

B ○ Transferring

C ○ Conditioning

D ○ Fusing

8 Which of the following forms the electrical field that charges the drum?

A ○ Transfer corona wire

B ○ Primary corona wire

C ○ Fusing roller

D ○ Cleaning blade

9 A dot-matrix printer with a 24-pin printhead is capable of producing

A ○ Letter-quality print

B ○ Daisy-wheel quality print

C ○ Near-letter quality print

D ○ Graphics only

10 Bidirectional communications on a parallel cable was standardized by

A ○ IEEE 232

B ○ VESA

C ○ Laser printers

D ○ IEEE 1284

Answers

1 **D.** Most paper jams happen right in the paper pickup area when more than one sheet, a crumpled sheet, or a twisted sheet of paper tries to feed into the paper pickup rollers. *See "Troubleshooting Common Printer Problems."*

2 **C.** In this step of the laser printing process, the drum is put into the right condition to receive the print image. *Charge over to "Printing with a laser printer."*

3 **B.** Remember "California Cows Won't Dance The Fandango." *See "Printing with a laser printer."*

4 **A.** I know this seems pretty basic, but forgetting the basics gets many PC technicians in trouble. *Check out "Troubleshooting Common Printer Problems."*

5 **D.** This step "writes" the blips on the drum where toner will be placed during the developing step. *Read "Printing with a laser printer."*

6 **C.** I include this question to drive home the comment I make for Prep Test Question 5. Putting toner on the drum "develops" the print image so that it can be transferred to the paper. *Review "Printing with a laser printer."*

7 **D.** Okay, this is the last question of the laser printer's process steps. In the fusing step, the toner is heated to about 350 degrees Fahrenheit and pressed down hard by the fusing rollers. *Take one more look at "Printing with a laser printer."*

8 **B.** To separate the two corona wires in your mind, just remember that the primary corona goes first and charges the drum. The transfer corona is second and charges the paper. *Look at "Inside the laser printer."*

9 **C.** About the best a dot-matrix printer can do with round dots is getting the print near the quality of print produced with a solid typeface. *Review "Dot-matrix printers."*

10 **D.** IEEE standard 1284 combines the SPP, EPP, and ECL parallel port standards that include bidirectional communications. *See "Keeping up with standards."*

Chapter 15

Portable Systems

▶ Identifying the unique components of portable PC systems

▶ Installing and upgrading components

*A*lthough the early laptop computers were smaller than the desktop devices of their time, they filled your lap completely and then some. Portables were also much too big for airline meal trays — a sure killer in the business market. Today, the *notebook computer* has finally established a package size that the market can truly use just about anywhere. Solitaire anywhere, anytime, anyplace! The latest evolution in portables is the ultimately small palmtop. Technology has finally developed a full-fledged Windows computer that you can literally hold in your hand or fit in your briefcase — or even conveniently tuck into your little zippered planner. Even smaller systems are available that fit into the category of personal digital assistant (PDA), but these devices are still cataloged as personal electronics and have not yet earned the very exclusive moniker of "computer."

The exact role of the professional PC service technician with these devices in the future remains to be seen, which explains why the A+ Core Hardware exam has only a few questions on portable systems.

Quick Assessment

Identifying the unique components of portable PC systems

1 _____ is the most popular type of portable PC today.

2 A(n) _____ is the power system that allows a notebook computer to be portable.

3 Because of its weight and long life, the _____ type of battery is probably the best choice for a portable PC.

4 Portable PCs use a special kind of memory module called a(n) _____.

Installing and upgrading components

5 Before physically installing a larger internal hard drive on a notebook computer, you can add _____, _____, or _____ by using an existing port.

6 The type of LCD display that supports each pixel with its own transistor is called _____.

7 Type I PCMCIA cards are used to add _____ to a notebook computer.

8 A modem is an example of a(n) _____ PC Card.

9 Type III PCMCIA cards can be up to _____ millimeters thick.

10 Changing a PC Card while the system is running is called _____.

Answers

1   *Notebook.* Flip to "Checking Out Portable PC Types."

2   *Battery.* Look at "Portable PC power systems."

3   *Li-Ion.* See "Portable PC battery types."

4   *SODIMM.* Take a look at "Adding memory."

5   *Zip, Jazz, or tape drive.* Review "Upgrading the hard drive."

6   *Active matrix.* Scan "Comparing active and passive LCD displays."

7   *Flash memory.* See "Focusing on PC cards."

8   *Type II.* Check into "Focusing on PC cards."

9   *10½.* Take a look at "Focusing on PC cards."

10 *Hot-swapping.* Look at "Expanding capacity on the fly."

Relating Portable Systems and the A+ Exam

The areas that you need to study about portable systems are the following:

- AC/DC power sources
- Hard drives
- Keyboard
- Mouse
- Motherboards
- Memory
- Video and other adapter cards
- Displays
- Docking station and port replicators

The next few sections cover a little history and terminology. If you want to cut to the chase on portable PCs for the A+ Core Hardware exam, go to the section "Expanding capacity on the fly" later in this chapter.

Powering the Portable

Adaptable, lightweight, and long-life power sources play a large part in the usability of a portable PC system. Essentially, three general types of power sources are available for portable PCs — each designed to provide it with power either in the office or on the road:

- **AC/DC adapter:** Works very much like the power supply in a desktop computer to convert the wall socket AC power into DC power. AC adapters are also used to recharge the portable PC's battery. You are probably very familiar with this type of device because it's used on a wide range of electronic products — including games, calculators, and external computer peripherals.

- **Battery:** An integral part of any portable PC because without it, the PC would not be as portable. Instead, users would need very long extension cords and have to depend on having an AC outlet everywhere they go. Look for more details on batteries later in this section.

✔ **Docking station:** In addition to the power that it provides the PC, the docking station enables the PC to connect to full-sized expansion cards and additional ports, and allows the portable PC to connect to and drive the peripherals (monitor, printer, and so on) that are usually connected to a desktop computer. *Port replicators* are typically smaller versions of the docking station that provide only for additional I/O ports.

Portable PC power systems

The power supply of a portable PC is focused on power conservation rather than power regulation, as is a nonportable PC power supply. A portable PC runs on DC power just like other PCs, but the portable runs straight from a battery. This means that the portable PC supply does not convert AC to DC to power the motherboard, processor, video display, and peripheral devices. AC power is used to recharge the battery, but it does not power the PC.

Managing portable PC power

Virtually all portable PCs now have some kind of a power management system, most commonly in the form of a software battery monitor. This system tracks the reserve power of the battery and reports its strength as a percentage. A report of 70 percent means that you've used only 30 percent of the battery's capacity. Many power management systems also check to see if the PC is in use and if it's not, the power management system suspends the PC to conserve the battery's power. Conserving a battery and extending its life is a much better — and less expensive — choice than replacing the battery.

Portable PC battery types

Be prepared to see a question about portable PC battery characteristics on the A+ Core Hardware exam. In this section, I cover the differences of the battery types that are used in portable PCs.

Portable PCs use four types of batteries: alkaline, nickel-cadmium (NiCad), NiMH (Nickel-Metal Hydride), and Lithium-Ion (Li-Ion). The following is a list of their characteristics:

✔ **Alkaline:** The same batteries that you commonly rely on for operation of your calculator, TV remote control, and portable tape player. This type of battery is used in some palmtop computers.

✔ **Nickel Cadmium (NiCad):** The most popular and durable type of rechargeable battery. This battery is also the heaviest, yet least expensive, of the portable PC battery types; it is also quick to charge and has a reasonable life of around 700 charge-and-discharge cycles.

✔ **Nickel-Metal Hydride (NiMH):** Unlike NiCad batteries, these batteries are environmentally friendly because they don't contain heavy metals that can be toxic. They also store up to 30 percent more power than NiCad batteries of the same battery weight. Some of the disadvantages of NiMH batteries are that they have a shorter life (around 400 charge-and-discharge cycles) and cost about 30 percent more than NiCad batteries.

✔ **Lithium Ion (Li-Ion or LiON):** Very lightweight with a long battery life, this type of battery is made with one of the lightest metals (Lithium) around. LiON batteries hold about twice the power as a NiCad battery in about half the weight, and compared to a NiMH of equal weight, a LiON delivers twice the run time from each charge. This battery type has about the same life cycle as NiCad and NiMH batteries. LiONs are not generally available for all models and are typically more expensive than other battery types. A LiON is probably the best choice of battery for a portable PC — although it can be more expensive than the other choices.

Looking inside the portable PC

Portable PCs resemble their nonportable computer cousins only in their functions. Their internal components, such as processors, motherboards, and memory, vary in size, capacity, speed, mounting, and other characteristics contributing to a PC's portability.

Computing power for the portable

Intel's Pentium family of processors includes the most popular CPUs used in notebook computers; among these are the mobile versions of its Pentium II, Mobile Celeron, Pentium II PE (Performance Enhanced), and Pentium III processors. AMD is gaining popularity with its K6-2 and K6-III processors. When producing a mobile version of a processor, the manufacturers are primarily concerned with size, power usage, and heat generation — all of which they try to reduce. The packaging of a mobile CPU provides much of the cooling for the processor, which is normally handled by fans and heatsinks in nonportable systems.

Upgrading the Portable PC

The two main disadvantages of notebook PCs are that they are difficult to work on and upgrades are expensive. Upgrade parts are expensive because they are usually proprietary and not generally interchangeable between manufacturers — or even between models from the same manufacturer, in many cases.

You can assume three things about questions regarding repairs on a portable PC:

 ✔ The type of portable PC in question is a notebook computer, unless otherwise stated.

 ✔ The notebook computer has a Pentium or higher CPU.

 ✔ The only upgrades that are performed internally are to the RAM and hard drive.

Adding memory

RAM upgrades, at least on most high-end and name brand portable PCs, are accomplished through a porthole or trap door on either the bottom or the side of the portable PC. The hard drive, which on some units is an inter-changeable unit, can be easily removed and replaced.

If after installing new RAM on a notebook PC, the RAM is not showing up in the BIOS POST display, chances are that the RAM is not properly seated. Shut down the notebook and reseat the RAM.

Notebook PCs and many other portable computers use *Small Outline Dual Inline Memory Modules (SODIMM)*. A SODIMM is a smaller, narrower, and taller version of the DIMM module that is used in desktop PCs. On most newer notebook designs, memory is added through the bottom of the PC's case. The SODIMM is mounted flush to the mainboard and lies flat to save space.

Here are the general steps used to install a SODIMM in a notebook PC:

1. **Remove the old SODIMM module. Push the plastic retaining clips outward and tilt the SODIMM up and out of the socket.**

2. **Install the new SODIMM by aligning the edge connector notches to the slot.**

3. **Place the SODIMM in the slot at a slight angle.**

   The retaining clips prevent the module from laying flat in the socket.

4. **Gently but firmly press the SODIMM into the slot until the detents on the retaining clips line up with the notches on the module.**

5. **Press the SODIMM until the plastic clips snap.**

   The plastic clips lock the SODIMM into place and hold it flat in the mounting.

Older notebook PCs may use single inline memory modules (SIMMs), which are installed in much the same manner as the SODIMM. However, portable systems often prescribe both the total memory that it can support and the increments that you can use to add it. Consult the owner's manual to determine the right choices.

Another way to add memory to a PC is to insert a PC Card, also known as a Personal Computer Memory Card International Association (PCMCIA) card. (See "Focusing on PC Cards" later in this chapter for more information.)

Upgrading the hard drive

The secondary storage units of some notebook models are located under the keyboard for easy interchange or replacement. In these models, replacing the hard drive is a snap: Snap out the old and snap in the new. On other models, however, the hard drive is internally blended into the notebook's system. If you really want to increase the hard drive space, you may want to use a less arduous way of increasing the PC's storage capacity.

The following is a list of options that you should eliminate before attempting to replace an internal hard drive on a notebook PC:

✔ You can add removable storage very easily through an existing port. For example, you can add a Zip, Jazz, or tape drive via a serial, parallel, or USB port.

✔ You can add a hard drive card in a PC Card slot.

✔ If a portable PC supports it, you can interchange the floppy disk or CD-ROM with a second removable hard drive.

✔ You can use disk space compression utilities to increase the effective space of the hard drive.

Notebooks and other portable computers don't have standard internal layout and designs like those provided by the form factors of desktop and tower PCs. Because of this, you need an upgrade kit to change the hard drive in a notebook PC. The upgrade kit usually includes the new hard drive, a PC Card, and data transfer cables. The PC Card and cables are used with data transfer software that is also included in the kit to temporarily hold and transfer the data from the old hard drive to the new one.

Focusing on PC Cards

PCMCIA offers a standard for adding more memory and peripherals to portable computers using credit card-like cards — also called PC Cards. All PC Cards are 85.6 mm long and 54 mm wide, or approximately 3.4 inches by

2.1 inches, and use a 68-pin connector. PC Cards are matched to designated slots on the portable PC, and each is defined to one of the three particular types and sizes of cards.

The three standards of the thickness of the card are as follows:

✓ **Type I:** At 3½-mm thick, these slots have one row of sockets and are used primarily to add *flash memory,* or SRAM (static RAM). This type of memory is common on PCMCIA cards because it requires less power. You can read more about flash memory in Chapter 5.

✓ **Type II:** At 5½-mm thick, these slots have two rows of sockets and are used to add modems and NICs to a notebook computer. These cards usually have a pop-out connector for an RJ-11 or RJ-45 connector.

✓ **Type III:** At up to 10½-mm thick, these slots have three rows of sockets and are used to install hard drives or support adapters for external CD-ROM, DVD, and tape drives.

More information is available on PC Card standards from PCMCIA's Web site (www.pc-card.com).

The magic of the PC Card

Adding a function through the PC Card slots of the notebook PC is as easy as pressing the card (firmly) into its slot. You can even do this while the notebook is up and running. The card's function is instantly recognized by the PC — provided that the card services and sockets are running.

PC Card sockets and services

Portable PCs contain two layers of software designed to detect and support a PC Card when you insert it into the computer:

✓ **Socket services:** A layer of BIOS-level software that detects when a card is inserted or removed.

✓ **Card services:** Software that manages the assignment and allocation of system resources to the PC Card, such as IRQ and I/O addresses, after the socket services software has detected the card.

Count on at least one portable PC question involving one of the three PC Card types. Just remember, the higher the type number, the thicker the card; a hard drive (Type III) is thicker than a modem (Type II), which is thicker than memory (Type I). Also remember which type of card supports which type of device.

Expanding capacity on the fly

You can change PC Cards without shutting down the system with a procedure called *hot-swapping.* Hot-swapping enables you to remove any existing card from its slot and install a new card while the PC is on and the operating system is running.

Expect a question on hot-swapping, something such as "What is changing a PC Card without powering off the system called?"

PC Cards use the 32-bit CardBus standard, which is essentially identical to the PCI bus architecture with some minor electrical differences. CardBus supports bus mastering, accommodates cards at different voltages, and includes advanced power-management features that can idle or turn off PC Cards to increase battery life.

Comparing active and passive LCD displays

Liquid crystal diode (LCD) displays are used on notebook computers because LCD displays have lower power requirements than the CRT-style monitor and can be configured into a flat panel.

Any exam question about notebook computer displays is likely to explore these two major types of LCD displays:

- ✔ **Active matrix:** If you have an LCD display on your watch, you have an active matrix display. This type of LCD display has a transistor for each pixel and creates a very crisp image that is easy to read from an angle and has very good resolution. The downside is that all those transistors take a lot of power. An active matrix display can clean out a battery in less than two hours. Active matrix displays are TFT (Thin-Film Transistor).

- ✔ **Passive matrix:** This type of LCD display has two groups of transistors: one along the top edge of the display containing one transistor for each vertical column of pixels, and the other along the left side of the display containing one transistor for each horizontal row of pixels. Wires form a matrix that interconnects the transistor rows and columns. To darken a particular pixel, power is sent to the transistors on the same row and column as the pixel and down the wires to the intersection point where the pixel sits. This method uses much less power, but it is much slower and produces a lower-quality image. Passive matrix displays are usually either the older Double-layer Supertwist Nematic (DSTN) or the newer High Performance Addressing (HPA). HPA improves the response of the display over DSTN, but it still produces an inferior display image compared to active matrix (TFT) screens.

Both types of LCD displays are flat and about ½-inch thick. TFT displays produce the best image and cost the most. HPA and DSTN screens are hard to see except by looking straight at the display. An HPA screen does have one advantage: Only the operator has a clear look at the screen. People trying to see the screen from the side are out of luck, which may be desirable when working with secure data.

Because LCD displays are covered with a thin sheet of plastic, avoid any abrasive cleaners and cloths. Use a mild detergent or low-sudsing, general-purpose cleaner and a lint-free soft cloth.

Prep Test

1 **A Type I PC Card is used to**

- **A** ○ Add SRAM to the system
- **B** ○ Add network capabilities to the system
- **C** ○ Add a device, such as a modem, to the system
- **D** ○ Connect an external device such as a CD-ROM drive

2 **A PC Card hard drive fits into a**

- **A** ○ Type I slot
- **B** ○ Type II slot
- **C** ○ Type III slot
- **D** ○ Type IV slot

3 **Hot-swapping means**

- **A** ○ Installing new devices without the need for a driver
- **B** ○ Removing and adding internal devices without rebooting
- **C** ○ Removing and inserting PCMCIA cards while the system is up and running
- **D** ○ All of the above

4 **SODIMM stands for**

- **A** ○ Special Operations for Digital Image Multimedia
- **B** ○ Some Other Dual Inline Memory Module
- **C** ○ Small Outline Dual Inline Memory Module
- **D** ○ None of the above

5 **After inserting a PC Card into a notebook computer, the system does not recognize the card. What could possibly be the problem?**

- **A** ○ No drivers were installed for the card.
- **B** ○ The card was inserted in the wrong type slot.
- **C** ○ The notebook computer does not support PCMCIA.
- **D** ○ Socket or card services have not recognized the card.

6 **A modem generally fits in a _____ PCMCIA slot.**

- **A** ○ Type I
- **B** ○ Type II
- **C** ○ Type III
- **D** ○ Type IV

7 PC Card socket services software _____.

A ○ Allows PC Cards to emulate ISA devices

B ○ Traps PC Card internal errors

C ○ Detects the insertion and removal of PC Cards

D ○ Is used to eject PC Cards

8 Which of the following are types of passive matrix displays? (Choose two.)

A ❑ TFT

B ❑ DHCP

C ❑ HPA

D ❑ DSTN

9 Which of the following resolution standards are used for notebook computer displays? (Choose three.)

A ❑ UGA

B ❑ SVGA

C ❑ XGA

D ❑ SXGA+

10 The video display on a portable PC is powered by

A ○ AC power only

B ○ DC power only

C ○ AC power when the PC is plugged in or DC power when it is not plugged in

D ○ Either AC or DC at the user's choice

Answers

1 **A.** Type II cards are used to add network adapters and modems, and Type III cards are used to plug in external drive adapters. *See "Focusing on PC Cards."*

2 **C.** Type III slots support hard drives. *Review "Focusing on PC Cards."*

3 **C.** Hot-swapping is removing and inserting PC Cards (PCMCIA) without shutting down the system. *Take a look at "Expanding capacity on the fly."*

4 **C.** Because they must mount flush to the mainboard of the portable computer, specially designed modules (SODIMM) are built for each make and model of notebook computer. *Visit "Adding memory" one more time.*

5 **D.** Unless the socket services software detects the card, Card services will not allocate its system resources. *Refer to "PC Card sockets and services."*

6 **B.** Type I cards are used for memory, Type II cards are used for modems, Type III cards are used to add hard drives and NICs, and Type IV cards do not exist. This is the last question on the PC Card types, I promise. *Review "Focusing on PC Cards."*

7 **C.** Socket services software detects when a PC Card is inserted or removed. *Check out "Focusing on PC Cards."*

8 **C** and **D.** Passive displays produce a lower-quality display that does not adapt to rapid changes quickly, but it does produce a good image and doesn't use much power. *Look at "Comparing active and passive LCD displays."*

9 **B, C,** and **D.** Depending on the size of the display, different resolution standards are used to produce the best possible image for the dots per inch (dpi) resolution available on the notebook computer. *Check out "Comparing active and passive LCD displays."*

10 **B.** All systems in a portable PC are powered with low-power DC current. AC is converted to DC by the AC/DC converter. *See "Portable PC power systems."*

Part IV
Putting the Hard in Hardware

The 5th Wave — By Rich Tennant

"Drive carefully, remember your lunch, and always make a backup of your directory tree before modifying your hard disk partition file."

In this part . . .

The three chapters in this part of the book provides information for about 75 percent of the Core Hardware exam, covering the "Installation, Configuration, and Upgrading," "Diagnosing and Troubleshooting," "Preventive Maintenance," and "Motherboard/Processor/ Memory" domains of the exam.

The chapters in this part review the procedures used to disassemble a PC, put it back together again, upgrade key components, determine the source of a problem, and care for the PC. This part summarizes the technical tasks associated with working as a PC service technician and the safety precautions used to protect both you and the PC in the process.

Chapter 16

Disassembling the PC and Putting It Back Together

Exam Objectives

▶ Identifying electrostatic discharge (ESD) safeguards

▶ Removing and replacing field replaceable modules (FRMs)

▶ Identifying system modules and their normal operations

▶ Working safely with high-voltage modules

*Y*ou probably won't have to worry about being asked to list the steps used to disassemble (or reassemble) a PC on the A+ Core exam. You do need, however, background knowledge of the process used to remove (or install) an FRM (field replaceable module) and the safeguards used to protect them and you from ESD. The best way to review the procedure for removing and replacing PC FRMs, such as hard drives, adapter cards, the motherboard, and so on, is to go step-by-step through the processes.

Taking the PC apart isn't difficult, but being able to remove the modules without disrupting everything else is what separates the professional PC repair technician from the hobbyist. The essential skill involved in this process is knowing the difference between an FRM, such as the power supply, and other modules. In addition to your personal safety, your primary concern is to keep working parts working.

When you disassemble a PC, you can see all the modules that you must remove. When you put a computer back together, however, you start with a pile of pieces and assemble them back into correct order (with none left over). If the computer isn't assembled (or reassembled) correctly, it will probably have serious problems functioning.

Review this chapter for four important factors about FRMs: how an FRM is removed, how an FRM is protected, how an FRM is replaced, and the ESD issues that are involved.

Quick Assessment

Identifying electrostatic discharge (ESD) safeguards

1 You should always wear a(n) _____ when working on the PC system unit.

2 You should have _____ and _____ available when working inside the PC so that you can note or diagram the identifying features, orientation, and position of components.

Removing and replacing field replaceable modules (FRMs)

3 You should handle adapter cards and other circuit boards by their _____ to avoid touching the electronic contacts.

4 _____ and _____ memory modules are installed in stand-up edge connector sockets.

5 Controller card failures are likely a cause of the card not being _____.

Identifying system modules and their normal operations

6 Ribbon cables, used to connect data connections for hard drives, have a color stripe that identifies pin _____ on the cable.

7 If you detached the CMOS battery during disassembly, you must update the _____.

8 Not installing a(n) _____ can result in a boot disk failure.

Working safely with high-voltage modules

9 Not installing the _____ can cause the power supply to explode.

10 The cable that provides power to the front panel of the PC carries _____ power.

Answers

1 *Antistatic protection device or ESD wrist strap.* Zap over to "Avoiding shocking developments."

2 *Paper and pen.* Review "Checking in: Is the patient ready, nurse?"

3 *Edges.* Peruse "Taking out the adapter cards."

4 *SIMM; DIMM.* See "Reinstalling memory modules."

5 *Seated properly.* Review "Testing the Results."

6 *1 (one).* Become one with "Relating to the Zen of ribbon cable."

7 *CMOS configuration information.* See "Checking the CMOS and Configuration Data, or Where Did the Battery Go?"

8 *Drive power connector.* Check out "Stating your preference: The adapter or the drive first?"

9 *Motherboard power connectors.* Take a look at "Testing the Results."

10 *110V AC.* Charge over to "Grasping the power and removing it."

Getting Ready and Taking Precautions

Two important preparations must be made before working on the PC, regardless of what you are planning to do: ESD preparations and general surgery preparations.

A person can feel a static charge beginning at about 3,000 volts, but electronic circuits can be damaged by a charge of only 30 volts.

Avoiding shocking developments

I can't over-emphasize the importance of protecting the PC and yourself from ESD and its potential damage and hazards. You can do this in a number of ways:

✔ For use in emergencies only — not recommended for general use: If you are trapped inside a system case without any other form of ESD protection, keep yourself in contact with the metal frame of the PC at all times.

✔ The minimum precaution against ESD is to wear an antistatic wrist strap with the strap attached to the metal PC chassis with an alligator clip. When working inside the PC, you cannot avoid becoming a grounding circuit for any static electricity built up in the system. The ESD strap contains a resistor that slows down the discharge and protects you and the PC. In addition to wearing the ESD strap, use an antistatic mat under the PC case. That way, if you accidentally knock off the clip, you won't pass along a charge to whatever you're holding at the time. Several mat and strap combinations are available on the market.

✔ A supply of antistatic bags is good to have on hand to protect cards and smaller FRMs outside of the case. ESD lurks everywhere. Never let your guard down and always protect your computer parts.

✔ In the past, you could leave the pre-Pentium PCs plugged into an AC power source, which provided a connection to an earth ground. These systems did not provide fast power-up or instant-on motherboards. However, with newer Pentium-class PCs, remove the power plug from the electrical source when working on the them.

Checking in: Is the patient ready, nurse?

A year or two ago, I would have said that it's rare for a PC repair technician to completely disassemble a PC — especially at a customer's site. Today's customers, however, are trying to maximize their investment in PC hardware by upgrading their older units. Replacing the motherboard, processor, power supply, and adapter cards when upgrading an older PC isn't unusual. The information I give you in this chapter goes beyond just getting you ready for the A+ exam.

I use the word *disassemble* (and as many derivatives as I can get away with) to mean the disconnection from cables, extraction of fasteners, and removal of a module to a location outside the case — onto a workbench or in a box, for example. *FRM* (field replaceable module) is used on the A+ exams to refer to any component that is replaced as a whole unit and can be installed at a customer site.

You will remember this information better if you have a PC that you can use as a model as you review this chapter. Nothing compares to a hands-on experience to help you learn.

Before beginning surgery on your PC, take these actions:

- ✔ Have your tools standing by and ready for use. If you are lucky enough to have a surgical assistant for this process, all the better — but you're probably on your own. So, to avoid the hassle of clipping and unclipping your wrist strap (and the possibility of forgetting to clip up again) as you run off for a forgotten tool, have your tools ready to go.

- ✔ Have paper and pen standing by so that you can write down or diagram the placement, orientation, and identifying features of the modules, cables, cards, and other vital organs that you remove. Your notes and diagrams are your guide when it's time to reassemble the PC.

- ✔ Use any system that works for you to sort, store, and secure the screws and other fasteners that you remove from the patient. They can easily get lost, scratch the case, or worse — they make an awful screeching sound if you drag the case across the workbench with a piece trapped underneath.

- ✔ Gather all the support and reference disks for the devices installed in the PC. Taking this action is even more important if the PC is an IBM Micro-Channel Architecture (PS/2) computer. If you cannot find them — and even if you can — do not disconnect the battery from the motherboard.

Taking inventory

As a precaution against the unlikely event that you accidentally disconnect or dislodge the CMOS battery (which would unfortunately result in losing the CMOS setup information), you should boot the system and write down the system setup configuration data, such as its RAM size and its CMOS setup information.

If you are working on a 286 or newer PC, do not disconnect the battery from the motherboard or you will certainly lose the CMOS setup information.

Record the model and serial numbers of each major FRM as you go — especially in the shop environment. As you reassemble the PC, verify that the parts that came out are the ones going back in. Inadvertently replacing a good part with a faulty one, and thus introducing new problems to a system, is a "bad thing."

Straight from the "Duh" file comes this reminder: Always close all running programs, shut down the operating system, and turn off the computer before disassembling it.

Removing the Major Components

You need to remember only a few general procedures for disassembling a PC, and each procedure relates specifically to a particular FRM, such as the case, the power supply, adapter cards, RAM, and the motherboard — which just about covers everything.

Opening the box

The logical place to begin the disassembly of the PC is the case of the system unit. To remove the case from any PC, the only tool that you need is a Phillips screwdriver. Some newer cases don't require any tools at all (or so it is said).

Unless you are the warranty service provider, be sure not to void the warranty on someone's PC by opening the system unit. Some manufacturers, but not all, put little stickers over the edges where the case parts fit together to warn you that you may be wiping out the warranty by removing the cover.

Be sure that you have on your ESD protection and that you avoid touching any of the internal parts when removing the cover.

System cases come in a variety of types and sizes, and each is opened using a slightly different technique:

> ✔ **Disconnect the cables.** Remove all peripheral device connectors and get them out of the way. Disconnect the parallel, serial, game port, video, and other cables connected to the back of the unit. Unplug the mouse and keyboard as well. You may want to use masking or other light tape to label the cables and the plugs to where they were connected. Some manufacturers now color code their connectors, which doesn't go unappreciated. (Now, if they could only do that for the rest of my life.)

✔ **Clean the case.** Although not the most technical of steps, this is a practical one. While the case is intact and with peripheral devices removed from its top (desktop models, of course), this is a good time to clean the dust bunnies from the top, back, and sides of the unit. This eliminates the chance that any accumulated gunk will fall inside the case when you remove the top.

✔ **Remove any protection or appearance bezels.** Some older desktop cases and full-size tower cases have plastic panels mounted on either the back or front for reasons known only to the case designer. If you are working on a PC that has such a panel, you should be able to pull it right off. You may need to encourage it with a tweaker to get it started. Check the back of this panel for dust, clean it if needed, and set it aside.

✔ **Remove the case cover.** Manufacturers are designing new ways to open and close cases, but in general, the most common cases are opened in these ways:

- **Tower cases:** These cases have the most variations, ranging from a screwless, to a removable single side panel, to a two-piece case that consists of a base and a U-shaped cover. On other cases, you can find usually two to four Phillips or thumbscrews located on the back edge of the case. Release the fasteners and remove the case. Consult with the PC's documentation to be sure you are removing the case properly and not ignorantly removing the power supply screws.

- **Standard desktop case:** This is the case type that has been around since the original PC, although it now seems to be fading away. The two pieces of this case fit together in an "L7" fashion, with the front panel attached to the case top, and the back panel attached to the case bottom. In some variations of this design, just the top of the case is popped off by pressing clips on the sides. On older cases, be sure you know which screws are case screws and which screws hold the power supply. After you remove the screws (that is, if you need to remove screws), push the top forward, lift it off, or continue pushing forward, depending on the type of case. When in doubt, check out the PC's documentation.

    Be very careful not to remove screws that connect internal components (such as the power supply or some connectors) to the inside of the case. Always verify what a screw is attached to before removing it.

- **Screwless case:** These cases have a release mechanism on the front or top that allows the front or side to be removed without a screwdriver. This type of case, available as either a tower or desktop, can be opened without tools (except for the occasional need to pry a panel loose with a screwdriver). The screwless case comes apart in a number of pieces (front, side, and top panels) that slide-lock into place.

Taking out the adapter cards

After the case cover is off and stored in a safe place, remove the adapter cards. Generally, you can follow the process in Lab 16-1 for every card.

Lab 16-1   Removing Adapter Cards

1. **Write down or diagram the expansion slot and type (ISA, VL-Bus, PCI, AGP, and so on) that the adapter card occupies before you pull it out.**

   This saves you some time when you reassemble the PC. Label any cables attached to the card before you disconnect them.

2. **If possible, record all jumper settings and DIP switch settings before removing the adapter card.**

   A little dental mirror comes in handy for this step. If you wait until after you've removed a card and handled it, can you guarantee that you haven't accidentally changed a setting?

3. **Remove the mounting screw that holds the adapter card in place.**

4. **Examine the card for any cables or wires that may be attached to it.**

   In addition to diagramming any cables or wires that you find, tag any cables or wires with a small piece of tape. (Small address labels are good for tagging parts and cables.)

5. **Grasp the card along its front and back edges and gently rock it front to back until it releases.**

   Avoid touching other circuit boards and the contacts on the bottom of the board with your hand. Handle cards and circuit boards only by their edges or port mountings and avoid touching the edge connectors.

6. **Lift the card out slowly and look for attached wires or cables that you may have overlooked.**

7. **If you're not going to replace the card, insert a port spacer.**

   A *port spacer* is a flat metal space holder used to block port openings on the back of the case. The cooling system needs all of these slots filled in order to do its job efficiently.

8. **Store the card in an antistatic bag and do not stack the cards on top of each other.**

If an ESD wrist strap or ankle strap is not available, lean your forearm on one of the metal beams that run across the chassis, and leave your arm in constant contact with the chassis while you lift out the adapter cards.

Undocking the bay

On a case manufactured in the past five or so years, the hard drives are probably installed in metal enclosures called *drive bays*. The standard drive bay is designed to hold a variety of drives requiring a general drive size standard called *half-height*. These enclosures allow drives to slip into place either from the front or the back. Removing a floppy disk, tape, or CD-ROM drive is much easier than installing one. Installing a hard drive can involve mounting problems, cabling considerations, and formatting (see Chapter 9 for more information). However, removing one requires only that you disconnect a few cables, remove a few screws, and slide it out. Okay, it's a little more complicated than that, but not much.

You must consider three things when removing a hard drive or tape drive from the PC:

✔ The drive is powered by the power supply through a connector.

✔ The drive is controlled by either an adapter board or a connection directly on the motherboard through one or more cables.

✔ The drive is attached to the chassis, so it won't move about when in use or when the PC is moved.

Removing the power connections

The power connections for hard drives and tape drives are fairly easy to find. The wires of their connectors extend back to the power supply. You will encounter only two types of connectors: a larger milky-white four-wire connector (usually a Molex connector) and a smaller and similarly colored four-wire connector (a Berg connector) that probably has a clip latch to hold it in place. See Chapter 10 for more information on the PC's power connections.

Here's how to remove them:

✔ **Molex connector:** Grasp the connector and gently move it from side to side to slip it out of the plug. Don't yank on it. You can break the connector right off the drive circuit board (and then you have to install a new drive).

✔ **Berg connector:** Pry it open gently and slide it apart. Use a tweaker or a small screwdriver to lift the latch tab just enough to pull the connectors apart. Again, don't pull on the wires. If you need to, use your needle-nose pliers to grasp the plug to pull it out.

You don't need to label drive power connectors (unless you feel compelled to do so). Drive power connectors come in only two types (each device takes only one type), and may already be labeled. You can use only the connectors that you have on the power supply, and the plugs are keyed so that you can't install them incorrectly.

Removing adapter cables

Depending on the drive and the form factor of the motherboard (see Chapter 4), a hard drive is connected to either an adapter card inserted in an expansion slot or directly to the motherboard. In either case, you need to remove these cables before proceeding any further in disassembling the PC. Label each cable and its orientation to the power supply (always a good landmark inside the case). Recording the orientation of a hard drive cable means to note the location of the color-striped edge (on which side of the cable) and its orientation to the power supply. If the cable doesn't have an edge reference, use a permanent marker to create one.

Gently pull out the drive adapter cables, keeping them level. In other words, don't yank them off, and pull in the direction of the pins to avoid breaking or bending the pins, which are easily bent or broken, on the connector.

Detaching a drive from the chassis

The first thing you should do when detaching a drive is to make a note of the size, height, and placement of the bay in which the hard drive is installed. The location and access to drive bays vary with the case, and although two cases may be of the same form factor, the bays may be accessed differently. In some of the newer mid- and full-tower cases, many 3½-inch drive bays are hidden inside the case.

Some XT cases are still around; these have one full-height bay. Two half-height devices can be stack-mounted in this bay by using a side bracket. This bracket holds one drive above the other with enough space between them so the electronics don't contact each other and for airflow. When removing a drive (or pair of drives) from an XT case, don't forget the retaining screws in the bottom of the drive bay. XT drives pull out through the front.

AT cases have two (or more) half-height bays that receive drives from the front. A drive is held in place with a pair of small L-shaped retaining brackets, which are fastened with a single screw on each side of the drive. To remove the drive, use a screwdriver to extract the retaining brackets and slide the drive forward out of the bay.

Taking out the motherboard

If you're not wearing your ESD wrist strap, put it on right now! At this stage of disassembling a PC, you can do some major and expensive damage without it. Worse yet, the damage may not show up right away; it may show up later after the damaged component is stressed further, causing an intermittent or misleading error condition.

At this stage, the only item of significance left inside the case should be the motherboard. Depending on the PC's vintage, the remaining steps range from extremely easy to slightly complicated. Note or diagram all jumpers, DIP switches, and connectors that require special orientations on the motherboard. After it is removed, the motherboard should be carefully protected in an antistatic bag and placed away from other circuit boards, preferably in a protective box or case.

PC XT motherboards have one small plastic connector that connects the motherboard to the speaker. Disconnect the speaker connector and remove the two or three screws that mount the motherboard to the chassis, and the motherboard is out.

IBM AT and its clones also have a speaker connector, but they also have a keylock connector. Remove the speaker and keylock connectors slowly because they are adjacent to the memory-size jumper on the AT motherboard. Be careful not to dislodge any jumpers on the board.

AT and related motherboards also have a lithium battery or a pack of AA batteries that are usually attached to the side of the chassis or case with Velcro. The battery or battery pack should be removed with the board and kept connected to the board. Newer AT boards have the battery mounted directly on the motherboard, so just be careful that you don't dislodge it. If this connection is broken, the CMOS chip loses the system setup configuration information.

Newer AT, Baby AT, ATX, LTX, NLX, and other form-factor motherboards are mounted on plastic spacer anchors and are held in place with two or three screws attached to the chassis. To remove these motherboards, extract the mounting screws and then slide the motherboard laterally toward the open end of the case to disengage the spacers, and then lift the motherboard out of the case by its edges. Leave the spacers in the motherboard.

Pulling out the memory modules

If you also want to remove the memory modules — single inline memory modules (SIMM), dual inline memory modules (DIMM), or dual inline packages (DIP) — be absolutely sure that you are grounded. When working with memory, just touching the case or power supply may not protect memory modules from possible ESD damage. See Chapter 8 for more information on memory modules.

Follow the steps in Lab 16-2 to remove memory modules.

Lab 16-2   Taking Out SIMMs and DIMMs

1. **Using your fingers, a slotted screwdriver, or a tweaker, push back the metal tabs holding the chip in the socket.**

   The tabs are located at the end of each memory module socket. With these released, you can then tilt the module.

2. **Gently tilt the first module one way and then the other to release it.**

3. **Tilt each module away from the locking prongs that fit into the holes at each end of the module.**

   Never rock the module side to side or yank it straight up. Record which socket each module comes out of by noting the bank, the socket numbers, and the chip number. You can use stickers, such as small price stickers, to identify the module.

4. **Place each module in a separate antistatic bag, and store them without stacking them on each other.**

You have your hands full removing a bank of DIP memory chips. Keep these tips in mind:

- ✔ Be antistatic. Memory chips are sold in antistatic tubes that you should be able to round up.

- ✔ Use a slotted screwdriver, such as the tweaker, to start the process of removing the chip and then gently pry it up and out of the socket with your fingers. You can use an IC puller, but don't blame me for all the bent pins.

- ✔ Mark each chip with its bank and socket number and mark the sockets accordingly.

Grasping the power and removing it

These days, the power supply and case are usually purchased together as a single unit. Rarely would you actually remove the power supply, but you may find it necessary on occasion. For example, the power supply or cooling fan in an older AT or XT PC can wear out and need replacement. Or you may find yourself removing a system's modules one at a time in an attempt to isolate the source of an intermittent problem. Unless you have a compelling reason to remove the power supply from the case, however, it is typically better to leave it in.

Treat the power supply and the main cooling fan as a single module and don't open it for any reason. Don't even be curious. If any part of the power supply is not working, remove it, dispose of it properly, and install a new one. A new power supply is not expensive enough to risk injuring yourself. Inside the power supply are big nasty capacitors that pack quite a wallop and can hurt you seriously if you touch them — even if you're wearing an ESD strap.

ATX and later form-factor motherboards contain power at all times, even when the power supply is turned off. Be sure that you know this for your safety and the A+ Core Hardware exam.

Lab 16-3 takes you through the process of removing the power supply.

Lab 16-3	Removing the Power Supply

1. **Turn off the power supply.**

   I'm sure you did this long before getting to this point, but I feel obligated to mention it.

2. **Remove the power cord from the power supply.**

3. **Diagram the orientation or use a grease pencil to mark the edges of the power supply connectors to the PC's front panel, motherboard, and hard drives, and then disconnect them in that order.**

   Use rubber bands to bind the motherboard and hard drive connectors in separate groups.

   The thick black cable that extends to the front panel from the power supply in many AT and ATX PCs carries live 110V AC power straight from the wall socket! This power is passed through the power supply directly to the cable that connects to the front panel.

   If your system has this cable, be absolutely sure that you draw a diagram of this connector configuration (illustrating where each of the four wires is connected by color). If you connect the wrong wire in the wrong place, it causes the system to catch fire, not to mention shocking you big time.

4. **Locate and remove the screws (either Phillips or hex-head) that hold the power supply to the back of the case, the sidewall, and the chassis.**

5. **Inspect the power supply for faulty, frayed, or broken wires or connectors, and use compressed air to blow out the fan and vents.**

Putting Everything Back in Its Place

If you have built or reassembled many PCs, then you are probably reasonably prepared for the A+ exam. For review, then, write down the steps that you use to build or reassemble a PC along with any safeguards and safety and performance checks that you use along the way. Then jump to the last section of this chapter — "Testing the Results" — and review it for common device failure modes, several of which will be on the exam.

For the A+ exam, make sure you know the general sequence of assembly and the relationship of the major FRMs to each other. You won't see questions that directly ask how a PC is assembled, but you do run into questions that assume knowledge or directly ask how FRMs are installed and how any associated cables and wires are attached.

FRMs are reassembled in essentially the reverse order that they were re-moved. Assuming that the power supply wisely wasn't removed from the system case (a wise decision), the motherboard (with its memory reinstalled) goes in first, then the hard drives, the adapter cards, and finally, the case parts. If the power supply was removed, it must be reinstalled first, with the other components following in their natural sequence.

Selecting the tools for the job

You need a few more tools to reassemble the PC than you did to disassemble it. You need your ESD grounding strap; a Phillips screwdriver, a slotted screw-driver, a tweaker, a pair of needle-nosed pliers, and a small flashlight. Mature eyes may also want a small magnifying glass. The most important tool for this job, however, is patience. Take your time. If something isn't right, and no smoke was involved in reaching that decision, take the computer apart and do it again. Chapter 3 provides more detail on the tools commonly used by a PC repair technician.

Protecting the PC and its FRMs from ESD damage is just as important when putting the system back together as it was when taking it apart. Use your grounding straps or take other appropriate precautions. Remember that together, you and ESD are the most threatening element to a PC. Whatever you can do to reduce this threat gives additional life to the PC. Makes you feel kind of powerful, doesn't it?

The greatest threat of ESD damage to the PC is working on the PC with its case open without proper ESD protection in place.

Putting back the power supply

The power supply is fairly easy to reinstall. Just line up the fan with its hole in the case, and match the power supply to the screw holes and then insert the screws. The only safeguard you need to take is to make sure that the power supply's cables are not trapped under the case or along its sides.

This may sound obvious, but when you install the power supply, it shouldn't be plugged into an AC power source. After you install the power supply, plug it in and operate it very briefly to test the fan — and the fan only. If the fan turns, all is well. If the fan doesn't operate, check the power supply's voltage selector to see whether it is set correctly and check that the power cord is seated tightly.

Do not, I repeat, do not try using a screwdriver, your finger, or anything else to goose the fan blade along. If all is well, and the fan still doesn't turn, replace the power supply.

Reinstalling the motherboard

As you reassemble the PC, pay your greatest attention to the motherboard and its cables and connections. Putting a floppy disk drive in backwards is a mistake that's easily corrected and normally does no harm, but some of the connectors on the motherboard can do extreme damage to the motherboard and other components if they are installed incorrectly or connected wrong. So take care as you work.

Do not begin to reassemble the PC without first putting on your ESD ground strap and connecting it to the PC case or ground mat. Do you get the impression that I think this is very important?

If you are installing a new motherboard in an existing system case, you need to verify several items, including that the motherboard is compatible with the form factor of the case and power supply, and that the devices in the PC are compatible with the motherboard, and its BIOS and chipset. Most of this information is available in the motherboard's documentation or on the manufacturer's Web site. Look up this information before you try installing the new motherboard; it saves you and your customer money in the end.

Lab 16-4 shows you how to reinstall the motherboard.

Lab 16-4   Reinstalling the Motherboard

1. **Orient the motherboard so that its spacers (also called standoffs), shown in Figure 16-1, are aligned with the slots in the bottom of the case.**

2. **Laterally slide the motherboard toward the power supply until the standoffs are firmly snug in their slots.**

3. **Reinsert the mounting screws to anchor the motherboard in place.**

   Most motherboards are attached to the case with screws. Some new case designs allow the motherboard to be attached to a hinged plate with only the spacers locking it into place. If screws are used, use either Teflon or plastic washers under the mounting screws when attaching the motherboard to the system case, which prevents the screw heads from contacting circuitry on the motherboard. Be absolutely sure that the electronic contacts and cut pins on the motherboard are not in contact with the metal case lining. Contact will definitely give you trouble — if it doesn't short out the motherboard. Look under the motherboard to verify that it is not touching the case anywhere.

4. **To complete this task, reattach the speaker, keylock, and battery connectors.**

   If the motherboard has a separate battery supply, you should keep it connected to the motherboard throughout this process. If it was removed, or if the system battery was removed, however, you need to set the system's configuration using the CMOS setup utility the first time you boot the PC.

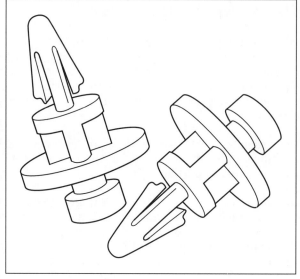

Figure 16-1:
Spacers
are used
to keep
the mother-
board from
grounding
against the
system
case.

Reinstalling memory modules

Memory modules are installed in a stand-up arrangement in an edge connector socket. Lab 16-5 takes you through reinstallation of either a SIMM (single
inline memory module) or a DIMM (dual inline memory module).

Lab 16-5   Reinstalling a SIMM or DIMM

1. **Insert the module into the socket at about a 45-degree angle.**

2. **Slowly stand the module up, applying even pressure on both side
   edges, until it snaps into place.**

   If the module doesn't seat into the socket, it may be backwards.

Installing DIP (dual inline package) memory chips takes a very steady hand
and a lot more patience than is needed with a SIMM or DIMM module.
Although a SIMM or DIMM requires only that you get the module into a slot,
DIP memory requires all of its pins to be inserted into separate holes at the
same time. If you removed the memory chips during disassembly, by now
you are probably asking yourself why. Don't use a chip insertion tool; instead,
use tweezers to line the chip over the DIP socket and lightly press one side
down. Inspect the other side's pins for alignment, and slowly and gently press
it down. When both sides are started (all the chip's pins are in the proper
socket holes), use your finger to press it into place.

Connecting the power source

The procedure and the level of caution that you should use to connect the motherboard to the power supply depends on its form factor. You use a different process and different connectors for AT form factor motherboards than for ATX or later motherboards.

 ✔ **AT motherboards:** The two six-wire power supply connectors for AT form factor motherboards should be labeled as P8 and P9. These two connectors are installed side-by-side into a 12-pin connector on the motherboard. You face a danger of possibly reversing the positions of these two connectors. If you do reverse them, you will definitely need a new motherboard. However, because you labeled them and drew a diagram when disassembling the PC, you know exactly which goes on the right and which goes on the left of the connector. Remember that the four black wires (two on each plug) must be aligned together in the middle.

> If you forget to connect the motherboard power connectors (P8 and P9) when you turn on the power, the power supply may explode — or at the least make loud, ugly noises. So, don't forget to install these plugs.

 ✔ **ATX (and later) motherboards:** You can easily distinguish the power connector on these form factor motherboards by its unique size and shape, and installation is easy because of its connector key. The connector has 2 rows of 10 pins in a rectangular shape. You should have it labeled and included on your diagram.

See Chapter 4 for more information on motherboard form factors.

Connecting the front panel

If the PC has a power cable for the front panel, which means it has a main power switch on the front of the PC, unplug the PC for the duration of this operation. The front panel cable that comes from the power supply carries 110V AC power that is passed straight from the AC wall socket. This isn't something with which you should take chances. Even if you diagrammed the front panel power switch connector during disassembly, check the power supply's documentation, if available, for the wire color scheme.

The power switch on the front panel closes a circuit that allows the AC power to flow to the power supply. To allow this flow, the power switch has both hot (live) and return (to the power supply) leads.

Stating your preference: The adapter or the drive first?

Some technicians prefer to install the hard drives before the adapter cards, and others like to do the reverse. Whatever you do first, the same rules apply, just in a different order. Follow your diagram, and reinstall the adapter cards and drives, keeping the cables and cards spaced evenly to allow for good airflow. Place the hard drive as far from the power supply as possible to allow for maximum air circulation inside the cabinet.

You may want to take this opportunity to clean the edge connectors of the adapter cards with an edge connector cleaner and protector. You can find these products at most computer supply stores.

For the A+ Core Hardware exam, it really doesn't matter which (drives or adapter cards) you install first, but be ready for questions on how cables are connected to adapter cards and the power supply.

A common installation error is forgetting to attach the power cables to hard drives. This error can be a result of the full attention required to align the drive in the bay correctly, making sure that round-headed screws are used to anchor the drive in the bay, and that the data connection (the dreaded ribbon cable) is attached correctly. If you don't attach the power connector to the drive, a POST (Power On Self Test) boot disk failure usually results.

Relating to the Zen of ribbon cable

In general, ribbon cables connect the same way on either end. However, this versatility can get you into trouble. You must connect the cable so that the wires connect to their counterparts on both connections. To help you with this connection, the wire representing pin 1 on the cable and connector is usually marked with a red or dark blue stripe along the edge of the cable.

You may have two or more ribbon cables to reinstall. The cable for the floppy disk drive is slightly different from the cable for the hard drive or other drives. Be sure to reattach the correct cable to the correct device, although this shouldn't present a big problem, because usually they won't attach to the wrong device anyway.

Excuse the veiled sports metaphor here, but an easy way to remember the orientation of a ribbon cable is the phrase "Big Red is Number 1." If you forget this phrase, just ask anyone from Nebraska to tell you who's Number 1, and he or she will most likely reply with the Big Red phrase, and you'll be reminded that the red stripe edge of the ribbon cable aligns to pin number 1. See how simply that works? For ribbon cables with a dark blue edge, you'll have to find somebody from Michigan or Duke to help you.

Finding pin 1 on the circuit board is the next step to completing the match. So, how do you tell which end of the connector is pin 1? A small numeral "1" should be printed next to or above the end of the connector that is pin 1. A magnifying glass may come in handy in this situation, along with a flashlight. If you can't find the printed number, examine the solder pads on the back of the circuit board where the connector is attached. Pin 1 has a square solder pad. These general rules are not universally applied, though, which is why your diagrams are so important.

Watch out for these three common ribbon cable connection errors:

✔ The connector is reversed — sadly, this can do major damage, so chant the mantra "Big Red/Blue is Number One" as you connect ribbon cables.

✔ The connector is attached to only one row — easy to do given the size of the connector and the pins. If caught before the power is turned on, no damage should result.

✔ The connector is shifted to the left or right, missing a pair of pins — also easy to do and just as dangerous.

Closing the lid

Reattach the case top. You may want to put the top in place, but leave the screws out until after you've had a chance to test the results. When reattaching the case top, watch that you don't snag or trap cables. Cables can get damaged by little nicks or breaks. They may also pull out of connectors, if dragged or dinged by the case top. If the case lid doesn't slide freely into place, investigate why.

Checking the CMOS and Configuration Data, or Where Did the Battery Go?

If you were overly zealous about disassembling every possible FRM in the PC and you removed the battery pack or the lithium battery from the motherboard, you are now faced with the challenge of resetting the CMOS setup configuration data. If the system boots okay, you need to press the appropriate key (depending upon your BIOS version) to open the CMOS setup utility and enter the appropriate data. You did write the CMOS information down, didn't you?

CMOS stands for *complementary metal oxide semiconductor*, which is a common integrated circuit technology. For more information on CMOS, see Chapter 5.

Okay, so you did remove the CMOS battery. Well, now what you need to do is re-enter the CMOS information that you captured before you started the disassembly of the PC. The data that you need to enter varies slightly with the BIOS version, but generally it includes the following:

- ✔ Floppy disk size and density
- ✔ Hard drive type and configuration in cylinders, heads, sectors, capacity, and other unique attributes, such as the landing zone (LZone) and others
- ✔ RAM size by type
- ✔ Time and date
- ✔ Parallel port type
- ✔ Serial port type and status
- ✔ Other stuff very specific to your system

If you didn't write down your CMOS settings and then either purposely or inadvertently removed the CMOS battery, you need to do some research in order to reconstruct the settings accurately. Most newer system CMOSs can detect some of the configuration of the PC, such as RAM size, but you need the manuals for the motherboard and peripherals to get it right.

Testing the Results

The real proof that you have reassembled the PC correctly comes when you turn on the power and everything works. However, don't panic if you don't get these results — unless, of course, smoke or flames billow out of the PC.

The following are some common problems associated with reassembling a PC:

- ✔ **Motherboard power connector(s) not installed:** This error is by far the most disastrous and can result in a damaged motherboard or an exploded power supply.
- ✔ **Motherboard solderside contacts touching the case:** On the backside of any circuit board (called its solderside) are the clipped contacts (cut pins) of the electronic components installed on the circuitside of the board. If these contacts touch the metal case lining, some or all of the board may short out.
- ✔ **Reversed data and control cables:** This error can damage a device and changes how the computer operates — if it operates at all. Align the colored edge to pin 1.
- ✔ **Drive power connectors not installed:** This one isn't so bad; it usually just gets you a boot error beep code or disk boot failure.

✔ **Speaker, keylock, and battery connectors not installed:** A very minor problem that comes under the heading of "What a nuisance."

✔ **Hard drive, video display, and other peripheral failures:** The adapter card may not be seated properly, may not be anchored with a mounting screw, or may be installed in an incorrect architecture slot.

✔ **Floppy drive failure:** The ribbon cable may not be connected properly. The first floppy disk drive (A) should be connected after the twist, or at the end of the cable.

✔ **Keyboard failure:** The keyboard connector may not be installed or not pushed on all the way. Also, if the PC has a PS/2 mouse and its connector is not installed properly, the keyboard may not function.

✔ **No lights, no action:** Did you plug it in?

Always be sure that the power supply is switched off before changing any power supply or signal cable connections.

Prep Test

1 The correct way to remove an adapter card circuit board is to detach any connectors, remove the retaining screw, and then

   A ○ Ensure that the power is off

   B ○ Grasp the card's front and back edges and rock it gently back and forth

   C ○ Grasp the card's top edge and pull straight up

   D ○ Grasp the card's front and back edges and rock the board gently from side to side

2 When servicing a PC, to which of the following would you not attach the ESD ground strap?

   A ○ To the inside of the case

   B ○ To the ground mat

   C ○ To the static shielding bag that came with the computer

   D ○ To a wall outlet

3 After a circuit board is removed from the system, it should be stored in

   A ○ A cool, dry, dark place

   B ○ An antistatic bag

   C ○ A stack with other circuit boards

   D ○ A clean, zippered plastic bag

4 The term *FRM* refers to

   A ○ Front or rear module

   B ○ Fully replaceable modem

   C ○ A slang term used by PC technicians to confuse customers

   D ○ Field replaceable module

5 Forgetting to attach which motherboard cable can cause damage to the power supply?

   A ○ The power supply connector

   B ○ The front panel power connector

   C ○ The speaker connector

   D ○ The keyboard connector

6 **What is the likely result of forgetting to attach the power connector to a hard drive during reassembly?**

A ○ The power supply explodes.

B ○ A disk boot failure.

C ○ A 601 POST error.

D ○ The hard drive dies an agonizing death.

7 **The colored edge of the ribbon cable represents**

A ○ Pin 40

B ○ Pin 1

C ○ The Cornhuskers

D ○ The power connector

8 **You just installed a hard drive, but it's not working. Why?**

A ○ It is connected to the wrong IDE controller.

B ○ The floppy disk drive is not connected properly.

C ○ The ribbon cable is aligned to pin 1 on the drive.

D ○ The ribbon cable is aligned to pin 40 on the drive.

9 **The biggest threat to the PC when being serviced is**

A ○ ESD

B ○ Accidental breakage of a component

C ○ Improper tools damaging a component

D ○ Placing components on the wrong type of surface to work

10 **The motherboard is mounted**

A ○ On brass standoffs

B ○ On plastic standoffs

C ○ On copper mounting brackets

D ○ Directly on the case's metal lining

Answers

1 **B.** Answer A is not a bad first step, but that should have been done before you opened the system case. You must avoid stressing the card by bending it side to side or harming the edge connectors by yanking the card straight up. *See "Taking out the adapter cards."*

2 **C.** Unless the static shielding bag is grounded to a solid ground, it won't do you much good. If you have the type of grounding system that plugs into the third (round) hole on an AC wall outlet, be very careful when plugging it in. *Charge over to "Avoiding shocking developments."*

3 **B.** Never stack circuit boards on top of each other (even if they are in antistatic bags) and never store a circuit board where it can gather static electricity. *Look at "Taking out the adapter cards."*

4 **D.** CompTIA uses this term to refer to all components of the PC that can be replaced at a customer site. *Check out "Checking in: Is the patient ready, nurse?"*

5 **A.** The power supply requires some electrical draw and without it can be damaged or worse. *Visit "Connecting the power source."*

6 **B.** The BIOS looks to the hard drive to boot from and not finding the drive, displays a disk boot failure. *Check out "Stating your preference: The adapter or the drive first?"*

7 **B.** The colored edge indicates how the cable's connector should be oriented to the adapter or motherboard connector. *Look up "Relating to the Zen of ribbon cable."*

8 **D.** The ribbon cable, which provides the data connection to the drive, must be correctly connected for the device to work properly. *Review "Relating to the Zen of ribbon cable."*

9 **A.** Besides the technician, the biggest threat to the PC when being serviced is electrostatic discharge (ESD). *Take a look at "Selecting the tools for the job."*

10 **B.** Also called spacers, the motherboard sits up off the case, allowing for air space under the board. *Check out "Reinstalling the motherboard."*

Chapter 17

Preventive Maintenance

● ●

Exam Objectives

▶ Performing preventive maintenance procedures

▶ Identifying the purpose of preventive maintenance products and when to use them

▶ Using preventive maintenance products appropriately

▶ Complying with environmental guidelines for cleaning products

▶ Creating data backups and storing backup media

▶ Detecting and removing viruses

● ●

*1*t has always seemed somewhat foolish to me for someone to invest a couple of thousand dollars into a computer system, run it until it dies, and then call the repair technician to perform a Lazarus miracle and raise it from the dead. I'm not talking about the usual, everyday kinds of stuff — you know, the 44-ounce soft drink dumped on the keyboard, the flower vase that spilled water inside the monitor, the metal fingernail file that somehow slipped inside the case, the paper clip stuck in the floppy disk drive slot, or the correction fluid painted on the screen. I'm talking about the truly scary abuse.

I've seen power supplies so choked with dust, smoke residue, and chalk dust that they looked like miniature replicas of Carlsbad Caverns. I've also seen a virus that could devour an entire hard disk and half of Cleveland. I won't mention any others for fear that children may read this book. Where's the Computer Protection Services agency when you need it?

The A+ people, CompTIA, recognize the value of preventive maintenance and have included it throughout the objectives of the Core Hardware exam. In fact, five percent of the A+ Core Hardware exam is devoted to the Preventive Maintenance domain, which means that you can absolutely expect questions on the test that challenge your knowledge and skills of protecting, cleaning, and caring for the PC while protecting yourself and the environment. You should expect the emphasis of the questions from this domain to deal with preventive maintenance issues or computer viruses. So, on a test where every question is equally important, you can't afford to dismiss this chapter as unimportant. You absolutely need to know this stuff.

Quick Assessment

Performing preventive main-tenance procedures

1 The purpose of a(n) _____ is to prolong the effective life of the computer.

`2 _____ is used to check a hard disk for possible surface errors.

3 You should never wear an ESD grounding strap when working on a(n) _____.

Identifying the purpose of preven-tive main-tenance products and when to use them

4 _____ is used to blow out the dust and debris found in the keyboard and in many other FRMs.

5 To clean a mouse ball, use a(n) _____.

6 A(n) _____ is used to clean the floppy disk drive.

Using pre-ventive mainte-nance products appropri-ately

7 Do not use _____ on a mouse ball, because it may shrink or misshape its rubber material.

Complying with envi-ronmental guidelines for cleaning products

8 A(n) _____ lists the hazards, proper handling, and storage procedures for a chemical solution.

Detecting and remov-ing viruses

9 A(n) _____ contains a virus program but is not suspected because it imitates a legitimate application.

Creating data back-ups and storing backup media

10 Tapes and other backup media should be stored in a(n) _____ and _____ location.

Answers

1 *Preventive maintenance program.* Review "Applying regular maintenance."

2 *ScanDisk.* Zip over to "The hard disk drive."

3 *Monitor or CRT.* Check out "The monitor."

4 *Compressed air.* Scoot over to "The keyboard."

5 *Damp cloth.* See "The mouse."

6 *Floppy drive cleaning kit.* Check out "The floppy disk drive."

7 *Alcohol.* Take a look at "The mouse."

8 *MSDS.* Review "Using the right cleaning supplies."

9 *Trojan horse.* See "Horses, worms, and germs."

10 *Cool, dry.* Take a look at "Storing data on tape."

Housekeeping, Safeguarding, and Other Chores

When your computer's worth more than your car, as mine is, you should want to keep it in good running order by performing regularly scheduled maintenance inspections. Just like a car needs regular oil changes, lubrication, and cleaning, a PC also benefits from a preventive maintenance program that's regularly applied. Without regular care and maintenance, your PC won't perform as it should — it may even stop working altogether, just like a car would without some form of regular attention.

Experienced with preventive maintenance programs and how the PC and its components are cleaned and checked for wear and tear? You can skip most of this chapter. However, it won't hurt you to quickly review this chapter to remind you of some helpful hints you may have forgotten.

Applying regular maintenance

The purpose of any *preventive maintenance (PM)* program is to reduce the need for repair and extend the effective life of the computer. You can accomplish this goal only if you perform PM on a regular basis following a well-defined procedure. Virtually all PC owner manuals include a chart or table detailing exactly the maintenance, adjustments, inspections, and cleaning that should be performed at specific, periodic intervals. For example, if you look in any automobile owner's guide, you can find such a guide tied to the mileage on the car. Like the car, every computer should have a similar guide. Table 17-1 shows an example of what the guide should include.

Table 17-1	PC Maintenance Schedule Guide	
Frequency	*Module*	*Maintenance Actions*
Daily	System	Run a virus scan of the memory and hard disk.
	Hard disk	Create a backup (if you have updated important data or program files).
Monthly	Hard disk	Defrag the drive and recover lost clusters.
	Keyboard	Clean the keyboard with compressed air and check for and repair stuck keys.
	Mouse	Clean ball and rollers and check for wear.
	Monitor	Turn off power and clean screen with soft cloth or antistatic wipe.

Frequency	Module	Maintenance Actions
	Printer	Clean with compressed air to remove dust and bits of paper.
On failure	Floppy disk drive	Clean floppy drive head.
Yearly	Case	Clean with compressed air to remove dust and other flotsam and jetsam.
	Motherboard	Check chips for chip creep and reseat if needed.
	Adapter cards	Clean contacts with contact cleaner and reseat.
As required	CMOS	Record and back up CMOS setup configuration.
	System	Keep written record of hardware and software configuration of PC system.

Table 17-1 doesn't contain everything that could be included, but I listed most of the biggies. I don't include tasks such as clearing temporary files, checking printer cartridges, and other common-sense preventive measures — such as don't drop, kick, or drop-kick the PC; don't blow cigarette smoke into the floppy disk drive; and don't spill water on the keyboard — but you often see them in PM plans.

For the A+ Core Hardware exam, you don't have to memorize this or any other preventive maintenance plan, but you should try to remember the kinds of tasks that should be included in one.

The frequencies used in Table 17-1 are examples, and depending on the usage of the PCs involved, some tasks may need to be performed more or less frequently. Some things, such as daily backups or cleaning a floppy disk's heads only when it fails, are fairly fixed in their schedules in any situation. Whatever the situation, a schedule of maintenance helps achieve the goals of preventive maintenance: It saves time and money.

Using the right cleaning supplies

The liquid cleaning compounds used to clean or condition the computer's components, case, and glass surfaces present safety and environmental problems to the user, the technician, and other people. Many of the chemical solvents, cleaners, and their containers may require special handling because they're poisonous (or harmful in other ways).

Finding the right information

The best tool available to find out whether a chemical solution poses a threat to you, the user, or the world in general is a *Material Safety Data Sheet (MSDS)*. An MSDS is available for every potentially hazardous chemical product. I use two Web sites to look up any product that I'm not completely sure of:

> ✔ **Northwest Fisheries Science Center:**
> http://research.nwfsc.noaa.gov/msds.html
>
> ✔ **Vermont Safety Information on the Internet (SIRI):**
> http://siri.org/msds/index.html

However, the first place to look for safety information on a product is on its label. Usually, if a problem may exist in using the product for either you or the PC, the label cautions you.

An MSDS lists the proper handling and storage procedures for chemical cleaning solutions.

Performing Preventive Maintenance

The process used to clean and maintain a PC and its components are one of the focuses of the A+ Core Hardware exam. Review this section to remind yourself of the general steps and cleaning products used on each FRM.

Before you do anything else, you should perform one often-overlooked step — make sure that the PC works! When I was young and foolish and still searching for each computer's bit bucket, I once cleaned a PC until it shined all over, only to find that it didn't have a motherboard. It may not have worked so well and my time was surely wasted, but it sure did sparkle!

The following sections each concentrate on the preventive maintenance steps of a different FRM. Review this information to get a general understanding of the steps, materials, and products used to clean and protect the PC and its parts. Most of the cleaning questions on the A+ Core Hardware exam deal with the kinds of products (for example, a mild cleaner) and materials (for example, a lint-free cloth) used for cleaning a particular device.

The keyboard

Other than the monitor screen, you probably clean the keyboard more often than the rest of the PC. This is because it sits open-faced most of the time and collects debris, flotsam, jetsam, and all the other gunk that floats by or falls in.

To clean the keyboard, use the steps shown in Lab 17-1.

Lab 17-1   Preventive Maintenance on the Keyboard

Here are the preventive maintenance steps for the keyboard:

1. **If you really want to get the keyboard clean or want to also do a close visual inspection of it, remove the keyboard cover.**

   Otherwise, you can open a cleaning hole by removing the key caps of the -, +, and Enter keys in the numeric pad at the far-right end of the keyboard. You can remove the key caps by using a small screwdriver or tweaker and gently prying off the key caps.

2. **Using compressed air, blow out the keyboard, sweeping with the air toward the removed key caps or use a keyboard vacuum to clean the keyboard.**

   If you removed the cover, you can turn it over, shake it out, and then use the compressed air to clean the internal and cover pieces.

   Special small vacuums are available that can be used to clean the keyboard, as well as other small parts of the PC. These vacuums usually have a small brush head attached with a gooseneck that can be bent around to provide the best angle for cleaning.

3. **Use non-static brushes or probes to loosen any large or stubborn pieces.**

   If the keyboard has had soda pop or the like spilled into it, you may need to wash it. If so, use warm, non-soapy water to rinse the guck away. Just be extra sure that the keyboard's completely dry before you power it up.

4. **Replace the key caps or reassemble the keyboard cover.**

   You can replace the keycaps by gently pressing them back onto their mounting.

5. **To clean the keys and keyboard case, use a soft, lint-free cloth and isopropyl alcohol or a non-sudsing general-purpose cleaner to wipe away any guck, ink, or other indescribable yuckies.**

   Isopropyl alcohol is good because its evaporation removes any worry about the keyboard being wet. As I said before, be sure that the keyboard is dry before you send power to it.

6. **Reboot the system, observing the POST for keyboard errors, and test the keyboard by pressing every key and verifying its action.**

The mouse

Just as it's the mud puddle's fault that the kid is dirty, it's the mouse pad's fault that the mouse gets dirty and needs cleaning. Like the keyboard, the mouse pad sits in the open most of the time and gets dusty, wet, slimed, and everything else that happens on your desktop. The mouse then rolls over whatever has collected on the mouse pad and it gets inside, gumming up the works.

To clean the mouse, follow the steps listed in Lab 17-2. To clean the mouse pad, wipe it off occasionally with a damp cloth or just get a new one.

Lab 17-2   Preventive Maintenance for the Mouse

Here are the preventive maintenance steps for the mouse:

1. **After you make sure that no open applications are running on the PC, roll the mouse gently onto its back and, without tickling, remove the ball access slide cover.**

2. **After you make sure that your hands are clean, remove and closely examine the ball for pits, cracks, or canyons. Also check to see whether the ball is lopsided or oval-shaped.**

   If the mouse ball has any of these problems, replace it or the entire mouse unit (recommended). Inspect the hole in which the ball sits for guck, lint, hair, string, ant colonies, or beaver dams. I'm only kidding about the last two, but you can find some pretty weird and extremely yucky stuff inside a mouse.

3. **Inspect the rollers inside the hole where the ball goes for debris or sticky or greasy buildup.**

   To clean the rollers, use a small, flat-blade screwdriver or tweaker (you know, the little pocket screwdriver) to scrape off the guck.

4. **Blow any dust from inside the mouse using compressed air.**

   Don't blow the dust out with your mouth for two reasons: spit inside the mouse and dust in your eyes.

5. **Use a damp, lint-free cloth to clean the mouse ball. Don't soak it or scrub it, just wipe it clean and let it dry before reinserting it in the hole where the mouse ball goes.**

   Don't use alcohol to clean the mouse ball. Alcohol may shrink the ball or cause it to be lopsided, just like it does to humans.

6. **Place the mouse ball back into the hole where the mouse ball goes, replace the slide cover, and lock it in place.**

   If needed, you can use isopropyl alcohol or a general-purpose cleaner to clean the exterior of the mouse or the mouse pad. Check the mouse pad to see whether it's worn, frayed, torn, or hollow in its center. A beat-up mouse pad can cause lint, bits of rubber, or other guck to get inside the mouse. Mouse pads come cheap, and you can usually garner freebies from stores, manufacturers, or at trade shows (one good reason to go). Your employer may even have some promotional mouse pads for you to give your customers.

7. **Test the mouse, using something other than Solitaire or another game — it just doesn't look right to the customer.**

Clean the mouse ball with a damp cloth; don't use alcohol on it. Alcohol can dissolve the mouse ball material and cause flat spots and distortion.

The monitor

Monitors are usually covered with a special coating that can be permanently streaked if the wrong solutions are used to clean it. Ammonia-based cleaning products can dissolve the coating on the monitor, which may damage the display. You can find antistatic cleaners designed specially for cleaning monitor and LCD screens.

You should not wipe the screen while it is on and warm. This can generate static electricity that can be harmful to the monitor and to you. The best way to clean your monitor's screen is to dry-dust it with a lint-free cloth. Remember that water, of which most liquid cleaners are made of, is an excellent conductor of electricity. Another caution is that, because of the mechanics and high voltage inside the monitor, you should never open the monitor's cover.

Lab 17-3 shows the proper cleaning procedure for the monitor.

Lab 17-3   Preventive Maintenance for the Monitor

After you make sure that the monitor works, the preventive maintenance steps for it are as follows:

1. **Turn the monitor off and unplug it.**

   Wait a few minutes before you begin, and *do not* wear an ESD grounding strap. As I explain in Chapter 13, an ESD grounding strap, whether worn on a wrist or ankle, is a dangerous thing to wear while working on a monitor.

2. **Using compressed air or a slightly damp, lint-free cloth, clean any dust from the top of the monitor, being careful not to blow it into the open vents.**

   Never open the cover of the monitor! Mean and nasty high voltage lurks inside.

   You can use either isopropyl alcohol or a general-purpose cleaner to clean the outside of the monitor case. The alcohol is probably the better choice, if you can stand the fumes, because it doesn't create a safety hazard if dripped inside the case.

3. **Use an antistatic cleaner to clean the glass of the monitor.**

   Never wash the monitor glass with the power on. You can buy antistatic cleaning packets that come individually wrapped just like the little moist towelettes you get from the fried-chicken place.

4. **Reconnect the monitor and test the video.**

If nothing displays, check that the power switch is on, and check the power cord and video connections and the brightness and contrast settings. These connections and settings may have been inadvertently loosened or changed during the cleaning.

The case

Not a lot needs to be done to the case itself to keep it functioning properly. After all, the case doesn't do a heck of a lot — it mostly just gets dusty. However, some preventive maintenance activities exist that you can perform at the system (or case) level to keep the general system functioning as it should.

Lab 17-4 lists the activities you can use to keep the system case in working order.

Lab 17-4	System-Level Preventive Maintenance

1. **After you turn off the PC and remove the power cord, carefully remove the case cover.**

Before you do anything else, visually inspect inside the case to assess any problems that may be written in the dust. Normally, the inside and outside vents have dust accumulated on them, but if dust is gathering in a place that it shouldn't, the case may have a crack in it, a part may be missing, or some other problem may have developed. A common problem is that one or more of the slot covers that should be filling empty expansion ports on the case are missing.

Look the case over thoroughly for dust, corrosion, leaking battery acid, dead bugs, moose droppings, and birds' nests. If only lightly dusty, use compressed air to blow it out, using caution not to blow it into your eyes. If you must remove boulders and other chunks, pick them out with tweezers, or if big enough, your fingers. Since you are working inside the case, you most definitely must use ESD protection and safeguards.

2. **Check cables and wires for loose connections.**

Using compressed air, blow out the outside vents of the power supply first, and then its inside vents, the drive bays, adapter cards, and finally the outside vents of the case.

You can also use a small vacuum cleaner to clean the inside of the case. In fact, it may actually be better for some systems than compressed air. Blowing the dust around can merely move it from one place to another inside the case. Sucking out the dirt and grime is sometimes better than blowing the dust under the edge of a loose component or connector.

3. Replace the case cover (be sure not to snag any cables).

4. With your bucket of isopropyl alcohol or the general-purpose cleaner, swab down the case, being careful not to slop the mop inside the case.

5. Power on the PC and monitor the POST process for errors.

The floppy disk drive

To perform preventive maintenance on a floppy disk drive or to clean it when it begins to fail, use the steps listed in Lab 17-5.

Lab 17-5	Preventive Maintenance for the Floppy Disk Drive

1. Verify that the floppy disk drive works.

2. Using a floppy disk drive cleaning kit and following its directions clean the read/write heads.

   This is an excellent place to use a small handheld vacuum with a brush head to clean any dust from the opening on the floppy disk drive.

3. Test the drive.

The hard disk drive

The preventive maintenance tasks for the hard disk deal more with optimizing its storage than with physical cleaning tasks. You have no cleaning tasks to perform because the hard disk is a sealed unit. The PM tasks for a hard disk involve the following:

✔ Backing up the data on the hard disk.

✔ Running ScanDisk, Norton, or another disk-diagnostic software tool to check the surface of the hard disk for errors.

✔ Running Defrag, Norton Speed, or an equivalent disk-optimization program.

Saving the earth

Several components in a PC require special handling when you dispose of them. The list includes batteries, mercury switches, the CRT in the monitor, and more.

Disposing of dead batteries

PC batteries, which are usually the lithium battery used to provide power to the CMOS memory, should not be disposed of in either fire or water. Batteries should not be casually discarded, but should be disposed of according to local restrictions and regulations covering the disposal or recycling of all batteries.

Leaking batteries should be handled carefully; make sure that you do not get the electrolyte, the stuff on the inside of the battery, in your eyes.

Yes, I know this all sounds like overkill, but it is the right answer for the exam.

Getting rid of a monitor

Believe it or not, a monitor contains the following contaminants: solvents and solvent vapors, metals (including a very high level of lead), photoresist materials, deionized water, acids, oxidizers, phosphor, ammonia, aluminum, carbon slurry, and a long list of other chemicals and caustic materials. A monitor should not be simply thrown in the dumpster. It should be disposed carefully. Probably, the best way to "throw out" a monitor is through a disposal service that handles computer equipment.

Handling other PC problem components

Other items related to the PC must be disposed of carefully and cautiously. Most are common-sense items, but you may see a question on the exam that relates them together as hazardous PC waste. Included in this bunch of items are laser-printer toner cartridges, refill kits, and the used or empty containers of chemical solvents and cleaners.

The best place to find information on how an item should be disposed is in its documentation, such as the information that comes with the printer cartridge, or the MSDS or WHMIS information on a chemical product.

Virus Detection and Protection

Viruses are nasty pieces of software that have taken on the characteristics of an infectious disease, spreading germs that infect unsuspecting and unprotected PCs. You can expect a couple of questions on the exam that deal with what a virus is, how it spreads, and how it is detected.

The following characteristics define a computer virus:

- ✔ A virus attaches itself to another piece of programming code in memory, on a floppy disk, or on a downloaded file, or it has the form of an executable file and runs when opened on the target system.

- ✔ A virus replicates itself and infects other systems, propagating itself from one computer to another.

Horses, worms, and germs

Not all viruses do catastrophic damage to a system. Many viruses are just nuisances or pranks, playing music, simulating system meltdowns, or displaying misinformation during the system boot. Viruses that are malicious can and do cause considerable damage in the form of lost data.

Many different types of programs are classified as viruses, including many that aren't actually viruses:

- ✔ **Trojan horse:** Based on Greek mythology. Like the gift horse that hid the attacking army, the viral Trojan horse hides a virus program by imitating or camouflaging itself as a legitimate application. When executed, it springs the virus, often creating other Trojan horses to avoid detection.

- ✔ **Worm:** A self-contained program that spreads itself to other systems, usually over a network connection. Worms create many different nasty effects when they run.

- ✔ **Virus impostor or gag programs:** Demented jokes created by programmers with not enough to do, obviously. These programs simulate the effects of a virus, scaring users into believing that they've been infected. It's not unusual for users to hear the truth from the jokester, about halfway through the apparent reformatting of their hard disk.

Also keep in mind that some of the nastiest viruses are not viruses at all. Virus hoaxes spread through the rumor mill (especially on the Internet) and tell of untold horrors that will happen at 13 minutes after midnight on the day the creator of a certain candy bar was born, or something like that. Before it gets started, I just made that one up.

Viruses and how they spread

Computer viruses are a form of electronic warfare developed solely to cause human misery. The evil, sick, and talented minds that develop computer viruses would like nothing better than to have your boot sectors catch cold or have your disk drives develop dysentery. Five major virus classes exist, each with many subclasses:

- ✔ **Boot sector viruses (system viruses):** These viruses target the boot program on every bootable floppy disk or hard disk. By attaching itself to the boot sector program, the virus is guaranteed to run whenever the computer starts up. Boot sector viruses spread mostly by jumping from disk to disk.

✔ **File viruses:** File viruses modify program files, such as .exe or .com files. Whenever the infected program executes, the virus also executes and does its nastiness. File viruses spread by infected floppy disks, networks, and the Internet.

✔ **Macro viruses:** The newest general class of virus, macro viruses take advantage of the built-in macro programming languages of application programs such as Microsoft Word and Microsoft Excel. Macro languages allow users to create macros, script-like programs that automate formatting, data entry, or frequently repeated tasks. A macro virus, most commonly found in Microsoft Word documents, can cause as much damage as other viruses and can spread by jumping from an opened document to other documents.

✔ **BIOS program viruses:** This type of virus attacks flash BIOS programs by overwriting the system BIOS program and leaving the PC unbootable.

✔ **E-mail viruses:** The latest trend in viruses and the ones getting most of the press these days. The Melissa virus was an e-mail virus that spread by e-mailing itself from one computer to another using the PC's e-mail address book.

Because a virus is a program, it can only infect programs. A virus can't hide anywhere that it doesn't blend into the scenery. Viruses that infect graphic files, e-mail, or text files are just myths. It would be like trying to hide a bright red ball among bright white balls. However, viruses can be attached to text files or e-mail and transmitted or copied to a new host system.

Playing hide and seek with viruses

As virus detection software becomes more sophisticated, so are the viruses. Most antivirus software works by recognizing a predefined pattern of characters unique to individual viruses, a sort of fingerprint, called its *signature*. As viruses get more devious, they include new ways to elude the virus detectors. These tricks, as a group, are called *cloaking*. Some of the cloaking techniques used are the following:

✔ **Polymorphing:** Allows viruses to change their appearance, signature, and size each time they infect a system.

✔ **Stealth virus:** Hides its damage in such a way that everything appears normal.

✔ **Directory virus:** Hides itself by lying. It changes a directory entry to point to itself instead of the files it is replacing. No actual change is made to the affected files, and they appear normal on directory lists and in Windows Explorer lists, which allows the virus to avoid detection.

Combating viruses

Viruses manifest themselves on a PC in a wide variety of ways, including spontaneous system reboots; system crashes; application crashes; sound card or speaker problems; distorted, misshapen, or missing video on the monitor; corrupted or missing data from disk files; disappearing disk partitions; or boot disks that won't boot.

In spite of the efforts of the virus developers, the best defense against virus infection is antivirus software, also called *scanners* or *inoculators*. Don't you just love all this medical talk?

Here are the general types of antivirus software in use today:

- ✔ **Virus scanner software:** This run-on-demand software scans the contents of memory and the disk drive, directories, and files that the user wants to check. This type of software is the most common form of antivirus program.

- ✔ **Memory-resident scanner software:** This kind of scanner stays in memory, automatically checking the environment, including incoming e-mail and browser documents for viruses.

- ✔ **Behavior-based detectors:** A more sophisticated form of memory-resident scanner, a behavior-based detector looks for suspicious behavior typical to virus programs. Some stereotyping is involved, and some good processes may be interrupted, but safe is better than sorry.

- ✔ **Startup scan antivirus software:** This software runs when the PC boots and does a quick scan of boot sectors and essential files to detect boot sector viruses before the PC boots up.

Most antivirus software uses a database of virus profiles and signatures for reference, commonly referred to as *DAT,* short for data or database, files. This database should be updated frequently; most antivirus packages include a provision for a set number or an unlimited number of updates.

Keep in mind that not all detected viruses are viruses. On occasion, what may look like a virus to the virus scanner may be an innocent look-alike program or data file. This detection of the look-alike is called a *false positive*. Before you don your surgical robes and glove up, investigate the virus to find out more about it — how it works and what damage it does. This investigating may save you from removing an important file from a customer's PC because you suspected it to be a virus. Don't get me wrong; most scanner alarms are for viruses, but proceed with caution, especially on a customer's machine.

Maintaining Your Integrity

Although you won't see it referred to as integrity on either of the A+ exams, where it is more likely to be called *data backups,* be ready to answer at least one question on when data backups should be created and possibly where you should store the backup media.

Data backups are a form of preventive maintenance. They ensure that, should a problem develop with your PC or system that jeopardizes your data, you have a copy of the data to restore when the problem is solved. On top of that, they just make good sense. There are any number of threats to the integrity of your data, hardware failures, beta-test software, operator error, and viruses. It may seem a bit paranoid, but just because I'm paranoid doesn't mean they aren't really trying to get me.

Creating a data backup

Tape is a good medium to use for creating a backup of hard disk data. Making a backup of files is a safety precaution taken to ensure that data outlives the device on which it's stored. A cardinal rule of computing: Back up files regularly, and then back up the backups.

Most operating systems include utilities for creating a backup (see Part V) and backup software is usually included with tape, recordable CD, and other writable media drives. Of course, a variety of software packages specifically designed to perform backups are available for purchase.

Backup software offers some advantages over just copying a file to a removable medium. Most offer data-compression techniques to reduce the number of disks or tapes needed to hold the archived data. Many also offer cataloging routines and single directory or file-restore capabilities.

You can create four different types of backups:

- **Archival backup (or full backup):** Contains every file, program, table, and so on from the hard disk.
- **Incremental backup:** Contains only the files that have been modified since the previous backup.
- **Differential backup:** Copies all the data added or modified since the last full backup.
- **Copy backup:** Created by using a copy command to write a duplicate of a file, directory, or disk to another media.

It's wise to rotate a series of tapes or other media relative to the number of increments to be regularly captured. For example, if daily backups are made, you should use seven sets (or possibly only five, if the office works only five days a week) of backup media. It's also good practice to make an archival backup at least once per cycle with two or more incremental backups filling out the cycle. For example, you can create an archival backup once a week and create a daily incremental backup during the rest of the week. Whatever cycle you use, the backup should be a comfortable safety net for the system that matches how frequently, and how much of the data is affected by changes.

Storing data on tape

Back in the dark ages of personal computing, back even before floppy or hard disks, the only permanent storage media available was cassette tapes — the same ones used for music. Before then, except for some very early use of punched paper tape, you just didn't store data between runs of the PC. Each time you wanted to run your BASIC program, you had to re-enter it and the data. Regardless of how you feel about tape today, at one time, it was a godsend.

Tape is a somewhat unique medium in comparison to the other writable permanent data storage media available to PC users today. Whereas most of the other media are direct access, tape is a serial, or physically sequential, access media. If you want to hear the third song on a music cassette, you must first fast forward over the first two songs. The same holds true for accessing the third record of a tape file.

Tape is primarily a backup media today, and many larger systems, especially network servers, have either an internal or external tape drive. This is a good use of the media, its serial nature, and its relative compact size. Some problems exist with using tape, but they're avoidable with proper care and diligence. You should rotate tapes regularly, store them in a cool, dry place (look for this tidbit on the test), and replace them at least once a year.

If intermittent problems begin showing up in a rotated group of tapes that are used for daily backups, the problem could be the age of the tapes or perhaps the tape heads need cleaning.

Prep Test

1 Backup media, especially tape cartridges, should be stored in a

A ○ Warm, humid location

B ○ Warm, dry location

C ○ Cool, humid location

D ○ Cool, dry location

2 Information on the hazard of a chemical solution and its safe handling and storage is contained on a

A ○ MSSC

B ○ MSDS

C ○ MSCE

D ○ DHCP

3 To open a hole on the keyboard for dirt and debris to blow out, remove the

A ○ Tab, Caps Lock, Shift, and Control keys from the left end of the keyboard

B ○ Spacebar

C ○ Arrow keys

D ○ Minus, Plus, and Enter keys from the right end of the keyboard

4 The monitor glass should be cleaned

A ○ When the monitor is on

B ○ When the monitor is off

C ○ Anytime using a wet cloth

D ○ Never

5 The major steps for preventive maintenance on a hard disk are

A ○ Defrag, ScanDisk, backup

B ○ Fdisk, Format, ScanDisk

C ○ Backup, ScanDisk, Defrag

D ○ Disassembly, blow dust out, reassembly

6 E-mail-transferred viruses are transmitted in what form?

A ○ Text messages

B ○ Binary data hidden in text messages

C ○ An e-mail attachment that contains executable code

D ○ All e-mail borne viruses are hoaxes

7 You should never wear ESD grounding attachments when working on which FRM?

A ○ Memory module
B ○ Monitor or CRT
C ○ Motherboard
D ○ Expansion card

8 Which of the following are backup types capture files changed since the last previous backup? (Choose two)

A ❑ Incremental
B ❑ Partial
C ❑ Differential
D ❑ Copy

9 The unique data image that's used by antivirus programs to detect and remove a virus is its

A ○ Profile
B ○ Fingerprint
C ○ Mug shot
D ○ Signature

10 The contacts of a memory module or expansion card are cleaned with which type of cleaner?

A ○ Non-sudsy cleaner
B ○ Clean, lint-free cloth
C ○ Contact cleaner
D ○ Ammonia

Answers

1 **D.** In fact, just about all recordable media should be stored in a cool and dry location, although some is less affected by the environments than others. *See "Storing data on tape."*

2 **B.** Material Safety Data Sheets contain information on all aspects of using, handling, and storing chemical products. *Take a look at "Using the right cleaning supplies."*

3 **D.** These three keys open up a slot on the end of the keyboard through which the chunks can fall out. *Check out "The keyboard."*

4 **B.** The monitor glass carries quite a charge of static electricity, and cleaning it when it is on, especially with a wet solution or cloth, can light up your life. *Look at "The monitor."*

5 **C.** Before you do anything to a hard disk, back it up. Then you can scan it for surface defects and optimize it by defragging it. *Review "The hard disk drive."*

6 **C.** Many viruses, like the infamous Melissa.vbx virus, are transmitted as attachments to e-mail messages. *See "Viruses and how they spread."*

7 **B.** A rather nasty danger lurks inside the monitor in the form of a very large capacitor that is just looking for a way to discharge its thousands of volts of stored electricity to the first grounded entity it can find. Don't let it be you! *Check out "The monitor."*

8 **A, C.** Both an incremental backup and a differential backup copy files that have been updated (meaning written to and saved) since the last backup was created. *Take a look at "Creating a data backup."*

9 **D.** Each virus program has a digital signature that uniquely identifies it. *See "Playing hide and seek with viruses."*

10 **C.** The contacts of memory modules and expansion cards should be cleaned periodically with contact cleaner to remove any oxidation that may have accumulated. *Review "Using the right cleaning product."*

Chapter 18

Troubleshooting PC Hardware

· ·

Exam Objectives

▶ Defining basic troubleshooting procedures and good practices

▶ Troubleshooting and isolating problems on a PC

▶ Identifying common symptoms and problems associated with FRMs

· ·

*F*ortunately, the job of a PC repairperson isn't just the drudgery of building up new customer PCs and upgrading the hard disk or video system. It also includes the part of the job that attracts and holds the very best PC technicians — troubleshooting and diagnosing a problem on a PC.

If you've looked under the hood of a car lately, you'll agree that the days when you could work on your car at home in the garage with just your trusty toolbox are long gone. Well, if you've looked inside the system unit of a PC lately, and I know you have, you know that like the car, the PC has become very complicated and nearly as hard to work on. This is a good news/bad news situation. The good news is that the PC user is less able to work on the PC, meaning that there is more work for you, the trained and skilled professional PC repairperson. The bad news is that troubleshooting and isolating a problem on the PC has become much more difficult. Oh sure, you still have the occasional data cable missing and keyboard errors, but now you must also deal with DMA channel conflicts and chipset problems that have to be chased down.

It is safe to say that the overriding focus of the A+ exams is troubleshooting. I'd say that more than half of the test involves troubleshooting, diagnostics, and problem solving in one form or another. Officially, diagnosing and troubleshooting is 25 percent of the Core Hardware exam, but questions on how to deal with common FRM problems can be found on all parts of the exam.

Quick Assessment

Defining basic troubleshooting procedures and good practices

1 The best source for information on a PC's problem is _____.

2 Before troubleshooting a hard disk, it is a good practice to create a _____.

3 Windows 2000 requires the BIOS to be _____-compliant.

Trouble-shooting and isolating problems on a PC

4 The POST signals errors with _____ and _____.

5 Floppy disk drive POST error codes are in the _____ series.

6 Expansion slot covers are technically part of the _____ system.

7 The highest value that can be represented on a three-pole jumper is _____.

8 _____ and _____ are applied to the CPU to solve overheating problems.

Identifying common symptoms and problems associated with FRM

9 IDE disk drives are configured as either a _____ or a _____.

10 The AT command used to reset a modem to its default settings is _____.

Answers

1 *The user.* See "Arriving on the scene."

2 *Full backup.* Review "Backing up before you move forward."

3 *ACPI.* Check out "Matching up the OS and the BIOS."

4 *Beeps, error codes.* Look over "Decoding the beeps" and "Numbering the error messages."

5 *600.* Study "Numbering the error messages."

6 *Cooling.* See "Cooling problems and the CPU."

7 *Seven.* Review "Troubleshooting SCSI hard disk drives."

8 *Heatsinks, fans.* Take a look at "Cooling problems and the CPU."

9 *Master, slave.* Check out "Troubleshooting IDE hard disk drives."

10 *ATZ.* Study "Troubleshooting modems."

Troubleshooting Can Be Fun

For the A+ Core Hardware exam, you must know the processes used in troubleshooting, diagnosing, and isolating a problem on a PC. I don't mean all of the little tricks and shortcuts that you and I have devised over the years. I mean the straightforward, down-the-middle, by-the-book way of identifying the source of a problem on a PC. So, even if you are a well-seasoned veteran and can tell a PC's problem by the sound it is making, you should at least skim through this chapter — especially this first section — to familiarize yourself with the terminology and processes the test assumes you know and use.

Getting ready to start

Chapter 3 discusses the tools you are likely to need when working with and troubleshooting the PC. However, it fails to include what may be the most valuable tools for troubleshooting a PC's hardware problem — paper and pen. You will have a lot to write down as you begin troubleshooting the PC, including what the user has to say, the current BIOS settings, the location and arrangement of expansion cards and their cables and the devices to which they are attached. They may even come in handy for writing down the customer's address and the directions to their location.

Always, repeat, always be absolutely sure that you have ESD protection with you. Your ESD wrist strap should be like the famous credit card that you should never leave home without. Remember that when you do not use proper ESD precautions at a customer site, you are risking not only the customer's systems, but also, perhaps, your reputation, or worse, your job.

Arriving on the scene

Observe the customer's environment as carefully as you can, especially the electrical setup used for the PC in question. Is it attached to a wall socket, plug strip, surge suppressor, or UPS? How many devices are sharing the electrical supply? Is the environment dust-free and otherwise clean? Is it humid or overly dry? All of these conditions tell you about the stresses and strains to which the PC is subjected.

Do not jump to any conclusions based on what you see, however. Ask the user how long the PC has been in its current location and electrical situation. Also don't jump to conclusions about what the apparent problem may be without first speaking with the user. Okay, if the PC is not plugged in, you can go ahead and see if that may be the problem, but anything else, ask first, listen to the response, and then begin troubleshooting.

Some questions you should use to learn more about the problem are:

1. When did the problem first happen?

2. Did you add hardware or software to the PC right before the problem appeared?

3. Can you recreate the problem?

4. Did smoke come out of the PC or monitor?

When dealing with a user directly, always use the five C's (courtesy, concern, consideration, conscientiousness, and cooperation) and the three L's (listen, listen, and listen) of customer care. You don't need to remember this for the test, but it can't hurt you to know this for real life.

Troubleshooting FRMs

Expect to see questions on the A+ Core Hardware exam about identifying common symptoms, troubleshooting, and isolating problems on the following FRMs (I pronounce FRM as FRAM, just to make it easy to read):

- ✔ BIOS and CMOS
- ✔ CPU
- ✔ Floppy drive
- ✔ Hard drives
- ✔ Memory
- ✔ Modems
- ✔ Monitor and video cards
- ✔ Power supply
- ✔ Sound card and speakers
- ✔ USB

I wouldn't worry too much about anything not in this list.

Be sure you know all about expansion slot covers. Not too much to diagnose, but at least know what kind of problems they prevent and their purpose.

Troubleshooting the BIOS

Unless there was a power failure halfway through a flashing operation on the BIOS, there is really not much that can go wrong with the BIOS itself. So, most of the troubleshooting questions on the A+ Core Hardware exam relate to boot sequence problems. However, you should know about a couple of situations that directly effect the BIOS directly. For more information about PC BIOS, see Chapter 5.

Upgrading the BIOS

If a PC has an apparent compatibility problem with a FRM, don't leap to the conclusion that a BIOS upgrade is automatically needed. The BIOS comes under the heading of *If it isn't broke, don't fix it.* The BIOS should not be upgraded except to solve an isolated specific (and documented) compatibility or performance issue. Use only the BIOS or motherboard manufacturer's flashing software and apply only the BIOS versions (obtained from the manufacturer only) that are listed as compatible to your motherboard, processor, and chipset.

Troubleshooting after a BIOS update

If you have flashed your BIOS (close the raincoat, please), but the system will not boot because it can't see the hard disk (and perhaps other devices as well), one or more CMOS settings might need adjustments. Using the written record of the CMOS settings before you flashed the BIOS, enter the Setup program and verify that all of the BIOS configuration settings are correct. The BIOS CMOS will have default settings, and any that were changed in the past will need to be changed again.

Matching up the OS and the BIOS

If you are installing a Windows 2000 operating system, the type and compliance of the PC's BIOS is very important. Windows 2000 requires the BIOS to be compliant to the Advanced Configuration and Power Interface (ACPI). If the BIOS is not ACPI-compliant, expect Windows 2000 to have boot errors and crash frequently. ACPI includes the *OnNow* standard that can start the PC from a single keystroke. Without this compatibility, the Windows 2000 setup program may not be able to communicate with the PC's hardware devices.

To verify that the BIOS is ACPI-compliant, check the BIOS or motherboard's documentation, the Windows 2000 Hardware Compatibility List (HCL), or contact the PC's manufacturer.

Dealing with BIOS errors

If the BIOS has the most current and compatible version, then most likely any problems generated by the BIOS will be during the Power-On Self-Test (POST) and boot processes. See Chapter 5 for information on the details of the boot sequence.

BIOS systems use two different means of notifying you of a problem during the boot sequence:

✔ **Beep codes:** The system speaker (the little one built into the system case) emits a series of short and long tones to indicate a problem in an essential system component during the hardware phase of the boot sequence.

✔ **Error messages:** The BIOS displays error messages on the monitor that indicate a problem has occurred in the final stages of the boot cycle.

Unfortunately, each BIOS manufacturer has a unique set of beep codes it uses to signal boot errors. Fortunately, the A+ folks see the difficulty in testing on beep codes and don't expect you to memorize all of the beep codes in the standard IBM, Award, and AMI BIOSes. The error messages issued from each different BIOS are fairly standard and generally describe the problem well enough.

Decoding the beeps

Every BIOS system has one beep code in common, which is a single beep tone to indicate the end of the POST. However, a single beep tone can also mean a memory problem on the AMI (American Megatrends, Inc.) BIOS (a very popular BIOS).

Don't worry about memorizing BIOS error codes for the exam. Just understand that if an error should occur during the POST, it will be identified by the BIOS program's beep codes.

Here are some general guidelines on what you should do for a few of the more common POST problems signaled by beep codes:

✔ **0 beeps:** If no beeps are sounded, most likely there will also be nothing displayed on the monitor. The problem is most likely power. Make sure the PC is plugged into an AC power source. If it is, check to see if the motherboard is getting power. Use the motherboard's documentation to locate the Power LED connector and plug the LED wire on it. If it lights, you know the motherboard is getting power. Otherwise, there is a problem with the power supply.

✔ **1 beep, 2 beeps, or 3 beeps:** Reseat any newly added memory or replace the memory with known good chips. One beep is also used to indicate a successful POST. If you hear one beep and the boot does not continue, you have a memory problem.

The term "known good" is used frequently on the exam to describe FRMs, components, and software configurations that you absolutely, positively know to be good, working parts.

✔ **4 beeps, 5 beeps, 7 beeps, or 10 beeps:** The motherboard has a serious problem and may need to be replaced or sent to the manufacturer for repairs.

✔ **6 beeps:** If the motherboard has a separate keyboard controller chip, try reseating it. If not, check the keyboard connection and the keyboard itself. It is unlikely that the Super I/O chip in the chipset is bad, so the problem must be with the physical components of the keyboard.

✔ **8 beeps:** Reseat the video card and check its memory to ensure it is also seated properly on the card. If the problem persists, replace the video card.

✔ **9 beeps:** You need to be sure that it is 9 and not 10 or 8. This indicates a faulty BIOS chip, which cannot be corrected by reseating the chips. Check with the motherboard supplier or the BIOS manufacturer. The BIOS may need to be updated.

Deciphering BIOS error messages

Depending on the BIOS in use, the on-screen BIOS error messages all indicate one thing — a serious system problem. Here are examples of boot cycle error messages for topics you are likely to find on the A+ Core Hardware exam:

✔ **BIOS ROM checksum error - System halted:** The American Heart Association has recognized this message as a major cause of minor heart attacks. In a nutshell, the BIOS is hosed and you need to contact the motherboard or BIOS manufacturer for recovery procedures, if there are any. This error could be caused by an incomplete or faulty flash upgrade and there may be recovery procedures available.

✔ **CMOS battery failed:** The CMOS battery is dead and needs to be replaced. Of course, you will need to re-enter the system configuration as well.

✔ **CMOS checksum error - Defaults loaded:** This message indicates that the CMOS has become corrupt. The cause is likely a weak battery that needs to be replaced.

If the system clock is losing time, the cause is likely a dying CMOS battery. Like the batteries in your room smoke detectors, the CMOS battery should be checked regularly and replaced when weak.

✔ **Display switch is set incorrectly:** Some motherboards have a jumper that sets the type of video display being supported. This error indicates that the jumper and the video configuration in CMOS are different.

✔ **Floppy disk fail:** The BIOS cannot find the floppy disk controller (FDC). If the PC does not have a floppy disk drive, set the CMOS Disk Drive value to None (or Auto). If the FDC is included in the chipset, make sure the drive's cables are all seated properly.

✔ **Hard disk install failure:** This is a similar error to the floppy disk fail error message. The POST cannot find or initialize the hard disk controller (HDC). Make sure the adapter card, if there is one, is seated snugly and that the drive cables are connected properly.

✔ **I/O card failure:** This error indicates that an expansion card has failed or has a parity error at a certain address.

✔ **Keyboard error or no keyboard present:** Make sure that the keyboard is attached correctly and no keys are pressed during POST. Make sure that nothing is lying on the keyboard, such as a book.

✔ **Memory test fail:** This message indicates an error was detected during memory testing. The message should also include information about the type and location of the memory error, such as a memory parity error at XXXX, where XXXX would be the location of the memory error.

✔ **Primary/Secondary master/slave hard disk fail:** The POST process has detected an error in either the primary or secondary master or slave IDE hard disk drive. Check the cabling and the master/slave jumpers.

Numbering the error messages

Most system BIOSes display a 3 or 4-digit error code along with the error message to help pinpoint the apparent source of the problem. The documentation for the BIOS system or the motherboard should list the exact codes used on a particular PC.

PC error codes are grouped by device or service types in even one-hundreds. For example, a 600-series error indicates a problem with the floppy disk drive or the floppy disk drive controller. The actual error code displayed will be a number between 600 and 699 with each separate number identifying a specific problem.

Table 18-1 lists the PC error codes you should know for the A+ Core Hardware exam.

Table 18-1	PC Error Codes
Series	*Category*
100	Motherboard errors
200	RAM errors
300	Keyboard errors
600	Floppy disk drive errors
1100	COM1 errors
1700	Hard disk drive errors
3000	NIC errors

Troubleshooting other boot problems

A boot failure is very typically a loose or missing component, including, but not limited to, the CPU, BIOS ROM, chipset, memory, expansion card, or cable. If you are unable to pinpoint the component causing the boot to fail, begin removing expansion cards one at a time until the system will boot. Eventually, you should find the culprit and can then focus on why it is causing the problem.

Remember that many boot and operational problems on a PC are miraculously fixed merely by rebooting the PC. Therefore, rebooting should always be a standard first step in your troubleshooting procedure.

Troubleshooting CPU problems

The first thing you must know about the CPU is that if it is broken and you can't fix it; it must be replaced. But, problems with the CPU are usually not a problem with the CPU itself. More likely a problem with the CPU is the result of cooling (or the lack of it), power (or the lack of it), or compatibility issues with the motherboard and chipset.

Here are the symptoms of a CPU that is beginning to fail:

- ✔ The PC will not boot
- ✔ The PC does boot, but will not start the operating system
- ✔ The PC crashes during startup and when running applications
- ✔ The PC has sudden POST parity error problems in many devices
- ✔ The PC lock ups after a few minutes of operation

Chapter 7 provides more information on processors and CPUs and their environments.

Cooling problems and the CPU

If a PC boots without problems, but consistently halts or freezes after a few minutes, chances are the CPU is overheating. One way to verify this is to turn it off and wait a few minutes to let it cool a bit before turning it back on. If the same problem happens after the PC operates for a while, it is very likely that the CPU has a cooling problem.

Processors are designed to run within a certain temperature range. The operating temperature varies among processors and their packaging types. On average, processors operate in the range of 40 degrees Celsius (around 100 degrees Fahrenheit) to 90 degrees Celsius (around 200 degrees Fahrenheit). For example, a Pentium III in a SECC (Single Edge Connector Container or Slot 1) package should run at 75 degrees Celsius (167 Fahrenheit), but in its FC-PGA (Flip Chip — Plastic Grid Array) package, it will run at 85 degrees Celsius (185 degrees Fahrenheit). These are *die temperatures,* which means the temperature at the core of the processor packaging, and not the temperature at which the processor dies.

If the CPU is not fitted with a heatsink or a cooling fan and it is a Pentium-class or higher processor, you have found the problem. A heatsink and fan (usually they come as a single unit) should be attached using liberal amounts of thermal paste.

Some troubleshooting steps you can use to check out the CPU, heatsink, and fan are

1. Examine the heatsink and fan to see if they are in place or are cracked or broken.

2. Carefully grasp the heatsink (test it for heat first — it can be very hot!) and try to move it slightly back and forth. If it is loose, it may not have the proper seal between the heatsink and fan.

3. Remove the heatsink and fan and verify that the CPU is properly secured in its socket or slot. If a ZIF (zero insertion force) socket is in use, make sure that the ZIF arm is locked and anchored. Reattach the heatsink and fan, making sure it is attached securely and properly.

For some reason, expansion slot covers (you know, those narrow metal plates that are used to cover empty expansion card slots on the back of the case) are a hot topic on the A+ exam. They are a part of the cooling system and are primarily used to close up holes in the case to preserve the engineered airflow.

Timing is everything

If the PC displays the same symptoms as an overheating problem, but the system is not overheating, the problem may be that the system clock jumpers on the motherboard or the BIOS settings for the system timers are incorrectly set. If the CPU and the motherboard are using different clock timings, it may take a while for them to get so far out of synch that the system halts. Refer to the documentation for the motherboard and CPU to get the proper clock setting and adjust it accordingly.

Remember to shut down and unplug the PC before removing the CPU and observe all standard anti-static procedures when handling the CPU. Be very careful not to bend any of the pins, because you may want to reinstall the CPU later. Use care when installing the new CPU because bent pins will almost always ruin the PC. If a new CPU fails to correct the problem, then replace the motherboard.

Power problems and the CPU

If the PC is sounding a POST beep code indicating a CPU fault, chances are the CPU is not getting power. Using a multimeter (see Chapter 3), check the power outputs to the motherboard. If any of the leads is low or dead, replace the power supply. If the power is as it should be, then you may have a dead CPU and it should be replaced. If the new CPU fails to solve the problem, you have isolated the problem to the motherboard itself.

Checking out the CPU

If the system boots okay, but freezes up consistently when running a certain application or group of applications, the situation is too weird for normal diagnostics. Try running repetitive tests on the CPU using a third-party diagnostics package, such as Pc-check from Eurosoft (`www.eurosoft-usa.com`) or AMIDiag from AMI (`www.ami.com`). If the diagnostics indicate a CPU problem, replace the CPU and test again. If the same problem appears, expand the testing into the motherboard and chipset. You may end up testing the system completely only to find the problem is a corrupted file in the application software.

Troubleshooting the floppy disk drive

For a device that was supposed to disappear, floppy disk drives are still found on a large number of systems. Virtually every PC sold today includes a 1.44MB 3.5-inch floppy disk drive. In fact, floppy disk drives are so commonplace that they have become disposable technology. If a PC has a problem with its floppy disk drive, it is often much less expensive to replace it than to fix it.

Troubleshooting a floppy disk boils down to determining if the floppy disk drive is the source of a problem or not. If it is the problem, it is replaced. If not, then the focus shifts to other devices.

Booting from the A: drive

If a PC will not boot from the floppy disk drive, there are several reasons, all of which you need to know for the exam:

- ✔ **CMOS settings:** The boot device setting in CMOS may not have the A: floppy disk drive listed as the first boot drive or the floppy disk drive may not be listed as a boot device at all.

- ✔ **Media issues:** The disk may not be a bootable disk, which means it does not contain the system files needed to boot the system.

- ✔ **Drive problems:** It is possible that the floppy disk drive's power supply connector or data cable is partially disconnected, or if either or both of these cables were removed during some work you did inside the case perhaps one or both was not completely reconnected. This could result in intermittent operational errors. However, this type of error is typically caught during the POST.

Dealing with a floppy failure

If the POST indicates that the floppy disk drive is bad or missing through its beep codes or by displaying an error message in the 600 series (see Table 18-1 earlier in the chapter), the problem may be a general failure of the floppy disk drive, which is a truly rare event. However, some things you can check are

- ✔ **Power connector:** Check the power supply connector for a snug connection and make sure the cable is not crimped or loose in the connector. You may want to try a different power supply connector if one is available or check the voltage with a multimeter. The problem could be the power supply.

✔ **Cabling:** Make sure the data cable is connected properly and is not on backwards or shifted one pin over. The location of Pin 1 can vary by manufacturer and even model, so verify its location and check that the cable is installed correctly. One surefire way to tell that the floppy drive's data cable is on backwards is that the drive LED comes on with the boot and stays on solid while the PC is powered on.

✔ **Connecting two drives:** Many older systems had two floppy disk drives, typically one 5.25-inch and one 3.5-inch drive. Floppy disk drives have jumpers to indicate which is installed without the twist in the cable and which is installed with the twist in the cable. Check the cable and the drives against the drives' documentation. In most cases, the A: (first floppy disk drive) gets the twist.

✔ **CMOS:** The floppy disk controller can be disabled in the CMOS setup data. Verify that the controller is enabled. Also check that the CMOS has the correct drive types indicated for the A: and B: drives.

✔ **Resource conflicts:** Floppy disk resource conflicts are very rare, because virtually every PC system reserves IRQ 6 and DMA channel 2 for the floppy disk controller, and peripheral device manufacturers avoid these resources. However, devices that work on the floppy drive interface and with the floppy controller, such as a tape drive adapter, may try to use these resources.

✔ **Motherboard issues:** If the floppy disk controller is built-in to the motherboard or its chipset, the problem could be a motherboard issue.

Troubleshooting hard disk drives

Hard disk drive problems cause more frustration than most other PC problems. Not only will the PC not boot up, but there is the threat that all of the user's data, programs, and treasured MP3 files may be lost. Because of this, the A+ Core Hardware exam places an emphasis on hard disk drives and a majority of the questions that deal with troubleshooting relate to hard disk drives.

A hard disk problem can be any one of a variety of issues, including some on the drive itself, the hard disk controller, a SCSI host adapter, and the associated cabling. The hard disk types you need to know for the exam are IDE (Integrated Drive Electronics) and SCSI (Small Computer System Interface). If you run into ESDI (Enhanced Small Devices Interface) or ST-506 or other legacy disk drive types on the exam, they are definitely wrong answers.

Backing up before you move forward

Troubleshooting a hard disk drive always poses the risk of destroying any data stored on the hard disk. Always make a full backup of the drive and test it by restoring a few random files before you begin working on the hard disk. Of course, this assumes that you can access the disk drive. If you are unable to access the drive, ask the user to have the latest backup handy for possibly restoring the drive when you are finished.

Troubleshooting IDE hard disk drives

As discussed in Chapter 9, most PCs support either one or two IDE channels. Each IDE channel supports up to two disk drives, which are designated as a master and a slave. Master actually means disk0 and slave means disk1 and neither is the boss of the other. The BIOS assigns a logical device name to the master of the primary channel first, then the primary channel slave, and then to any drives on the secondary channel if one is installed. For example, the master drive on the primary IDE channel (assuming it has only one partition) is assigned the logical name of C: . The slave on the primary channel is assigned D: and the secondary channel drives are E: and F: . The master drive on the primary channel is the boot drive.

Each IDE drive has a jumper that must be set to indicate that the drive is either a master or a slave. You cannot have two masters or two slaves; it just won't work that way. Two IDE drives (a master and a slave) on the same channel connect to a common data cable in series. It really doesn't matter which of two drives is designated as the slave or the master. If two drives will not work with each other in any configuration as master and slave, there is something wrong with the drives.

To begin troubleshooting any disk drive problem, you should boot the system from a floppy disk drive that has minimal, if any, AUTOEXEC.BAT and CONFIG.SYS files. This is called a *clean boot* and may indicate a conflict exists in these system files.

IDE hard disk problems are caused by a variety of issues and here are some you need to be familiar with for the A+ Core Hardware exam:

- ✔ **The CMOS hard drive configuration is incorrect:** Check the CMOS configuration for each hard disk drive. The information you need should be in the documentation for each drive.

- ✔ **Newly added hardware is conflicting with hard disk drive:** Check the system resource settings in the Device Manager to verify that a resource conflict has not been created by the installation of a new piece of hardware.

- ✔ **The boot partition on the hard disk may be corrupted:** If the system files on the boot partition are corrupt, the system cannot boot properly. Use the SYS command (from a MS-DOS or command prompt) to transfer the system files back onto the hard drive. It may be necessary to format the partition and reinstall the operating system, should this fail to solve the problem. Also verify that the boot partition has not been accidentally removed.

- ✔ **The hard disk may be infected with a virus:** Many viruses can corrupt the master boot record on the hard drive and cause errors that show up as hard disk errors. If an anti-virus program is not installed on the PC, install one and scan the hard disk.

✔ **The hard disk cable may be bad or not connected properly:** If the front panel drive LED lights up and stays on constantly, it is very likely that the drive data cable is not properly connected, if at all. This condition should also cause a POST error message that says there is no boot device available. Check both ends of the cable, at the device and on the motherboard or adapter card. Also check the power supply connectors.

✔ **The hard drive may just be defective:** It can and does happen. Every disk drive makes some noise and users get accustomed to it. However, that louder than usual noise the drive has been making for over a month may have been the bearings seizing up.

Some of the common PC system error messages for hard disk problems are

✔ **Hard disk configuration error:** An incorrect CMOS configuration or a loose data cable causes this message.

✔ **Hard disk 0 failure:** Disk 0 is the master drive on the primary IDE channel. This message is caused by an incorrect CMOS configuration or a bad connection to the power supply.

✔ **Hard disk controller failure:** Check the connection of the data cable on the drive and the power connectors.

Troubleshooting SCSI hard disk drives

You can expect to find several questions on the A+ Core Hardware exam about SCSI systems and hard drives, although most of this information has been pushed off to the new Server+ exam. Look for my new *Server+ Certification For Dummies* book at your local booksellers soon. I have no shame, obviously.

For the exam, you should know the following facts about SCSI drives for troubleshooting situations:

✔ **CMOS setup:** The hard disk drive settings in CMOS should be set to None or Auto-detect.

✔ **SCSI device drivers:** SCSI devices require device drivers. Make sure the latest drivers are installed.

✔ **Host adapter and hard disk IDs:** The SCSI host adapter is always device 7 on the SCSI chain and the first SCSI hard disk drive on the channel should be assigned SCSI ID 0. If you have two or more SCSI hard disks, or any other SCSI devices, on the same SCSI cable, each must have a unique SCSI ID number. The ID is set through a three-pole jumper.

✔ **Termination:** If the SCSI hard disk is the only internal device or the last on the internal SCSI channel, it must be terminated.

A three-pole jumper can be set to 8 values, which are usually 0 through 7. Should you be asked what the highest value that can be set on a three-position jumper, the answer is 7.

Tempting fate: Mixing hard drive types

If a PC has both SCSI and IDE (ATA) hard disks, the choice must be made as to which is the boot disk. Because the SCSI is usually a higher performance disk drive, the user may want it to be the boot drive. If the BIOS on the user's PC doesn't allow a SCSI drive to be designated in the boot disk hierarchy, it can't happen.

Before giving up completely on assigning the SCSI hard disk as the boot drive, check with the motherboard or BIOS manufacturer for an upgrade that supports SCSI boot disks. The only other option is to remove the IDE drives altogether and go with only a SCSI drive, which should boot with the IDE drives gone.

Troubleshooting memory

After the hard disk drive, memory is the next largest block of troubleshooting questions on the A+ Core Hardware exam. Memory problems on a PC are typically one of three general types of errors:

- **Configuration:** The amount of memory installed is more than the PC or operating system supports or the BIOS CMOS settings are incorrect

- **Hardware:** At least one memory module is defective or the memory modules installed are not compatible

- **Installation:** The memory chips or modules are not properly seated in their sockets or a socket is bad or needs cleaning

One problem with diagnosing memory problems is that other components of a PC, such as software or the motherboard, can cause what may appear to be a memory problem.

Identifying memory problems

Knowing when a memory problem happened is often the best clue to its source. Memory problems typically occur in one of five instances:

- **The first time a new PC is started up:** The problem could be any number of things, but most likely the memory chips need to be reseated (in the best case) or are missing (in the worst case). If the problem does not appear to be memory related, it may well be a bad motherboard. Check with the manufacturer or the vendor.

✔ **Immediately after new memory is installed:** Check the part numbers and speed of the memory that was installed. Also verify that the memory was properly installed or configured in memory banks and that if DIP (Dual Inline Packaging) or SIMM (Single Inline Memory Module) memory is in use, that each bank was filled before memory was placed in another bank. You may also want to verify that the memory is appropriate for the motherboard, chipset, and processor. For example, the memory bus on a Pentium III PC is either PC100 or PC133-compliant and so must be the memory modules.

There are different memory standards available for a PC, but you must match the memory to the system. The part number of the memory holds a clue as to what it is. For the most part today, if the memory's part number ends with a dash and a number, such as "-60," it is industry standard EDO (Extended Data Output) or FPM (Fast Page Mode) memory. If the part number ends with a slash and a number, such as "/32," it is industry standard SDRAM (Synchronous DRAM). SDRAM part numbers also indicate the standard to which they conform. For example, a Kingston Technology memory with the part number KTM66X64/128 is compliant with the Intel 66 MHz standard and is a 128MB DIMM. For more information on memory modules, see Chapter 8.

✔ **Immediately after new software or operating system is installed:** More recent versions of software and operating systems typically require more memory than older versions. New software, especially beta versions, is notoriously buggy and can produce memory errors. The first step to correcting these errors, other than uninstalling the beta software, is to check for a BIOS upgrade or a service patch for the software.

✔ **Immediately after hardware is installed or removed:** New hardware installed incorrectly or a connector or cable dislodged while removing a device can in some instances cause what appear to be memory errors accompanied by memory error messages. After checking the cables and connectors, check for the new hardware's manufacturer for newer device drivers or BIOS updates.

✔ **For no apparent reason:** If a PC has been running okay and suddenly begins having memory problems, check for corrosion on the contacts of the memory modules. Another likely cause is heat. The PC could have been running too hot for a while and has finally damaged the motherboard, memory, or processor to the point of errors. Another suspect should be the power supply.

Dealing with memory errors

Typically, the PC will inform you of a PC problem in predicable ways. In most cases, it will be one of the following ways and you should perform the action listed for it.

✔ **The PC fails to boot and sounds a beep code:** Check the memory to ensure it is properly installed and is configured to the BIOS properly.

✔ **The PC boots, but the display is blank:** A dislodged card, a memory module not fully seated, or a memory module that the system doesn't support will most commonly cause a blank screen. Confirm that all expansion cards and memory modules are seated in their sockets and verify that the memory installed is compatible with the system by checking its part numbers. Putting nonparity RAM in a PC that has error-checking code (ECC) memory, or SDRAM in a PC that supports only EDO (Extended Data Output) memory will cause the screen to be blank at boot up, as the boot sequence cannot complete.

✔ **The PC boots up but the memory count is wrong:** The POST does a memory count that is displayed on the monitor. If the number displayed is not correct (it will always be less than it should be if it is wrong), the PC didn't recognize all of the installed memory. This could be caused by a wrong memory type being installed, such as dual-bank memory added to single-bank memory, in which case the POST will see only half of the memory added. Also certain systems will only accept specific memory modules or the system cannot see more than a certain amount of RAM.

✔ **The PC displays a memory error message**, such as:

- `Memory mismatch error`

- `Memory parity interrupt at nnnnn`

- `Memory address error at nnnnn`

- `Memory failure at nnnnn, read nnnnn, expecting nnnnn`

- `Memory verify error at nnnnn`

Where *nnnnn* is the physical address of the fault memory.

These errors typically point out problems between old memory and new memory or a failing memory module. If removing a newly installed memory module eliminates the error, replace the old memory with the new memory. If the error shows up again, the new memory is either defective or not compatible with the system. However, these error messages can show up when there is a motherboard problem as well.

✔ **Other memory problems:** The dreaded nemesis of any PC repairperson is the intermittent memory problem, which shows up sporadically as an error message, system crash, or a spontaneous reboot. There are literally hundreds of possible causes, including ESD (Electrostatic Discharge), overheating, corrosion, or a faulty power supply.

✔ **Software-related memory problems:** The problems under this category include registry errors, general-protection and page faults, and exception errors. Registry errors happen when the Windows operating system writes parts of the registry to a defective portion of RAM. Software bugs cause faults and exception errors. For example, an application may release its memory when completed or tries to occupy the same memory address as another. Rebooting the PC usually solves these problems.

Troubleshooting modems

Once it is installed and configured properly, a modem rarely causes problems. Software device drivers, changed connection settings, or another device causing resource conflicts are the causes of most modem problems. Upgrading or replacing the device driver can usually fix software problems. If another device causes a resource conflict, and most likely it will be contention for a particular COM port, change to a different COM port using the Modems icon on the Windows Control Panel.

However, if the problem is apparently on the modem, there are two levels of problems: a bad modem card or external unit, or the modem needs to be reset using the AT commands set. To reset the modem to its default values using the AT commands set use the command ATZ.

Troubleshooting the video system

The two elements you must deal with when troubleshooting the video of a PC are the monitor and the video card. The video card is perhaps the most complicated of the two, but you can see any problems it causes with your own eyes. However, unless part of the picture is missing, like with a failing television set, the video card rarely causes video problems on a PC.

Clearing up video problems

The most common problems with a video card are refresh rates, and resolution and color depth settings. Fortunately, these problems can be fixed through Windows using the Display Properties settings.

If the displayed image is scrambled or distorted or has multiple layers of the same image, the monitor is unable to handle the output of the video card. Other symptoms of this mismatch are a blank screen or an irritating high-pitched tone coming from the monitor.

Until such time that the monitor can be replaced with a better quality monitor, these problems can be handled by changing the settings for the display and video card. Using the Display Properties window, which is accessed by right-clicking the Windows Desktop in an open space, the color depth and the resolution can be set to lower levels.

If the screen is blank or dark and you've already checked to see if it is plugged into a power source and the power cord is connected to the monitor, check the cables connecting the monitor to the PC. Many newer monitors use a double-ended VGA cable that has a HD-15 connector at the monitor end as well as the video card end. If the cables are okay, then reseat the video card.

Your monitor and video card documentation should have a recommended refresh rate for the monitor. The tools you need to change the refresh rate are accessed through the Advanced button on the Windows Display Properties window.

If after changing the refresh rate the monitor image is unreadable, reboot the PC into Windows Safe Mode and use the lower refresh rate and reboot the PC into normal mode.

Driving the device

It is common for a video device driver to cause problems of the video kind. Video cards are mass-produced and they sit on store and warehouse shelves before they are installed in PCs. Because of this, the device driver included with the device is often obsolete when it is installed. The device drivers in the Windows device library also suffer from the time factor. Always download the latest device drivers available from the manufacturer's Web site whenever you suspect a driver problem.

Troubleshooting the power supply

A weak or faulty power supply can cause a number of problems to the devices attached to it, including the motherboard and disk drives. If unexplained and intermittent memory or hard disk errors begin showing up that cannot be isolated, the problem could very well be the power supply.

A faulty power supply can make a good hard disk or motherboard appear to be bad. Extended periods of low voltage can damage the hard disk drive as much as over voltages can burn out the motherboard and memory. Troubleshoot the power supply by testing each of its power connectors for the proper voltages. Test the +12VDC and +5VDC supplies with a multimeter. Most power supplies have adjusting screws that can be used to dial in the voltages. Turning the screw clockwise increases the voltage and counter-clockwise decreases it.

Troubleshooting the sound system

If the PC's sound system is having problems, it is usually easy to hear the problem, but it can be very difficult to isolate the source of the problem. However, here are some troubleshooting steps you can take to find the problem:

✔ **Resource conflicts:** Use the Windows System Information window (shown in Figure 18-1), from the Accessories and Systems Tools menus, to determine if there are any resource conflicts (IRQ, DMA, or I/O address) between the sound card and other devices. If a conflict exists, reassign the conflicting device or the sound card. The most common conflict is an IRQ.

✔ **Speakers:** Troubleshooting the speakers is a fairly straightforward process:

- Make sure the sound card is connected to the speakers and the correct cable is plugged into the correct jack on the sound card. Match up the color-coded plugs to the jacks or look carefully at the little pictures on the jacks.

- Make sure the volume on the sound card and the speakers is turned up. The sound card's volume can be set either with an adjustment knob or dial on the sound card or by clicking on the speaker symbol in the tray on the right end of the Task bar to open the Play Control panel. Make sure that the volume on the speakers is turned up.

- Make sure that the speaker wires are not crimped or broken and that all of the jacks are seated in the appropriate plugs.

✔ **Device drivers:** Sound cards are completely dependent on their software device drivers. Verify that the latest version of the sound cards driver software is installed by checking the manufacturer's Web site.

✔ **EMF (Electromagnetic Field):** Sound cards are very susceptible to EMF emissions from other devices and cards. If placed too close to a disk drive or the power supply, the sound card may have problems. Place the sound card in an open expansion slot as far away from other components as possible.

Figure 18-1:
The
Windows
System
Information
window can
be used to
display the
hardware
configura-
tion of a PC.

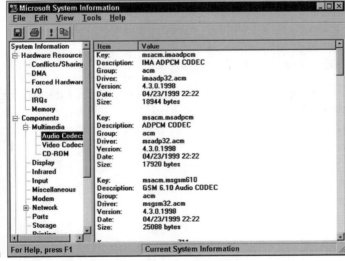

Prep Test

1 When you arrive at a customer site, what is the first thing you should do?

A ○ Go straight to the problem PC and begin work.

B ○ Ask the user about the problem and actively listen.

C ○ Ask the user about the problem and passively listen.

D ○ Explain your qualifications and experience to the user to put him or her at ease.

2 The POST uses which of the following to signal a problem with essential hardware? (Choose two)

A ❏ Beep codes sounded through the system speaker

B ❏ Error messages and codes displayed on the monitor

C ❏ An ASCII display illustrating the problem device

D ❏ Verbal messages played through the sound system

3 Before troubleshooting a hard disk drive, what is the first thing you should do?

A ○ Disconnect the power supply connector.

B ○ Shut down the PC.

C ○ Back up the hard disk.

D ○ Recreate the problem.

4 A PC's clock is consistently losing time and recently the PC has failed to boot on occasion. What is likely the problem?

A ○ The time setting in the CMOS needs correcting.

B ○ The time should be adjusted on the Windows Desktop.

C ○ The BIOS needs to be updated.

D ○ The CMOS battery needs to be replaced.

5 A POST error message with an error code in the 600 series indicates a problem with which FRM?

A ○ Hard disk drive

B ○ CPU

C ○ Floppy disk drive

D ○ Motherboard

E ○ Keyboard

6 Which of the following ensure that a PC's cooling system is able to work at its best? (Choose two)

A ❑ All case parts are attached and secured.

B ❑ An oversize fan has been installed.

C ❑ All empty expansion slots have slot covers in place.

D ❑ Extra venting holes have been added to the sides of the case.

7 Which of the following could be the problem if a PC will not boot from a floppy disk drive? (Choose three)

A ❑ The floppy disk drive may not be first in the CMOS boot device settings.

B ❑ The diskette in the floppy disk drive may not be boot disk.

C ❑ The floppy disk drive does not have power.

D ❑ The system has a CD-ROM drive installed.

8 How is an IDE/ATA hard disk drive designated as either a master or a slave?

A ○ DIP switch on the drive

B ○ Where it is connected to the drive data cable

C ○ By the drive's installation software

D ○ Jumpers on the drive

9 What is the highest numerical value a three-pole jumper can represent?

A ○ 8

B ○ 7

C ○ 6

D ○ 4

10 A customer has purchased new memory with a part number that ends with –70. He wants you to install it in his Celeron PC100 system. What should you do?

A ○ Proceed with the installation, putting the new memory in a different memory bank.

B ○ Explain to the user that this is the wrong memory and he should return it.

C ○ Remove all existing RAM and install the new memory.

D ○ Proceed with the installation, changing the PC's CMOS settings.

Answers

1 **B.** One of the best sources of information about a problem is the person having the problem. Actively listen to the user to gain all of the information you need, but avoid chitchat if you can. *Check out "Arriving on the scene."*

2 **A, B.** When the video system is not available, the POST uses the system speaker. After the video's BIOS is loaded, error messages can be displayed. *See "Dealing with BIOS errors."*

3 **C.** It is an excellent practice to completely back up a hard disk before troubleshooting it. You just never know what might happen. *Look over "Backing up before you move forward."*

4 **D.** Another clue is that the CMOS begins losing its contents and gives intermittent device not found errors. *Review "Deciphering BIOS error messages."*

5 **C.** Don't worry about memorizing all of the BIOS error code numbers and what they represent. But, you should know the first five or six series just to be safe. *Take a look at "Numbering the error messages."*

6 **A, C.** Trust the engineering of the case and keep all of its parts in place and close up all empty expansion slots with slot covers. *See "Cooling problems and the CPU."*

7 **A, B, C.** Perhaps if a tape drive is installed, you may want to also check out the system resource assignments for conflicts, which is not a bad idea anyway. *Review "Booting from the A: drive."*

8 **D.** The jumper positions are usually marked as "MS," "SL," or the like. Check out *"Troubleshooting IDE hard disk drives."*

9 **B.** Think of the poles of the jumper as bits. A seven is the highest value that can be represented by three bits in binary. *Take a look at "Troubleshooting SCSI hard disk drives."*

10 **B.** Expect to see a question very much like this one on the exam using different memory part numbers and processors. You should know what the part number represents and to which processors or motherboard standards each is compatible. *Study "Identifying memory problems."*

Part V
The Softer Side of Systems

"You know, this was a situation question on my A+ Certification exam, but I always thought it was just hypothetical."

In this part . . .

Okay, calm down! Yes, there does seem to be more material in this book about the Core Hardware exam than for the OS Technologies exam. However, that is actually an optical illusion. There is some overlap between the two exams and a significant amount of what you need to know for the OS Technologies exam is embedded in the chapters seemingly dedicated to the Core Hardware exam.

The A+ exam expects you to be conversant with DOS, Windows 3.*x*, Windows 9*x*, Windows 2000, and just a wee bit of Windows NT. You must know how they are installed, configured, and manipulated to perform well on the test.

Also included in this part of the book is a chapter that covers Networks and networking for both exams. Of particular interest should be how to configure, install, and enable network interface cards (NICs) and how to connect, navigate, and use the Internet and World Wide Web.

Chapter 19

Operating System Basics

● ●

Exam objectives

▶ Identifying the popular operating systems

▶ Detailing the functions of operating systems

▶ Defining the major system files

▶ Listing commonly used DOS commands

● ●

*T*he A+ Operating Systems (OS) Technologies exam has greatly expanded on the DOS/Windows content of the previous (1998) version of the exam. The new exam expects you to know what amounts to a history of the Windows operating systems. Oh, there is some mention of the UNIX and Linux operating systems and Novell in the networking domain, but make no mistake — this is a Windows exam! So, in covering the basics of an operating system, it makes sense to me that I should give you the basic knowledge of Windows you need and point out what it is about Windows you need to study.

The A+ exams assume you to have at least 6 months of on-the-job experience as a professional PC repairperson. If you have been working as PC repairperson for at least 6 months, you know how much of the job is installing, configuring, and troubleshooting the Windows operating system. Without that hands-on experience, the A+ OS Technologies exam may be a bit of a struggle. Some questions on the test that assume you can recognize a situation from your experience. For example, a question may start out "The Video Adapter Properties window is displayed on the screen, what is your next action to change. . . ." Only because you've used this particular window many times on the job are you be able to recognize the situation and intelligently answer the question. Or at least that's what the test assumes.

To prepare yourself completely for the A+ OS technologies exam, I highly recommend that you get as much hands-on experience as you can with the Windows operating system. Concentrate on the processes of installing, configuring, and debugging it on a PC, networked and standalone. Also take time to learn the commands entered at the command line prompt in Windows 9*x* and Windows 2000 Professional and Me.

Quick Assessment

Identifying the popular operating systems

1 _____ is the most popularly used operating system.

2 The non-Windows operating systems that are also commonly used are _____, _____, and _____.

Detailing the functions of operating systems

3 Windows operating systems are distinctive for using a(n) _____ user interface.

4 Support for FAT32 file system was introduced in _____.

Defining the major system files

5 The three core components of Windows 9x are _____, _____, _____.

6 Before installing Windows 2000, the compatibility of the hardware should be verified on the _____.

7 _____ means the operating system supports more than one program or application at a time.

8 In Windows 9x systems, the _____ file now handles most of the commands previously performed by CONFIG.SYS and AUTOEXEC.BAT.

Listing commonly used DOS commands

9 The DOS command prompt that is displayed on the C: drive root directory is _____.

10 The command used to change the file attributes of a file is _____.

Answers

1 *Windows.* See "Meeting the Operating System."

2 *UNIX, Linux, and OS/2.* Check out "Getting down to specifics."

3 *Graphical.* Review "Interfacing with the Windows GUI."

4 *Windows 95 OSR2 or Windows 95b.* See "Differentiating Windows 95 and Windows 98."

5 *Kernel32.dll, User32.dll, GDI32.dll.* Take a look at "Getting to know Windows 98."

6 *HCL (hardware compatibility list).* Review "Getting to know Windows 2000."

7 *Multitasking.* Study "Multitasking, multiprocessing, and multithreaded."

8 *IO.SYS.* Look over "Windows 95/98 system files."

9 *C:\>.* See "Interfacing with the DOS and Windows command prompt."

10 *ATTRIB.* Review "Changing file attributes."

Meeting the Operating System

Most of the time the operating system is taken for granted — that is until there's a problem. It is at that moment that the user realizes how very little he or she knows about it and how very complicated it can be. To most users, the PC is one altogether thing and when there is a problem, the PC is down. It is rarely that the operating system has created a page fault or a memory exception, it is that "The dumb computer has locked up again and that they are tired of this happening all the time," which means this problem has happened before but was never reported.

In its most basic form, the operating system provides an interface to the hardware and system software that makes the system and its resources available to the user in a useful way. By far, the most popular operating system in the world is the Microsoft Windows operating system, in all of its various versions. For this reason, the A+ Operating Systems (OS) Technologies exam focuses on the Windows operating system. Windows is the operating system you are most likely to encounter on the job. However, Windows is not the only operating system mentioned on the test. So, I must expand your horizons a bit.

Getting down to specifics

The operating systems you should know for the A+ Operating System (OS) Technologies exam are:

- ✔ **DOS (Disk Operating System):** No reference is made to a particular type of DOS. I assume the DOS to be MS-DOS, but it really doesn't matter. What you need to know are the DOS commands that are used to prepare a system to take an operating system or in troubleshooting errors on the system.

- ✔ **Novell NetWare:** This network operating system (NOS) is exclusively related to the networking domain of the exam. You need to know the protocols it uses to connect a Windows client to a NetWare server, its file system, and how user and file permissions are managed.

- ✔ **Windows 3.***x:* This version of Windows is mentioned once or twice, and you need to know how it relates to DOS and to Windows 95.

- ✔ **Windows 95:** There are questions on the exam about Windows 95's registry and installation. Among other specifics, you need to know about the OSR2 (OEM) release and what features it added.

- ✔ **Windows 98:** The bulk of the questions on the Windows operating system are about this version. In addition to other topics, you need to know the features of the SE update and just about everything else involved with installing, configuring, and troubleshooting this Windows version.

✔ **Windows CE:** Windows CE (which allegedly stands for "consumer elec-tronics") is the version implemented on palmtop and other handheld PC and computing devices. It is mentioned in a couple of questions, and all you really need to know for the test is that it is never the right answer.

✔ **Windows Me (Millennium edition):** You really don't need to know very much about Windows Me, which is the home-users edition of Windows, beyond what I've just told you.

✔ **Windows NT 4.0 Server:** For some reason, Windows NT Workstation gets little or no mention on the exam, but you will see Windows NT Server mentioned. Remember that this is not the Server+ or MCSE exams so don't sweat NT.

✔ **Windows 2000 Professional:** Referred to as Windows 2K Pro, you need to know how this version differs from Windows 98 and the other versions of Windows 2000. In the portion of the exam that deals with desktop and client PC issues, assume this is the Windows 2000 version in the question.

✔ **Windows 2000 Server:** This is the big daddy of the Windows 2000 family of operating systems. In the 15 percent of the exam dealing with networking, you should assume it is the version in the question, unless otherwise indicated.

Speaking operating system

A number of terms were used in the preceding sections that should be defined before you run into them on the test and are still not sure what they mean.

Protected versus real mode

Protected mode operations limit an application to its own memory space, but that space can include memory above the 1MB barrier of real mode. Protected mode gets its name from the fact that programs in this mode are protected from other programs desiring its memory. Real mode restricts applications to addressing only the first 1MB of RAM.

All Windows versions after 3.x run in protected mode, which can lead to some problems. For example, when a Windows system is booted into DOS mode, DOS can't load any protected-mode device drivers. In order to use these devices in real mode, real-mode drivers must be loaded. The devices affected may include the CD-ROM, the sound card, and other devices not widely implemented before Windows 95. An additional problem is that load-ing these drivers to real mode could fill up memory very quickly.

Multitasking, multiprocessing, and multithreaded

Multitasking means the operating system supports more than one program at a time. Windows 3.x supports what is called *cooperative multitasking*, which means that the programs running on the PC are expected to give way when another program requests use of a resource. If a program hogs a certain resource, there is no way of policing it. The other programs have to wait until the program releases the resource needed. Windows 95 and 98 support *preemptive multitasking,* which gives the operating system the authority to suspend a program that is monopolizing a needed resource.

Multiprocessing means that a computer has more than one processor. This is not anything you need to worry about for the OS Technologies exam, but the term does come up on the Core Hardware exam.

Multithreading means that a single program has the ability to create (*spawn* is the technical term) several activities under its control that all run concurrently. The example usually given for this is a word processor that can run a repagination process while it is also running a spell checker and a grammar checker.

Symmetrical multiprocessing

Symmetrical Multiprocessing (SMP) is the capability that enables an operating system to utilize more than one microprocessor on a single computer. SMP divides the work and assigns tasks to each of the different processors, which results in each processor getting better utilization. Windows NT Workstation supports two processors on the same PC, and Windows NT Server supports four to eight processors.

The opposite of SMP is *Asymmetrical Multiprocessing (ASMP),* which assigns a particular program or portion of a program to a particular processor that runs the program to its end.

Interacting with the operating system

As a PC repairperson, your interaction with the operating system, regardless of which one it is, is through its command line prompt. There really are only two very distinctive command line formats used in the operating systems on the exam — the DOS/Windows command line prompt and the shell prompt of the UNIX and Linux operating systems.

Interfacing with the DOS and Windows command prompt

In my opinion, the DOS command line should be easily recognized, but I have finally come to grips with the fact that most PC users have never used anything other than the Windows operating system. In computer years, the fact that I at one time worked directly with the DOS operating system makes me the equivalent of Methuselah.

For the OS Technologies exam, you really should know the command line prompt of DOS by sight:

```
C:\WINDOWS>_
```

This same command prompt is used for all versions of the Windows operating system and is very close to that use for Novell NetWare (although you really don't need to know it).

In this prompt, the C: indicates the active disk drive and the \WINDOWS indicates the active directory (folder). If the active directory is a subdirectory of another directory, the command prompt shows the entire directory pathname of the active directory, for example: C:\WINDOWS\COMMAND, is the command prompt displayed when the COMMAND subdirectory of the WINDOWS directory is the active directory.

This prompt can be totally customized to include a variety of information, but the format shown is the default format in DOS and all versions of Windows. The prompt command is used to customize the command line prompt in DOS and Windows.

Interfacing with the Windows GUI

If Figure 19-1 is not something you've ever seen before, you have either been living in a cave for around ten years or need to trade-in your PC XT for a newer computer. The Windows interface is a graphical user interface (GUI) and the user interfaces through a mouse (or another type of pointing device) and the keyboard.

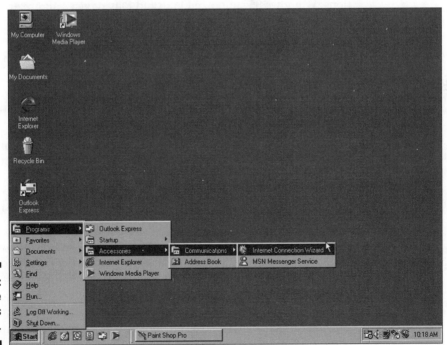

Figure 19-1:
The
Windows
GUI.

Getting to Know the Operating Systems

It may not be easy for you to track down a version of each of the operating systems you need to know for the exam (see "Getting down to specifics" earlier in the chapter). So, the following sections give you a brief overview of the features of each OS.

For the OS Technologies exam, you must have an understanding of the foundation components of the various versions of the Windows operating systems, including their interfaces, 16-bit and 32-bit support, and all the virtual stuff that's really there.

Getting to know Windows 95

In addition to an updated and improved user interface, Windows 95 brought 32-bit capabilities to PCs with Intel processors. The differences to the earlier Windows 3.*x* are the following:

- ✔ **Backward compatibility:** Windows 95 supported legacy devices requiring system file (AUTOEXEC.BAT and CONFIG.SYS) support to load device drivers. It also supported most 16-bit DOS and Windows 3.*x* applications. Windows 95 supported Plug and Play devices and referred to all non-Plug and Play cards as *legacy* cards.

- ✔ **Setup and configuration:** Windows 95 could be installed from a network server or from a CD-ROM and included auto-detection of hardware and Plug and Play support during setup.

- ✔ **Improved user interface:** Windows 95 added the Start button, taskbar, and properties sheet (along with a use for the right mouse button) and eliminated the program groups from the desktop.

- ✔ **Protected mode:** Windows 95 allowed applications to run in protected mode where DOS and Windows 3.*x* restricted applications to real mode.

- ✔ **32-bit application support:** Windows 95 runs 32-bit applications with private memory space, preemptive multitasking, and multithreaded execution. Windows 95 also supports the 16-bit code of the DOS/Windows 3.*x* environment.

- ✔ **Peer-to-peer networking:** Although first introduced in Windows for Workgroups, Windows 95 (and later Windows 98) improved its capabilities, operation, and setup. Windows 95 also added peer services for Novell networks.

- ✔ **Virtual machine:** Windows 95 implemented the concept of the *virtual machine,* which allowed it to run applications from other operating systems (primarily DOS and Windows 3.*x*) in a nearly native environment.

Getting to know Windows 98

Perhaps the best way to review an operating system for the OS Technologies exam is practice navigating around the various Properties functions of Windows 98, including those accessed by right-clicking the desktop and the My Computer icon. You should also review the functions on the Settings menu and the System, Printers, Modems, and Network icons of the Control Panel. The exam has questions about how to access each of these functions and the kinds of actions available on each.

Windows 98 (and Windows 95) supports both 16-bit and 32-bit applications through the Windows Application Programming Interface (API). The API provides application developers with a library of utilities that perform a variety of tasks in the Windows environment. The primary components of the API are the following:

- **Kernel** (KERNEL32.DLL) contains the essential operating system functions, including memory, file, and I/O management, and application support.

- **User** (USER32.DLL) controls the user interface including the mouse, keyboard, I/O ports, and the desktop layout.

- **GDI** (GDI32.DLL) manages graphics and controls printing.

When an application creates a window, the window resource is stored in the USER.DLL resource table; when an application loads a picture or graphic, it is stored in the GDI.DLL resource table; and when an application opens a disk file, the file's information is stored in the KERNEL.DLL resource table. If an application does all three, the resources required to support the application in memory is tripled. This arrangement creates USER, GDI, and system KERNEL resources instead of general system resources.

The Windows Resource Meter (see Figure 19-2), a utility that is available on Windows 9*x,* monitors the utilization of Windows' resources by all the applications, applets, and utilities running on the system.

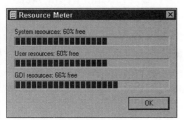

Meeting Windows 98 Second Edition (SE)

In the confusion surrounding just what Windows 2000 was replacing or enhancing, Windows 98 Second Edition (SE) was released. Operationally, it is not different from Windows 98, but it did fix many bugs of the first edition, improved some device support, and added a few new features, including Internet Connection Sharing.

Internet Connection Sharing (ICS) allows home, home-office, and small office users to share a single Internet connection, such as a dialup proxy server, a DSL (Digital Subscriber Line) connection, a UNII (unlicensed national information infrastructure) wireless line, or perhaps a frame relay connection over a peer-to-peer or local area network. ICS assumes a network to be present and isn't fussy about the type of network or the media used. More on ICS in Chapter 22.

Differentiating Windows 95 and Windows 98

Windows 95 and Windows 98 are actually pretty much the same. They share the same architecture and function the same in every major area. Windows 98 is often described as Windows 95 OSR2 with Internet Explorer, a few new device drivers, and some housekeeping utilities added.

Windows 98 did add some features and functions that do differentiate the two operating systems including the following:

- ✔ **Active Desktop and Internet Explorer:** Windows 98 allows the desktop and folders to be viewed as a Web page and includes Internet Explorer.
- ✔ **Fixes, patches, and additions:** Windows 98 incorporated all the user service packs and OEM updates (OSRs) that had been released for Windows 95. Most prominent among these were the following:

  - **System Configuration utility:** Used to modify the startup files (AUTOEXEC.BAT, CONFIG.SYS), the Registry, and so on.
  - **FAT32 Converter:** Converts an existing FAT16 disk format to the more efficient FAT32 format. However, this action cannot be reversed.
  - **Task Scheduler:** Typically, used to set up regular runs for maintenance tasks, but can be used to run any program at a set time or date.
  - **Dr. Watson:** This utility is used to aid troubleshooting of application program crashes.
  - **Registry checker:** Automatically repairs, compresses, and backs up the Registry files.

✔ **New device support:** Windows 98 included support for several new
devices, including:

  • USB and IEEE 1394 (FireWire) devices

  • OnNow and ACPI (Advanced Configuration and Power Interface),
    which allow the PC to be put to sleep instead of powered down.

  • DVD (Digital Versatile Disc) drives and TV tuners

  • Multiple monitors

Comparing Windows 9x features

Many of the features in Table 19-1 indicated as not available on one or both of
the Windows 95 versions could be added through downloads and application
software. For example, Windows 95 did not include device drivers for a DVD,
and the drivers had to be downloaded from the manufacturer; also, Active
Desktop had to be implemented through Internet Explorer 4.0. The information in Table 19-1 shows the native features of each Windows 9x release for
comparison purposes. You will see questions on the test that require you to
know which versions had which features.

Table 19-1	Features of Windows 9x Versions			
Feature	*98 SE*	*98*	*95 OSR2 (95b/OEM)*	*95a (Retail)*
ACPI support	Y	Y	N	N
Active Desktop	Y	Y	N	N
Backup Utility	Y	Y	N	N
Dial-Up Networking	Y	Y	Y	Y
Disk management	Y	Y	N	N
DVD support	Y	N	N	N
FAT32	Y	Y	Y	N
FAT32 Conversion	Y	Y	N	N
Internet Connection Sharing	Y	N	N	N
Multiple monitors	Y	Y	N	N
OnNow support	Y	Y	N	N
Task Scheduler	Y	Y	N	N
USB support	Y	Y	Y	N
Windows Update Utility	Y	Y	N	N

In late 1996, Microsoft released a Windows 95 update to PC manufacturers and resellers known as OEM (Original Equipment Manufacturer) Service Release 2 (OSR2). This release, which also became known as Windows 95b, included a number of bug fixes along with new support for enhanced power management, FAT32, IDE bus mastering, 32-bit Card Bus, and Desktop Management Interface (DMI).

The last release of Windows 95 (Windows 95c) was an OEM release in 1997 that fixed bugs, installed Internet Explorer 4.0, and introduced some of the user interface enhancements that were to be part of Windows 98.

For the exam, you should know that FAT32 support was released in Windows 95b, also known as OSR2.

A quick look at Windows NT

Because the A+ exam blueprints do not specify a particular version and because an A+ certified repairperson works on client issues more often than not, I'm assuming that when the blueprint mentions Windows NT it means Windows NT Workstation. At their cores, both Windows NT Server and Windows NT Workstation have the same functionality, so there isn't too much risk in my assumption. Besides, there really isn't that much about Windows NT on the exam, anyway.

Windows NT is a multithreaded, multitasking operating system that runs its applications in protected mode memory space. This means that an unruly application cannot crash the entire system and a problem with one application can't cause problems in other applications.

Windows NT requires a logon, which then assigns security and control permissions through the user's profile. Windows NT is designed for use in a networked environment and includes support for Internet protocols such as TCP/IP, IPX, and dialup networking. It also works very well in a standalone mode.

Windows NT can run on a wide variety of hardware, because it isolates any unique programming needed to support a specific piece of hardware in what is called the *Hardware Abstraction Layer (HAL)*. Windows NT has releases compatible with the Intel x86 architecture, the MIPS RISC architecture, Digital Alpha, and Motorola PowerPC RISC. In comparison, Windows 2000 only runs on the x86 and Digital Alpha platforms, so far.

One area where Windows NT (and Windows 2000) does outperform Windows 9*x* is security. The logon sequence begins with the Ctrl+Alt+Del keys, which as you know are typically used to warm start the PC. This prevents a program from spoofing the logon to steal your account name and password. By the way, after you've logged in, the Ctrl+Alt+Del keys display the Windows NT Security dialog box.

Windows NT supports *RAID (Redundant Array of Inexpensive Disks)* on SCSI drives. RAID is a high-availability, high-reliability, and data redundancy feature usually reserved for servers. See Chapter 9 for more information on RAID systems.

Table 19-2 compares the technical features of Windows NT and Windows 9*x*. Don't bother memorizing any of the hardware requirements (RAM, hard disk, and CPU), but do take a hard look at the networking support and the file systems.

Table 19-2	Technical Comparison of Windows 9*x* and Windows NT		
Feature	*Win 95 (OSR2)*	*Win 98*	*Win NT 4.0*
Min. RAM	16MB	16MB	32MB
Min. hard disk	50MB	80MB	100MB
Min. CPU	486-25	486-66	Pentium 100
Networking	NetBIOS	NetBIOS	NetBIOS
	IPX	IPX	IPX
	TCP/IP	TCP/IP	TCP/IP
	DHCP	DHCP	DHCP
	Dialup Network	Dialup Network	Dialup Network
File systems	FAT16	FAT32	FAT16
NTFS			

Don't forget about Windows Me

Windows Me is a home-user alternative to Windows 2000. It is not the merger of Windows 98 and Windows 2000 as rumored. This version of Windows is actually an updated version of Windows 98 and is referred to as Windows 98 Third Edition by some. Windows Me is intended to serve as an interim solution for home and small-office users until a personal edition of Windows 2000 (now code-named "Whistler") is available.

Getting to know Windows 2000

Windows 2000 is the next version of Windows NT, and was known for a short while as Windows NT 5.0. There are four distinctive versions of Windows 2000, but only Windows 2000 Professional (the name Professional replaces the name Workstation for business desktop systems) and Windows 2000 Server are mentioned on the A+ OS Technologies exam. The other versions, just to satisfy your curiosity, are: Windows 2000 Advanced Server and Windows 2000 Data Center Server.

You can upgrade to Windows 2000 from Windows 98, and its setup program includes a process to guide you. Windows 2000 has a very Windows 98-like interface and will read and support FAT32 files — something Windows NT 4.0 wouldn't do.

Microsoft lists the minimum system requirements for Windows 2000 Professional to be a Pentium 133 or better with 64MB RAM. Windows 2000 Server requires at least a Pentium 133 or better with 256MB RAM. However, before installing Windows 2000 on any system, check the Windows 2000 hardware compatibility list (HCL) for all the FRMs installed.

Check Windows 2000's hardware and software compatibility lists to see if your hardware and software are listed, and then convert your operating system to Windows 2000. Take a few minutes to orient yourself to the HCL by visiting Microsoft's Hardware and Software Compatibility Web site at www.microsoft.com/windows2000/upgrade/compat/.

If you find that your hardware is not supported, check with the manufacturer for information on when a Windows 2000 driver will be available. Until then you must wait.

Displaying the Windows version number

To display the version number of the Windows 9x installed on a PC, right click My Computer, click Properties, and select the General tab (see Figure 19-3). From the command prompt, the version of the operating system is displayed from the DOS command VER.

As shown in Figure 19-3, the version number has three parts. Actually, the first two are considered the version number, such as 4.10, and the third part of the number is the *build number,* or the current release of a particular version. Build numbers are used more extensively in beta versions and reflect the evolution of the trial system. When the system is released, the build number usually becomes arbitrary.

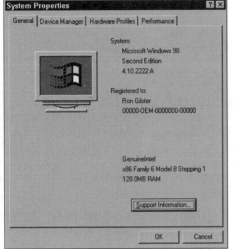

Figure 19-3:
The General
tab on the
System
Properties
window
includes the
Windows
version
number.

The version numbers that have been released are:

- **Windows 95**: 4.00.950, 4.00.950A, 4.00.950B, and 4.00.950C
- **Windows 98:** 4.10.1998 and 4.10.2222 (Windows 98 SE)
- **Windows 2000 Professional:** 5.00.2195

To display the version (and the latest service pack installed) on a Windows 2000 system, click the Start button, click Run, type **winver** in the Run box, and press Enter. A display box appears with version and service pack information. This same method can be used on a Windows 98 system, but all that it displays is that it is a Windows 98 system.

Tracking Down the System Files

One of the major emphasis areas of the OS Technologies exam is the system files of the various operating system versions. This includes knowing what they are, how they are used, where they are located, and what's inside each one. Although the system files you need to know are for the most part the same for most versions of Windows, some files are unique to a particular version or release. Make sure you know which files are supported by which versions of Windows, including the following:

- AUTOEXEC.BAT
- BOOT.INI and .INI files in general
- CONFIG.SYS

  ✔ IO.SYS

  ✔ MSCDEX.EXE

  ✔ MSDOS.SYS

Windows 95/98 system files

On the OS Technologies exam, you are expected to know the role of each of the system files in the boot process and in establishing the operating environment for the hardware and operating system. I'm starting with the Windows 9*x* files because the DOS and Windows 3.*x* files that are on the test are still in use in Windows 9*x*.

Here are the files you should know and what you should know about them:

  ✔ **AUTOEXEC.BAT:** This file is used to load real-mode drivers when a protected-mode driver isn't available. For example, on a Windows 3.*x* system or on a Windows 9*x* system with an incompatible CD-ROM device, the MSCDEX (Microsoft CD extensions) file is loaded from this file. The drivers listed in the AUTOEXEC.BAT file are loaded before the 32-bit portion of the operating system is loaded. On most Windows 9*x* systems, the AUTOEXEC.BAT is mostly empty with its functions covered by the IO.SYS file. See "AUTOEXEC.BAT commands included in IO.SYS" later in this section.

  ✔ **BOOTLOG.TXT:** A logged record of the Windows 9*x* boot sequence that is created when a logged boot is requested.

  ✔ **COMMAND.COM:** The Windows 9*x* command-line processor. A boot to just the command line prompt would end with this file.

  ✔ **CONFIG.SYS:** Like its companion the AUTOEXEC.BAT file, this file is only used on Windows 9*x* systems, to load real-mode device driver. Most of what the CONFIG.SYS file did for DOS and Windows 3.*x* is now performed in the IO.SYS file, see "CONFIG.SYS commands included in IO.SYS" later in this section. However, if EMM386.EXE is loaded, it is still done from the CONFIG.SYS file. The statements used are shown in Figure 19-4.

Figure 19-4:
The contents of a CONFIG.SYS file on a Windows 9*x* system.

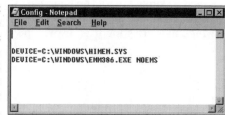

```
Config - Notepad
File  Edit  Search  Help

DEVICE=C:\WINDOWS\HIMEM.SYS
DEVICE=C:\WINDOWS\EMM386.EXE NOEMS
```

✔ **DETLOG.TXT:** This log file tracks the automatic hardware-detection processes in Windows 9*x*. Each time a new piece of hardware is detected, an entry is made to this file. If the system crashes during the hardware-detection process, Windows uses this file to determine the source of the problem.

✔ **IO.SYS:** This file is the Windows 9*x* equivalent of the DOS IO.SYS, MSDOS.SYS, CONFIG.SYS, and AUTOEXEC.BAT files all rolled into one. See "CONFIG.SYS commands included in IO.SYS" and "AUTOEXEC.BAT commands included in IO.SYS" later in this section, which summarize the commands included in the IO.SYS.

✔ **LOGO.SYS:** This is actually the 320 x 400 bit-mapped wallpaper that is displayed during the boot sequence. If you wish to replace it with something of your own, create a 320 x 200 bit-mapped (8-bit) file in MS Paint or another drawing package and save it as LOGO.SYS in the C: drive's root directory. Be sure to back up the original LOGO.SYS first, just in case.

✔ **MSDOS.SYS:** Unlike its DOS binary file predecessor, the Windows 9*x* file is a text file that contains the locations ([Paths]) of other Windows files (such as the Registry) and any modifications ([Options]) made to the boot process. Figure 19-5 shows a sample MSDOS.SYS file that includes a boot option for multiple operating systems.

✔ **SCANDISK.LOG:** A log file that records the results of the most recent ScanDisk operation that is overwritten each time this disk utility runs.

✔ **SETUPLOG.TXT:** A log file record that is created and updated during the installation process of Windows 9*x* by the Setup program. Should Setup crash, Windows uses this file to help identify the problem.

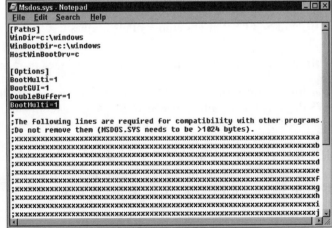

Figure 19-5:
The contents of a sample MSDOS.SYS file.

CONFIG.SYS commands included in IO.SYS

Many of the commands that were included in the CONFIG.SYS file on DOS and Windows 3.*x* systems are included in the IO.SYS file on Windows 9*x* systems. The IO.SYS file is not used on Windows NT or Windows 2000 systems; see "Windows 2000 system files" later in this section.

Here is a list of the commands that the IO.SYS file loads on Windows 9*x* systems:

- ✓ **DOS=HIGH:** Indicates that DOS (kernel) should be loaded into the high memory area. A UMB parameter is included if EMM386.EXE is loaded from the CONFIG.SYS file. IO.SYS won't load EMM386.EXE.

- ✓ **DEVICE=HIMEM.SYS:** Enables real-mode memory managers, specifically EMM386.EXE. HIMEM.SYS must be loaded before Windows 9*x* can start up.

- ✓ **DEVICE=IFSHLP.SYS**: Enables file and print sharing and 32-bit disk access.

- ✓ **DEVICE=SETVER.EXE:** This command allows the operating system to appear to be whatever operating system version a legacy application requires, which is most typically a DOS version.

- ✓ **FCBS=4:** Sets the number of file control blocks (FCBs) that the system can have open at one time.

- ✓ **SHELL=COMMAND.COM /P:** Sets the permanent (/P) command interpreter for the system. Permanent means that the command interpreter should not be unloaded from memory.

- ✓ **DOS Compatibility commands:** Some commands used only by DOS and Windows 3*x* systems are also included:

  - • **FILES=60:** This command sets the number of DOS file handles.

  - • **LASTDRIVE=Z:** Sets the highest drive letter that can be assigned to a device or a network drive.

  - • **BUFFERS=30:** Sets the number of file buffers the system should create.

  - • **STACKS=9,256:** Sets the number and size of stack frames.

To override any setting in the IO.SYS file, enter the command into the CONFIG.SYS file. It is loaded after the IO.SYS file, and any commands and parameters will supersede those loaded from the IO.SYS file.

AUTOEXEC.BAT commands included in IO.SYS

The IO.SYS file also loads many of the commands loaded from the AUTOEXEC.BAT file on earlier versions of Windows, including:

- ✓ **TMP=C:\WINDOWS\TEMP:** This command assigns the folder for temporary files.

- ✓ **PROMPT=PG:** This command establishes the format of the command prompt to C:\>.

- ✔ **PATH=C:\WINDOWS; C:\WINDOWS\COMMAND:** This command and its two parameters adds the two pathnames to the DOS search path.

- ✔ **COMSPEC=C:\WINDOWS\COMMAND\COMMAND.COM:** This command specifies the location of the command interpreter file.

Entries in an AUTOEXEC.BAT file in the root directory of the boot disk override or add to those in the IO.SYS file.

Windows 2000 system files

Windows 2000, in all of its versions, uses a completely different set of system files than the previous versions of Windows. The Windows 2000 system files are located in the root folder of the system partition, which must be on the first physical disk of the system. The Windows 2000 system files included on the OS Technologies exam are all boot files. Here are the Windows 2000 system files you need to know:

- ✔ **NTLDR:** The bootstrap loader program.

- ✔ **BOOT.INI:** Contains information on multiple operating systems that a system could boot.

- ✔ **BOOTSECT.DOS:** Contains information on operating systems other than Windows 2000.

- ✔ **NTDETECT.COM:** Collects data on the current hardware configuration for use in building the Registry key HKEY_LOCAL_MACHINE\HARDWARE.

- ✔ **NTOSKRNL.EXE:** Loads the Windows 2000 kernel.

- ✔ **HAL.DLL:** Hardware Abstraction Layer (HAL) data libraries.

Starting Up the Operating Systems

The processes used to start up a PC running the Windows operating system are basically the same through the completion of the BIOS POST operation. At that point, which is when the operating system will be started, Windows 9x and Windows 2000 systems use completely different methods to start up.

Booting to the command prompt

Starting the system to only a command prompt requires a boot disk (typically a floppy disk in the A: drive) that contains at a minimum the DOS system files. To create a boot disk on a diskette, you can either use the File➪Format disk option of the Windows Explorer, or type the following DOS FORMAT command entry at a command prompt:

```
C:\>FORMAT A: /S
```

Another way to add the system files to any formatted diskette or hard disk partition is through the SYS command. Its format is:

```
C:\>SYS A:
```

If you wish to create a boot disk that includes other commands and perhaps CD-ROM support, you may need to follow the SYS command with the following entries:

```
C:\>COPY AUTOEXEC.BAT A:\
C:\>COPY CONFIG.SYS A:\
C:\>COPY \WINDOWS\HIMEM.SYS A:\
C:\>COPY \WINDOWS\COMMAND\FDISK.EXE A:
C:\>COPY \WINDOWS\COMMAND\MSCDEX.EXE A:
```

The MSCDEX.EXE (Microsoft CD Extensions) file is the native DOS/Windows device driver for the CD-ROM drive. If you wish to have the CD-ROM available after booting the system to the command prompt, you need to add the following line to the CONFIG.SYS file:

```
C:\WINDOWS\COMMAND\MSCDEX.EXE /D:MSCD001 /M:10
```

The files that must at minimum be loaded to boot the system to the command prompt are IO.SYS, MSDOS.SYS, and COMMAND.COM.

Starting Windows 9x

The steps used to start up a Windows 9x system are:

1. After the BIOS performs the POST, and if the PC has a Plug and Play BIOS, Plug and Play devices are configured.

2. The partition table is accessed, and the boot record activates IO.SYS.

3. The Windows 9x boot sequence starts in real mode and then switches to protected mode. Beginning at this point, the boot sequence is in real mode.

4. The MSDOS.SYS is checked for any user-defined parameters (such as BootMulti or BootMenu).

5. If all is normal, the message "Starting Windows 9x" displays, and the sequence pauses for two seconds to wait for a function key. LOGO.SYS is displayed.

6. If file compression is in use, DRVSPACE.BIN loads.

7. The Registry (SYSTEM.DAT) is checked, and if it's valid, it loads.

8. Windows 9*x* performs hardware detection and identifies any new hardware.

9. If the CONFIG.SYS and AUTOEXEC.BAT files exist, IO.SYS processes their commands.

10. The boot sequence switches to protected mode, and WIN.COM is loaded.

11. The VMM32.VXD file and all virtual device drivers included in the Registry or the SYSTEM.INI file load.

12. The Windows 9*x* core components — Kernel, GDI, and User — load, along with Windows Explorer and all configured networking components.

14. Any applications in the Startup (Run Once) section of the Registry start.

15. The boot sequence ends.

If the Windows 9*x* startup sequence has any problems, restart it and immediately press the F8 key after the message "Starting Windows 9*x*" appears. This action displays the boot menu, which includes the option to boot the system in Safe mode. Safe mode boots Windows 9*x* without its startup files, which results in only the essential device drivers being loaded. If the computer can successfully boot in Safe mode, you know that the problem is in a device or its driver.

Another boot menu option that can help you to isolate a boot problem is the selection for Step-by-Step Confirmation. This choice forces the system to boot by displaying system file entries one at a time for you to include or exclude from the boot process with keyboard entries. Answering "No" to every option is the same as booting in Safe mode, and Windows 9*x* reverts to that mode automatically.

If Windows 9*x* won't boot to Safe mode, the system may have any of the following problems:

- The CMOS settings are incorrect.
- A hardware conflict exists, such as advanced BIOS settings, IRQ conflicts, duplicated COM ports, or defective memory modules.
- The MSDOS.SYS file contains an erroneous setting.
- The video drivers are not compatible.

You may also want to examine the contents of the BOOTLOG.TXT file located in the root directory. This file contains a log file of the results of device driver activation. The last line should list the driver attempting to load when the error occurred. If you suspect the video driver is the problem, set the video drivers to either VGA.DRV or VGA.VXD, both of which you can find on the Windows 9*x* CD-ROM.

Starting Windows 2000

Windows 9*x* systems start up by loading the IO.SYS file followed by MSDOS.SYS, and then COMMAND.COM, but Windows 2000 neither implements nor does it use any of these files in its startup process. The Windows 2000 startup process (and Windows NT as well) is executed each time the computer is powered on or rebooted. This process includes the following steps:

1. After the system POST completes, the system BIOS locates the system partition and loads the bootstrap loader program NTLDR, which loads the operating system files from the boot partition.

2. If the system is configured for a multiple boot, the user is prompted to choose an operating system to boot. The available operating systems on the computer are listed in the BOOT.INI system file.

3. After the operating system is selected (or if there is only one), NTDETECT. COM auto-detects the hardware and passes a list of the computer's hardware configuration to NTLDR.

4. NTLDR loads the operating system kernel, the hardware abstraction layer (HAL), and the Registry key HKEY_LOCAL_MACHINE\SYSTEM.

5. The system kernel initiates the Windows 2000 Professional splash screen (LOGO.SYS), and the "Starting Up" progress bar is displayed across the bottom of the display. When the status bar completes, NTOSKRNL sets up any network information relating to the system.

6. Although the system may still be initializing network device drivers, the Windows subsystem automatically starts WINLOGON.EXE, which displays the Begin Logon dialog box.

The actions of the NTLDR

As indicated in the numbered list in the preceding section, NTLDR, which must be located in the root folder of the startup disk, controls the operating system selection and hardware detection phases of the Windows 2000 startup process before passing control over to the Windows 2000 kernel.

The actions that NTLDR performs or controls are:

1. Switches the processor to run in 32-bit memory mode. All PCs run in real mode when first started, but because NTLDR and the rest of Windows 2000 are 32-bit programs, the processor must be switched to 32-bit mode.

2. Starts the file system. NTLDR contains the code to access NTFS (NT File System), FAT16, or FAT32 file systems.

3. Reads BOOT.INI. The operating system choices, if more than one, are displayed on the screen. If an operating system other than Windows 2000 is selected, NTLDR loads the BOOTSECT.DOS file and passes control to it, which starts the selected operating system. If Windows 2000 is chosen or if it is the only operating system listed in BOOT.INI, NTLDR starts NTDETECT.COM, which collects the computer hardware data.

4. Startup completes. The computer hardware data is passed to NTOSKRNL.EXE, which completes the startup.

Selecting the OS from the BOOT.INI

BOOT.INI contains the list of available operating systems on a computer. Each entry in the BOOT.INI file contains the path of the boot partition for each operating system, the text that is displayed on the boot loader screen, and any optional parameters that are used by the operating system when it starts up. In addition to starting multiple versions of Windows 2000, BOOT.INI will start Windows 95, Windows 98, Windows NT 4.0, MS-DOS, and OS/2.

The following is a sample BOOT.INI file:

```
[boot loader]
timeout=30
default=multi(0)disk(0)rdisk(0)partition(1)\WINNT
[operating systems]
multi(0)disk(0)rdisk(0)partition(1)\winnt="Microsoft Windows
          2000 Professional" /fastdetect
C:\="Windows 98"
```

The information of the BOOT.INI is displayed on the boot loader screen and looks something like this:

```
Please select the operating system to start:

Microsoft Windows 2000 Professional
Microsoft Windows 98

Use your arrow keys to move the highlight to your choice.
Please touch Enter to choose.

Seconds until highlighted choice will be started
          automatically: 29

For troubleshooting and advanced startup options for Windows
          2000, press F8.
```

The default operating system is always listed first. If the operating system has not been selected before the countdown timer reaches 0, the default operating system (Windows 2000 Professional in this example) is started.

Working at the Command Prompt

If you peruse the A+ OS Technologies exam's blueprint, you see a number of different DOS commands that are included on the test. What you should know for the commands I have included in this section are its command line syntax (how to enter the command and its parameters) and its actions (what it does).

Viewing hidden files

To view system files on any Windows version, you must be able to view hidden files in Windows Explorer or in the My Computer window. Lab 19-1 details the steps you can use in any Windows version to view hidden files.

Lab 19-1	Showing Hidden Files in Windows Explorer

1. **Right-click the Start button and choose Explore.**

2. **On the Tools menu, choose Folder Options, and then click the View tab to display the file view options. Figure 19-6 shows the file options in Windows 98.**

3. **In Windows 9x and NT, under the Hidden Files options, change the selection to Show All Files. In Windows 2000, change the option to Show Hidden Files and Folders.**

4. **Click OK.**

The following files are hidden by default on a Windows system (the files are listed by their filename suffixes):

- ✔ **386 files:** Virtual device driver
- ✔ **DLL files:** Program extension files
- ✔ **DRV files:** Device drivers
- ✔ **INI files:** Program initialization files
- ✔ **SYS files:** System files
- ✔ **VXD files:** Virtual device drivers

Changing file attributes

Another file-related action you need to know for the exam is how to change file attributes. Four file attributes can be set on a file (or folder) in Windows:

✔ **Archive:** This attribute indicates a file that is marked to be backed up.

✔ **Hidden:** This attribute prevents a file from appearing on directory listings.

✔ **Read Only:** This attribute indicates a file that can be read but cannot be changed or deleted.

✔ **System:** This attribute indicates a file that is used only by the operating system and is not typically displayed on a directory listing.

The ATTRIB command is used to display and modify the file attributes of a file. To view or change the file attributes for one or more files from the command prompt or through Windows Explorer, follow the processes in Labs 19-2 and 19-3.

Lab 19-2   Changing File Attributes from the Command Prompt

1. **To display the current attributes of a file change to the directory of the file and enter the following command:**

```
ATTRIB MYFILE.DAT
```

The system displays something like this:

```
A SHR   MYFILE.DAT
```

The series of letters at the beginning of this line are the first letters of the current attributes: A stands for Archive; S for System; H for Hidden; and R for Read-only.

2. **To remove an attribute from a file, use the minus sign (–). For example:**

```
ATTRIB -S -H -R MYFILE.DAT
```

This command removes the System, Hidden, and Read-only attributes from the file.

3. **To add an attribute to a file, use the plus (+) sign. For example:**

```
ATTRIB +H MYFILE.DAT
```

This command adds the Hidden attribute to the file.

Lab 19-3   Changing File Attributes in the Windows Explorer

1. **In the Windows Explorer, right-click the file and select Properties.**

In the Attributes section of the Properties window, the attributes that are enabled have checkmarks.

2. **To remove or add an attribute to a file, simply check or uncheck the attributes as you desire.**

3. **To change the System attribute, you must do it from the command prompt (see Lab 19-2).**

Other DOS commands you should know

Here is a list of other DOS (command line) commands that you should know for the OS Technologies exam:

- ✔ **COPY:** This command is used to create a copy of a file and place it into another directory or disk drive. Its format is COPY FILENAME.EXT NEWFILE.EXT.

- ✔ **DEFRAG:** As files are created, modified, and removed, the disk can become fragmented. Disk fragmentation can impact system performance, because disk drive heads must perform multiple seek operations to access a file. The DEFRAG command reorganizes the disk to eliminate fragmentation. The DEFRAG command can be executed from the command prompt or this same action can be started from the desktop. Use the Start⇔Programs⇔Accessories⇔System Tools⇔Disk Defragmenter path to start it. The command line format is DEFRAG X: (where X is the disk drive to be defragged).

- ✔ **DIR:** This command lists the file and subdirectories in the active directory.

- ✔ **EDIT:** This command opens a text line editor that can be used to make changes to some system and user-defined text-format files, such as INI files, and the AUTOEXEC.BAT and CONFIG.SYS files.

- ✔ **FDISK:** This command is used to partition hard disks prior to formatting them for use with a system. This command is discussed in more detail in Chapter 20.

- ✔ **MEM:** This command displays the current usage of system memory. Commonly used options of this command are:

    - View memory usage by classification — MEM /C

    - View memory usage by module — MEM /M module-name

    - View the amount of free memory — MEM /F

- ✔ **SCANDISK:** This command runs automatically at the next startup after a Windows 9x system is shut down improperly. The SCANDISK command fixes errors on hard disks, floppy disks, a RAM drive, and DBLSPACE compressed drives. It can be started from the System Tools list on the Accessories menu or executed from the command line with the format SCANDISK X: (where X is the drive letter of the disk to be repaired).

- ✔ **XCOPY:** This command is used to copy directories, subdirectories, and files to and from a fixed disk. Using its extensive list of options, the files or directories copied can be expanded or limited as desired by a variety of options, including only files with an archive attribute. XCOPY has some problems handling long file names, though. Its format is XCOPY A:*.* C:*.* /S, where the /S switch tells the command to copy the contents of all subdirectories as well.

✔ **XCOPY32:** This command is used to copy files and directory trees to another disk drive or to a backup media on Windows 9*x* systems. XCOPY32 has a more robust list of options than the older XCOPY command. The format for XCOPY32 is XCOPY32 A: C: /S, where the /S switch indicates that the contents of all subdirectories are to be copied.

Prep Test

1 Which of the following can be used to display the version and build numbers of a Windows 9*x* system? (Choose two)

A ❏ VER

B ❏ Winver

C ❏ My Computer, Properties, General

D ❏ Right-click desktop, Properties, About

2 Support for FAT32 was introduced in which Windows version?

A ○ Windows 95a

B ○ Windows 95b

C ○ Windows 98

D ○ Windows NT

3 Which of the following system files are used when starting a Windows 2000 system? (Choose two)

A ❏ IO.SYS

B ❏ NTDETECT.COM

C ❏ MSDOS.SYS

D ❏ NTLDR

4 Which of the following file types are hidden by default in the Windows Explorer display? (Choose two)

A ❏ SYS

B ❏ EXE

C ❏ DLL

D ❏ COM

5 The attributes assigned to DOS and Windows files are:

A ○ System, archive, read-only, hidden

B ○ Archive, reserved, read-write, hidden

C ○ Hidden, system, private, write-only

D ○ System, archive, read-only, reserved

6 Which of the following is the command prompt displayed for the COMMAND subdirectory of the Windows directory on the primary hard disk drive?

A ○ A:\COMMAND

B ○ C:\WINDOWS\COMMAND>

C ○ D:\WINDOWS\COMMAND>

D ○ A:\WINDOWS\COMMAND>

E ○ C:\COMMAND>

7 The core components of the Windows 9x API are:

A ○ Kernel, Graphics, Printers

B ○ GUI, User, Registry

C ○ Kernel, User, GDI

D ○ GDI, DMI, ACPI

8 To multi-boot a Windows 2000 system, which file must be modified?

A ○ BOOTSECT.DOS

B ○ BOOT.INI

C ○ BOOT.DLL

D ○ MSDOS.SYS

9 The command that would best be used to copy Windows 9x files from one disk to another is:

A ○ XCOPY

B ○ DIR

C ○ XCOPY32

D ○ COPY

10 The program that enables real-mode memory managers that must be loaded before Windows 9x can start is

A ○ EMM386.EXE

B ○ DOS=HIGH

C ○ LOGO.SYS

D ○ HIMEM.SYS

Answers

1 **A, C.** The WINVER command will run on a Windows 9*x* system, but it shows only the operating system, such as Windows 98, and not the version and build numbers. *See "Displaying the Windows version number."*

2 **B.** The FAT32 file system and a number of other features were included in the OSR2 release (Windows 95b). *Review "Comparing Windows 9x features."*

3 **B, D.** The NTDETECT.COM utility gathers information on the installed hardware of the system and passes to the NTLDR (boot loader) for use in creating the hardware configuration Registry entry. *Check out "Windows 2000 system files."*

4 **A, C.** The other file types that are hidden by default have the following suffixes: 386, DRV, INI, and VXD. *Take a look at "Viewing hidden files."*

5 **A.** The archive, read-only, and hidden attributes can be modified through a file's properties window. However, the system attribute must be managed through the ATTRIB command line command. *Study "Changing file attributes."*

6 **B.** Yes, I do make the assumption that the primary disk drive is the C: drive, because it will always be so. *See "Interfacing with the DOS and Windows command prompt."*

7 **C.** These files are commonly referred to as the core component files of Windows 9*x*. You'll need to know what they control on a summary level. *Look over "Getting to know Windows 98."*

8 **B.** The BOOT.INI is a system file unique to Windows 2000. In Windows 9*x* systems, multi-boot parameters are entered in the MSDOS.SYS file. *Check out "Windows 2000 system files."*

9 **C.** Actually, if there is no concern for long filenames being lost and files perhaps overwritten as a result, COPY or XCOPY could be used. XCOPY32 handles the long filenames and file systems of Windows 9*x* systems. *Review "Other DOS commands you should know."*

10 **D.** I'm willing to bet that you see a question very much like this one on the exam. *Study "CONFIG.SYS commands included in IO.SYS."*

Chapter 20

Windows 9x and Me

• •

Exam Objectives

▶ Identifying the procedures used to install or upgrade Windows 9x and Windows Me

▶ Defining commonly used DOS and Windows files and commands

▶ Explaining the procedures used to add hardware and device drivers

▶ Creating an emergency boot disk

▶ Recognizing common error and startup messages

• •

*T*he A+ OS Technologies exam could easily be called the A+ Windows exam because it focuses heavily on the processes of installing, configuring, and troubleshooting the various versions of Windows. Although the exam is focused primarily on the Windows 9x versions (Windows 95, Windows 95b, Windows 98, and Windows SE), you will also find references to both the earlier (Windows 3.x and Windows NT) and later (Windows Me and Windows 2000) versions, as well as an occasional mention of the pre-Windows operating system, MS-DOS.

Say what you will about Windows, but it is the most commonly used operating system for PCs in the world. For this reason, a professional PC repairperson should have a good working knowledge of the impact the Windows OS can have on the PC hardware as well as the effect that the hardware can have on the OS. PC technicians are called on to solve software problems as much as, if not more than, hardware problems these days. You need to know how to add Windows to a PC, how to configure it properly for either standalone or networked operation, and how to fix problems.

There isn't much you don't need to know about the Windows 9x systems. Spend time opening every icon on the Control Panel and testing what each icon controls, exploring Explorer, navigating file systems, and checking into the Registry. After you do all of that, you are about ready for a big part of the OS Technologies exam.

Quick Assessment

1 The Windows 95 version created with the application of OSR2 is _____.

2 The LFN "Committee minutes for 6/30/01.DOC" has the DOS alias of _____.

3 Windows 3.*x* and Windows 9*x* will not start up if _____ is not loaded.

4 The two primary files of the Windows 9*x* Registry are _____ and _____.

5 _____ can be used to back up, restore, or fix the Windows Registry.

6 The _____ file includes the BootMulti parameter that controls a system's capability to boot to multiple operating systems.

7 A (n) ____ device can be automatically configured and assigned a device driver by Windows.

8 The _____ command is used to create an emergency repair disk (ERD).

9 0E and 0D error messages reflect errors with _____ and _____, respectively.

10 A Windows Protection Error is associated with a(n) _____.

Answers

1 *Windows 95b.* See "Check out the file system before you start."

2 *COMMIT~1.DOC.* Review "Checking for names."

3 *HIMEM.SYS.* Check out "Installing Windows 95 over Windows 3.*x*."

4 *USER.DAT, SYSTEM.DAT.* Take a look at "Windows Files and Commands."

5 *SCANREG.* Study "Working with Windows utilities."

6 *MSDOS.SYS.* Review "Modifying MSDOS.SYS."

7 *Plug and Play (PnP).* Look over "Installing Hardware in Windows 9*x*."

8 *RDISK.EXE.* See "Running with the ERD."

9 *Memory, video.* Check out "Friendly Windows 9*x* error messages."

10 *Virtual device driver (VXD).* Take a look at "Dealing with Windows protection errors."

Putting in the Windows

You should understand the steps used to install each of the Windows versions as well as the procedures used to upgrade from one version to the next. Practice installing as many of the Windows versions as you can. However, if you lack all of the various versions, concentrate on installing Windows 95 or 98 and upgrading it to Windows 2000.

First, some DOS facts

Before I get too deep into the Windows world, here are some DOS commands, files, and features that you'll encounter on the exam. Although there are no questions about the DOS operating system itself, you will need to know some of its files and commands because they are still in use by the Windows operating system. Remember the following:

- ✔ CONFIG.SYS is not required for DOS or Windows to start up.

- ✔ COMMAND.COM displays the DOS command prompt, contains the internal DOS commands, and is required for DOS and Windows 3.*x* to boot.

- ✔ EMM386.EXE enables expanded memory and the use of upper memory as system memory.

- ✔ The boot sequence for a DOS system is IO.SYS, MSDOS.SYS, CONFIG.SYS, COMMAND.COM, and AUTOEXEC.BAT.

- ✔ DOS memory is divided into *conventional* memory (640K), *expanded* or *upper* memory (384K), and *extended* memory (above 1,024K) areas.

To boot to a DOS command prompt, only the IO.SYS, MSDOS.SYS, and COMMAND.COM files are required to load.

Refreshing your Windows 3.x

The name *Windows 3.x* is the all-inclusive name used on the A+ OS Technologies exam for any version of Windows that came before Windows 95. The exam barely acknowledges that Windows existed before Windows 95, but it expects you to know in minute detail the differences between Windows 3.*x* versions and later versions. The exam also refers to Windows 3.*x* as Windows for Workgroups, although this was specifically Windows 3.11.

These Windows 3.*x* facts may show up on the test:

✔ Program icons are arranged in Group files (GRP) with one group file representing one window.

✔ INI files are initiation files that contain startup parameters for Windows and applications. INI files can be edited with a text editor. The WIN.INI file controls how the desktop looks and how file types are associated.

✔ The file manager in Windows 3.x is called the File Manager. Fancy that!

✔ Device drivers are identified in the SYSTEM.INI file.

✔ The desktop windows are defined in PROGMAN.INI.

✔ Windows 3.x filenames are limited to eight characters plus a three-character extension. (I refer to this as the 8.3 filename later in this chapter.)

Don't waste your time studying the user-oriented accessories, games, tools, and applications included in any Windows release. Concentrate on the operating system functions (device management, memory management, and so on) and the functions of the Control Panels icons of Windows 9x.

Installing Windows 9x

The A+ OS Technologies exam includes both Windows 95 and Windows 98, with a slight edge towards Windows 98. You are probably very familiar with these operating systems, but if you do not have much experience installing them or dealing with installation problems, study the following carefully.

Check out the file system before you start

Windows 98 and Windows 95b — the version created by OEM Service Release 2 (OSR2) — provided two choices for file systems: FAT16 and FAT32. DOS and Windows 3.x users knew FAT16 simply as FAT, which meant File Allocation Table.

All Windows versions, including 3.x and 2000, and DOS support FAT/FAT16. However, only Windows 95b, Windows 98, and Windows 2000 support FAT32. This means that FAT32 is not supported by MS-DOS (except for the Windows 98 MS-DOS Mode), Windows 3.x, Windows NT, and the versions of Windows 95 that are referred to as 95a, which are versions 4.00.950 and 4.00.950a. Windows 3.x and Windows 95a supported FAT/FAT16 and VFAT (Virtual FAT), which was an interface between the FAT and applications.

See Chapter 21 for more information on these and other file systems.

Checking for names

A feature of both FAT16 and FAT32 on Windows 9x is long filenames (LFNs). Some LFN facts you should know are

✔ Each LFN has a DOS 8.3 (8 filename characters and 3 file extension characters) file name alias that consists of the first six characters of the LFN followed by a tilde (~) and a number that increments for multiple occurrences of filenames with the same first 6 characters. For example, the long file name THIS IS MY FILE NAME.DOC has an 8.3 alias of THISIS~1.DOC, as illustrated in Figure 20-1.

✔ An LFN is limited to 255 characters, but an 8.3 name is limited to its 11 characters. A LFN full-directory pathname is limited to 260 characters, but an 8.3 pathname is limited to 80 characters.

Backing up before you start

Before installing or upgrading any version of Windows, create a full backup of the hard drives. Windows 98 did include an uninstall, but if the installation fouls, you may not be able to boot to Windows 98, which means that you will not be able to run its uninstall feature.

Removing all barriers

Before upgrading to Windows 98 from Windows 95, halt all applications that are running, including the anti-virus software. Windows upgrades the master boot record on the disk, which is usually tenaciously protected by the anti-virus software. If you forget to stop a BIOS-level anti-virus routine and get a warning message because Windows is trying to change the master boot record of a disk, click whatever button continues the process and allows Windows to proceed.

```
MS-DOS Prompt

Auto

C:\>dir th*.*

 Volume in drive C has no label
 Volume Serial Number is 0F65-14E2
 Directory of C:\

THISIS~1 DOC        19,456  01-09-01  8:03p this is my file name.doc
         1 file(s)          19,456 bytes
         0 dir(s)        9,980.70 MB free

C:\>
```

Figure 20-1:
Long filenames (LFNs) also carry DOS filenames for backward compatibility.

If memory management utilities, such as QEMM or 386MAX are in use on a Windows 3.x system, they need to be halted. The only memory manager that should be running when you install or upgrade to Windows 9x is HIMEM.SYS.

Meeting the minimums — Windows 9x

Microsoft has two sets of minimum hardware requirements for the Windows 9x systems: a bare minimum on which the system will run (but, who knows how well) and a recommended minimum on which the system will actually run. For the A+ exams, remember both. Table 20-1 lists Microsoft's minimum and recommended system requirements for Windows 95, Windows 98, and Windows Me.

Table 20-1   Minimum System Requirements for Windows 9x

System	Component	Minimum	Recommended
Windows 95	Processor	386DX/20	486DX/66
	Memory	4MB	16MB
	Hard drive	10MB	500MB
	Video card	VGA	SVGA
	CD-ROM	Optional (2X)	Optional (2X)
	Mouse	Required	Required
Windows 98	Processor	486DX/66	Pentium
	Memory	16MB	24MB
	Hard drive	180MB	295MB
	Video card	VGA	SVGA
	CD-ROM	Required (2X)	Required (2X)
	Mouse	Required	Required
Windows Me	Processor	Pentium/150	Pentium/150
	Memory	32MB	32MB
	Hard drive	480MB	645MB
	Video card	VGA	SVGA
	CD-ROM	Required (2X)	Required (2X)
	Mouse	Required	Required

Installing Windows 95 over Windows 3.x

The steps used to install Windows 95 over Windows 3.x are

1. Setup.exe is selected and executed from either the CD-ROM or the Disk One floppy disk using the File Manager.

2. The Windows 95 files are copied to the hard drive, and the system is restarted. DOS is replaced, and program folders are created from the Windows 3.x program groups.

3. The Windows 3.x INI (initialization) files (SYSTEM.INI, WIN.INI, and PROTOCOL.INI) are migrated to Windows 95, and the Registry is created.

4. Select the type of installation you want: Typical, Portable, Compact, or Custom. Typical is the default. Portable customizes the installation for portable PCs. Compact enables only the minimum files required to run Windows 95. Custom installation enables you to select the specific options to be installed.

5. The Setup Wizard searches for hardware devices on the system. Only the Custom installation type has an option on which devices to install. The other installation types automatically install the devices found.

6. The installation concludes with the system being rebooted.

Windows will not load or run if HIMEM.SYS is not loaded to memory.

Installing Windows 98

The process used to install Windows 98, which is a completely different installation process than used for Windows 95, involves five major steps:

1. System check: SETUP.EXE verifies that the minimum hardware requirements are met, that anti-virus software is not running and performs a SCANDISK to check the integrity of the disk.

2. Information collection: Windows 98 collects the information it needs to complete the installation. The information may come from the user, a script, or an existing Windows 95 version that is being updated. This information includes the type of installation (Typical, Compact, Portable, or Custom), the user's name, the PC's name, and more.

3. Copying files: The Windows 98 files are copied to the hard drive.

4. System restart: The PC is restarted into Windows 98 and makes its modifications to the system files (WIN.INI, SYSTEM.INI, and the Registry) and adjusts the CONFIG.SYS and AUTOEXEC.BAT files, if present.

5. Hardware setup: Windows 98 searches for any Plug and Play and legacy devices on the system and configures them. The system is restarted once again after this step.

All versions of Windows install from the SETUP.EXE command. Windows 95 could be installed from floppy disks or a CD-ROM, but Windows 98, Windows Me, and Windows 2000 are typically installed from a CD-ROM. Windows 9x and Windows 2000 can be installed across a network as well.

The SETUP.EXE command can be executed either from the Windows Explorer or from a command line prompt in addition to the autorun on the CD-ROM.

Dealing with installation problems

During the installation process, the Windows 9x systems create a variety of log files — in the root directory of what is called the destination disk (the disk on which Windows is being installed) — that are used to recover from installation crashes. These files are

- ✔ **BOOTLOG.TXT:** Contains the results of the initial boot of the Windows 9x system.
- ✔ **DETLOG.TXT:** Lists the results of the hardware detection steps.
- ✔ **DETCRASH.LOG:** An internal file used by Windows 9x to recover from a crash during installation.
- ✔ **MODEMDET.TXT:** This file, which is found in the Windows directory, contains the results of autodetecting a modem on the PC.
- ✔ **NETLOG.TXT:** Lists the results of the network software startup.
- ✔ **SETUPLOG.TXT:** Contains a log of Setup's actions before and after hardware detection.

Dual-booting Windows 9x

One of the options available with Windows 9x systems is to create a dual-boot environment on a PC. Here are some things you should know about creating this situation:

- ✔ **Disk space:** Enough disk space must be available to support both operating systems. If the dual-boot is with MS-DOS, the DOS version must be able to support disk partitions greater than 32MB.
- ✔ **Private directory:** Windows 9x must be in its own directory with no other version of Windows present.
- ✔ **Compatibility:** Windows 95 and Windows 98 can be dual-booted with MS-DOS, OS/2, and Windows NT.

Modifying MSDOS.SYS

Entries in the MSDOS.SYS file tell the system that you want to choose the system to boot from a boot menu that is displayed before the operating system is loaded each time the PC starts up. To select which OS should boot, the following command is added to the [OPTIONS] area in the MSDOS.SYS file:

```
BootMulti=1
```

This option causes a boot menu listing the operating systems present on the PC to be displayed. If the BootMulti option is set to zero, only Windows 9*x* will boot.

Set BootMulti to 0 (zero) to indicate that only Windows 95 should boot. Other system options controlled by entries in the MSDOS.SYS file are the Windows splash screen, logo pages, and other displays, as well as a few other system-level attributes and characteristics.

If you edit the MSDOS.SYS file, make sure that the file remains greater than 1,024 characters in length when you are finished.

Using the ATTRIB command

To access the MSDOS.SYS and other system files, you may need to use the ATTRIB command to change the file's attributes to permit the change. The different attributes that can be assigned to files are

- ✔ **A (archive):** This attribute indicates that a file is available for archiving (backing up).
- ✔ **H (hidden):** Files with this attribute are not displayed on the Windows Explorer by default and are hidden from view.
- ✔ **R (read-only):** Files with this attribute can be read, but they cannot be modified or deleted.
- ✔ **S (system):** This attribute marks a file as an operating system configuration or environment file.

The ATTRIB command can be used to display the current attributes of a file. Figure 20-2 shows a series of ATTRIB commands and their results.

Attributes can be removed from a file by using a minus sign and the letter of the attribute in an ATTRIB command, as shown on the second command line of Figure 20-2. Typically, you would display the current attributes of the file first, as in the first command line in Figure 20-2. Attributes can be added to a file by using the plus sign and the letter representing the attribute to be added, as shown in the fourth command line of Figure 20-2. I don't mean to hammer this too hard, but this is on the test.

To change the MSDOS.SYS file, you must remove its blocking attributes using the same command shown on the second command line in Figure 20-2. After this is done, you can use a text editor to modify the file. Remember to replace the attributes when you are finished.

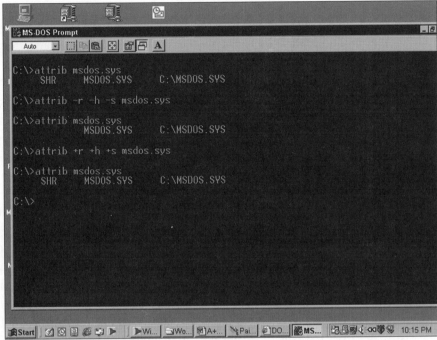

Figure 20-2:
The ATTRIB
command
shows the
attributes of
a file.

Installing Windows Me

Windows Me (Millennium Edition) is actually just an upgrade of Windows 98 targeted at the home user. Installing Windows Me involves the same steps used to install Windows 98. You should back up the hard drive and create a DOS boot disk before you upgrade to Windows Me, because Windows Me can't create a boot disk because most of the DOS support in the earlier versions has been removed.

DOS and Windows 3.*x* systems cannot be upgraded to Windows Me, so a clean installation should be used. A clean installation should involve formatting the hard drives and then installing Windows Me on a clean hard drive. Windows 95 and Windows 98 can both be upgraded to Windows Me, provided the hardware is adequately sized. (See Table 20-1 earlier in the chapter.)

Installing and running application software

Four processes can be used for installing application software:

✔ The application may come with a self-extracting or self-installing application, which is titled SETUP.EXE, INSTALL.EXE, or the like.

✔ The application is distributed on a CD-ROM that has an autorun applet that starts automatically to an installation window.

✔ The name of the installation applet is entered in the Start menu's Run box.

✔ The application is installed through the Control Panel's Add/Remove Software icon.

Windows Files and Commands

Well, some of these files can be classified as DOS files as well, but if you see them on the A+ OS Technologies exam, they will be in a Windows context. The files you should remember are

✔ **COMMAND.COM:** This is the command processor for DOS and Windows 9*x*. It displays the DOS prompt and processes the commands typed at the command prompt.

✔ **HIMEM.SYS:** This is the device driver for extended and high memory. If it is not loaded during startup, Windows 9*x* displays an error message and boots to a command prompt.

✔ **IO.SYS:** This binary executable file is loaded during the boot sequence. This file contains many of the commands and actions that were previously run from the CONFIG.SYS and AUTOEXEC.BAT files in DOS and Windows 3.*x*.

✔ **MSDOS.SYS:** This text file contains a number of startup and configuration variables and settings, including the BootMulti and BootMenu parameters used to indicate a system with multiple operating systems.

✔ **REG.DAT:** This is the Registry file used with Windows 3.*x* systems.

✔ **SYSTEM.DAT:** With USER.DAT, this is one of the two files in the Registry for a Windows 98 and NT/2000 system. The Registry is a database of configuration data about a PC's hardware and operating environment. The Registry actually has two files: USER.DAT and SYSTEM.DAT. Many of the entries formerly in the WIN.INI and SYSTEM.INI files of Windows 3.1 are now in the Registry.

✔ **SYSTEM.INI:** This system initialization file describes a PC's system environment, including device drivers, how DOS applications are executed, and internal Windows settings.

✔ **USER.DAT:** With the SYSTEM.DAT file, this is one of two files in the Registry for a Windows 9*x* and NT/2000 system.

✔ **VMM32.VXD**: This file is created during the Windows 9x setup. It includes all virtual device drivers (VXDs) required by the system. It is much faster at startup to load this one large VXD file than each of the individual drivers.

✔ **WIN.INI:** INI files are initialization files that describe or define the Windows environment. The WIN.INI file contains entries that tell Windows which programs to load and run and defines the screen, keyboard, mouse, display, and fonts. This file is read by the Windows operating system during startup.

The command line prompt

Recognize the following as the DOS/Windows command line prompt:

```
C:\>
```

This version of the command line prompt indicates that the C: drive is the active disk drive, and the active directory (folder) is the root (\) directory. Commands that can be entered in the Run box on the Start menu can also be entered at the command line prompt and vice versa. To display the command line prompt (in its own window), enter COMMAND or command in the Start menu Run box, as shown in Figure 20-3.

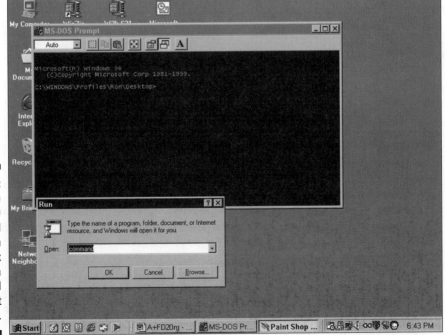

Figure 20-3: The COMMAND command entered in the Run box opens a command prompt window.

On a Windows 9*x* system, you can also open the command prompt in a window from the Program menu, but on Windows NT and 2000 systems, RUN COMMAND is used. When you open a command line prompt, the prompt reflects the current active directory.

Working with Windows utilities

The OS Technologies blueprint lists a wide variety of Windows system utilities that you should know for the exam. As I recall, just about all of them are mentioned on the exam, either in a question or as an answer (good or bad). Know the following commands:

- **ASD.EXE:** ASD stands for Automatic Skip Driver. Whenever a driver cannot be loaded or Windows 9*x* simply skips loading a driver, it is recorded in a log file. ASD.EXE displays the contents of this log file so you can determine why a particular device driver may not be active. This command is executed from the Start menu Run box. Most of the time, ASD will respond that there are no current ASD critical operation failures on the PC.

- **CHKDSK:** This utility can be used to check FAT and directory errors on a disk. The /F option is required to fix any errors found.

- **EDIT.COM:** EDIT.COM is a DOS/Windows utility that can be used to modify or create a text file. This command line utility can also be used to print the contents of a text file.

- **EXTRACT.EXE:** This is a command line utility, which means that it doesn't have a GUI display; it's used to extract and uncompress a file or multiple files from a compressed disk. This command is used to replace a corrupted system file with one located in the cabinet files of a Windows installation floppy disk or CD-ROM.

- **HWINFO.EXE:** This command line utility opens a window that displays about everything you'd ever want to know about the hardware configuration and utilization of your PC. To execute this command, type **HWINFO.EXE /UI** in the Start menu Run box. Figure 20-4 shows the display from the HWINFO command.

- **MSCONFIG:** As shown in Figure 20-5, this Windows 9*x* command, which is started from the Run box on the Start menu, opens a window that contains a variety of tabs. Each tab shows the data and current selections of a number of system files. The General tab of this window controls the process used during the operating system startup.

- **REGEDIT.EXE:** This command, which is executed from the Start menu's Run box, is the Registry editor for 16-bit Windows systems. Both this and the 32-bit Registry editor (REGEDT32.EXE) are distributed with Windows NT and 2000. See "The Windows Registry," later in this chapter, for more information on the Registry.

✔ **REGEDT32.EXE:** This is the Registry editor for 32-bit Windows systems. Both this and the 16-bit Registry editor (REGEDIT.EXE) are distributed with Windows NT and 2000. REGEDT32.EXE allows for editing values in the Registry that are greater than 256 characters. See "The Windows Registry," later in this chapter, for more information on the Registry.

✔ **SCANDISK:** SCANDISK is used to find and repair errors on the disk, including the file system structure (such as lost clusters and cross-linked files), and rebuild the file allocation table (FAT) and the directory tree structure. It will not repair fragmented files, which is the job of DEFRAG.

✔ **SCANREG:** Windows 98 and Me include a very flexible Registry tool that can be used to back up and restore Registry files. Each time a Windows PC is started successfully, SCANREG, or the Windows Registry Checker, creates a daily backup of the system and Registry files, including SYSTEM.DAT, USER.DAT, SYSTEM.INI, and WIN.INI.

✔ **SYSEDIT:** SYSEDIT is short for system configuration editor. This utility is used to view or edit system files, including the AUTOEXEC.BAT and CONFIG.SYS files, the WIN.INI, SYSTEM.INI, and the PROTOCOL.INI initialization files. Each file is opened in a separate window (that is very much like the Windows Notepad text editor). Figure 20-6 shows the display of the SYSEDIT utility.

✔ **WSCRIPT.EXE:** This Windows 98 and 2000 utility enables you to run scripts (strings of instructions written in a scripting language, such as VBScript, Jscript, and PERL) in Windows.

Figure 20-4:
The HWINFO command displays the current configuration and status of a PC's hardware.

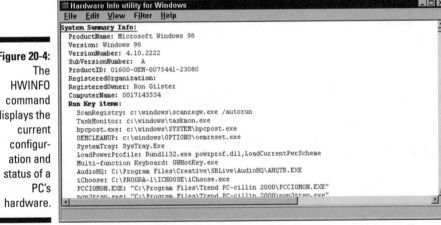

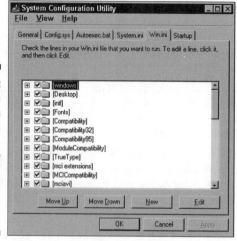

Figure 20-5:
The
Windows
System
Configur-
ation Utility
is started
from the
MSCONFIG
command.

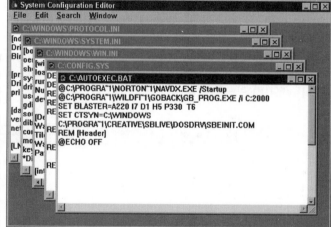

Figure 20-6:
The
SYSEDIT
windows
contain
initialization
and system
files for
viewing or
editing.

Dealing with Boot Sequence Errors

Much of the Diagnosing and Troubleshooting domain of the OS Technologies exam consists of knowing the sequence of events that occurs in the boot sequences of DOS, Windows 3.*x*, and Windows 95, and recognizing error messages and their associated corrective actions. Memorize the boot sequences and familiarize yourself with the error messages in each environment.

The DOS boot sequence

Yes, you will see references to the DOS boot sequence on the exams. Virtually every PC goes through about the same sequence of events when starting up, regardless of the operating system it uses. Memorize the DOS boot sequence and remember the sequence of the files.

After the POST completes, the MS-DOS system loads using the following steps:

1. The CMOS indicates the sequence in which the disk drives (A, C, and so on) are scanned for a boot record.

2. If the boot device is the C drive, the Master Boot Record (MBR) loads, and its program locates the boot partition.

3. If the boot disk is the A drive, or if the C drive boot is continuing, the DOS Boot Record (DBR) loads, and control passes to it.

4. The DBR loads the IO.SYS and MSDOS.SYS files (which is most of DOS) and passes control to them.

5. IO.SYS loads CONFIG.SYS (required by DOS systems), which sets the environment and loads the device drivers.

6. The COMMAND.COM command interpreter then loads, and control passes to it. COMMAND.COM loads and executes the AUTOEXEC.BAT and then displays the user interface (the command prompt).

The DOS boot sequence is IO.SYS, MSDOS.SYS, CONFIG.SYS, COMMAND.COM, and AUTOEXEC.BAT.

Following the DOS PATH

The DOS PATH= statement that is placed in the AUTOEXEC.BAT file is mentioned at least once on the exam. The context goes something like this: *Why would a certain file when entered on the command line prompt result in the message, "Bad or missing file name?"*

The PATH statement establishes the directory sequence and priority for where the operating system is to look for command-line files. For example, this statement in the AUTOEXEC.BAT file means that the system should look in the DOS directory first and then the Windows directory for a command entered on the command line.

```
PATH=C:\DOS;C:\WINDOWS
```

The Windows 3.x boot sequence

Because Windows 3.x isn't an actual operating system, but rather an operating environment, it actually uses the DOS boot sequence and then adds a few more steps. Typically, WIN.COM executes from the AUTOEXEC.BAT file.

Windows 3.x uses several configuration (called *initialization* or *.INI*) files to define the graphical user interface (GUI) and its input and output devices. These files contain such things as the size of the screen, the display font, the colors of the desktop, and the speed settings for the mouse. These files include the following:

- **CONTROL.INI:** Defines the user desktop, including colors, wallpaper, background, and any screen saver options in use.
- **MOUSE.INI:** Defines operational settings for the mouse.
- **PROGMAN.INI:** Defines the group windows and the icons included in each.
- **SYSTEM.INI:** Defines hardware settings, defaults, and the Windows multitasking parameters.
- **WIN.INI:** Defines the working relationships of Windows 3.x, including printers, fonts, file associations, and applications.

DOS/Windows 3.x error messages: Old favorites

An error message from the DOS/Windows 3.x boot sequence provides immediate feedback on any error you have made either by omission or commission. You have left something out or put in an error, ever so slight, but enough that DOS doesn't work. Here are some of the error messages you may encounter on the exam:

- **Missing operating system:** The MBR can't find a bootable partition. Either the disk hasn't been formatted and had the operating system copied to it, or a virus has clobbered the partition table or MBR. Either format the disk or use the SYS command to copy the system files to the disk or use an anti-virus program to scan and clean the disk.
- **Non-system disk or drive, replace and press any key to continue:** This usually means that you forgot to remove a floppy disk before you restarted the PC. Pop out the disk and hit the space bar to continue the boot.
- **Incorrect DOS version:** The COMMAND.COM file in the root directory of the boot disk is an incorrect or incompatible version. Replace it with the correct version or use the SETVER command to an older DOS version.

✔ **Bad or missing DRIVER.DRV:** If the CONFIG.SYS file can't load a device driver, it issues this message, replacing DRIVER with the name of the missing driver. Locate the driver and correct the entry in the CONFIG.SYS file.

✔ **HIMEM.SYS not loaded:** Windows 3.*x* will not run unless HIMEM.SYS is loaded. Correct the CONFIG.SYS statement that loads this file.

The Windows 9x boot sequence

The startup sequence used for Windows 9*x* is a little different than the startup sequence used for Windows 3.*x*. Windows 9*x* uses the following steps:

1. After the BIOS performs the POST, and if the PC has a Plug and Play BIOS, Plug and Play devices are configured.

2. The partition table is accessed, and the boot record activates IO.SYS.

3. The Windows 9*x* boot sequence performs partially in real mode and then switches to protected mode. Beginning at this point, the boot sequence performs in real mode.

4. The MSDOS.SYS is checked for any Windows parameters (such as BootMulti or BootMenu).

5. If all is normal, the message Starting Windows 95 displays or the Windows 98 splash screen is displayed. The system pauses for two seconds to wait for a function key to change the boot path.

6. If file compression is in use, DRVSPACE.BIN loads.

7. The Registry (SYSTEM.DAT) is checked, and if it's valid, it loads.

8. Windows 9*x* performs hardware detection and identifies any new hardware.

9. IO.SYS processes the commands in the CONFIG.SYS and AUTOEXEC.BAT files, if they exist.

10. The boot sequence switches to protected mode.

11. WIN.COM executes.

12. The VMM32.VXD file and all virtual device drivers included in the Registry or the SYSTEM.INI file load.

13. Windows 95 core components — Kernel, GDI, and User — load, along with the Explorer and network support.

14. Any applications in the startup (RunOnce) section of the Registry start.

15. The boot sequence ends.

If the Windows 9x boot sequence experiences any problems, restart it and immediately press and hold down the Control (Ctrl) key during the boot process to display the Startup Menu (from which you can boot the system in Safe mode).

If Windows 9x won't boot in Safe mode, the system may have any of the following problems:

✔ The CMOS settings are incorrect.

✔ A hardware conflict, such as advanced BIOS settings, IRQ conflicts, duplicated COM ports, or defective memory modules exists.

✔ The MSDOS.SYS file contains an erroneous setting.

✔ Set the video drivers to either VGA.DRV or VGA.VXD, both of which you can find on the Windows 95 CD-ROM.

You may also want to examine the contents of the BOOTLOG.TXT file located in the root directory. This file contains a log file of the results of device driver activation. The last line should list the driver attempting to load when the error occurred.

Friendly Windows 9x error messages

Because DOS and Windows 3.x used up all of the really good bad error messages, Windows 9x systems have had to resort to messages that actually make sense on occasion. Here are some of the very best errors that Windows 9x has to offer.

✔ **No error message:** The startup stops at a point after the POST but before Windows starts. Run FDISK from a command line prompt with a /MBR option to rebuild the MBR (master boot record). You may want to scan the disk with an anti-virus program first, because it is likely that the problem is a boot virus or some equally scary problem with the MBR.

✔ **General Protection Fault in USER.EXE:** The User core component has run out of file space. Add the line FILES=100 to the CONFIG.SYS file.

✔ **0E or 0D exception:** 0E errors refer to bad memory, and 0D errors are video problems. These errors are usually displayed on the "blue screen of death." Restart the system to clear the error. If the problem persists, check the CMOS for exceptions and verify the device drivers in use. To avoid the problem, try switching to standard VGA video mode.

✔ **Out of Memory:** This error is caused by memory leaks — programs that end without releasing their memory allocations. Reboot the system and reduce the activity on the system.

Booting Windows

Typically, when you start up your Windows 9x PC, the operating system is started through its normal startup procedure, which ends with the Desktop on the screen and all of the applications included in the startup procedure running. However, for the A+ OS Technologies exam, you should know how to access the Startup menu and start Windows 9x and Windows 2000 from it. Know what each selection on the Startup menu does.

Changing your boots

To access the Windows Startup menu, you can either press and hold the Control (Ctrl) key down while the PC is booting, or you can press the F8 key right after you hear a beep, after the "Starting Windows" message displays, or when the Windows splash screen appears.

The Windows 9x Startup menu includes the following entries:

1. Normal: This selection is just what it sounds like, the normal Windows boot. Choosing this option (by entering 1) continues the boot as usual.

2. Logged (\BOOTLOG.TXT): This selection completes a normal startup, but with all startup actions recorded in the BOOTLOG.TXT file in the root directory or the startup disk.

3. Safe mode: Completes the startup, but bypasses the system files and loads only the essential system device drivers. You can go straight into Safe mode during the startup by pressing F5 right after the "Starting Windows" message (Windows 95) or the Windows splash screen appears (Windows 98, Me, and 2000) or by entering the command WIN /D:M at a command line prompt.

4. Safe mode with network support: This selection starts Windows in Safe mode but also loads the drivers to allow access to a network.

5. Step by step confirmation: This selection allows you to confirm each of the actions contained in the system files one at a time. For each action, you are required to respond with a "Y" or an "N" to start it or not. Pressing F8 also starts this option.

6. Command prompt only: This selection startups up the operating system and loads the normal system files and the Registry but displays only a command line prompt in place of the Windows Desktop.

7. Safe mode command prompt only: This selection starts Windows in Safe mode but displays only the command line prompt. Pressing Shift+F5 will also start this option.

8. Previous version of MS-DOS: This selection starts MS-DOS, if it is installed on the PC. This option appears only if BootMulti=1 is set in the MSDOS.SYS file. Pressing F4 can also start this option.

You cannot multitask Windows and DOS programs together if you boot into a MS-DOS mode from a Windows 9x system.

The function key options that can be used to select the Windows startup options are controlled by the BootKeys variable in the MSDOS.SYS file. If the BootKeys variable is set to 1, which is its default, the function keys are available for use during startup. Setting this variable to 0 or setting the BootDelay variable to 0, which removes the delay provided for you to press a function key, removes the ability to use function keys to change the startup process.

When Windows won't boot

If for any reason Windows does not start normally, you should try to start it in Safe mode, which bypasses the real-mode drivers and configuration to load a very minimal protected-mode configuration that disables the Windows drivers and a VGA display.

However, if Windows will not start in Safe mode, one of the following conditions is likely the cause:

- **The PC is infected with a virus:** Install and run an anti-virus program on the PC.

- **The CMOS settings are wrong:** If you can access the BIOS setup program and the configuration data, check it for accuracy. Hopefully, you have a paper backup of what the CMOS settings should be. If not, you may need to contact the manufacturer.

- **There is a system resource or hardware conflict:** Check for IRQ conflicts, duplicated COM ports, PCI BIOS settings, and possible defective RAM.

- **MSDOS.SYS has an incorrect setting:** Verify that there are no incomplete or invalid settings in this file.

- **A DriveSpace drive cannot mount a compressed volume file (CVF):** Follow the procedures in the Windows Help files for CVF files and troubleshooting DriveSpace.

- **There is a Registry error:** Boot to the Command prompt only startup option and run SCANREG from the command line prompt. See "Changing your boots," the preceding section, for information on Windows startup options.

When all else fails, reinstall Windows into a new folder to determine if the problem is something left over from the previous operating system or Windows version.

If Windows will boot to Safe mode, you should step through the startup process using the Selective Startup option of MSCONFIG (executed from the Start Run box) to try several different startup options.

Using Device Manager to isolate startup problems

If a PC will boot to Safe mode but the problem remains unsolved after scanning the Registry and startup process, the problem may be hardware related. Follow these steps to use the Device Manager to help isolate the problem:

1. Open the Device Manager from the Control Panel's System icon or by right-clicking the My Computer icon and choosing Properties.

2. On the Device Manager tab, disable all of the devices listed under the following device trees by right-clicking on each device, choosing Properties, and clicking the Disable in this hardware profile box, shown in Figure 20-7:

   - Display adapters

   - Floppy disk controllers

   - Hard drive controllers

   - Keyboard

   - Mouse

   - Network adapters (if present)

   - Ports

   - PCMCIA socket (if present)

   - SCSI controllers (if present)

   - Sound, video, and game controllers

Figure 20-7:
The Disable in this hardware profile box is used to disable a device from the Device Manager to isolate hardware problems on a Windows system.

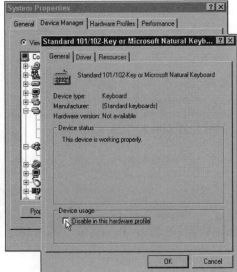

3. If the PC starts without the problem, begin enabling the devices in this order until the problem repeats:

- COM ports

- Hard drive controllers

- Floppy disk controllers

- Other devices

Restart the PC after enabling each device one at a time. Also check the Resources tab for the device to see if any problems are listed under the Conflicting Device List.

Using the Automatic Skip Driver

The Automatic Skip Driver (ASD) agent will attempt to enable any disabled device that may be causing the startup problem and report the problem. The ASD tool is located on the Accessories menu. To access it, click Start➪Programs➪Accessories➪System Tools➪System Information➪Tools➪ASD.

Dealing with Common Problems

The OS Technologies exam includes a number of questions about a variety of common Windows errors that a PC repairperson should know in order to isolate and solve problems on a user's PC.

When the system crashes

When Windows or one of its applications is seriously malfunctioning, it typically will halt, also known as crash, hang, freeze, lock up, or die, and display an error message. General Protection Faults (GPFs) and Invalid Page Faults are memory protection errors that are commonly the problem. These errors typically cause the crash of one or more Windows 9x programs and perhaps even Windows itself. They can either be the indicators of very serious problems or something very trivial that is fixed with a restart.

Computer crashes, GPFs, and page faults are caused by Windows trying to store information in a space already in use by another program. Yes, it should know better and keep better records, but at the speeds that it is swapping data in and out of RAM and with programs starting and stopping, it is easy on occasion to become confused. Other error messages you may see when the system crashes are: Access Violation, Exception Error, Illegal Operation, Segment Load Failure, and Violation of System Integrity. (I just love the presumption in this one.)

GPF messages usually indicate where the error is occurring. The message is typically "General Protection Fault in module . . . at address. . . ." or "Program Name . . . has caused a general protection fault in module. . . ." and might include an error code as well.

In most cases, restarting the PC will clear the problem, but if the problem persists, you will need to track it down and stamp it out.

Elementary, Dr. Watson

If you can imagine when you are investigating the mystery of a system crash, that you are Sherlock Holmes, then Windows 3.x, 98, NT, 2000, and Me will offer assistance to help you track down the culprit, with a software-environment sleuth named Dr. Watson.

Dr. Watson, although a valuable tool, is not included on the Programs menus. It is located in the Windows directory, and you can start it in background by entering DRWATSON in the Start Run box. In order to isolate software failures, Dr. Watson must be running in background at all times, which means that it must be added to the StartUp folder. An icon is displayed in the Task Bar tray when it is running. When you click this icon, Dr. Watson takes a snapshot of the system and displays any errors it finds or possible problems it foresees, as shown in Figure 20-8.

Other sources of help

If you isolate which program is causing the system to crash, check the publisher's Web site for troubleshooting help or upgrade information. A very good example of a publisher's troubleshooting Web site is Netscape's GPF pages at http://help.netscape.com/kb/consumer/19970702-6.html.

Figure 20-8:
Dr. Watson is a Windows software diagnostic tool that can help you isolate the cause of General Protection Faults.

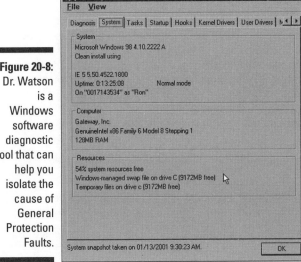

Dealing with Windows protection errors

A Windows Protection Error may appear when you start up or shut down a Windows system. During startup, you may see an error message like:

```
While initializing device ... Windows Protection Error
```

The device name is inserted after the word device. When you are shutting down Windows, the error message is simply:

```
Windows Protection Error
```

A Microsoft Windows Protection Error happens when a virtual device driver (VXD) is being loaded or unloaded. Typically, if the error occurs when a driver is being loaded, the message will contain the name of the device, which makes it very easy to isolate and fix the problem. However, they can also occur from several other problems, including

- ✔ A real-mode driver and a protected-mode driver have been loaded on the same device.
- ✔ The Registry is corrupted.
- ✔ WIN.COM or COMMAND.COM is damaged or infected with a virus.
- ✔ A file referenced in SYSTEM.INI, WIN.INI, or the Registry is invalid.
- ✔ The CMOS settings for peripheral devices built into the motherboard (cache, hard drive controller, and others) are incorrect.
- ✔ The BIOS program's Plug and Play feature is not working.
- ✔ The motherboard, system cache, or memory is not working properly.

Other Windows problems

The OS Technologies exam also references other Windows problems in the context of *if this or that happens, what is your next action?* In most cases, the action to take is a choice between one or two common-sense items. Count on questions that give you scenarios and ask you what your action is. For example, if you encounter a question about an Illegal Operation error, what you should do depends on the cause of the error. Here are the most common cases:

- ✔ **After new hardware or software is installed:** Remove the new item and reboot.
- ✔ **In only one software application:** Uninstall the program, delete its folder, and reinstall it.
- ✔ **If the problem appears to be power related:** Move the power supply's cord to a new electrical outlet.
- ✔ **Undetermined hardware problem:** Remove all external devices and add them back one at a time to find the problem device.

See Chapter 18 for more information on troubleshooting procedures for
hardware issues.

A few other Windows errors you may want to store away are

- ✔ **Invalid working directory:** This error typically occurs when the user is
  trying to start a program from a shortcut or icon. This message means that
  the working directory of the program (the one used to store temporary
  files or where initialization data is located) is not valid or is missing. Either
  the entry in the icon's properties has a typo, or the directory has been
  inadvertently deleted. Either correct the icon's Start In line on its
  Properties window or restore the folder.

- ✔ **System busy:** This message usually accompanies the blue screen of death
  and suggests that you wait for the system to become available or reboot.
  Depending on your patience, you can wait awhile before you reboot.

- ✔ **Application will not start or load:** Enough system resources may not be
  available to start the job, or the application's EXE file may be corrupted.
  If the application should be able to load but won't, then uninstall,
  reboot, and reinstall it. You may also need to add more memory or hard
  drive space. One other reason for this problem may be that it's a DOS
  application that may not be able to run in a Windows DOS window. Try
  running it after rebooting into MS-DOS mode.

- ✔ **Cannot log on to network:** Let me count the ways: The network configuration has been changed or corrupted; the cable is missing from the NIC;
  the network itself is down; the user has been removed from the network
  users list; and so on. On a Windows 9x system, check out the Network
  settings on the Control Panel and, if all is well, check the network end
  before opening the hardware. Chapter 22 covers networking and networking problems in more detail.

- ✔ **Windows printing problems:** The OS Technologies exam's blueprint
  lists a number of printing errors that you should know for the exam. The
  good news is that there are virtually no questions about this area on the
  exam. Chapter 14 details how a printer is added and set as the default
  printer on a Windows system, which is what you need to know about
  printing for the exam.

Dealing with Windows clock problems

For some reason, the A+ exams think that you should be an expert at setting
the Windows clock. Understand first that the Windows clock is not the
system clock. In fact, the Windows clock can lose time if the system is not
reset periodically so it can resynchronize to the system clock.

Remember these two rules for dealing with the Windows clock:

- ✔ **If the time zone is correct:** Adjust the time or drag the hands on the clock to the proper settings.

- ✔ **If the time zone is not correct:** Choose the correct time zone from the list box and verify that the time is correct.

These adjustments are made to the Windows clock settings only and not to the system clock, which must be set in the BIOS. You can access the clock by either double-clicking the time displayed in the Task Bar's right-corner tray or through the Date/Time icon on the Control Panel.

Running with the ERD

The OS Technologies exam definitely contains at least one question on how to create an emergency repair diskette (ERD), particularly relating to Windows NT/2000. The ERD is created during or after installation, with the utility RDISK.EXE, which is executed from a command line prompt or in the Start Run box.

The command used to create an ERD that backs up the Registry, system files, and the SAM (Security Accounts Manager) is

```
RDISK.EXE /S
```

This command opens a dialog box that provides you with two ERD options. The first is Update Repair Info, which creates a Repair folder in the system folder that contains the files to be placed on the ERD. The second option, Create Repair Disk, formats a disk and then copies the system's critical files to the disk.

Installing Hardware in Windows 9x

In the hazy, lazy days of Windows 3.x and DOS, installing hardware was a simple matter of plugging in the hardware and editing the CONFIG.SYS file to load the hardware's device driver. Installing hardware may not have been *that* simple, but that's a fairly close description of the process.

On a Windows 9x system, hardware is classified into four hardware groups:

- ✔ **Plug and Play (PnP):** Windows 9x systems (including Me) are PnP operating systems that configure PnP devices even when the PC's BIOS is not PnP-compliant. On some systems, you may need to disable the BIOS program's PnP settings and just let Windows take care of it.

✔ **32-bit supported devices:** Windows 9*x* carries a variety of 32-bit device drivers for peripheral devices that are directly supported. These drivers are included on its CD-ROM and are loaded automatically when the devices are detected.

✔ **Unsupported 32-bit devices:** These devices may be compatible with a user's computer, but Windows may not include drivers for them. The manufacturer usually supplies compatible drivers on a floppy disk, which means that when you are installing the device, you should use the "Have disk . . ." option.

✔ **Legacy cards and adapters:** These 16-bit or 8-bit adapters and interface cards may cause system resource conflicts. They are usually configured through DIP switches and jumpers.

If Windows recognizes the device as a supported device, hardware installation proceeds with virtually no external input needed. If a device is supported device (other than PnP), Windows suggests system resource assignments and prompts for confirmation to complete the installation. Intervention from the user is usually needed for legacy cards or unsupported devices to supply a device driver to be loaded.

The Windows Registry

Windows 3.*x* is a virtual forest of INI files that contain the configuration and execution instructions for Windows and its installed applications, but beginning with Windows 95, a lot of this information has been consolidated into the Registry. Windows 3.*x* and Windows NT had perfunctory registries in a file named REG.DAT. The Windows 9*x* and Windows 2000 Registry is a special hierarchical database that contains a complete profile of the system configuration and program settings, eliminating the need for most of the INI files.

The Registry records the overall hardware and software configuration and associations of the Windows system. Expect to see at least three or four test questions about the Windows Registry. The questions do not drill down to a specific Windows version and are very generic, recognizing that at PC repairperson should not necessarily be mucking about in the Registry.

Know these facts about the Registry:

✔ The two Registry files are USER.DAT and SYSTEM.DAT.

✔ The file extension for backups of the Registry files is .DA0.

✔ The acronym HKEY stands for Handle for a Key.

✔ If you export part of all of the Registry to back it up, the exported data is placed in a file with a .REG extension.

✔ The Registry is organized in a tree hierarchy around six major keys. Each key is a major branch of the registry database and holds information relating to the subject of the branch.

The six major keys of the Windows Registry are the following:

- ✔ **HKEY_CLASSES_ROOT:** File associations and OLE (Object Linking and Embedding) data.
- ✔ **HKEY_USERS:** User preferences, including desktop setup and network connections.
- ✔ **HKEY_CURRENT_USER:** On a PC with only a single user, this key is a duplicate of the HKEY_USERS key. However, on a PC with multiple logins, it contains the preferences of the currently logged-in user.
- ✔ **HKEY_LOCAL_MACHINE:** The hardware and software installed on the system.
- ✔ **HKEY_CURRENT_CONFIG:** In addition to duplicating the KEY_LOCAL_MACHINE key when running, this key also contains any configuration changes made in the current session and information on the printers and fonts installed.
- ✔ **HKEY_DYN_DATA:** Records system performance information and keeps information on Plug and Play devices.

You need to know that the Registry is organized into keys and the contents of each key. The A+ exam doesn't ask you to match the key to the type of information it contains, but it may include a key name in a question, and you need to know the context it connotes.

Editing the Registry, if you dare

Use the REGEDIT.EXE program to edit Registry files. Make changes to the Registry only with extreme caution and care. Be sure that you back up both the SYSTEM.DAT and the USER.DAT files before making any changes to the Registry. You may want to back up these files before you install new Windows software to the system as well, because each installation modifies the Registry. Figure 20-9 is a screen capture of this program displaying the contents of a Windows 98 Registry.

Getting Around in Windows without a Mouse

Many different key combinations can be used to manipulate, navigate, and configure Windows straight from the keyboard. Here are the ones you should know for the OS Technologies exam:

- ✔ **Alt (or F10):** Moves the cursor control to the Menu bar of the current application or back.

- ✔ **Alt+Esc:** Cycles through the applications running in the Task Bar.

- ✔ **Alt+F4:** Closes the current application. If there are no running applications, this key set displays the Shut down box.

- ✔ **Alt+Spacebar:** Displays the Control menu of the current application window. Alt closes the menu.

- ✔ **Alt+Tab:** Shows a menu and cycles through the icons of the applications running in the Task Bar.

- ✔ **Ctrl+Alt+Delete:** When not from an error screen, this key set displays the Close Program box. From the Blue Screen of Death, it will restart the system.

- ✔ **Ctrl+Esc:** Shows the Start menu and Task Bar.

- ✔ **Ctrl+Tab and Ctrl+Shift+Tab:** These key sets move you through the tabs on a dialog box.

- ✔ **Shift:** In addition to its other primary use, if you hold down the Shift key when inserting a CD-ROM, any autorun programs on or associated with the CD will not run.

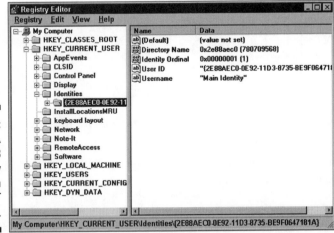

Figure 20-9:
A Windows 98 Registry displayed in a REGEDIT window.

Prep Test

1 The file attributes that can be set with the ATTRIB command are (Choose three)

- **A** ❏ Sharing
- **B** ❏ Read-only
- **C** ❏ Write-only
- **D** ❏ System
- **E** ❏ Hidden
- **F** ❏ Reserved
- **G** ❏ Encrypted
- **H** ❏ Compressed
- **I** ❏ Archive

2 The Scandisk utility will fix errors in which of the following? Choose two.

- **A** ❏ Directory tree structure
- **B** ❏ Fragmented files
- **C** ❏ File system structure
- **D** ❏ Media defects

3 The key set used to display the Windows 9x Start menu and Task Bar is

- **A** ○ Ctrl+Alt+Del
- **B** ○ Alt+Tab
- **C** ○ Ctrl+Esc
- **D** ○ Alt+F4

4 The F5 key is used during system startup to start Windows in which mode?

- **A** ○ Command prompt only
- **B** ○ Safe mode command prompt only
- **C** ○ Safe mode with network support
- **D** ○ Safe mode

5 Which of the following files are required in a Windows 9x CONFIG.SYS file?

- **A** ○ HIMEM.SYS
- **B** ○ FILES=
- **C** ○ UBM=
- **D** ○ DOS=HIGH
- **E** ○ None of the above

6 **The minimum requirements for Windows Me are**

A ○ 100 MHz Pentium or better processor, 16MB of RAM, 120MB of free disk space

B ○ 233 MHz Pentium or better processor, 8MB of RAM, 200MB of free disk space

C ○ 150 MHz Pentium or better processor, 32MB or RAM, 480MB of free disk space

D ○ 133 MHz Pentium or better processor, 32MB of RAM, 650MB of free disk space

7 **To dual-boot a Windows 9x system, the BootMulti variable must be set in which system file?**

A ○ IO.SYS

B ○ AUTOEXEC.BAT

C ○ MSDOS.SYS

D ○ CONFIG.SYS

8 **Which of the following are files of the Windows 98 Registry? Choose two.**

A ❑ SYSTEM.DAT

B ❑ USER.DAT

C ❑ SYSTEM.SYS

D ❑ REG.DAT

9 **Which of the following utilities and applications can be used to troubleshoot an application error?**

A ○ SCANREG

B ○ HWINFO.EXE

C ○ Dr. Watson

D ○ MSCONFIG

10 **A Windows 9x system has displayed an error message and booted to a command line prompt. What is likely the problem?**

A ○ HIMEM.SYS did not load.

B ○ VMM32.VXD is corrupted.

C ○ A file referenced in SYSTEM.INI is invalid.

D ○ The Registry is missing.

Answers

1 **B, D, E, I.** The ATTRIB command is used to add or remove these four file attributes to either restrict or permit access to files and folders. *See "Using the ATTRIB command."*

2 **A, C.** This command is used during installation to verify the integrity of the disk and during startup to check the disk when the system has not been shut down properly. *Check out "Working with Windows utilities."*

3 **C.** For some unknown reason, CompTIA has decided that you need to know these keystrokes to pass the A+ exams. *Review "Getting Around in Windows without a Mouse."*

4 **D.** You could also press F8 and choose Safe Mode from the Startup menu. *Take a look at "Changing your boots."*

5 **E.** Okay, so this is way too much like a trick question, but the lesson here is to examine every available answer choice. Yes, the CONFIG.SYS file itself is not required for a Windows 9x system, which means that there are no required entries in it. *See "The Windows 9x boot sequence."*

6 **C.** I wish I knew a shortcut to remembering these numbers, but I don't. You'll just need to memorize them. *Look over "Meeting the minimums — Windows 9x."*

7 **C.** The MSDOS.SYS file contains many startup variables that are used to set the operating environment for Windows. *Review "Modifying MSDOS.SYS."*

8 **A, B.** These are the primary files in the Registry database on Windows 98 systems. *Check out "The Windows Registry."*

9 **C.** Dr. Watson can be executed to run in the background monitoring all applications, or it can be run periodically, to take a snapshot of the system. *Investigate "Elementary, Dr. Watson."*

10 **A.** If I haven't already told you, HIMEM.SYS must be running for Windows 9x to start up. *Take a look at "Windows Files and Commands."*

Chapter 21

Moving Up to Windows 2000

• •

Exam objectives

▶ Identifying the function, structure, and system files of Windows 2000

▶ Explaining the process used to upgrade a Windows 9x system to Windows 2000

▶ Detailing the startup and shutdown procedures used by Windows 2000

▶ Recognizing Windows 2000 error messages

• •

Make no mistake: The OS Technologies exam is essentially a Windows 98 exam, but you will see questions about Windows NT and 2000 on the exam. Although the focus is primarily on Windows 2000 Professional, at least a couple of questions require you to have some knowledge of Windows 2000 Server as well as its predecessor, Windows NT 4. To my best recollection, Windows NT Workstation doesn't get much more than a passing reference in a wrong multiple-choice response.

The OS Technologies exam deals only with personal computer operating systems in the context of the PC repairperson's ability to install, configure, and troubleshoot the entire PC, including its operating system. You need to be aware of the problems an operating system has so that you can separate software problems from hardware problems.

You don't need to know Windows 2000 (or any other operating system) so thoroughly that you threaten to put Microsoft's technical support hotline out of business. However, you must be able to set up a Windows 2000 PC and use its utilities and applets to troubleshoot and isolate problems.

As the hardware of the PC becomes more mature and sophisticated, software plays an increasing role in the PC repairperson's daily life, not to mention a huge role in his or her certification.

Quick Assessment

1 The _____ is used to verify if a hardware device or computer is compatible with Windows 2000.

2 The _____ contains the device drivers and control software used by the kernel to communicate with the hardware on a Windows 2000 system.

3 The editing tool used to add or change settings in the Windows 2000 Registry is _____.

4 The _____ utility can be used to check for system resource and file-sharing conflicts.

5 To display the command line prompt from a Windows 2000 system, enter the command _____ in the Start Run box.

6 The phases of the Windows 2000 setup are _____, _____, and _____.

7 The command used to create a set of Windows 2000 startup disks is _____.

8 _____ is the bootstrap loader program for Windows 2000.

9 The boot mode that starts up Windows 2000 with only essential device drivers and services is _____.

10 Windows 2000 _____ messages are also known as blue screen messages.

Answers

1 *HCL (Hardware Compatibility List).* See "Upgrading to Windows 2000."

2 *HAL (Hardware Abstraction Layer).* Review "Meeting HAL."

3 *REGEDT32.EXE.* Check out "Managing a Windows 2000 computer."

4 *MSINFO32EXE.* Take a look at "Managing a Windows 2000 computer."

5 *RUN CMD.* Read over "Displaying the Command Prompt."

6 *Setup loader, text-mode setup, GUI-mode setup.* See "The phases of the Windows 2000 setup."

7 *MAKEBOOT.EXE.* Review "Creating startup disks."

8 *NTLDR.* Look over "Starting Up Windows 2000."

9 *Safe Mode.* Check out "Playing it safe."

10 *Stop.* Study "The joy of Windows 2000 stop messages."

Checking out Windows 2000

Windows 2000 is not just an update for Windows NT, as Windows Me is just an update (or bug fix) with some bells and whistles added to Windows 98. Although Windows 2000 is largely based on Windows NT (in fact, the opening splash screen advertises this fact proudly), it is a new operating system with several new additions and features.

Don't worry about memorizing the features of Windows 2000 for the OS Technologies exam. I will spotlight the specific features you need to know in this chapter and Chapter 20. I am only including this overview of features to provide contrast between the Windows 9x and 2000 versions. Whenever I use Windows 2000 without specifying a version (Server, Professional, Advanced Server, or Data Center), I mean Windows 2000 Professional (or as its often called, Pro).

Microsoft lists the following as the major features of Windows 2000:

✔ **Ease of use:** A number of new Wizards are included for installing, configuring, and setting up a Windows client, such as the Setup Manager and the System Preparation Tool.

✔ **Cost of ownership:** This new marketing term is used to describe all types and forms of technology. Here it means that Windows requires less time to install and maintain — something that should interest an A+ technician.

✔ **Windows NT technology:** Windows 2000 builds on the good part of Windows NT with added reliability, scalability, interoperability, and security — all of which translate to fewer headaches for support and repair personnel.

Setting the record

Rumors, myths, and other spurious information always float around when a new operating system or version hits the streets. Here are some things you should know about Windows 2000 for the exam:

✔ **Windows 2000 Server is not required to support Windows 2000 Professional.** In fact, Windows 2000 Pro will run in Windows NT or UNIX environments as well.

✔ **Windows 2000 is not the next version of Windows 98.** That honor goes to Windows Me. However, it is claimed that Windows 2000 Pro is 50 times more reliable than Windows 98 and 17 times (there's a strange number) more reliable than Windows NT Workstation.

✔ **Windows 2000 has compatibility issues.** Some hardware and software is not Windows 2000-compatible, but virtually all hardware and software will be compatible in the future. In the meantime, check the hardware and software on the PC for compatibility before proceeding with the installation (more on this later in "Upgrading to Windows 2000").

✔ **Windows 2000 can be installed remotely and unattended.** New tools, such as disk duplication utilities, contribute to the ease of installation of Windows 2000.

Learn the system files used in Windows 2000 and how they replace or compare to the files used in Windows 9*x*. Remember that you are getting certified as PC repairperson. Don't get sidetracked studying the functions of Windows NT Server or Windows 2000 Server. That part of operating system technology has been reserved for the new Server+ exam, for which you'll be sure to need a copy of my newest adventure, *Server+ Certification For Dummies,* coming to your local or online bookseller soon.

Installing Windows 2000

You need to know the steps used to prepare for and install Windows 2000 on a PC for the exam. Know how to verify compatibility between the operating system and the hardware and the files and utilities used during the installation.

When installing Windows 2000 on a PC, whether it's a fresh installation or an upgrade from an earlier Windows version, a few steps must first be taken to ensure that installation will take and not cause some serious operating problems on the PC.

Making sure it will fit

The minimum system requirements for a Windows 2000 Professional installation are the following:

✔ **Processor:** 133 MHz or higher Pentium-compatible CPU.

✔ **Memory:** 64 megabytes (MB) of RAM minimum, but of course, more is better. Remember that there is a 4GB maximum.

✔ **Hard drive space:** Requires at least 2GB hard drive with a minimum of 650MB of free space.

The minimum system requirements for a Windows 2000 Server installation are

 ✔ **Processor:** 133 MHz or higher Pentium-compatible CPU.

 ✔ **Memory:** 128MB of RAM minimum, but 256MB is recommended. There is a 4GB maximum.

 ✔ **Hard drive space:** Requires at least a 2GB hard drive with a minimum of 1GB of free space (or more if installed over a network).

Both the Professional and Server versions of Windows 2000 require the use of a CD-ROM drive because that is the standard media used for the distribution discs.

Loading up Windows 2000

Whether you're installing Windows 2000 on a fresh hard drive or upgrading a previous version of Windows, the process is essentially the same. Of course, there are some preparation steps you must complete, some of which are required and some that are just highly recommended (which you should interpret as required).

Upgrading to Windows 2000

You must do five actions before upgrading a Windows PC to Windows 2000. These actions must be done even before you put the Windows 2000 installation CD-ROM in the drive. Make sure that

1. The current Windows version is upgradeable. Table 21-1 lists the Windows versions that can and cannot be upgraded to Windows 2000. A Windows version that cannot be upgraded must be installed from a clean start, which means using newly partitioned and formatted hard disk drives. When possible, all installations of Windows 2000 should be made on a clean system.

2. The hardware and application software are compatible. Windows 2000 claims to support a wide selection of PCs, peripheral devices, and application software. However, there is also a wide selection of hardware and software that it does not support as well. Before you begin, verify that the PC meets the minimum system requirements (see "Making sure it will fit" earlier in the chapter). Next, check the Hardware Compatibility List (HCL) on the CD-ROM, or better yet, visit Microsoft's Windows 2000 homepage at `www.microsoft.com/windows2000/upgrade/compat/ default.asp`, which includes recent updates to the compatibility list. Figure 21-1 shows this page and its options. You can also check the compatibility of your software applications on the Web site, as well.

   If the PC or any of its components are not listed, check with the appropriate manufacturer for Windows 2000 upgrades.

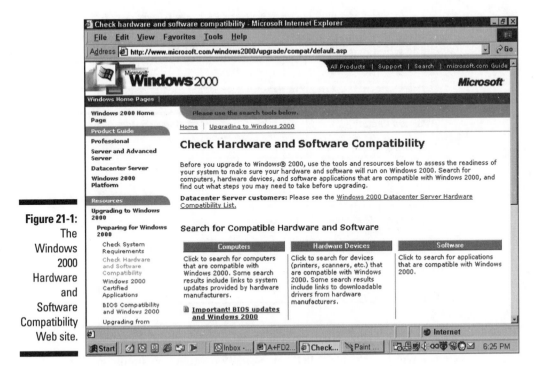

Figure 21-1:
The
Windows
2000
Hardware
and
Software
Compatibility
Web site.

3. **The device drivers are Windows 2000 compatible.** If the hardware checks out, verify that the device drivers are Windows 2000 compatible. Make sure you have compatible versions of all device drivers before installing Windows 2000, especially for essential devices, such as the monitor and printer. It's very hard to know what is going wrong when Windows will not complete the boot because of an incompatible video driver.

The Support folder on the Windows installation CD-ROM contains tools to help you with the previous two steps. It contains the HCL, the Application Compatibility tool, and the Windows 2000 Support Tools. During installation, you are asked if you want to run a System Compatibility report. Answer yes, and heed what it says.

4. **The PC's BIOS is current and compatible for Windows 2000.** If the BIOS is not the latest version available, the worst that can happen is that the advanced power management and device configuration features of Windows 2000 may not function. See Chapter 5 for information on updating the system BIOS.

5. **You have a recovery plan.** Windows 2000 cannot be uninstalled. There are a couple of points in the installation process where you can cancel it, but once Windows 2000 is installed, removing requires that you format the hard disks and start clean to reinstall the previous (or another) operating system. I recommend taking a full archive backup before beginning a Windows 2000 installation.

The documentation included with the Windows 2000 installation CD-ROM contains additional information on checking compatibility and the options available when installing the operating system.

Table 21-1	Upgradeable Windows Versions
Windows Version	*Upgradeable*
Windows 3.*x*	No
Windows 9*x*	Yes
Windows Me	No
Windows NT Workstation 3.51 or 4.0	Yes
Backoffice Small Business Server	No
Windows NT Server 3.51 or 4.0	Yes
Windows NT Server 3.51 with Citrix	No

Checking out the disk

On the Windows 2000 CD-ROM are some tools that you should know about:

- ✔ **BOOTDISK folder:** This folder contains the image files used to create the four-disk boot disks for Windows 2000 and the MAKEBOOT.EXE and MAKEBT32.EXE command line programs used to create the book disks.

- ✔ **I386 folder:** This folder contains a variety of files and folders that make up the Windows 2000 installation set. Included are the command line programs that can be used to execute the Windows 2000 setup from either a DOS or Windows 9*x* boot-disk (WINNT.EXE) or directly from Windows 9*x*, Windows NT, or Windows 2000 (WINNT32.EXE). Of course, you can also let the Autorun on the CD-ROM just take off.

  To suppress the Autorun feature on a Windows installation CD-ROM, press the Shift key when closing the CD-ROM tray.

- ✔ **SETUPTXT folder:** This folder contains two Windows 9*x* Notepad-compatible files that contain the release notes and setup documentation for Windows 2000.

- ✔ **SUPPORT folder:** This folder contains the TOOLS folder, which has a subset of the full Windows 2000 Resource kit, a version of the HCL current to some date in the past (for example, many are dated December 7, 1999), and the APCOMPAT.EXE utility, which is the Windows 2000 version of the DOS SETVER command. Use the HCL on the CD-ROM first. Visit the Microsoft Windows 2000 Web site to check compatibility.

Running Setup

Depending on the PC and its operating system, the Windows 2000 setup program can be started three ways:

- ✔ **From a DOS or Windows 9x command line:** Execute WINNT.EXE.
- ✔ **From a Windows 9x or Windows NT Start Run box:** Execute WINNT32.EXE.
- ✔ **From any upgradeable system:** Allow the CD-ROM's Autorun to start the Setup program.

The phases of the Windows 2000 setup

The three general phases of a Windows 2000 installation are

- ✔ **Setup Loader:** This setup phase is initiated by WINNT.EXE or WINNT32.EXE from a command line prompt or by the Autorun function on the CD-ROM. The Setup Loader copies the installation files and SETUPLDR to the hard drive and either creates or modifies the BOOT.INI file.

  SETUPLDR is a special version of NTLDR (see "Starting Up Windows 2000" later in the chapter) that loads NTDETECT.COM and NTBOOTDD. SYS, which perform initial hardware detection, load the drivers for the hard disk controller, and pass control to the kernel.

  If setup was started from WINNT32.EXE or the CD-ROM's Autorun, the End-User License Agreement (EULA — pronounced "you-la") and the Product ID dialog box are displayed in this phase.

- ✔ **Text-mode setup:** This phase is distinctive for its blue screen. It performs an inventory and check of the system hardware (CPU, motherboard, and hard drives), creates the Registry, detects the Plug and Play (PnP) devices, parti°482tions and formats the hard disk, and creates the file systems or converts an existing NTFS (NT File System) file system.

- ✔ **GUI-mode setup:** The Setup wizard is displayed on the screen in GUI-mode, which detects and configures the devices found on the computer, and creates the Setup log files in the installation directory on the hard drive.

Keeping the logs

During the Windows 2000 setup, a number of log files are created that can be used to help troubleshoot any installation problems that may happen. The log files are in a text format and can be opened with the Windows Notepad. The log files created by setup are

- ✔ **SETUPACT.LOG:** Information on the files copied to the PC during setup.
- ✔ **SETUPERR.LOG:** Information on any errors that occurred during setup.

- ✔ **SETUPAPI.LOG:** Information on the device driver files copied to the PC during setup.
- ✔ **SETUPLOG.TXT:** Additional information on the device driver files copied to the PC during setup.

The final part of the setup asks for a login and password and allows you to customize the system for a variety of options, including accessibility, regional, and networking.

Creating startup disks

The Windows 2000 installation CD-ROM contains the MAKEBOOT utility that is used to create system boot and startup disks that can be used to start a PC that is unable to start from the system CD-ROM. Lab 21-1 lists the steps used to create a set of startup disks.

Lab 21-1	Creating a set of Windows 2000 Startup Disks

1. **You need four blank, formatted 3.5-inch 1.44MB floppy disks. Label them as Windows 2000 Startup Disk 1, 2, 3, and 4.**
2. **Insert the first floppy disk in the floppy drive.**

   This procedure can be performed on any PC running Windows or MS-DOS with a floppy disk drive and a CD-ROM drive.
3. **Insert the Windows 2000 CD-ROM into the CD-ROM drive.**
4. **Either open the Start⇨Run box and enter the following command or enter the command at the DOS command line prompt:**

   ```
   D:\BOOTDISK\MAKEBOOT.EXE A:
   ```

   Adjust the D to the drive letter of the CD-ROM on your PC.
5. **Follow the prompts on the screen to complete the startup disks.**

Before starting a computer using the Windows 2000 operating system CD-ROM or the floppy disks, try starting the computer in safe mode.

Starting Up Windows 2000

The Windows 2000 startup process is very different from the process used to start up MS-DOS, Windows 95, or Windows 98. In these systems, the IO.SYS file is loaded followed by the MSDOS.SYS and COMMAND.COM program. Windows 2000 does not use these files, and you will only find them on PCs that are configured for a multi-boot and early Windows version or MS-DOS.

The general startup sequence used to start a Windows 2000 system is

- ✔ **Power-on self test (POST):** This is the same regardless of the operating system.

- ✔ **Initial startup:** After the POST, the system BIOS looks for the disk from which it should start the operating system. The storage devices are checked in the sequence prescribed in the BIOS. A number of different error messages can be displayed if the operating system is not found.

- ✔ **Bootstrap loader:** The bootstrap loader program NTLDR loads the operating system's files into memory from the boot partition. If the PC is set to Multiboot, a multiple-boot menu is displayed from which the operating system to be started is chosen. NTLDR processes the operating system selection and the hardware detection processes before passing control to the Windows 2000 kernel. NTLDR must be located in the root directory of the boot partition.

- ✔ **Operating system selection:** If the PC is configured as Multiboot, the system file BOOT.INI contains the list of available operating systems, including the path to its boot partition. Windows 2000 can multiboot with multiple Windows 2000 versions, as well as Windows 95, Windows 98, Windows NT 4.0, MS-DOS, and OS/2. Here is an example of the contents in the BOOT.INI file:

```
[boot loader]
timeout=30
default=multi(0)disk(0)rdisk(0)partition(1)\WINNT
[operating systems]
multi(0)disk(0)rdisk(0)partition(1)\winnt= "Microsoft
        Windows 2000
Professional" /fastdetect
C:\="Windows 98"
```

- ✔ **Hardware detection:** After the operating system is selected on a multiboot PC, or when only Windows 2000 is on the PC, NTDETECT.COM detects the hardware, creates a list of the installed hardware, and passes the list to NTLDR. The information that NTDETECT.COM passes includes the computer ID and information on the bus and adapters installed, keyboard, COM ports, floppy disk controller, mouse, and LPT ports.

- ✔ **Hardware profile selection:** Windows 2000 supports more than one hardware profile to allow for multiple non-Plug and Play configurations of the PC. If multiple hardware configurations are defined, NTDETECT.COM prompts for the hardware profile to use. If only one hardware profile is in use, the default settings are used. One choice available on the hardware profile screen is the Last Known Good Configuration, which will overlay all changes in the Registry and control set since the last good boot. After the hardware profile is chosen, control passes back to NTLDR.

✔ **Windows 2000 kernel loads:** NTLDR loads the Windows 2000 kernel and the hardware abstraction layer (HAL) into memory. (See "Meeting HAL" later in this section.) NTLDR then loads the registry key HKEY_LOCAL_MACHINE\SYSTEM from the folder %SystemRoot%\system32\Config\System and uses it to create the control set that is used to initialize the PC. This control set is used to start the operating system.

✔ **Logon:** WINLOGON.EXE and the Local Security Administration are started and the Begin Logon box is displayed. Windows 2000 is still loading drivers and such, but you can log in. After the logon is complete, the Desktop is displayed and the Last Known Good control set is created.

Meeting HAL

The HAL (hardware abstraction layer) contains the device drivers and control software used by the elements in the kernel to communicate, control, and manipulate the PC's hardware. Because each PC is slightly different, the contents of the HAL vary by PC. The HAL is a common communication interface between Windows 2000 and the hardware.

Solving startup problems

A goodly share of a PC's problems occurs at startup. This is when hardware, software, and even operators break down the most frequently. This section covers some things you should know about problems during a Windows 2000 system startup.

Now where'd I put that darn OS?

If the BIOS cannot find a system partition from which to load the operating system, it will display one or more of the following messages:

✔ **Non-system disk or disk error:** A floppy disk that is not a boot disk is loaded in the floppy drive. This message appears when the A: drive and is designated as the first boot drive.

✔ **Invalid partition table:** If the BIOS is directed to a hard drive partition (C:, D:, and so on), and the partition is not a system partition, this message or "Error loading operating system," "Missing operating system," or "Missing operating system" is displayed.

Playing it safe

Most startup problems happen immediately after new hardware or software is installed and are typically directly related to that activity. The first step to troubleshoot a startup problem that occurs right after you've installed new stuff in the PC is to remove the new stuff and reboot to see if that really was the problem.

However, if nothing new was added, modified, or reconfigured on the PC, you must start at the beginning and drill down to the facts. If the PC freezes up during startup, displays any error messages, including those from the preceding section, or you lose the function of any peripheral device, your best bet is to boot into Safe Mode.

Safe Mode loads only a minimal configuration of the operating system and only those device drivers absolutely essential to starting Windows and allowing you to interface, such as a VGA driver for the monitor, the keyboard, mouse, hard drive, and floppy disk. Other drivers, such as serial and parallel ports and network support are not loaded in Safe Mode. If the PC will not boot to Safe Mode, check for system resource conflicts, a corrupt Registry, or device drivers that are incompatible with Windows 2000.

To enter Safe Mode on a Windows 2000 system, press F8 when the prompt "For troubleshooting and advanced startup options for Windows 2000, press F8" appears. Safe Mode can be selected from the Advanced Options Menu.

If the problem is suspected to be a corrupted Registry, the best course of action is to reboot, press F8 to enter the Advanced Options Menu and select the Last Known Good Configuration option to reset the PC's configuration to what it was the last time it booted successfully.

Getting the system information

If you are able to boot an ailing PC into Safe Mode, the Windows 2000 System Information utility (MSINFO32.EXE) should be used to check for system resource and device and file sharing conflicts.

If you find any conflicts, disable the device or devices in question and reboot to see if the problem is solved. It's also a good idea to check the devices against the HCL to make absolutely sure it is compatible with Windows 2000. The Windows Update can be used to search for compatible drivers, but the manufacturer's Web site is likely a better choice.

If no hardware conflicts exist, check the Software Environment of MSINFO32 for a list of the programs that are started when the PC starts. To see if the problem is in one of these programs, disable them and restart the PC.

If the problem still exists, check the boot log file, NTBTLOG.TXT.

Managing a Windows 2000 computer

Windows 2000 includes a utility that helps you manage both local and remote PCs, called Computer Management. This tool combines several Windows 2000 administration tools into a single Explorer-like tree arrangement, as illustrated in Figure 21-2. The Computer Management window is opened from the Administrative Tools icon on the Control Panel.

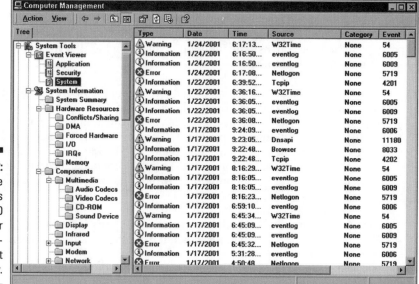

Figure 21-2:
The
Windows
2000
Computer
Manage-
ment
window.

In addition to the Computer Management tools, Windows 2000 also provides a variety of other tools that are used to maintain, troubleshoot, or update the system. Table 21-2 lists the ones that you may encounter on the OS Technologies exam.

Table 21-2	Windows 2000 Maintenance and Update Tools
Tool	*Application*
Disk Defragmenter	Optimizes disk performance by rearranging files, folders, programs, and unused space on the hard drive.
AVBoot	MAKEDISK.BAT can be used to create a boot disk that also scans for and removes MBR (master boot record) and boot sector viruses from RAM and the hard drive.
Windows Update	An online repository of product updates, service packs, device drivers, and operating system updates.
MSINFO32.EXE	The system information utility will collect and display information on the PC's hardware, system components, and software.
REDEDT32.EXE	The editing tool used to add and change settings and create subkeys in the Windows 2000 Registry.

Shutting out shutdown problems

During the shutdown process on a Windows 2000 system, messages are sent to the peripheral devices, system services, and application programs to alert them that the system is shutting down. The system waits for responses from each of these elements, especially the applications, before beginning to close down the device drivers, services, and applications. If a device driver, system service, anti-virus software, or application does not respond, the shutdown process can hang.

Windows 2000 File Systems

The primary file systems supported by Windows 2000 are NTFS (NT File System) and FAT32 (File Allocation Table 32-bit). The NTFS released with Windows 2000 is a version called NTFS 5.0, which includes support for Dynamic Disk features.

Here are the files systems supported by Windows 2000:

- **FAT (File Allocation Table):** This is the legacy file system first used with MS-DOS and Windows 3.*x* systems.

- **FAT32:** Windows 2000 allows FAT32 volumes of up to 2TB (terabytes) in size to be used. Larger volumes are supported, but only if they were created under Windows 98. FAT32 is also the file system used for dual-boot systems with Windows 98.

- **NTFS (NT File System):** Windows 2000 fully supports this file system with volumes of up to 16 terabytes (trillions of bytes) in size. Windows 2000 will upgrade NTFS volumes to NTFS 5.0, but only Windows 2000 or NT 4.0 with service pack 4 (SP4) or later can read an NTFS 5.0 volume.

- **CDFS (CD File System):** A legacy CD file system that is being replaced by the UDF format.

- **UDF (Universal Disk Format):** A newer file system supported by newer CD-ROMs, DVDs, and other optical disks.

The joy of Windows 2000 stop messages

To make sure that you don't get too lonely for your old pal, the blue screen of death, it has been included in Windows 2000. Whenever Windows 2000 has an error it cannot recover, it displays a stop message — the blue screen message. Two types of stop messages are generated on a Windows 2000 system:

✔ **Stop messages:** This type of message is displayed when the Windows 2000 kernel detects a condition from which it cannot recover. These messages are displayed in full blue screen glory with each error type identified by a hexadecimal error code and a symbolic name for the error. A stop message display looks something like this:

```
Stop 0x0000000A or IRQL_NOT_LESS_OR_EQUAL
```

Stop messages are grouped into four categories:

- **Normal operations messages:** Can be from a number of hardware or software sources.

- **Installation messages:** Are typically HCL problems.

- **Initialization messages:** Are caused by a device or system component failing to initialize.

- **Software trap messages:** Is an error in an applications or system service that is detected by Windows 2000.

✔ **Hardware malfunction messages:** Are displayed when the CPU detects a hardware problem that Windows 2000 cannot recover. These messages are typically in the form of

```
Hardware malfunction.
Call your hardware vendor for support.
```

Encrypting and compressing files

Windows 2000 has the capability to encrypt a file for private use simply by choosing a file property. The encryption method is a standard 56-bit encryption. Microsoft recommends that an NTFS folder be created and the folder marked for encryption. Lab 21-2 details the steps used to encrypt a file in Windows 2000.

Lab 21-2	Encrypting a File or Folder in Windows 2000

1. **Right-click the file or folder to be encrypted from the Windows Explorer and choose Properties.**

2. **Under Attributes, click the Advanced button to display the Advanced Attributes box, as shown in Figure 21-3.**

   Your choices are to encrypt your files or folders or to compress your files.

   To encrypt your files or folders: Choose "Encrypt contents to secure data" to encrypt the folder or file or deselect this box to decrypt a file or folder.

   To compress a file or folder: Choose the "Compress contents to save disk space" option on the Advanced Attributes window. To decompress the file or folder, deselect the Compress option.

Figure 21-3:
The
Advanced
Attributes
window is
used to
encrypt and
compress a
file on a
Windows
2000 system.

3. Click OK to close the dialog box.

The file or all of the files in the folder are not encrypted (or decrypted). If you encrypted a folder, any new files added to the folder will be encrypted, and encrypted files cannot be shared.

 Remember that encrypted files cannot be compressed, and compressed files cannot be encrypted.

Displaying the Command Prompt

One small, but very important command you absolutely need to know for the OS Technologies exam is how to display a command line prompt (otherwise known as the DOS prompt) in Windows 2000.

 To do so, open the Start Run box and enter CMD in the Open box and click OK or enter RUN CMD at a command line prompt. That's it; that's all there is to it.

Prep Test

1 Which of the following is not a minimum system requirement of Windows 2000?

A ○ 133MHz or higher Pentium processor
B ○ At least 2GB of free disk space
C ○ At least 256MB of main memory (RAM)
D ○ A CD-ROM drive

2 Which of the following is used to verify if a PC, peripheral device, or application is Windows 2000 compatible?

A ○ HAL
B ○ MSINFO32
C ○ Computer Management
D ○ HCL

3 Which of these Windows versions can be upgraded to Windows 2000? (Choose two.)

A ❑ Windows 9*x*
B ❑ Windows Me
C ❑ Windows 3.*x*
D ❑ Windows NT 4.0

4 The log file created during the Windows 2000 setup process that contains information on any errors that occurred during the setup.

A ○ SETUPERR.LOG
B ○ ERRSETUP.LOG
C ○ STUPERR.TXT
D ○ W2KERR.LOG

5 During the Windows 2000 startup, a list of the installed hardware is created and passed to NTLDR by which function?

A ○ HAL
B ○ HCL
C ○ NTDETECT
D ○ W2KDETCT

6 Which of the following can be used to enter Safe Mode during a Windows 2000 startup?

A ○ F5 key during boot process

B ○ F8 key during boot process

C ○ F8 when prompted and select Safe Mode from the Advanced options menu

D ○ Delete key

7 A Windows 2000 system will not start up, and you have determined the cause to be a corrupted Registry. What course of action can you use to start the system?

A ○ Reinstall Windows 2000 to rebuild the Registry.

B ○ Access the Advanced Options Menu and choose the Last Known Good Configuration option.

C ○ Use REGEDT32 to rebuild the Registry

D ○ Delete SYSTEM.DAT, rename SYSTEM.DA0, and reboot.

8 This utility can be used to download and install product updates, service packs, device drivers, and updates to Windows 2000.

A ○ MSINFO32

B ○ Windows Update

C ○ MAKEDISK

D ○ SETUPAPI

9 To configure a Windows 2000 system to multiboot with Windows 98, which Windows 2000 system file must be edited?

A ○ MSDOS.SYS

B ○ NTLDR.EXE

C ○ BOOT.INI

D ○ SYSTEM.INI

10 Windows 2000 supports which of the following file systems? (Choose three.)

A ❑ FAT

B ❑ FAT32

C ❑ NFS

D ❑ NTFS

Answers

1 **C.** The minimum RAM requirement of Windows 2000 Professional is only 64MB. Windows 2000 Server requires a minimum of 128MB, but 256MB is recommended. *See "Making sure it will fit."*

2 **D.** The Hardware Compatibility List (HCL) is used to check a device, PC, or application's compatibility with Windows 2000. A version is included on the distribution CD-ROM, but an up-to-date version is available online. *Review "Managing a Windows 2000 computer."*

3 **A, D.** Windows NT 3.51 (the non-Citrix version) can also be upgraded to Windows 2000. *Study "Upgrading to Windows 2000."*

4 **A.** Log files are text files and can be examined using either the Windows Notepad or another text editor or word processing application. The SETUPERR. LOG file should be empty most of the time, but should errors occur, they are recorded in this file. *Check out "Keeping the logs."*

5 **C.** NTDETECT.COM is the full name of this program. All of the installed devices on the PC are recorded in the list passed to the NTLDR which compares it to the hardware profile used to configure the system. *Take a look at "Starting Up Windows 2000."*

6 **C.** When the "For troubleshooting and advanced startup options for Windows 2000, press F8" prompt appears, you have about 2 seconds to press F8 and display the advanced options menu. Safe Mode can be selected from this menu. *See "Playing it safe."*

7 **B.** The Last Known Good Configuration is created each time the system startups up completely and trouble free. *Review "Playing it safe."*

8 **B.** Windows Update is the online extension of the Windows 2000 operating system that can be used to keep the operating system and the services it supports up to date relatively automatically. *Look over "Managing a Windows 2000 computer."*

9 **C.** BOOT.INI lists the multiple operating systems and includes a path statement that directs the system to the boot partition for each operating system. *Check out "Starting Up Windows 2000."*

10 **A, B, D.** Windows 2000 also supports the EFS (Encryption File System — not on the exam), and the CDFS (CD File System) and UDF (Universal Disk Format), which are mentioned on the exam. *Study "Windows 2000 File Systems."*

Chapter 22

The Hard and Soft of Networking

● ●

Exam Objectives

▶ Understanding networking concepts

▶ Swapping and configuring network interface cards

▶ Connecting to the network

▶ Networking DOS and Windows

▶ Identifying Internet concepts

▶ Accessing the Internet

● ●

*E*ven if you know the Father of Ethernet and truly understand the basic concepts of networking and how the common network topologies are used, you should still review this chapter. Sometimes the way that I understand something works for general purposes, but my knowledge may not be insightful enough to answer some of the questions on a test. I recommend that you review the networking fundamentals in this chapter as a part of your test preparation. Also give this info a quick review before you take the test, just in case.

About 15 percent of the A+ Core Hardware and OS Technologies exams require that you understand the following items:

✔ Basic networking terms and concepts, including protocols, cabling, and the different ways you can connect a PC to a network

✔ How to tell whether a PC is networked

✔ The process used to swap and configure network interface cards (NICs)

✔ The ramifications of improperly repairing a networked computer

Even though this chapter is in the part of the book that deals with operating systems and the OS Technologies exam, its contents actually covers the information you need to know for both A+ exams.

Quick Assessment

Networking DOS and Windows

1 On a Windows network, the server that manages user logons and the permissions of the domain resources is the _____.

Connecting to the network

2 A(n) _____ is the networking device that is used to reduce broadcast storms on a network.

3 Before working on a PC, determine whether it is a(n) _____ PC.

4 The two most commonly used connectors for network hardware are the _____ and the _____.

Swapping and config- uring network interface cards

Under- standing networking concepts

5 A(n) _____ address is the 48-bit address assigned to a NIC by its manufacturer.

6 192.168.1.100 is an example of a(n) _____ address.

7 The command used to reset a modem to its default settings is _____.

8 _____ is the most widely used network protocol.

Identifying Internet concepts

9 The software facility used to resolve the domain name to its associated IP address is _____.

Accessing the Internet

10 The protocol used to transfer files across a network is the _____.

Answers

1 *PDC (Primary Domain Controller).* See "Domain controller."

2 *Router.* Review "Passing around the signals."

3 *Networked.* Look up "Working on a Networked PC."

4 *RJ-45 and BNC.* Check out "Just call me NIC."

5 *MAC (media access control).* Take a look at "Addressing the network."

6 *IP (Internet Protocol) address.* Study "Addressing the network."

7 *ATZ.* See "AT commands."

8 *TCP/IP.* Connect to "Protocols and other niceties."

9 *DNS (Domain Name System) or WINS (Windows Internet Naming Service).* Review "Addressing protocols and services."

10 *FTP (File Transfer Protocol).* Check out "Protocols and other niceties."

The Hardware Side of Networking

A network is two or more computers that have been connected together for the purposes of exchanging data and sharing resources. Networked shared resources range from printers, CD-ROMs, and modems to files and hard disks. Networks vary in size and scope.

Many types of computer networks exist, but you need only be concerned with the following:

- **Peer-to-peer network:** This type of network includes two or more PCs connected to share data files, a printer, or other resources.

- **Local area network (LAN):** A small business or corporate department may install a LAN interconnecting from two to hundreds of PCs, using permanently installed cabling or perhaps a wireless technology.

- **Wide area networks (WAN):** A corporation may maintain a WAN using dial-up, leased, or other dedicated communication means.

Also be familiar with the following network terminology and characteristics:

- **Topology:** The geometric arrangement of any network is its topology. The most common topologies are the bus, star, and ring topologies.

- **Protocol:** To operate efficiently, any communications-based system must have an established set of rules — its *protocol* — to govern its operation. Popular protocols for LANs are Ethernet, token ring, and FDDI.

- **Data packets:** Data, messages, and tokens that are transmitted on any network must conform to the size and format prescribed under the network's protocol. Data packets also vary between network operating systems (NOS) on the same protocol.

- **Architecture:** Any network can be classified as either a peer-to-peer or client/server architecture. When all nodes on a network are equal and resources are shared equally, the network is a true peer-to-peer network. When one computer is designated to host programs or files for the rest of the network, it is a server, and the other nodes are clients.

- **Media:** Nodes on a network are connected by twisted-pair copper wire, coaxial cable, fiber-optic cable, or wireless radio wave connections.

- **Server:** A network computer from which workstations (clients) access and share files, printers, communications, and other services. Servers can be dedicated to a single service, such as file servers, print servers, application servers, Web servers, and so on. Servers can also be the software that performs, controls, or coordinates a service or resource.

- **Node:** Any addressable network point, including workstations, peripherals, or other network devices. The term *node* is commonly used interchangeably with workstation.

> ✔ **Workstation:** A personal computer that runs application or utility software and uses data stored locally or provided by a network server to which it is connected by a cable or media. Workstations are also known as clients.

The network's domains

A domain has several different uses. The three common uses of domain in networking are the following:

> ✔ **Windows NT/2000 domain:** A group of network servers and devices that appear to end-users as a single network.
>
> ✔ **Internet domain:** An element of the Domain Name Server (DNS) naming hierarchy.
>
> ✔ **NetWare domain:** The memory segment within NetWare used to separate NetWare Loadable Modules (NLMs) from the operating system.

Internet domains

The highest level of domains defined by the DNS is standardized to group domain names by the type of organization or geographical location. The top-level Internet domains are

> ✔ **.com:** for companies intending to make a profit (such as `hungryminds.com`)
>
> ✔ **.edu:** for schools, colleges, and universities (such as `purdue.edu`)
>
> ✔ **.gov:** for the not-secret government agencies (such as `whitehouse.gov`)
>
> ✔ **.int:** for international organizations outside of the U.S. (such as `europa.eu.int`)
>
> ✔ **.mil:** for the U.S. Armed Forces (such as `pentagon.mil`)
>
> ✔ **.net:** for networking services providers (such as `innw.net`)
>
> ✔ **.org:** for charitable and other nonprofit organizations (such as `redcross.org`)

Network domains

Servers and workstations are classified into domains by the role they play on the network. Network domains and their controllers and the names of the resources in a domain are important things to know for the exam:

Domain controller

In the context of a Windows NT Server or Windows 2000 Server network, a domain is a collection of hardware and software resources and the user accounts that have access to them. The resources may include multiple servers, printers, CD-ROM drives, RAID, and other devices attached to the network.

On a domain, one server is designated as the Primary Domain Controller (PDC) and manages user logons and the permissions assigned to the domain resources. One or more of the other servers on the network are designated as a Backup Domain Controller (BDC). The BDC serves as a backup controller to the PDC, but also maintains the user account database for the network. Like the first runner-up in a beauty pageant, a BDC can be promoted to PDC if the PDC is for some reason unable to fulfill its official duties.

Share names

Resources are made available to the domain through share names, which are assigned by the network administrator. To access any resource on a domain, a user needs two things: the appropriate access permissions and the share name of the device. For example, a printer shared over the network may be named GUTENBURG, the PDC named BUSH, and the BDC named CHENEY. These names are then used to access these devices over the network. Share names provide network users with an easily remembered reference to use in lieu of physical hardware addresses. I cover share names more in "Sharing print and file services" later in this chapter.

Hello, I'll be your server

Several types of servers can exist on a network, each one performing a different task for the network and its workstations. A server is usually thought of as a computer, but a server is actually the software that performs, controls, or coordinates a service or resource. One computer can physically house many different software servers. To network clients, each server can appear to be a completely separate device, when that is not usually the case. Table 22-1 lists the most common types of servers implemented on a network.

Table 22-1	Server Types
Function	*Description*
File server	Stores network users' data files
Print server	Manages the printers connected to the network and the printing of user documents on the network printers
Communications server	Handles many common communications functions for the network, such as e-mail, fax, or Internet services
Application server	Shares network-enabled versions of common application software and eliminates the need for software to be installed on each workstation
Database server	Manages a common database for the network, handling all data storage, database management, and requests for data

A network devices primer

The A+ Core Hardware exam focuses on the hardware used to connect a PC to a network, which boils down to the network interface card (NIC) and the cabling to which it attaches. Other hardware devices are used on a network to improve its performance or to provide an interface between different types of networks, and you should at least review these for background.

Cabling the network

In order for one computer to carry on a conversation with another computer, both computers must be able to transmit and receive electrical impulses representing commands or data. The computers and peripherals of a network are interconnected with a transmission medium to enable data exchange and resource sharing. Cable media has laid the foundation on which networks grew — literally.

Although near and dear to my heart, wireless networks are not included on the A+ exams.

Primarily three types of cabling are used on most networks:

- **Coaxial (coax) cable:** Similar to the cable used to connect your TV set to the cable television service. Two types of coaxial cable are used on networks: thick coaxial cable (commonly called 10Base5, thickwire, or thicknet) and thin coaxial cable (10Base2, thinwire, or thinnet).

- **Twisted pair (no, not the upstairs neighbors) cable:** Available in two types: unshielded twisted pair (UTP) and shielded twisted pair (STP). UTP, which is by far the most commonly used network cabling, is similar to the wiring used to connect your telephone.

    For use in networks, unshielded twisted pair (UTP) is clearly the most commonly used. UTP is referred to in many different ways: 10BaseT or 100BaseT, Cat 3 or Cat 5, or simply as Ethernet wire. These all translate loosely to "The moon is made of green iMacs," but they all refer to copper twisted pair wiring.

    You may encounter some terminology relating to twisted pair copper wiring on the exams. Don't worry too much about the really technical issues surrounding each term.

- **Fiber-optic cable:** Glass or polymer fibers carry modulated pulses of light to represent digital data signals. Although a few different types of fiber-optic cables exist, you care about only one specific kind, and it's generally referred to as fiber-optic. Fiber-optic is also known as 10BaseF or 100BaseF.

Passing around the signals

Here are descriptions of the networking terms you may encounter on the A+ exams. These devices play a key role in the performance of the network. You don't need to memorize them, but understand how they're used.

- **Repeater:** An electronic echo machine that has no other function other than to retransmit whatever it hears, literally in one ear and out the other. A repeater is used to extend the signal distance of the cable by regenerating the signal.

- **Hub:** Used to connect workstations and peripheral devices to the network. Each workstation or device is plugged in to one of the hub's ports. A hub receives a signal from one port and passes it on to all of its other ports and therefore to the device or workstation attached to the port. For example, if an eight-port hub receives a signal on port 4, it immediately passes the signal to ports 1, 2, 3, 5, 6, 7, and 8. Hubs are common to Ethernet networks.

- **Bridge:** Used to connect two different LANs or two similar network segments to make them operate as though they were one network. The bridge builds a bridging table of physical device addresses that is used to determine the correct bridging or MAC (Media Access Control) destination for a message. Because a bridge sends messages only to the part of the network on which the destination node exists, the overall effect of a bridge on a network is reduced network traffic and a reduction of message bottlenecks.

- **Router:** Routes data across networks using the logical or network address of a message to determine the path it should take to arrive at its destination.

Too many workstations broadcasting too many messages to the whole network causes a *broadcast storm*. A router helps prevent broadcast storms by routing messages only to certain segments of the network.

- **Switch:** A switch is a device that segments a network. The primary difference between a hub and a switch is that a switch does not broadcast incoming messages to all ports, but instead sends it out only to the port on which the addressee workstation exists based o a MAC table created by listening to the nodes on the network.

- **Gateway:** A combination of hardware and software that enables two networks with different protocols to communicate with one another. A gateway is usually a dedicated server on a network because it typically requires large amounts of system resources. Three different types of gateways exist:

    - **Address gateway:** Connects networks with different directory structures and file management techniques.

    - **Protocol gateway:** Connects networks that use different protocols. This is the most common type of gateway.

- **Format gateway:** Connects networks using different data format schemes, for example, one using the American Standard Code for Information Interchange (ASCII) and another using Extended Binary-Coded Decimal Interchange Code (EBCDIC).

Just call me NIC

The network interface card (NIC), also known as a network adapter, is central to the concepts of networking covered on the A+ exams.

The NIC is a physical and logical link for a PC to a network. It is installed inside the computer in an open expansion slot. NICs are available for most of the expansion bus architectures, so getting a card for an available slot is easy. However, the most common bus used for NICs is the PCI (Peripheral Component Interconnect), but many legacy ISA (industry standard architecture) cards are still in use.

When choosing a NIC for a system, try to get one that is Plug and Play (PnP) compatible to make setup easier. Even with PnP, a network card can be a pain to set up. Some NICs use DIP switches or jumpers, and some use software to configure its identity and compatibility to the network.

The setup needed for the NIC is controlled by two factors: the PC itself and the NOS (network operating system, such as Windows NT/2000 or Novell NetWare). If you have the choice, do yourself a big favor and use the same brand and model NIC in every PC on the network. Mixing NICs on a network can be a pain, and you know where.

The NIC is a translator that works between the network and the PC. Networks transmit data in a serial data format (one bit at a time), and the data bus of the PC moves data in a parallel format (eight bits at a time). The NIC acts as a go-between to convert the signal from serial-to-parallel or parallel-to-serial, depending on its direction. The NIC also formats the data as required by the network architecture.

The NIC attaches a PC or other networked device to the network cabling and the network system. The primary purposes of the NIC are to serve as a transceiver, a device that transmits and receives data to and from other NICs (installed in the other networked nodes and devices), and to connect to the network cabling. Here are a few NIC characteristics you should know:

- ✔ **MAC (Media Access Control) address:** Each NIC is physically encoded with a unique identifying address that is used to locate it on the network. This address is 48 bits (6 bytes) long.

- ✔ **System resources:** A NIC is configured to the computer with an IRQ, an I/O address, and a DMA channel. A NIC commonly uses IRQ3, IRQ5, or IRQ10, and an I/O address of 300h.

- ✔ **Data bus compatibility:** NICs are designed with compatibility to a particular data bus architecture. ISA (Industry Standard Architecture) and PCI (Peripheral Components Interconnect) cards are the most common.

- ✔ **Data speed:** The NIC card must be compatible to the data speed of the network. The data transfer speeds of a network are determined by several factors, including the cable media, the topology, and the network connectivity devices in use. For example, a token ring network uses STP cable — the workstations attach to the network through MAUs (Multistation Access Units) — and typically runs at either 4Mbps or 16Mbps. An Ethernet network uses UTP cable (or coax), attaches its workstations through hubs or switches, and most commonly runs at either 10Mbps or 100Mbps. Many NICs have the ability to sense the data speed in use. A NIC designated as a 10/100 NIC has the ability to autosense between a 10Mbps and a 100Mbps network.

- ✔ **Connectors:** Several different connectors are used to connect NICs to network cabling. The type of connector depends mostly on the type of cable in use. Coax cabling primarily uses a BNC (for which they are several alleged meanings, none of which you need to know for the A+ exams) connector. Fiber-optic cabling is rarely used for cabling to workstations because of its cost. The most commonly used connector for networking is the RJ-45 connector, which is very much like the connector on your telephone, only a little bigger.

Working with NICs

An objective in the Networking domain of the A+ Core Hardware exam is that you can determine that a PC is networked before working on it. This requires special considerations and actions on your part. Not recognizing that the PC is on a network can result in damage to the PC and possibly to the network, including:

- ✔ Reduced bandwidth (the data transmission capacity and capability of the network) on the network caused by a faulty NIC signal or improperly set NIC

- ✔ A loss of data caused by an interruption in the network structure

- ✔ A slowdown in the general operation of the network

Some of the ways you can determine whether a PC is networked are:

- ✔ Look at the back of the PC for a network port with a cable attached to it. If you find one, you have a winner — a networked PC.

- ✔ If a network cable is not attached to the back of the PC, it doesn't mean it is not a networked PC; the customer may have already disconnected it. You can ask the customer.

✔ If no network cable exists, check to see whether a NIC is installed. No NIC — no network. However, if a NIC is in the PC, you can make other checks to determine whether the PC is networked.

✔ If you have access to the hard disk, search it for the telltale signs that the PC has been networked: folders or directories with names like NWCLIENT. Or look in AUTOEXEC.BAT or CONFIG.SYS for entries that start networking clients. (This is especially true for Novell software, which places entries in these files.)

✔ If you have access to Windows 9*x* or 2000, use the Windows Explorer to look for network drives. They usually have drive designators of E, F, or higher.

If you determine that the PC is a part of network, follow the steps in Lab 22-1 before and after repairing or replacing hardware on the PC.

Lab 22-1   Working on a Networked PC

1. **Check to see whether the PC is logged on to the network.**

   Open a drive or folder on a network device. If you can open a file, the PC is logged on. If the drive is not available, the PC may be a node, but it is not logged into the network.

2. **If you are working on the hard disk, make a backup of all files.**

   Especially important is backing up any networking information on the hard disk.

3. **Log off the PC as necessary.**

4. **Disconnect the network cable from the NIC card and proceed with the repair of the PC.**

5. **After the repair is complete, reconnect the network cable, verify that the network files are on the disk, and restore them if needed.**

6. **Ask the customer to log on to the network to verify that all is well.**

Installing and configuring a NIC

Although many manufacturers now include a NIC as a standard device in newer PC configurations, not every PC comes with a NIC installed. This is why the A+ Core Hardware exam expects you to be able to install and configure a NIC in a PC.

A NIC is installed in a PC to connect it to the network, or when a PC's NIC has gone bad. Lab 22-2 details the steps used to install a NIC in a PC.

Lab 22-2   Installing a NIC in a PC

1. **If the PC already has a NIC installed, and even if it is the very same manufacturer and model, uninstall the NIC from the operating system.**

   See Lab 22-4 later in the chapter for instructions on uninstalling a NIC from a Windows system. If the PC does not have a NIC installed, you must determine the type of slot available for the NIC. On most newer PCs expansion slots are usually available.

   If a PCI slot is open, obtain a PCI card, otherwise you'll need to use an ISA or EISA (Enhanced ISA) card depending on the expansion slots available, see Figure 22-1. You need to identify these expansion slots by sight on the exam, so take a very good look at this figure.

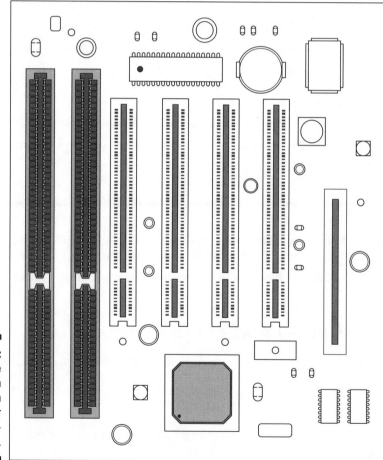

Figure 22-1:
The expansion slots on most newer PC motherboards.

2. **Before inserting the card in a slot, study its documentation to determine if any physical configuration steps are necessary.**

   Most PCI cards are Plug and Play but may still require a DIP switch or a jumper to be set. You absolutely want to do this before. Be sure to handle the card only by its nonconnecting edges.

3. **Open the case and install the NIC in the appropriate expansion slot.**

   Of course, I am assuming that you are wearing your ESD protection and you used the steps in Lab 22-1 to disconnect the PC from the network.

   The remainder of the installation, aside from replacing the case, is performed on the operating system. Lab 22-3 details the steps used to configure a NIC on a Windows system.

Please Accept My Topologies

Imagine an aerial view of a network. Picture the network's general shape. The pattern of connections that tie the workstations to the network is its *topology*. Here are the topologies you may encounter on the A+ exams:

- ✔ **Ethernet:** Or bus topology, uses a full range of network media (using copper or fiber optics) and operates at either 10 Mbps or 100 Mbps. The 100 Mbps Ethernet is called Fast Ethernet. An Ethernet network (LAN) can support about 500 nodes. This is the most commonly installed type of network, probably because it is the cheapest and simplest. Ethernet devices connect to either a hub or a switch that is connected to the network backbone.

- ✔ **FDDI:** (I've heard this pronounced as *fiddy,* but it's usually just spelled out.) Stands for Fiber Distributed Data Interface. A FDDI NIC contains a laser or diode transceiver that converts its digital data into light to be transmitted on a fiber-optic network or back to a digital signal from incoming light impulses for use by the PC. FDDI is a standard of the ANSI and the International Standards Organization (ISO) for data networks using ring topology and data speeds of 100 Mbps.

- ✔ **Token Ring:** Or ring topology, which also uses copper and fiber-optic cabling, operates at 4 Mbps to 16 Mbps, and supports about 260 nodes. A token ring network operates very reliably but can be a bear to troubleshoot. Because IBM is involved with the exams now, look for at least one token ring question.

Connecting a workstation to the network

Each network topology is associated with a network technology or protocol. Ethernet networking is the most common on a bus topology, and Token Ring is the most common on a ring structure.

The network technology in use is important because when you connect a PC to the network for the first time, you need to know the network identity requirements for a new workstation.

Addressing the network

The three addressing elements used on a network that you should know are

- ✔ **MAC (media access control) address:** Every NIC or network adapter is assigned a unique-to-the-world ID (called the MAC address) by its manufacturer when it is made. This address is burned into its firmware and cannot be changed. The MAC address is the basis for all network addressing and all other address types are cross-referenced to it. A MAC address is a 48-bit address that is expressed as 12 hexadecimal digits (4 bits to a hex digit). Figure 22-2 is the WINIPCFG command display showing the MAC address (Adapter address) of a NIC, which in this case is 44-45-53-54-00-00.

    To display this box on a Windows PC, enter WINIPCFG in the Start Run box.

- ✔ **IP (Internet protocol) address:** Many internal and all external networks use IP addresses to identify nodes on both LANs and WANs. An IP address for a network workstation combines the address of the network and the node into a 32-bit address that is expressed in four 8-bit octets (which means sets of eight). Figure 22-3 shows the results of the IPCONFIG command that displays the IP addressing information for a workstation. To run this command, open a command prompt and enter IPCONFIG on the command line.

    IPCONFIG displays the IP address assigned to the workstation (in this case, 192.168.1.100), its subnet mask (which is used to determine which part of the network the workstation is located), and the default gateway of the node.

- ✔ **Network names:** The most common form of a network name is the share name assigned to a workstation and is used to identify it to other network users who want to share its resources over the LAN. The most common network name used on a Windows network is the NetBIOS (Network Basis Input/Output System) name, which is a unique 15-character name that is periodically broadcasted over the network so that the Network Neighborhood function can catalog them. The NetBIOS name is the one that shows up on the Windows Network Neighborhood.

Addressing protocols and services

Many protocols and services can be used on a network to aid in the correlation and translation of one address form to another. The ones you need to know for the A+ exam are the following:

Figure 22-2:
The
WINIPCFG
command
can be used
to display
the MAC
(Adapter)
address of a
PC's NIC.

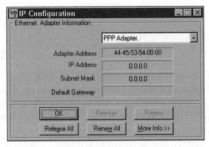

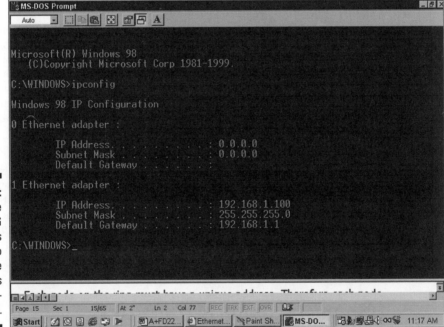

Figure 22-3:
The
IPCONFIG
command is
used to
display the
IP address
configura-
tion of a PC.

✔ **DHCP (Dynamic Host Configuration Protocol):** This is a protocol used to automatically configure a network workstation with its IP address data. Each time the workstation is logged on to the network, the DHCP server software, running on a network server or router, assigns or renews the IP configuration of the workstation. Typically, the address assigned is from blocks of IP addresses that have been set aside for use by internal networks. Depending on the network operating system, IPCONFIG or WINIPCFG can be used to view, renew, or release DHCP data.

✔ **DNS (Domain Name System):** DNS is used to resolve (translate) Internet names to their IP address equivalents. For example, when you request www.hungryminds.com from your browser's location line, a nearby DNS server (typically at your ISP), converts it to an IP address, such as 12.168.1.100, which is then used to request the data across the Internet.

✔ **WINS (Windows Internet Naming Service):** WINS is Microsoft's network name resolution software that converts NetBIOS names to IP addresses. Windows machines are assigned NetBIOS names (see "Addressing the network" earlier in this section), which are converted into IP addresses for use on a network using TCP/IP (Transmission Control Protocol/ Internet Protocol), the foundation protocol suite of the Internet. The use of a WINS server allows nodes on one LAN segment to find nodes on other LAN segments by name.

Connecting to an Ethernet network

When a new workstation is added to an Ethernet network, it identifies itself using its MAC address and computer name to the rest of the network. Those devices that need to hold this addressing information, such as a switch or bridge, store it in their MAC address tables. When requests come in for a particular IP address, the MAC address of the node is looked up and the message is sent to that workstation. Before you bury me in e-mails, please understand that this is highly simplified, but represents the essence of what happens.

Connecting to a Token Ring network

When you add a new node to a Token Ring network, it must establish first that its address is unique. The workstation sends out test frames with its ID address and the system responds with its own test frames sent to that address. If no other node responds (oops), the new ID address is accepted and established for the new ring node. If there is a duplication (it can happen), jumpers or DIP switches on the NIC can be used to alter the address.

Protocols and other niceties

In addition to the three network protocols described earlier in this chapter (Ethernet, token ring, and FDDI), other protocols can be used to interconnect PCs to other PCs or networks. For the test, you need to know their names, acronyms, and the scope of what they interconnect. Table 22-2 lists other protocols that you may find on the A+ exams.

Table 22-2	Networking and Communications Protocols	
Protocol/Layer	*Acronym*	*What It Does*
Point-to-Point Protocol	PPP	Used to connect and manage network communications over a modem
Transmission Control	TCP/IP	The backbone protocol of the Protocol/Internet Protocol Internet
Internetwork Packet Exchange/Sequenced	IPX/SPX	The standard protocol of the Novell network operating systems Packet Exchange
NetBIOS Extended User Interface	NetBEUI	A Microsoft protocol that is used only by Windows systems for LANs with no external connections; does not support routing (addressing through a router to other networks)
File Transfer Protocol	FTP	Used to send and receive files in client/server mode to or from a remote host
Hypertext Transfer Protocol	HTTP	Used to send World Wide Web (WWW) documents, which are usually encoded in HTML across a network
Network File Services	NFS	Allows the network node to access network drives as if they were local drives, files, and data; also performs the file access and data retrieval tasks requested of the network
Simple Mail Transfer Protocol	SMTP	Used to send electronic mail (e-mail) across a network
Telnet	Telnet	Used to connect and log in to a remote host

Dialing up a network

Modems don't hold the vaulted position on the A+ Core Hardware exam they have in the past, but expect to see questions on the exam about installing, configuring, and troubleshooting a modem, both internal and external.

Modem facts you should know

A modem (which is an acronym for modulator/demodulator) converts the digital data signal of the PC into the analogy data signal used on the plain old telephone system (POTS), which is also called the public telephone switched network (PTSN). Modems can be installed inside the PC in an expansion slot or attached to the PC externally through a serial or USB port.

You may hear or have heard of modems for other types of communications besides dialing into a network, such as an ISDN (Integrated Services Digital Network) modem or a DSL (Digital Subscriber Line) modem. You don't need to know about these for the A+ exam and they're not really modems anyway.

Modem types

The two general types of modems are the following:

- ✔ **Standard modem:** A standard modem can be an internal or external device. It can also be Plug and Play or legacy. Standard modems are operating system neutral and use generic device drivers.

- ✔ **Windows modem:** A Windows modem is an internal Plug and Play device that requires a device driver provided by the Windows operating system to function properly.

The best way to differentiate one type of modem from another is by reading the documentation that came with the system or visiting the manufacturer's Web site.

Internal versus external modems

An internal modem is installed like any other expansion card — into a compatible expansion slot. Modern modems do not require physical configuration, but some have DIP switches or jumpers to be set. Most of the configuration of the modem is done through the operating system, which is covered later in the chapter (see "Setting up a modem").

Modems use serial communications modes, which are explained in detail in Chapter 11. Be sure to read up on flow control and full- and half-duplexing.

AT commands

One modem topic that continues to be included on the A+ exam, although I'm not sure why in today's world of software configuration tools and Plug and Play modems, is the AT command set. AT does not mean Advanced Technology as it would with a motherboard or power supply. On a modem, AT refers to "attention" which is used to precede each command given to the modem from the AT command set.

The AT command set, which is officially know as the Hayes Standard AT Command Set, is used to drive and configure Hayes compatible modems. For the A+ Core Hardware exam, you should know the AT commands listed in Table 22-3.

Table 22-3	AT Modem Commands
Command	*Action*
AT DT XXX-XXXX	Dial the telephone number using touch-tone dialing
AT H	On hook (hang up)
AT L	Speaker loudness (volume)
AT Z	Reset the modem to default settings

There are other commands that can be used to control the modem during the dialing process. For example, if you are in an office or hotel where it is necessary to dial a 9 to get an outside line that can be entered into the string, along with pauses to wait for the second dial tone. For example, to dial out of an office the following command string might be used:

```
AT DT 9,,15095551212 (which means AT Dial TouchTone 9 pause
                 pause and the phone number).
```

Troubleshooting a modem connection

If the internal modem will not begin the dialup process, the problem is probably either a resource conflict or a device driver problem. Modems do not have a default IRQ assignment and must use an unassigned IRQ or share one with another device, such as a USB controller. Often an updated, newer version of a device driver can solve a modem/operating system conflict.

An external modem uses the resources assigned to the COM port it uses. Conflicts can arise when both an external modem and an internal device have both been assigned to the same IRQ. To remedy this situation, move the external modem's connector to a different COM port or reassign the internal device.

To check the resources and drivers assigned to a modem, use the System Information applet accessed from the Start⇨Programs⇨Accessories⇨ System Tools menus. Figure 22-4 illustrates the information available on the System Information display.

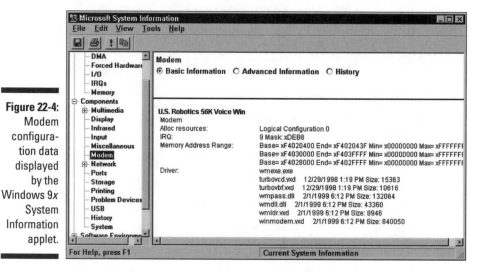

Figure 22-4:
Modem
configura-
tion data
displayed
by the
Windows 9*x*
System
Information
applet.

If the system has not detected the modem on startup after installing an internal modem, use the Add New Hardware icon on the Control Panel to start the New Hardware Wizard. Should that fail, open the system case, reseat the modem or move it to another open slot and reboot.

Connecting to a server

Windows NT and Windows 2000 Server support Remote Access Services (RAS), which is the service used to manage and control incoming dialup connections. Not all dialup access is made to Internet providers. A remote user may need to dial up the RAS services of a corporate server and log on to the corporate LAN and gain access to the WAN.

The Software Side of Networking

The OS Technologies exam also has an objective domain dedicated to networking. Although there is some overlap between it and the Networking domain on the Core Hardware exam, the OS Technologies exam focuses on the tools available in the Windows operating system to set up, configure, and access PCs on a local network. Expect about 8 to 12 questions on the OS Technologies exam from this area.

Setting up a modem

Any Windows 9*x* PC that uses a modem to connect to a network — whether it is a LAN, WAN, or the Internet — uses dial-up networking (DUN) to make the connection. DUN creates PPP connection between two computers over a telephone line. In effect, PPP causes the modem to act like a network interface card. PPP is the telephone line protocol that transports the actual network protocol over the telephone lines to carry out the network interaction by the connected PCs.

Dial-up networking automatically installs the Dial-Up Adapter (no abbreviation for this one) and the Client for Microsoft Networks (this one either). These tools carry out the network dialogue by configuring the outgoing data packets to fit the protocol of the remote network (whether it is NetBEUI, IPX/SPX, or TCP/IP) and translate the incoming data packets from the network protocol for local use. The remote network in this case is the network you have connected to using DUN. In order to communicate with it or any of its workstations, servers, or features, you must speak its language (protocol). DUN, Dial-Up-Adapter, and the Client for Microsoft Networks are the tools used to translate your messages into the format and form that can be understood by the remote network, and vice versa.

Virtually all PCs come with an internal modem installed. However, you may need to upgrade a PC by installing an internal modem or replace a faulty or outdated modem. After the modem has been physically installed, use the steps in Lab 22-3 to configure the modem in Windows.

Lab 22-3   Configuring a Modem on a Windows PC

1. **Open the My Computer window to determine if DUN is installed.**

   If Dial-up Networking is not already installed, insert the Windows distribution CD-ROM in the CD-ROM drive, open the Control Panel, and choose Add/Remove Program icon. When the Add/Remove Program window displays, select the Windows Setup tab. Double-click on the Communications option, and click the box to the left of Dial-up Networking to place a check in the box. Click OK on this and the next box to load the DUN files to the PC. When the installation is complete, click OK to restart the PC.

2. **Make a new connection by opening the My Computer window and double-clicking the Dial-up Networking icon. Assuming you need to create a new connection, double-click the Make New Connection icon, which starts the Make New Connection Wizard, of all things.**

   If the Wizard tells you that the modem you just installed is not recognized, don't take it personally; just agree to let Windows try to detect the modem again.

3. **Enter the dialing data from the user's ISP and contact the ISP's technical support for the dialing (and connection information) information needed to set up the connection, including the phone number to be dialed by the modem.**

4. **Create the PC's identification by opening the Control Panel and selecting the Network icon. Choose the Identification tab.**

Ask the user to give the computer a name, a workgroup, and a description. Entering this information updates the device information database and requires a system restart.

5. **To configure the network, open the Control Panel, select the Network icon, and choose the Configuration tab. Click the Add button. On the window that displays next, highlight the Protocol selection and click its Add button to display the Select Network Protocol window (see Figure 22-5). Highlight Microsoft and find TCP/IP in the right pane. Click OK to return to the Network window and OK to exit the window.**

Figure 22-5:
The Select Network Protocol window is used to add new dialup or network protocols to a Windows PC.

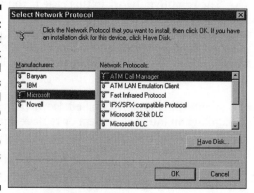

6. **Configure the protocol.**

Open the My Computer window and double-click the Dial-up Networking folder. Right-click the icon of the connection just created and choose Properties. Select the Server Types tab, and click the TCP/IP button near the right bottom corner to open the TCP/IP settings dialog box (see Figure 22-6). The settings on this box should be verified with the ISP or the network administrator, depending on the use of the modem and the network to which it is connecting. However, except for the IP addresses, which are unique to each ISP, the settings shown in Figure 22-6 are fairly typical.

Configuring a PC for network connection

Windows 2000 automatically configures a PC with a typical network setup during its installation processes. However, a Windows 9*x* PC does not have that feature and the software side of the configuration must be performed by hand. Actually, the NIC is configured to the network. The PC communicates only to the NIC through its device driver.

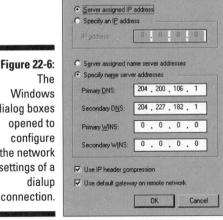

Figure 22-6:
The
Windows
dialog boxes
opened to
configure
the network
settings of a
dialup
connection.

The Network window (see Figure 22-7) is used to configure a PC's network environment. Four network components can be configured from the Network window. They are the following:

- ✔ **Adapter:** This choice identifies and loads the device drivers for a NIC. To configure a PC to a network, a NIC must be installed.

- ✔ **Protocol:** To communicate with a network, the PC must be using the same protocols as the network.

- ✔ **Client:** Network clients allow a PC to communicate with specific network operating systems, such as Windows NT, Windows 2000, or Novell NetWare. To communicate with the network, a PC must have at least one client configured.

- ✔ **Service:** Network services include specialized drivers that facilitate specialized capabilities, such as File and Print Sharing, and support for file systems on non-Windows systems.

Configuring a network adapter

When we last checked in on our old buddy NIC, he was just settling into his new home in a PCI or ISA expansion slot. Having NIC settled in his new home is fine, but that's only half the job of getting the PC connected to the network. Expect a question or two about adding devices to a Windows PC. The device in the question may not be a NIC, but beyond a few specific pieces of data, adding a NIC is like adding any hardware device.

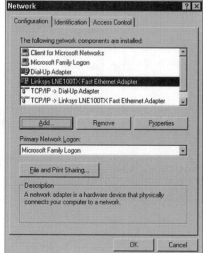

Figure 22-7:
The
Windows 98
Network
window is
used to
configure a
NIC.

That NIC card you just installed in your PC probably sat on a store or warehouse shelf just long enough for its device drivers to become obsolete. So, even though a disk is included with the card and Windows has an extensive library of NIC card drivers, always check with the manufacturer (online or by voice) to see if a later version is available.

After you are sure that you have the latest driver, there are three ways you can install the NIC from the software point of view:

- ✔ **Plug and Play:** If the NIC is a PnP device, it should be automatically configured after physically installing it when you restart the PC. If Windows cannot identify the adapter, you are prompted to insert a disk with the device driver on it.

- ✔ **Add New Hardware:** This wizard, which is started from the Control Panel, searches for and detects the new NIC.

- ✔ **Add adapter:** Use the Add button on the Configuration tab of the Network window to add the adapter to the PC.

Labs 22-4 and 22-5 detail the steps involved to configure a PC (actually its NIC) to a network and to uninstall a PC from a network. To prepare you for Lab 22-4, I am assuming that you have already physically installed the NIC in an expansion slot on the motherboard, and it has been properly configured with the system resources (IRQ, I/O addresses, and so on), and no conflicts exist, so you are ready to do the software configuration of the NIC.

Lab 22-4   Configuring a PC (NIC) for a Network

1. **Click the Start⇨Settings⇨Control Panel.**

2. **From the Control Panel, double-click the Networks icon to open the Network window, shown in Figure 22-7.**

   An alternative path to the Network window is right-clicking the Network Neighborhood icon and choosing Properties.

3. **On the Configuration tab, double-click the adapter to open the Properties window for the NIC.**

   The Driver Type tab should indicate an Enhanced mode (32-bit and 16-bit) NDIS (Network Device Interface Specification) driver for the NIC. The other choices are for cards without 32-bit NDIS support or NICs requiring ODI (Open Data-Link Interface).

   On the Bindings tab, you'll find a list of the protocols and services for which a binding is established. In most cases the bindings are preconfigured, but they can be modified. *Binding* is a network term for two protocols that perform different networking functions that have an active connection. If you are on an Ethernet network that has access to the Internet, your bindings will reflect your NIC card with a binding to TCP/IP protocols.

   The contents of the Advanced tab vary by NIC and the characteristics of the network. The properties list may reflect the media and connector in use or it may be used to turn on a log file.

4. **Click any Apply or OK buttons that appear.**

   You are asked for other network information, IP address, gateway, and DNS. The user or the network administrator should provide this information. The system will update its information database, and you may be asked to restart the system.

Lab 22-5   Uninstalling a PC from a Network

1. **Open the Networks icon from the Control Panel.**

2. **Highlight the adapter and click Remove.**

   This breaks the bindings of the protocols and services from the network. You can remove the protocols and adapters by highlighting each and clicking Remove.

3. **Click OK and allow the system to restart.**

Navigating the neighborhood and a few new places

Windows 9*x* has Network Neighborhood, and Windows 2000 has My Network Places. In both cases, the icons are located on the Windows Desktop and can be used to display the PCs and resources on the same network segment as your PC. The Network Neighborhood and My Network Places icons work like the My Computer icon. My Computer shows you the resources on your PC, and My Network shows you the resources on the network.

The network display creates a tree structure of the resources on the local network similar to in the files are displayed the Windows Explorer. The Windows Explorer can also be used to display the network structure. Figure 22-8 shows the Network Neighborhood on a Windows 98 PC connected to a Windows 2000 server.

Figure 22-8:
The Network Neighborhood displayed on the Windows Explorer.

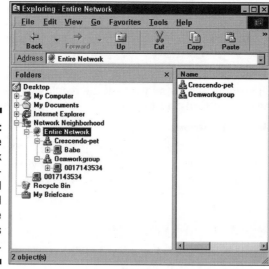

Many of the resources shown on the network are most likely directly available to you, such as printers, CD-ROMs, and modems. However, other networked PCs may not be accessible, and if they are, may require a password.

On those PCs to which you do have access, the files and resources for which you have permission to use display in the same tree structure used on the Windows Explorer. To open a file or access a device, double-click it.

Sharing print and file services

After a PC is configured as a part of a network, the user can grant other users on the network access to folders, files, or devices on the PC. Some minor dangers exist in sharing files, such as unknowingly sharing a virus across the network or others using your disk to save large files that would fill up their disk. However, this is an excellent way to avoid printing or copying files onto a disk in order to share a file or to share the wealth of that nifty new color laser printer you bought for yourself.

To set up file and printer sharing on a PC, follow these steps:

1. Double-click the Networks icon on the Control Panel.

2. Click the File and Printer Sharing button.

3. Select (place a check in the box) the option or both options you wish to enable. Your choices are "I want to be able to give others access to my files" and "I want to be able to allow others to print on my printer(s)." Notice the careful wording in these options. Just because you enable the options doesn't mean that all of your files and printers are immediately available to the world. You still need to grant permission and set up passwords.

4. Click OK a couple of times to close the boxes and restart the PC.

Sharing files

At this point, the File and Printer Sharing services are loaded, but nothing is really shared. To share files with other users on the network, use the following steps:

1. From the Windows Explorer, right-click any folder. Only folders can be shared. So, if you don't want to share all of the files in a folder, you'd better move the files you don't want to share to an unshared folder. Choose Sharing and complete the level of sharing and security you want for this folder. You may assign a password to read-only or to full-access levels of sharing.

2. Any share you create will appear on the Network Neighborhood under the PC's Computer Name, which is the name specified on the Identification tab of the Network properties window (the one opened from the Network icon on the Control Panel). If you want a more descriptive name, change it.

Sharing a printer

Here are the steps used to share a printer:

1. Open the Printers folder from either the Setting menu or the Control Panel.

2. Right-click the printer to be shared and choose Properties to display the properties window for the printer. Choose the Sharing tab.

3. On the Sharing tab, enter the share name of the printer and a password if you want to control who has access to the printer. Click OK.

4. The printer will not appear on the Network Neighborhood under the PC's name.

If you click the Network Neighborhood icon and no PCs are shown, check to see that you have enabled printer and file sharing and that other PCs on the network have also set up resources to be shared.

Keeping your finger on the network pulse

Windows 9x and Windows 2000 include a number of network monitoring and diagnostics tools that are used to troubleshoot and isolate network problems that directly affect a single PC. Here are the ones you should know for the exams:

- ✔ **IPConfig (IP Configuration):** This command line utility displays the current configuration for a PC connected to a TCP/IP network.

- ✔ **PING (Packet Internet Groper):** This Internet utility is used to determine whether an IP address is online or reachable. Either an IP address or a domain name can be pinged over a network.

- ✔ **TRACERT (Trace Route):** This TCP/IP utility is used to determine the path in use between one network point and another and if any problems exist along that path.

Working in the World of the Internet

For the A+ OS Technologies exam, you need an understanding of the basic protocols, terminology, and function of the Internet and how it is accessed. This includes all of the Internet's little protocol buddies — the ones known only by their initials.

Installing and configuring a browser

If you were to search the Web for "configuring a browser," and I did, you will find a long list of resources to help you configure a browser for everything from chat session tools, graphic tools, Telnet, and much more. Today's most popular browsers, Internet Explorer (www.microsoft.com), Netscape Navigator (http://home.netscape.com), and Opera (www.opera.com), are largely self-configuring. However, there are some areas where the configuration of the browser can affect the PC on which it is loaded. Here are the ones you should know for the exam:

- ✔ **Cached content:** To speed up the time required to display a downloaded Web page, browsers store the page and its objects in a disk cache on the hard disk. Internet Explorer (IE) calls this Temporary Internet Files. When you ask to see the page again, it is supplied from the cache, which speeds up the display and reduces the amount of bandwidth required to support your PC. By default the cache is emptied each time IE is started. However, you can change the caching settings so that the cache is never cleared, a page is never cached, or some setting in-between. One of the more important of the caching settings is the amount of the disk space you wish to assign to cache. If you have all the disk space in the world, then you can use more of the disk for caching, but if the PC is low on disk space, minimize the disk space used for Internet caching.

- ✔ **History files:** The History folder holds the addresses and links to sites you have visited on the Internet over a given time period. These links are displayed in the drop-down list of the Address line of the browser. Keeping a fewer number of days reduces the amount of disk space used for these links.

- ✔ **Players and handlers:** The latest releases of the most popular browsers include most of the players and handlers required for the majority of content on the Web. However, you may want to download customer players and handlers to display or playback the content on specific Web sites. The popular players and handlers are Adobe Acrobat (used to read PDF [portable data format] files), Flash (used to play Macromedia Flash animations), and Windows Media Player, Apple QuickTime, and RealPlayer (all used to play back streaming audio, video, and multimedia).

Connecting to the Internet

The process used to connect to the Internet relies on the connection configuration of a PC using either a dialup or network to connect. After the connection is made, the process is the same and the same protocols are in use.

Dialup connection

Dial-up Networking has a built-in dialer that invokes the necessary commands to the modem to dial the modems of the service provider and make a connection whenever an application, such as a browser or an e-mail client, is opened. The speed of a dialup connection is typically between 28.8 Kbps and 56 Kbps.

Dial-up networking uses PPP to send data packets over telephone lines. PPP picks up a packet that has been created by one of the other network protocols and which will be received by a remote PC running that same protocol. PPP is merely the intermediary that carries the data packet over the telephone line. If the packet begins the journey as a TCP/IP packet, it arrives at its destination as a TCP/IP packet.

An ISP typically assigns an IP address to PC though its NAS (network access services), or modem banks, and RADIUS (Remote Authentication Dial-In User Service) services, after a username and password combination is verified and the user is authenticated.

If a dialup connection will not connect, check the following areas:

- ✔ **Phone connection:** Nearly all modems use sound to enable the user to track the action of the connection (handshake) as it is being made. The first of these sounds is the dial tone from the phone line. If the modem is not connecting and you do not hear a dial tone, there is a problem with the wall jack connection or the phone line itself. Chances are that you will get an error message to the effect of no dial tone anyway.

- ✔ **Modem problems:** If the modem cannot complete the handshake with the other end, the modem might be configured incorrectly in terms of its character length, start and stop bits, and speed.

- ✔ **Protocols:** Another common problem, especially for new modems, is that TCP/IP or other protocols have not been properly configured. Dialup connections typically require the PPP protocol. Verify that the protocols are enabled and that the proper bindings are set for the protocols.

- ✔ **Remote response:** The NAS you are attempting to connect to might be down or having problems. Call the ISP to check.

- ✔ **Telephone company problems:** If there is sufficient static or crosstalk on the telephone line, it can cause the modem to disconnect very soon after completing the connection or cause enough data retransmissions that the line appears exceptionally slow.

Network connection

If a PC connects to the Internet through its LAN, its primary (or default) gateway is the router on the LAN that is used to connect to the WAN (Internet). The only real differences between establishing a dialup connection and a network connection is that the network connection remains in place and does not require a reconnection each time access is desired, and the user does not need to be authenticated except for secure services, such as e-mail or VPN (virtual private network). For more information on networking, read *Networking For Dummies,* by Doug Lowe and *Network+ Certification For Dummies,* by Ron Gilster (blush) both published by Hungry Minds, Inc.

IP addressing

IP addresses are four sets of numbers separated by periods (dots). An IP address is 32 bits long with each of the four numbers 8 bits long. The highest possible IP address is 255.255.255.255, because the highest value that can be represented in 8 bits is 255. Each of the four numbers is called an octet, which means a set of 8, and are referred to as the first, second, third, and fourth octets. Sounds a little like a singing group — the Octets and their new hit "Home, Home on the Domain."

IP addresses can be assigned as a static IP address (a fixed PC location) or as a dynamically assigned IP address (changeable). A static IP address is permanently assigned to a node when it is added to the network. Static IP addresses work as long as the network doesn't move, the NIC card is not interchanged with other PCs, or the network is never reconfigured. If a network will be reconfigured, however, it should use dynamically assigned IP addresses. Each time the PC is booted, the Dynamic Host Configuration Protocol (DHCP) server assigns it an IP address to use for that session. All versions of Windows 9*x* and Windows NT, and Windows 2000 have built-in DHCP clients.

Sharing an Internet connection

Internet Connection Sharing (ICS) is a feature included in Windows 98 SE and Windows 2000 Professional that allows home and small office users to share a single Internet connection. The type of connection isn't important, ICS assumes a network to be present and isn't fussy about the type of network or the media used.

ICS builds a type of LAN with one PC serving as the network gateway. The other PCs on the network use the gateway PC to connect to the Internet. The requirements are that each PC be connected to the gateway via a network connection and that a single modem, proxy server, DSL, ISDN, or other Internet connection line serves the entire network.

Prep Test

1 Which of the following are protocols in use in a dialup connection to the Internet? (Choose two.)

A ❏ ICMP

B ❏ PPP

C ❏ TCP/IP

D ❏ NetBEUI

2 The FRM responsible for converting the signal between the PC and the network media is the

A ◯ Router

B ◯ Bridge

C ◯ NIC

D ◯ Hub

3 A dialup connection to an ISP is successful but disconnects after a few seconds. What is possibly the problem? (Choose two.)

A ❏ The serial port UART is faulty

B ❏ Line noise on the telephone line

C ❏ Required protocols not configured

D ❏ The data speed of the line is too fast for the modem

4 The address 44-45-53-54-00-00 is an example of a(n)

A ◯ NetBIOS name

B ◯ IP address

C ◯ IPX address

D ◯ MAC address

5 A new PC is added to a token ring network. What will the network establish first?

A ◯ The unique ID of the new node

B ◯ MAC address

C ◯ IP address

D ◯ NetBIOS name

6 Also very popular on intranets, which of the following is the foundation protocol suite of the Internet?

A ○ TCP/IP

B ○ NetBEUI

C ○ IPX/SPX

D ○ NetBIOS

7 The protocol that automatically sets up the IP addressing configuration of network PCs is

A ○ TCP/IP

B ○ WINS

C ○ DHCP

D ○ DNS

8 UTP network cable typically has what type of connectors at each end?

A ○ RJ-45

B ○ RJ-11

C ○ AUI

D ○ BNC

9 The software service that resolves (translates) domain names on the Internet, such as www.hungryminds.com, to its IP address is

A ○ WINS

B ○ PING

C ○ DNS

D ○ DHCP

10 The Windows NT/2000 service that allows remote PCs to dial in is

A ○ PPP

B ○ IPX/SPX

C ○ RAS

D ○ MAU

Answers

1 **B, C.** PPP and TCP/IP are used to form network data into packets and transmit them from the sending to the receiving computer. PPP is used to encapsulate TCP/IP packets for transmission over the telephone line. *Review "Dialup connection."*

2 **C.** The NIC serves as an interface between the PC and the network. It is connected into both the PC and the network and translates the PC's data for transmission over the network and translates data from the network for transmission over the PC's bus. *Take a look at "Just call me NIC."*

3 **B, C.** Actually, there are many reasons, but of those listed, these are the best two. Line noise (static) and crosstalk on the telephone line are the cause of many connection problems, but without the appropriate protocols, the connection can't be held. *Check out "Dialup connection."*

4 **D.** This is a MAC (media access control) address, also known as a Layer 2 address (after the Data-Link Layer of the OSI Reference Model). *Study "Addressing the network."*

5 **A.** The token ring network requires each node to have a unique identity. Before the node is allowed to join the network, it must establish that its ID is unique. *See "Please Accept My Topologies."*

6 **A.** TCP/IP (Transmission Control Protocol/Internet Protocol) is actually a suite of protocols and services that form the foundation services of the Internet as well as most intranets. *Review "Getting down to specifics."*

7 **C.** DHCP (Dynamic Host Configuration Protocol) is used to configure network workstations with their IP addressing data. *Link up with "Addressing protocols and services."*

8 **A.** Looking like a big telephone connector, the RJ-45 connector is easy to work with and adapts well to use in buildings. *Review "Just call me NIC."*

9 **C.** Domain Name Service (DNS) is used to translate a domain name to its IP address or back again. *Take a look at "Addressing protocols and services."*

10 **C.** Remote Access Service (RAS) supports dial-up access to a Windows NT system. *Connect with "Connecting to a server."*

Part VI
The Part of Tens

The 5th Wave   By Rich Tennant

JERRY CRAMS FOR THE EMOTICON SECTION OF THE A+ CERTIFICATION EXAM.

@RICHTENNANT

Oo-I know this one! It's...uh...

C'mon Jerry. Over 800 more to go.

In this part . . .

After you have scheduled yourself to take the test, you can begin preparing for the test in earnest. This part includes some great places to get study guides, test demonstrations, and other information to help you prepare. Also included in this part is a list of things you should think about or do before, during, and after the test.

Chapter 23

Ten (Or So) Ways to Prepare for Your Test Day

. . . .

In This Chapter

▶ Get there early

▶ Review your lists

▶ Check in

▶ Write down memorized lists immediately

▶ Do the tutorial

▶ Take your time

▶ Relax

▶ Mark the difficult, move on to the easy

▶ Every question counts

▶ Celebrate in moderation

. . . .

Get to the Test on Time

When you schedule your exams, you are at the mercy of the testing center as to the time you can take the test. VUE (Virtual University Enterprises) and Prometrics are the two testing organizations that give the A+ Exams. The testing centers are commercial, governmental, or educational affiliates of these companies, but remember that the testing centers have another primary business.

The test center may have up to 8 testing stations. Your schedule must coincide with the testing center's hours of operation and the number of test stations available at any given time. The choice of the location, day, and time is up to you, within the operating times, days, and openings of the testing center. Of course, if you plan to take one of the boot camps being offered these days, your training company is likely also your testing center.

Schedule the test at a location and time that provides you a comfortable schedule to reach the testing center and at a time that does not put added pressure on you. Scheduling your exams when you know you'll be facing traffic jams is a bad idea.

Make sure that you arrive at the testing center at least one-half hour before your test time, or even earlier if you want to do some last-minute studying or cramming. The last thing you want is to be rushing to make the test appointment (that you set yourself, remember) and be agitated when you begin the test. Get there early, find a quiet place, relax, have a cup of coffee, tea, Postum, Mountain Dew, or whatever helps you relax, and go over the *A+ Certification For Dummies* Cheat Sheet and your notes.

Review Your Notes One Last Time

In the time right before you check in, review the things guaranteed to be on the test: IRQs and I/O addresses, processor specifications, hard disk configurations, memory allocations, laser printer operations, and the items marked with Remember and Instant Answer icons throughout this book. Trying to cram conceptual topics at the last minute is a bad idea, but going over the tables and bulleted lists in this book and from your notes is a good use of your time.

Check In on Time

A few minutes before your scheduled test time, check in with the test administrator. Be sure that you have the required two pieces of identification that you were asked to bring. One needs to be a picture ID, such as your driver's license, passport, or work badge (if it also has your signature on it). The second only needs to have your name on it. A credit card with your signature on the back or the like should do fine.

You can't carry your notes or books with you into the test area, so surrender them all willingly. Don't whimper or clasp your notes to your chest; keep yourself relaxed and focused on the test.

Do a Brain Dump, but Do It on the Paper

You're not allowed to bring your own paper into the testing center, but you will be supplied with two sheets (or more if you think you really need it) of paper. Some test centers give you a couple of sheets of plastic or a dry erase board and a dry erase pen. The writing materials issued to you must be surrendered immediately after the test. This prevents you from copying down the test during the exam time and sharing it later with your friends.

After you're situated at your test station and have been given your basic instructions, do a brain dump and unload all of the lists you memorized. Write down the sequences and special relationships, such as I/O addresses and IRQs, and the devices to which they are assigned. You can then refer to your notes during the exam without getting flustered about whether you're remembering something correctly.

Even if you're taking both exams on the same day, concentrate only on the test at hand. The tests are delivered online, and if you've never taken an online exam before, it is a good idea not to be sweating out the material on the first exam. However, when you pass your first exam, don't get overly confident about the second. The 2001 A+ exams overlap much less than the previous versions of the tests. In fact, almost nothing on the Core Hardware exam is repeated on the OS Technologies exam.

 Whether it is better to schedule the two tests on different days is really up to you. Some would advise you to schedule them a week apart so you can focus your studies on each test separately. It may be more difficult to take them together than in the past, but unless you absolutely must take them together because of travel or scheduling, give yourself a break. How far you must travel to take the exams can definitely be a factor. I had to drive 3.5 hours each way (uphill both ways, through the snow, in a Ford) to get to the testing center, which highly motivated me to take the tests together.

Do the Tutorial!

At the beginning of the test session, you will be offered a tutorial on the test from the test provider. Don't shortchange yourself by thinking that if you've seen one online test, you've seen them all. Take the time to casually move through the tutorial. Your time doesn't begin until you start the actual test, so the time you spend with the tutorial, which should be a minute or two tops, doesn't count against you.

The tutorial contains examples of each type of question included on the test. It also shows you how to display and hide illustrations and figures used with a question. Use the tutorial as a way to relax and get ready for the exam. There is nothing like answering that first question to settle your nerves, even if you can't really get it wrong.

Ready, Steady, Go

When you're ready to begin, take a deep breath, clear your head, and start the exam. You are allowed 75 minutes to answer the 70 questions on the Core Hardware exam and then 75 minutes for the 74 questions on the OS Technologies exam. If you're taking both exams on the same day, be sure you allow yourself around 3½ hours, including a break between the exams.

As you take the exam, notice that the time remaining is displayed in the upper right-hand corner of the display. Because CompTIA has decided not to use an adaptive format for these tests, you should have plenty of time to go back and review your answers at the end of the test. When the time is up, it is up! No finishing one last question; no nothing. When the test is over, it's over. So watch your time carefully.

Mark Questions You Want to Think About

The Prometric and VUE testing software allows you to mark questions with a checkbox in the upper left corner of the display for later review. If you aren't sure of an answer or flat don't know, mark it and come back to it. You just never know: Another question may trigger your memory or provide you with the answer (but don't count on that).

You may want to make a note on your scratch paper about why you marked the question:

✔ 33. Is it A or D? First impression is D.

✔ 41. B or D?

✔ 61. Isn't this asked a different way earlier in the test?

Avoid the temptation to mark every question. You don't need to mark a question to review it later. The test engine has the option to select all, if you really want to review the entire test (and have the time).

Answer Every Question

Some people recommend that you read the entire exam before you begin answering the questions. Don't waste your time! Instead, answer all the questions you're sure of and mark the ones you're not. If you're the least bit hesitant on a question, make your best guess and then mark it. This way you can't forget to answer it. Don't leave any questions unanswered. When in doubt, make as educated of a guess as you can, but give an answer. Blank is wrong!

Some questions require more than one answer, but don't worry about it. There are two surefire ways to tell if a question needs multiple answers. One, the radio button that is provided for each of the possible answers changes to a checkbox. The radio buttons allow only one response to be chosen, but the checkboxes allow multiple answers to be selected. The second way to tell if a question needs more than one response is that you are prompted to provide two (or three or four) responses. Plus, if you don't give enough answers, the question is flagged on the review screen as incomplete.

Chapter 24

Ten Really Great Sources for Study Aids

In This Chapter

▶ A+ exam study materials on the Web

▶ Other resources to prepare you for the A+ exams

*V*ariety is one of the keys to preparing for the A+ exams. By using a number of different study tools and aids, you will see the many different ways a question can be asked. This variety helps prepare you for the question formats that the A+ exams use. The Quick Assessments and Prep Tests included in each chapter of this book and the questions in the test engine on the CD are intended to help you gauge the areas you need to strengthen. However, you should try to use at least one other sample test set to gain another perspective of the exams.

A number of A+ Certification Web sites simulate the test content and format fairly accurately. Some are free and others cost slightly more. The free ones are certainly worth their cost; the others, well — *caveat emptor* (buyer beware). You need to balance how much you want to spend on study aids to prepare you for a pair of $132 tests. Of course, if you don't pass the first time, you'll have to pay to take the test again, and there are no discounts for multiple attempts. Be cautious when buying study aids and look for bargains.

Be especially alert for those study aids that were written for the old tests. One surefire way to determine whether the study aid is old is that it contains Macintosh, DOS, Windows 3.1, or the OSI Model information. Another tip-off is that Windows 98 and 2000 are not mentioned at all.

The Web sites and other resources listed in this chapter are sites that I believe you will find helpful without having to spend a fortune. Please understand that all of these sites did exist at the time this book was written. If any of these sites have disappeared, search for others. Remember that some search engines use the plus sign as part of the syntax of the search string, and searching for "A+" may get you nowhere. On these engines, you may want to search for "Aplus" or "certification." I've had the best luck using Google (www.google.com).

Listed next are a few Web sites and other sources of study aids that you may find useful. Starting after CompTIA, the sites are listed alphabetically to erase any bias I might have, so you can form your own opinions. I have either personally used or reviewed the products offered at these sites, unless otherwise indicated, and believe that they can be useful depending on your needs.

CompTIA.org

This should be your first stop when preparing for the A+ exams. This site is the proverbial "horse's mouth" for the A+ tests. CompTIA has attempted to answer many questions you may have about the exams, including information on test sites and costs in over 25 countries.

This well-organized site is where you can get the exam blueprints, which you should use as your study guides for the exams, and links to Prometrics and VUE for online test registrations.

```
www.comptia.org/certification/aplus/index.htm
```

The CompTIA site also displays banner ads from companies that sell training materials, prep courses, and practice tests.

AplusCentral.com

This site provides some useful links to other test prep companies, a freeware practice test, as well as an 85-page cram sheet with sample A+ questions and other A+ exam related information.

```
www.apluscentral.com/
```

Literally hundreds of companies, organizations, and individuals on the Web are eager to share, mostly at a price, their products with you. Most of them are listed on either the 2000 Tutor (www.2000tutor.com) or Exam Notes (www.examnotes.net) sites, which have links on this site.

AplusExam.com

Other than having a great name, this site offers a very good CD-ROM-based product. The product, called *A+ Certify,* contains a variety of sample tests for each of the A+ exams, as well as a cram guide for each exam. You can find a sample exam on the Web site that demonstrates the content on the CD.

```
www.aplusexam.com/
```

AplusExam.com's products are very accurate and the cram guides are among the best available.

BrainBuzz.com/Cramsession.com

BrainBuzz.com is a Web site that offers much more to IT professionals than just exam study guides. If you visit this site, take the time to browse around a bit. Several resources are available that can help you on the job as well.

```
http://cramsession.brainbuzz.com/cramsession/comptia/
```

Two of the great features of this site are a cram session document for each test that you can download and a question-of-the-day e-mail service that sends you a different question each day on a topic of your choice.

Cheet Sheets

This Web site has cheat sheets for sale that contain actual questions from various certification tests, including the A+ exams.

```
www.cheet-sheets.com/comptia.html
```

When last visited, the site did not have an A+ 2000 cheet sheet (sic), but I'm sure one will be available soon.

DaliDesign.com

Dali Design has created a product called *PREP! for A+ 2000* that is an excellent study and test prep aid. The sample test includes 54 questions that can be downloaded free. The folks at Dali Design tell me that the feedback from users reflects about a 97% pass rate.

```
www.dalidesign.com/prepap/apdef.html
```

The full *PREP! for A+* contains 540 questions that Dali Design has taken from "actual A+ Certification test experiences," so all the test topics are included. If you like the sample test, you might think that the price of the full test engine is very reasonable.

Companies that are members of CompTIA can offer test vouchers at a discount. Dali Design has a bundle, which includes their *PREP! for A+ 2000* test engine and vouchers for the two tests, for less than what the actual tests cost.

Marcraft International

Of the free downloadable practice tests, this one is probably the most challenging. The questions are written in a way that requires you to think about why an answer is correct as well as why the other answers are wrong. Marcraft's full-blown practice test is reasonably priced, and if you haven't already shot your bankroll on other study tools, it's worth buying.

www.mic-inc.com/Aplus

Absolutely don't buy a practice test or other study materials online without first trying out a demo. You may actually find a free one that does the job for you. If you plan to use interactive practice tests (a good idea in my opinion), then the Marcraft product is a good choice.

PCGuide.com

The PC Guide is not technically an A+ site, but it is without doubt the most comprehensive site on PC hardware on the Web. If you are new to PC hardware, this is a must visit as you begin your studies for the A+ Core Hardware exam. Charles Kozierok's has maintained this site to offer ". . . steak, not sizzle, since 1997." Even if you don't use this site to round-out your studies for the A+ Core exam, you should probably bookmark it for later reference.

www.pcguide.com/

Buy the CD-ROM version of *The PC Guide* and use it in your studies as well as on the job. Trust me, this is probably the absolute best bargain for PC hardware information available. Buying the CD will also encourage Mr. Kozierok to continue maintaining his most excellent Web site.

Sasasite.com

This Web site is a community effort by people who have taken various certification tests and contributed answers to various practice test banks, questions or topics from the actual tests. If you're okay with the ethical quandaries of such a site, then you will be able to find some information about the A+ exams here.

```
www.sasasite.com
```

A lot of information on this site is intended for other certifications, which may be of interest to you.

Self Test Software

This site offers one of the best freebie test demos on the Web. In fact, its practice test is very much like the actual test experience in terms of content, look, and feel.

```
www.selftestsoftware.com/
```

You can download a sample A+ test demo and a few other certification tests as well. The idea is that if you like the practice tests, you'll buy the full-blown test simulators.

Other Resources You Should Consider

You may also want to check with your local community or technical college for courses to prepare you for the A+ exams, especially if you are new to PCs, hardware, and operating systems. Commercial courses and training packages are also available, but a course at your local college is most likely a better value and provides all of the tools and equipment you need.

Another resource you may want to consider is books from my favorite publisher, Hungry Minds, Inc.

- *Upgrading & Fixing PCs For Dummies,* 5th Edition, by Andy Rathbone
- *PCs for Dummies,* 7th Edition, by Dan Gookin
- *Windows 98 For Dummies* by Andy Rathbone
- *Microsoft Windows Me Millennium Edition For Dummies* by Andy Rathbone
- *Networking For Dummies,* 5th Edition, by Doug Lowe
- *Windows 2000 Professional* by Sharon Crawford and Andy Rathbone

In spite of the shameless plug, these books are an entertaining and informative way to brush up on your PC repair, Windows, and networking knowledge. You need to have some fun while studying, and these books will surely give you a reason to smile.

Part VII
Appendix

"Our automated response policy to a large company-wide data crash is to notify management, back up existing data, and sell 90% of my shares in the company."

In this part . . .

This part contains information on the contents of the CD-ROM included with this book and instructions for accessing the sample tests and other tools to help you prepare for the test, including a test engine that generates practice tests for you in a variety of combinations.

The sample questions on the CD-ROM cover the domains of the two A+ exams to help you prepare for the test. Use these questions as indicators of the types of questions you can expect to see on the test. If you do fairly well on these questions, then you are probably reaching your peak. However, you should always use more than one sample test to measure your readiness for the actual exam. This is why a variety of commercial practice test demos are also included on the CD-ROM.

Appendix

About the CD

● ●

On the CD-ROM

▶ Practice and self-assessment tests to make sure you're ready for the real thing

▶ Demo versions of eight of the better A+ exam practice tests

● ●

System Requirements

Make sure that your computer meets the minimum system requirements shown in the following list. If your computer doesn't meet most of these requirements, you may have problems using the contents of the CD-ROM.

✔ A PC with a 486 or faster processor.

✔ Microsoft Windows 95 or later.

✔ At least 16MB of total RAM installed on your computer.

✔ At least 32MB of available hard drive space to install all the software on this CD-ROM. (You need less space if you don't install every program.)

✔ A CD-ROM drive — double-speed (2x) or faster.

✔ A sound card for PCs.

✔ A monitor capable of displaying at least 256 colors or grayscale.

✔ A modem with a speed of at least 28,800 bps.

Using the CD-ROM with Microsoft Windows

To install the items from the CD-ROM to your hard drive, follow these steps:

1. **Insert the CD-ROM into your computer's CD-ROM drive.**

2. **Click Start⇨Run.**

3. **In the dialog box that appears, type** D:\SETUP.EXE.

Replace *D:* with the drive letter for your CD-ROM drive, if needed.

4. **Click OK.**

A License Agreement window appears.

5. **Read through the license agreement and then click the Accept button if you want to use the CD-ROM. After you click Accept, you are never bothered by the License Agreement window again.**

The CD-ROM interface Welcome screen appears. The interface is a little program that shows you what's on the CD-ROM and coordinates installing the programs and running the demos. The interface enables you to click a button or two to make things happen.

6. **Click anywhere on the Welcome screen to enter the interface.**

The next screen lists categories for the software on the CD-ROM.

7. **To view the items within a category, just click the category's name.**

A list of programs in the category appears.

8. **For more information about a program, click the program's name.**

Be sure to read the information that appears. Sometimes a program has its own system requirements or requires you to do a few tricks on your computer before you can install or run the program, and this screen tells you what you may need to do, if necessary.

9. **If you don't want to install the program, click the Go Back button to return to the previous screen.**

You can always return to the previous screen by clicking the Go Back button. This feature enables you to browse the different categories and products and decide what you want to install.

10. **To install a program, click the appropriate Install button.**

The CD-ROM interface drops to the background while the CD-ROM installs the program you chose.

11. **To install other items, repeat Steps 7 through 10.**

12. **When you finish installing programs, click the Quit button to close the interface.**

You can eject the CD-ROM now. Carefully place it back in the plastic jacket of the book for safekeeping.

To run some of the programs on the *A+ Certification For Dummies* CD-ROM, you need to leave the CD-ROM in the CD-ROM drive.

What You'll Find on the CD-ROM

The following is a summary of the software included on this CD-ROM.

Dummies test prep tools

This CD-ROM contains questions related to A+ Certification. The questions are similar to those you can expect to find on the exams. I've also included some questions on A+ topics that may or not be on the current tests or even covered in the book, but they are things that you should know to perform your job.

Practice test

The Practice test is designed to help you get comfortable with the A+ testing situation and pinpoint your strengths and weaknesses on the topic. You can accept the default setting of 60 questions in 60 minutes, or you can customize the settings. You can pick the number of questions and the amount of time, and you can even decide which objectives you want to focus on.

After you answer the questions, the Practice test gives you plenty of feedback. You can find out which questions you got right or wrong and get statistics on how you did, broken down by objective. Then you can review all the questions — the ones you missed, the ones you marked, or a combination of the ones you marked and the ones you missed.

Self-Assessment test

The Self-Assessment test is designed to simulate the actual A+ testing situation. The only difference is that this test is not an adaptive test. However, it does try to put a little pressure on you in the same way that the actual test does. You must answer 60 questions in 60 minutes. After you answer all the questions, you find out your score and whether you pass or fail — but that's all the feedback you get. If you can pass the Self-Assessment test fairly easily, you're probably ready to tackle the real thing.

Links page

I've also created a Links page, a handy starting place for accessing the huge amounts of information about the A+ tests on the Internet. You can find the page, `Links.htm`, at the root of the CD-ROM.

Commercial practice test demos

The following are the eight practice test software demos that have been included on the CD-ROM. The demos give you a good idea of what the full practice test from each company is like so that you can find the ones that fit your style and focus. I recommend that you use at least two practice tests beyond the ones from this book to prepare for the test.

A+ Certify Exam 8.0 from Super Software

The Super Software (www.aplusexam.com) people produce some of the best practice exams available. Their reasonably priced CD-ROM contains sample tests, (usually more than one) some specific to each domain of the exam objectives, and tips and cram notes for the actual test.

A+CoreCert/A+WinCert from Transcender

Transcender is one of the best known names in certification test preparation. The quality of their MCSE products was carried over into their practice test products for the previous A+ exams, and I see no reason why they would do anything different for their products for the new A+ exams. Visit Transcender at (www.transcender.com).

A+ Test Bundle from Self Test Software

Make sure when you go to Self Test's Web site (www.selftest.co.uk) that you use the co.uk on the end of the URL. The com URL will take you to another company with a completely different type of self-test. Self Test Software practice tests are very good and the test software simulates the test very well.

Boson A+ from Boson Software

Boson's practice tests (www.boson.com) may be the hardest tests you'll see, which can be discouraging when just starting out in your test preparation. If you can pass a Boson test, you are ready for the real thing.

Demo A+ Exam from Vista Net

I don't have much first hand experience with Vista Net or their practice test, but I do trust the judgment of the person that recommended them to me. Check out the demo at www.vista-net.com and if you like it, go get the full test. Remember that you should use at least two different practice tests (meaning from two different suppliers) when preparing for the exam.

EasyCert from JRK Software

If you want a practice test that sticks to the test objectives without throwing in stuff you won't find on the test, you may want to check out the practice test at www.jrksoftware.com.

Prep! for A+ 2000 from Dali Design

Last, but certainly not least! Jeff Thorssell and the Dali Design team have consistently produced the very best practice tests available for the money. Typically, the Prep! tests are the first available and are usually right on target regarding what you need to study for the exams. Check out these tests at www.dalidesign.com/prepap/.

Diagnostic software demo

Troubleshooting is a major part of the A+ Core Hardware exam and the exam assumes you can use diagnostic software to diagnose, troubleshoot, and isolate problems quickly. Pc-Check from Eurosoft USA, Ltd., (www.eurosoft-usa.com) and the rest of Eurosoft's library of more specialized diagnostic software packages are excellent troubleshooting tools. A demo copy of Pc-Check is included on the CD-ROM for you to use to gain some experience with software diagnostic tools, should you need it.

If You've Got Problems (Of the CD-ROM Kind)

I tried my best to compile programs that work on most computers with the minimum system requirements. Alas, your computer may be somewhat different, and some programs may not work properly for some reason.

The two most likely culprits are that you don't have enough memory (RAM) for the programs you want to use, or that you have other programs running that are affecting installation or running of a program. If you get error messages such as Not enough memory or Setup cannot continue, try one or more of the following procedures and then try using the software again:

- ✔ **Turn off any anti-virus software monitors that you may have running on your computer.** Installers sometimes mimic virus activity and may make your computer incorrectly believe that it is being infected by a virus.

- ✔ **Close all running programs**. The more programs you're running, the less memory is available to other programs. Installers also typically update files and programs; if you keep other programs running, installation may not work properly.

✔ **In Windows, close the CD-ROM interface and run demos or installations directly from Windows Explorer.** The interface itself can tie up system memory or even conflict with certain kinds of interactive demos. Use Windows Explorer to browse the files on the CD-ROM and launch installers or demos.

✔ **Add more RAM to your computer.** This is, admittedly, a drastic and somewhat expensive step. However, if you use Windows 95, adding more memory can really help the speed of your computer and enable more programs to run at the same time.

If you still have trouble installing the items from the CD-ROM, please call the very nice and helpful people at Hungry Minds Customer Care phone number: 800-762-2974 (outside the U.S.: 317-596-5430).

Index

Notes

Notes

Notes

Hungry Minds, Inc.
End-User License Agreement

5. Limited Warranty.

(a) HMI warrants that the Software and Software Media are free from defects in materials and workmanship under normal use for a period of sixty (60) days from the date of purchase of this Book. If HMI receives notification within the warranty period of defects in materials or workmanship, HMI will replace the defective Software Media.

(b) **HMI AND THE AUTHOR OF THE BOOK DISCLAIM ALL OTHER WARRANTIES, EXPRESS OR IMPLIED, INCLUDING WITHOUT LIMITATION IMPLIED WARRANTIES OF MERCHANTABILITY AND FITNESS FOR A PARTICULAR PURPOSE, WITH RESPECT TO THE SOFTWARE, THE PROGRAMS, THE SOURCE CODE CONTAINED THEREIN, AND/OR THE TECHNIQUES DESCRIBED IN THIS BOOK. HMI DOES NOT WARRANT THAT THE FUNCTIONS CONTAINED IN THE SOFTWARE WILL MEET YOUR REQUIRE-MENTS OR THAT THE OPERATION OF THE SOFTWARE WILL BE ERROR FREE.**

(c) This limited warranty gives you specific legal rights, and you may have other rights that vary from jurisdiction to jurisdiction.

6. Remedies.

(a) HMI's entire liability and your exclusive remedy for defects in materials and workman-ship shall be limited to replacement of the Software Media, which may be returned to HMI with a copy of your receipt at the following address: Software Media Fulfillment Department, Attn.: *A+ Certification For Dummies,* 2nd Edition, Hungry Minds, Inc., 10475 Crosspoint Blvd., Indianapolis, IN 46256, or call 1-800-762-2974. Please allow four to six weeks for delivery. This Limited Warranty is void if failure of the Software Media has resulted from accident, abuse, or misapplication. Any replacement Software Media will be warranted for the remainder of the original warranty period or thirty (30) days, whichever is longer.

(b) In no event shall HMI or the author be liable for any damages whatsoever (including without limitation damages for loss of business profits, business interruption, loss of business information, or any other pecuniary loss) arising from the use of or inability to use the Book or the Software, even if HMI has been advised of the possibility of such damages.

(c) Because some jurisdictions do not allow the exclusion or limitation of liability for conse-quential or incidental damages, the above limitation or exclusion may not apply to you.

7. **U.S. Government Restricted Rights.** Use, duplication, or disclosure of the Software for or on behalf of the United States of America, its agencies and/or instrumentalities (the "U.S. Government") is subject to restrictions as stated in paragraph (c)(1)(ii) of the Rights in Technical Data and Computer Software clause of DFARS 252.227-7013, or subparagraphs (c) (1) and (2) of the Commercial Computer Software – Restricted Rights clause at FAR 52.227-19, and in similar clauses in the NASA FAR supplement, as applicable.

8. **General.** This Agreement constitutes the entire understanding of the parties and revokes and supersedes all prior agreements, oral or written, between them and may not be modified or amended except in a writing signed by both parties hereto that specifically refers to this Agreement. This Agreement shall take precedence over any other documents that may be in conflict herewith. If any one or more provisions contained in this Agreement are held by any court or tribunal to be invalid, illegal, or otherwise unenforceable, each and every other pro-vision shall remain in full force and effect.

Installation Instructions

To install the items from the CD-ROM to your hard drive, follow these steps:

1. **Insert the CD-ROM into your computer's CD-ROM drive.**

2. **Click Start⇨Run.**

3. **In the dialog box that appears, type** D:\SETUP.EXE.

   Replace *D:* with the drive letter for your CD-ROM drive, if needed.

4. **Click OK.**

   A License Agreement window appears.

5. **Read through the license agreement and then click the Accept button if you want to use the CD-ROM. After you click Accept, you are never bothered by the License Agreement window again.**

   The CD-ROM interface Welcome screen appears.

6. **Click anywhere on the Welcome screen to enter the interface.**

   The next screen lists categories for the software on the CD-ROM.

7. **To view the items within a category, just click the category's name.**

   A list of programs in the category appears.

8. **For more information about a program, click the program's name.**

9. **If you don't want to install the program, click the Go Back button to return to the previous screen.**

   You can always return to the previous screen by clicking the Go Back button. This feature enables you to browse the different categories and products and decide what you want to install.

10. **To install a program, click the appropriate Install button.**

    The CD-ROM interface drops to the background while the CD-ROM installs the program you chose.

11. **To install other items, repeat Steps 7 through 10.**

12. **When you finish installing programs, click the Quit button to close the interface.**

    You can eject the CD-ROM now. Carefully place it back in the plastic jacket of the book for safekeeping.

To run some of the programs on the *A+ Certification For Dummies* CD-ROM, you need to leave the CD-ROM in the CD-ROM drive.

FOR DUMMIES
BOOK REGISTRATION

Register
This Book
and Win!

We want to hear from you!

Visit **dummies.com** to register this book and tell us how you liked it!

✔ Get entered in our monthly prize giveaway.

✔ Give us feedback about this book — tell us what you like best, what you like least, or maybe what you'd like to ask the author and us to change!

✔ Let us know any other *For Dummies* topics that interest you.

Your feedback helps us determine what books to publish, tells us what coverage to add as we revise our books, and lets us know whether we're meeting your needs as a *For Dummies* reader. You're our most valuable resource, and what you have to say is important to us!

Not on the Web yet? It's easy to get started with *Dummies 101: The Internet For Windows 98* or *The Internet For Dummies* at local retailers everywhere.

Or let us know what you think by sending us a letter at the following address:

For Dummies Book Registration
Dummies Press
10475 Crosspoint Blvd.
Indianapolis, IN 46256

TM

...FOR
DUMMIES

BESTSELLING
BOOK SERIES